East Asian Art History in a Transnational Context

This is the first comprehensive English-language study of East Asian art history in a transnational context, and challenges the existing geographic, temporal, and generic paradigms that currently frame the art history of East Asia. This pioneering study proposes an important new framework that focuses on the relationship between China, Japan, and Korea. By reconsidering existing concepts of 'East Asia', and examining the porousness of boundaries in East Asian art history, the study proposes a new model for understanding trans-local artistic production – in particular the mechanics of interactions – at the turn of the 20th century.

Eriko Tomizawa-Kay is Lecturer in Japanese, University of East Anglia and Academic Associate at the Sainsbury Institute for Japanese Arts and Cultures.

Toshio Watanabe is Professor for Japanese Arts and Cultural Heritage at the Sainsbury Institute for the Study of Japanese Arts and Cultures, University of East Anglia and Emeritus Professor of History of Art and Design, Research Centre for Transnational Art, Identity and Nation, University of the Arts London.

Routledge Research in Art History

Routledge Research in Art History is our home for the latest scholarship in the field of art history. The series publishes research monographs and edited collections, covering areas including art history, theory, and visual culture. These high-level books focus on art and artists from around the world and from a multitude of time periods. By making these studies available to the worldwide academic community, the series aims to promote quality art history research.

Pop Art and Popular Music
Jukebox Modernism
Melissa Mednicov

Globalizing East European Art Histories
Past and Present
Edited by Beáta Hock and Anu Allas

Visual Typologies from the Early Modern to the Contemporary
Local Contexts and Global Practices
Edited by Tara Zanardi and Lynda Klich

Cultural Mobility in the Interwar Avant-Garde Art Network
Poland, Belgium and the Netherlands
Michał Wenderski

New Geographies of Abstract Art in Postwar Latin America
Edited Mariola V. Alvarez and Ana M. Franco

René Magritte and the Art of Thinking
Lisa Lipinski

The Paragone in Nineteenth-Century Art
Sarah Jordan Lippert

East Asian Art History in a Transnational Context
Edited by Eriko Tomizawa-Kay and Toshio Watanabe

For a full list of titles in this series, please visit www.routledge.com/Routledge-Research-in-Art-History/book-series/RRAH

East Asian Art History in a Transnational Context

Edited by Eriko Tomizawa-Kay and
Toshio Watanabe

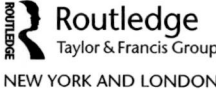

NEW YORK AND LONDON

First published 2019
by Routledge
52 Vanderbilt Avenue, New York, NY 10017

and by Routledge
2 Park Square, Milton Park, Abingdon, Oxon, OX14 4RN

Routledge is an imprint of the Taylor & Francis Group, an informa business

© 2019 Taylor & Francis

The right of Eriko Tomizawa-Kay and Toshio Watanabe to be identified as the authors of the editorial material, and of the authors for their individual chapters, has been asserted in accordance with sections 77 and 78 of the Copyright, Designs and Patents Act 1988.

All rights reserved. No part of this book may be reprinted or reproduced or utilised in any form or by any electronic, mechanical, or other means, now known or hereafter invented, including photocopying and recording, or in any information storage or retrieval system, without permission in writing from the publishers.

Trademark notice: Product or corporate names may be trademarks or registered trademarks, and are used only for identification and explanation without intent to infringe.

Library of Congress Cataloging-in-Publication Data
Names: Tomizawa-Kay, Eriko, editor. | Watanabe, Toshio, 1945– editor.
Title: East Asian art history in a transnational context/edited by
  Eriko Tomizawa-Kay and Toshio Watanabe.
Description: New York : Routledge, 2019. | Series: Routledge research in art
  history | Includes bibliographical references and index.
Identifiers: LCCN 2018052269 | ISBN 9781138480810 (hardback : alk. paper) |
  ISBN 9781351061902 (e-book : alk. paper)
Subjects: LCSH: Art, East Asian—19th century. | Art, East Asian—20th century. |
  Art and transnationalism.
Classification: LCC N7337 .E27 2019 | DDC 709.509/034—dc23
LC record available at https://lccn.loc.gov/2018052269

ISBN: 978-1-138-48081-0 (hbk)
ISBN: 978-1-351-06190-2 (ebk)

Typeset in Sabon
by Apex CoVantage, LLC

Every effort has been made to contact copyright-holders. Please advise the publisher of any errors or omissions, and these will be corrected in subsequent editions.

Cover: Onchi Kōshirō, Hakua (Soshū shoken) [White walls (Impressions of Suzhou)], 1940, woodblock print on paper, Chiba City Museum of Art

Contents

List of Figures vii
List of Color Plates xii
Notes on Contributors xiii
Notes on Translations and Names xvii
Acknowledgements xviii

Introduction 1
ERIKO TOMIZAWA-KAY AND TOSHIO WATANABE

PART I
Constructing the Idea of East Asian Art 13

1 Reconsidering the History of East Asian Painting: Painting from China vs. Chinese-style Painting in Japan 15
SHIMAO ARATA

2 The Imperial Treasures of the Shōsōin and the Collections of the Tang Emperors 32
ITAKURA MASAAKI

3 Overcoming Modernity: Towards a Concept of 'East Asian Art History' 52
SATŌ DŌSHIN

PART II
New Ways of Looking at Others 63

4 The Triangle of Modern Japanese *Yōga*: Paris, Tokyo, and East Asia 65
MIURA ATSUSHI

5 'Marginal Man' Pai Un-soung (1900–1978): His European Experience, His Views, and His Art 83
SHIN MIN-JONG

6 Reinventing Localism, Tradition, and Identity: The Role of Modern
  Okinawan Painting (1930s–1960s) 102
  ERIKO TOMIZAWA-KAY

7 The Evolution and Modernization of the Sculpture Genre in East
  Asia According to the Japanese Example 126
  KITAZAWA NORIAKI

8 War and Pornography in East Asia 152
  ADACHI GEN

PART III
Translation of Art within East Asia 167

9 Chinese Seal Carving in Modern Japan: Qian Shoutie's Relationship
  with Hashimoto Kansetsu 169
  AIDA YUEN WONG

10 'National Painting' Unbound: Modernizing Ink Painting in the
   Sino-Japanese Art World 188
   TAMAKI MAEDA

11 Korean Lacquerwork Craftsmen Who Went to Japan: Change
   and Innovation in Korean Lacquerwork during the Colonial Period 209
   ROH JUNIA

12 The Concept of Art in the *Meishu Congshu*: From Foreign Loan
   to National Tradition 227
   LIU YU-JEN

   Glossary 244
   Index 254

Figures

1.1	Framework of *Kara-e*, *Yamato-e*, and Chinese painting	17
1.2	Image of *Karamono Kazari* of the main room	19
1.3	Xia Gui, *Pure and Remote Views of Mountains and Streams* (detail), Southern Song dynasty. Ink on paper, 46.5 × 889.1 cm. The National Palace Museum, Taipei	21
1.4	[Signed] Ma Yuan, *Grand View of Rivers and Mountains* (detail), Ming dynasty. Ink and light colour on silk, 64.2 × 1276.4 cm. Freer Gallery of Art and Arthur M. Sackler Gallery	21
1.5	[Signed] Dai Jin, *High Mountains and Flowing Rivers* (detail), Ming dynasty. Ink and light colour on paper, 50 × 2073 cm. Guangzhou Museum of Art	22
1.6	Framework of 'global' and 'local'	23
1.7	Networks of external connection	24
1.8	Geiami, *Viewing Waterfall* (detail), 1486 (Muromachi period). Ink and light colour on silk, 106.0 × 30.3 cm. Nezu Museum	26
1.9	[Signed] Dai Jin, *High Mountains and Flowing Rivers* (detail), Ming dynasty. Ink and light colour on paper, 50 × 2073 cm. Guangzhou Museum of Art	27
2.1	*Catalogue of the Calligraphy of Wang Xizhi and Wang Xianzhi* (Daishō Ō Shinseki chō), 758. Ink on paper, 27.5 × 88 cm. Collection of the Shōsōin, North Warehouse	35
2.2	Wang Xizhi, *Letter on the Disturbances* (Ch: *Sang luan tie*, J: *Sōran jō*), Tang dynasty copy, 7th century. Ink on paper mounted on bamboo paper, 26.2 × 58.4 cm. Collection of the Imperial Household Agency	37
2.3	*Juka kōshi zu byōbu* (Nobleman under the trees), ca. 740. Screen of *Shuxia Gaoshi tu* (Nobleman under the trees), ca. 740. Guoxinzhuang, Xi'an	41
2.4	*Musicians Riding Elephants* (Kizō sōgaku zu), Tang dynasty (713 ∼ 766). *Biwa* plectrum guard painting, sappanwood dye and mother-of-pearl inlay on maple wood, 97.0 × 40.5 cm. Collection of the Shōsōin, South Warehouse	42

2.5 *Landscape* (Sansui zu tsuitate), ca. 740. Standing screen painting on the north wall of the Tomb of Han Xiu and His Wife, Guoxinzhuang, Xi'an 42
3.1 Framework and identity of 'art history' 55
3.2 Content and form of regional art history 59
4.1 Fujishima Takeji, *Orientalism* (Tōyō-buri), 1924. Oil on canvas, 63.7 × 44.0 cm. Private collection 69
4.2 Fujishima Takeji, *Sunrise in Inner Mongolia* (Mōko no hi no de), 1937. Oil on canvas, 72.5 × 100.0 cm. Kagoshima Prefectural Museum of Culture, 'Reimeikan' 71
4.3 Kojima Torajirō, *Autumn* (Aki), 1920. Oil on canvas, 200.0 × 136.0 cm. Centre Pompidou, Musée National d'Art Moderne, Paris 72
4.4 Yasui Sōtarō, *A Portrait of Chin-Jung* (Kin'yō), 1934. Oil on canvas, 96.5 × 74.5 cm. The National Museum of Modern Art, Tokyo 73
4.5 Umehara Ryūzaburō, *Scenery of Taiwan* (Taiwan Fūkei), 1933. Oil on canvas, 37.4 × 45.2 cm. Fuchū Art Museum, Tokyo 75
4.6 Fujishima Takeji, *The Rear Wooden Gate of the Mausoleum of Confucius at Tainan, Taiwan* (Taiwan Tainan Seibyō no Urakido), ca. 1933–1935. Oil on canvas, 53.0 × 40.8 cm. Kitano Museum of Art, Nagano 76
5.1 Pai Un-soung, *Self-Portrait* (Shaman), 1930s. Oil on canvas, 55 × 45 cm. Ethnologisches Museum, Berlin. Image courtesy Kim Bog-gi Collection of National Museum of Modern and Contemporary Art, Korea, donated by Kim Bog-gi 85
5.2 Pai Un-soung, *Self-Portrait with Hat*, 1930s. Oil on canvas, 54 × 45 cm. Private collection 86
5.3 View of the Korean Department of the Guimet Museum in the 19th century. Musée nationale des arts asiatiques Guimet, Paris 87
5.4 Pai Un-soung, *Family Portrait*, 1930–1935. Oil on canvas, 140 × 200 cm. Private collection. Image courtesy Kim Bog-gi Collection of National Museum of Modern and Contemporary Art, Korea, donated by Kim Bog-gi 88
5.5 Pai Un-soung, painting in Chinese ink in his atelier, 1935. Image courtesy Kim Bog-gi Collection of National Museum of Modern and Contemporary Art, Korea, donated by Kim Bog-gi 89
5.6 Invitation letter to Pai Un-soung's solo exhibition in Paris 91
5.7 Article on Pai Un-soung in *France-Japon* entitled 'The Exotic Artists of Paris: Korean Painter Pai Un-soung' and his illustration, 'Child of Korea'. *France-Japon* 27 (March 15, 1938). 92
5.8 Exhibition hall of the Japanese Artist Exhibitions in Paris. *Binokuni* 15, no. 8 (August 1939). 93
6.1 Fujita Tsuguharu, *Grandchildren* (Mago), 1938. Oil on canvas, 100.0 × 81.0 cm. Okinawa Prefectural Museum and Art Museum ©Fondation Foujita/ADAGP, Paris and DACS, London 2017. 107
6.2 Nadoyama Aijun, *Nostalgia* (Kyōshū), 1946. Oil on canvas, 100.3 × 80.2 cm. Okinawa Prefectural Museum and Art Museum 110
6.3 Ōmine Seikan, *Landscape of Nishihara Village in 1950* (Nishihara 1950), 1950. Oil on canvas, 91.3 × 117.3 cm. Okinawa Prefectural Museum and Art Museum 111

6.4	Tamanaha Seikichi, *Portrait of an Elderly Mother* (Rōbo-zō), 1954. Oil on canvas, 90.8 × 73.0 cm. Okinawa Prefectural Museum and Art Museum	113
6.5	Tamanaha Seikichi, *Shipwrecks* (Hasen), 1958. Oil on canvas, 65.6 × 101.0 cm. Okinawa Prefectural Museum and Art Museum	114
6.6	Ashimine Kanemasa, *Crowd* (Gunzō), 1950. Oil on canvas, 76.2 × 127.8 cm. Okinawa Prefectural Museum and Art Museum	116
6.7	Adaniya Masayoshi, *Nostalgia* (Bōkyō), 1965. Oil on canvas, 73.3 × 107.3 cm. Okinawa Prefectural Museum and Art Museum	117
7.1	Vienna World's Fair exhibition listing of classifications and divisions, January 1872	128
7.2	Matsuzaki Shinji, *Exterior View of the Fine Art Gallery at the First Domestic Industrial Exposition*, albumen silver print (*kenranshi*), 9.2 × 5.8 cm. Collection of the Amagasaki Shiritsu Bunkazai Shūzōko. Reproduced in *Meiji jū-nen naikoku kangyō hakurankai reppin shashin jō* [Photographs of exhibited objects at the Domestic Industrial Exposition in Meiji 10 (1877)], 11.6 × 19.5 × 7.5 cm	134
7.3	Takamura Kōun, Hayashi Biun, and Gotō Sadayuki, *Portrait of Saigō Takamori* (Saigō Takamori zō), 1898. Bronze, 363.6 × 360 cm. Ueno, Tokyo	138
7.4	Yonehara Unkai, *Portrait of Edward Jenner* (Zenna zō), 1904. Bronze, 180 × 190 cm. Collection of the Tokyo National Museum. Photograph courtesy TNM Image Archives	138
7.5	Yonehara Unkai, *Portrait of Edward Jenner in Wood* (Zenna kigata), 1897. Wood, height: 183.2 cm. Collection of the Tokyo University of the Arts	139
7.6	Takamura Kōtarō, *Hand* (Te), ca. 1918. Bronze, 38.6 × 14.5 × 28.7 cm. Collection of the National Museum of Modern Art, Tokyo. Photograph courtesy MOMAT/ DNPartcom	140
8.1	A photo of Koreans having sex and a cartoon of a Japanese man and a Korean woman, date unknown, in Takahashi Tetsu, *The Graphical History of Sex* (Tokyo: Kuboshoten, 1968), p. 98	156
8.2	Leaflet made by the Japanese army against the U.S. army, ca. 1943. Getty Images	159
8.3	Leaflet made by the U.S. army against the Japanese army, ca. 1944, in Ichinose Toshiya, *The Asia-Pacific War Seen in Advertisement Plotter Flyers* (Tokyo: Kashiwa Shobō, 2008), p. 51	159
8.4	Tomita Akihiro (Sasaoka Sakuji), 'Bathing of Soldiers'. In *A Picture Book of Soldiers* (Tokyo: Banchō Shobō, 1972), p. 83	160
9.1	Photograph of Qian Shoutie. Published in *Qian Shoutie yincun* [Seals of Qian Shoutie], ed. Wu Yiren and Qian Dali, p. 1	170
9.2	Select seals of Hashimoto Kansetsu by Qian Shoutie. Published in *Hashimoto Kansetsu* (Asahi Shinbunsha, 1994), p. 111	172
9.3	Hashimoto Kansetsu's poetic commentary on Qian Shoutie's seal album. Published in *Qian Shoutie yincun* [Seals of Qian Shoutie], ed. Wu Yiren and Qian Dali, p. 4	173
9.4	Hashimoto Kansetsu's residence in Kyoto, named Hakusasonsō (White Sand Village Residence), today's Hashimoto Kansetsu Memorial Museum	174

x Figures

9.5	Qian Shoutie, 'White Sand Village Residence', ca. 1920s–1930s. Published in *Qian Shoutie yincun* [Seals of Qian Shoutie], ed. Wu Yiren and Qian Dali, p. 51	175
9.6	Qian Shoutie, 'Shangwu' seal in Japanese style, ca. 1920s–1930s. Published in *Qian Shoutie yincun* [Seals of Qian Shoutie], ed. Wu Yiren and Qian Dali, p. 44	175
9.7	How to hold the knife for the double-hook (top) and single-hook (bottom) methods. Published in Ma Guoquan, 'Zhuanke jifa zhong de daofa wenti' [Issues concerning knife methods in seal carving techniques], p. 485	176
9.8	Qian Shoutie, 'Guanxue zijian' [Kansetsu's self-inspection], ca. 1920s–1930s. Published in *Qian Shoutie yincun* [Seals of Qian Shoutie], ed. Wu Yiren and Qian Dali, p. 51	177
9.9	Qian Shoutie in Japan, 1947. Published in *Qian Shoutie nianpu* [Qian Shoutie's chronology], compiled by Liao Lu and Qian Mingzhi, p. 12	181
10.1	Fu Baoshi, *Autumn Landscape with a Waterfall: In the Style of Wang Meng* (Fang Huanghe Shanqiao: Qiuhuo mingquan tu), 1933. Hanging scroll, ink on paper, 135.5 × 54.0 cm. Musashino Art University. In Musashino Bijutsu Daigaku and Chūgoku Bijutsu Gakuin Kōkanten Jikkō Iinkai, eds., *Fu Hōseki ten* [Fu Baoshi exhibition], p. 3	189
10.2	Fu Baoshi, *The Thatched Hut of Great Purity* (Dadi caotang tu), 1942. Hanging scroll, ink and colour on paper, 85.0 × 58.0 cm. Fu Family Collection. In Chen Lusheng, et al., *Fu Baoshi quanji* [Collected works of Fu Baoshi], vol. 1, p. 147	195
10.3	Fu Baoshi, *Beauty under Banana Leaves* (Yuan Xian bo ba yi dimi), 1945. Hanging scroll, ink and colour on paper, 85.2 × 54.5 cm. Nanjing Museum. In Xu Huping, et al., *Fu Baoshi Zhongguo hua: Fu Baoshi jiashu juanzeng, Nanjing Bowuyuan cang* [Chinese paintings by Fu Baoshi: donation of the Fu Baoshi family: collection of the Nanjing Museum], p. 30	197
10.4	Fu Baoshi, *After a Poem by Mao Zedong* (Mao Zedong [Huanghelou] ciyi), 1961. Album leaf, ink on paper, 34.0 × 49.0 cm. Fu Family Collection. In Shibuya Kuritsu Shōtō Bijutsukan, ed., *Fu Hōseki: 20-seiki Chūgoku gadan no kyoshō: Nit-Chū bijutsu kōryū no kakehashi* [Fu Baoshi: a great master of 20th-century Chinese painting: a Sino-Japanese bridge in art exchanges], Figure 74	198
10.5	Fu Baoshi, *Whispering Rain at Dusk* (Xiaoxiao muyu), 1945. Hanging scroll, ink and colour on paper, 103.5 × 59.4 cm. Nanjing Museum. In Xu Huping, et al., *Fu Baoshi Zhongguo hua: Fu Baoshi jiashu juanzeng, Nanjing Bowuyuan cang* [Chinese paintings by Fu Baoshi: donation of the Fu Baoshi family: collection of the Nanjing Museum], p. 26	199
10.6	Fu Baoshi, *Portrait of Sesshū* (Xuezhou huaxiang), 1956. In Fu Baoshi, ed., *Xuezhou*, [Sesshū] n.p.	200

Figures xi

10.7 Sesshū Tōyō, *Haboku Landscape* (Haboku sansui zu) (detail), 1495. Ink on paper, 148.6 × 32.7 cm. Tokyo National Museum. Photograph provided by the Tokyo National Museum 201
11.1 *Plaque*, early 20th century. Lacquered wood, inlaid with mother-of-pearl, 0.7 × 25.8 × 18.8 cm, British Museum 213
11.2 Jeon Sung-gyu (design by Kimura Tenkō), *Lidless Lacquered Box*, early 1920s. Lacquered wood, inlaid with mother-of-pearl, 5.1 × 23.0 × 30.3 cm, Gakushuin University Museum of History 215
11.3 Jeon Sung-gyu, *Mountain Peony-Phoenix Lacquered Brazier with Mother-of-Pearl Inlay*. Lacquered wood, inlaid with mother-of-pearl (from the catalogue of the 11th Crafts Exhibition of the Ministry of Agriculture and Commerce (Nōten)) 215
11.4 Jeon Sung-gyu, *Lacquered Dining Table*. Lacquered wood, inlaid with mother-of-pearl, ca. 1937, 35.3 × 121.1 × 85.3 cm, Korea Mother-of-Pearl Art Museum 216
11.5 Chung Hae-cho, *Black Lustre 0819*. Lacquer, hemp cloth, 2008, 21.0 × 37.0 × 37.0 cm, British Museum 217
11.6 Rokkaku Shisui, *Square Tray with Design of Deva of Arts*. Lacquered wood, 1927, 2.2 × 19.6 × 19.6 cm, Hiroshima Prefectural Art Museum 220
11.7 Kang Chang-gyu, *Dry-Lacquered Tray*. Lacquer, hemp cloth, 1933, 15.2 × 35.5 × 35.5 cm, National Museum of Korea 223
12.1 Advertisement for the ten-volume continuing series of the *Meishu Congshu, Meishu Congshu* 2, no. 10 (1914). SOAS Library 232

Color Plates

Between pages 125 and 126

1. Sesshū, *Long Landscape Scroll* (Sansui chōkan) (detail), 1486 (Muromachi period). Ink and light colour on paper, 39.8 × 1580.2 cm. Mōri Museum
2. *Catalogue of State Treasures* (Kokka chinpō chō), 756. Ink on paper, 25.9 × 1474.0 cm. Collection of the Shōsōin, North Warehouse
3. *Beauties Beneath Trees*, detail (Torige ryūjo zu byōbu), Nara period. Folding screen, polychrome paint on white ground with *yamadori* feathers. 136.0 × 56.0 cm. Collection of the Shōsōin, North Warehouse
4. Kuroda Seiki, *Maïko, Dancing Girl* (Maïko), 1893. Oil on canvas, 80.4 × 65.3 cm. Tokyo National Museum
5. Umehara Ryūzaburō, *Forbidden City* (Shikinjō), 1940. Oil and *iwae-no-gu* (Japanese mineral pigment) on *maniaigami* (traditional Japanese paper), 115.0 × 89.0 cm. Eisei Bunko Museum, Tokyo
6. Pai Un-soung, *Baron Mitsui and His Works*, 1935. Woodblock print, 55 × 43 cm. Museum für Völkerkunde, Hamburg. Photo credit: National Research Institute of Cultural Heritage, Korea
7. Adaniya Masayoshi, *Tower* (Tō), 1958. Oil and sand on canvas, 91.0 × 61.0 cm. Okinawa Prefectural Museum and Art Museum
8. *Statue of Prince Yamato Takeru* (Meiji kinen no hyō), 1880. Bronze and glass, 554 cm. Kanazawa, Ishikawa Prefecture
9. Ogiwara Morie, *Woman* (Onna), 1910. Bronze, 98.5 × 47 × 61 cm. Collection of the National Museum of Modern Art, Tokyo. Photograph courtesy MOMAT/DNPartcom
10. Leaflet entitled 'That Goes Double', made by the Japanese army (Ono Saseo) against the Australian army, ca. 1943. In Ichinose Toshiya, *The Asia-Pacific War Seen in Advertisement Plotter Flyers* (Tokyo: Kashiwa Shobō, 2008), p. 49
11. Fu Baoshi, *Landscape* (Manshen cangcui jing gaofeng), 1962. Hanging scroll, ink and colour on paper, 102.8 × 71.6 cm. Fu Family Collection. In Chen Lusheng, et al., *Fu Baoshi quanji*, vol. 4, p. 223
12. Kim Bong-ryong, *Lacquered Ceramic Vase*. Lacquered celadon, inlaid with mother-of-pearl, 1970, 35.0 × 18.5 cm, Wonju Museum of History

Notes on Contributors

ADACHI Gen

ADACHI Gen is an art historian and critic based in Tokyo. He is a lecturer in Japanese Cultural Studies at the Department of Literature, Nishōgakusha University. He published *Zenei no idenshi: Anakizumu kara sengo bijutsu e* [The meme of the Japanese avant-garde: from anarchism to postwar art] (Brücke, Tokyo, 2012).

ITAKURA Masaaki

ITAKURA Masaaki is Professor at the Institute for Advanced Studies on Asia, University of Tokyo. His latest research interests include 'Higashiyama Gomotsu' (as the Ashikaga shogunal collection was known); an investigation of how visual images in the East Asian cultural sphere were shared or differentiated; and an exploration of how visual images were created, transmitted, and received. His latest publications include Itakura Masaaki, ed. *Nihon bijutsu zenshū 6 – higashi ajia no naka no nihon bijutsu* [Japanese art collection vol. 6: Japanese arts in East Asia] (2015); "Xia Yong's 'The Yueyang Tower' as the Artist's Portrait: Its Beginning and Development," *Art Forum 21*, vol. 32 (2015); 'Liang Kai's "Shakyamuni Descending the Mountain after Asceticism": Issues and Questions', *Buddhist Art* 344 (2016).

KITAZAWA Noriaki

KITAZAWA Noriaki is currently Visiting Professor of Fine Arts at Musashino Art University, specializing in both art criticism and art history. His principal publications include *Me no shinden – Bijutsu juyōshi nōto* [Shrine of the eye: notes on the accepted history of 'fine art'] (1989), *Nihonga no ten'i* [Transition of nihonga] (2003), *Abangyrarudo igo no kōgei* [Craft since the avant-garde] (2003), and *'Rettō' no kaiga: 'nihonga' no reitō sutairu* [Painting in the archipelago: late style of nihonga] (2015).

LIU Yu-jen

LIU Yu-jen is Assistant Curator at the Department of Painting and Calligraphy, the National Palace Museum, Taipei. Her publications include 'Second Only to the Original: Rhetoric and Practice in the Photographic Reproduction of Art in Early

Twentieth-Century China', *Art History* 37, no. 1 (2014), and 'Stealing Words, Transplanting Images: Stephen Bushell and the Intercultural Articulation of "Chinese Art" in the Early Twentieth Century', *Archives of Asian Art* 68, no. 2 (2018). She is currently researching the reception to Giuseppe Castiglione in the early 20th century.

Tamaki MAEDA

A native of Kyoto, Tamaki MAEDA received her Ph.D. from the University of Washington, and taught at Wellesley College (USA), the University of British Columbia (Canada), and Heidelberg University (Germany). She was the recipient of major grants, including the Japan Foundation, Robert and Lisa Sainsbury, and Freeman fellowships. Her series of articles on Sino-Japanese interchanges was published in English, Japanese, and Chinese, and her article on the Kusunoki Masashige image (ca. 1660–1945) appeared in *Artibus Asiae* (2012). She is currently completing a book tentatively titled *Japan's Visual Dialogue with China, 1900s–1930s*. She is also collaborating with Joshua A. Fogel on an anthology project, *Modern Japanese Art and China*, funded by the Ishibashi Foundation.

MIURA Atsushi

MIURA Atsushi is Professor at the Graduate School of Arts and Sciences, University of Tokyo, and a Visiting Professor at Paris IV. He obtained his Ph.D from Paris-Sorbonne University (Paris IV) after postgraduate studies in Art History at the University of Tokyo. His recent major publications include *The Representation of Modern Artist – Manet, Fantin-Latour and the French Painting of the 1860s* (The Tokyo University Press, in Japanese, 2006); *Histoires de peinture entre France et Japon* [Histories of painting between France and Japan] in French and English (2009) and *Edouard Manet – Revolution of Western Painting* (2018) in Japanese. He has supervised various exhibitions including the 'Raphaël Collin' exhibition (1999), the 'French Painting in the 19th Century' exhibition (2009) and 'Japan's Love for Impressionism, from Monet to Renoir' (2015).

ROH Junia

ROH Junia is a researcher at the Kyujanggak Institute for Korean Studies, Seoul National University. She is a Ph.D. candidate of Cultural Resources Studies, Graduate School of Humanities and Sociology, the University of Tokyo. She has published several articles on the formation of the modern Korean craft concept and style in Korea and Japan.

SATŌ Dōshin

Dōshin SATŌ is Professor of Aesthetics and Art History at Tokyo University of the Arts. He has published extensively on the art of the Meiji period, and his work on the relationship between art and the nation-state in particular has transformed the way in which we understand the artistic production of the Meiji period. His *Meiji kokka to kindai bijutsu –Bi no seijigaku* (1999) won the Suntory Prize for Social Sciences and Humanities in 1999, and was translated into English as *Modern Japanese Art and the Meiji State: The Politics of Beauty* (Getty Research Institute, 2011).

SHIMAO Arata

SHIMAO Arata is currently Professor of Japanese Art History at Gakushūin University, Tokyo. His research interests focus primarily on ink painting, with a special emphasis on Sesshū: the most distinguished painter in the Muromachi period. His publications include *Hyōnen-zu* [A man catching catfish with a gourd] (1995), *Sesshū* [Sesshū] (1996), *Suibokuga to Katarau* [Discourse with ink paintings] (1997), and *Sesshū no Sansui-chōkan* ['Long Landscape Scroll' by Sesshū] (2001).

SHIN Min-jong

SHIN Min-jong is a Ph.D. candidate in Comparative Literature and Culture, at the University of Tokyo. She specializes in artistic exchange and the relationships among Korea, Japan, and France in the modern period. Her current research focuses on artists' migration between the West and the East, approaching various artistic topics from a historical perspective. Her latest publications include 'A Korean Painter under Japanese Colonization and His European Experience: Pai Un-soung, between the East and the West', *Sociology and Anthropology* 5, no. 8 (August 2017).

Eriko TOMIZAWA-KAY

Eriko TOMIZAWA-KAY is a lecturer in Japanese at the School of Politics, Philosophy, Language and Communication Studies, at the University of East Anglia. She specializes in modern Japanese style paintings (*nihonga*), particularly the formation of *nihonga* and its perception in the market. Her publications include 'Changes in the Japanese Art Market with the Emergence of the Middle-Class Collector: A Study of Hishida Shunsō (1874–1911)', *Journal of the History of Collections* 28, no. 2 (2016).

Toshio WATANABE

Toshio WATANABE is Professor for Japanese Arts and Cultural Heritage, Sainsbury Institute for the Study of Japanese Arts and Cultures, University of East Anglia and Emeritus Professor of History of Art and Design, University of the Arts London. His current research interests are: Modern Japanese gardens in a transnational context; historiography of Japanese art history; and Japonisme. His publications include *High Victorian Japonisme* (1991), *Japan and Britain: An Aesthetic Dialogue 1850–1930* (1991), and *Ruskin in Japan 1890–1940* (1997). He was Chair of the Association of Art Historians (1998–2001); member of the Tate Britain Council (2002–2005); Director of the Research Centre for Transnational Art, Identity and Nation (TrAIN), UAL (2004–2015); President of the Japan Art History Forum (2005–2011); and Vice President of Comité international d'histoire de l'art (2010–2016).

Aida Yuen WONG

Nathan Cummings and Robert B. and Beatrice C. Mayer Professor in Fine Arts, Brandeis University, USA. Aida Yuen WONG specializes in modern and contemporary Asian art. Among her publications are three books, *Parting the Mists: Discovering Japan and the Rise and National-Style Painting in Modern China* (2006), *Visualizing Beauty: Gender and Ideology in Modern East Asia* (ed., 2012), and *The Other Kang Youwei: Calligrapher, Art Activist, and Aesthetic Reformer in Modern China* (2016).

Notes on Translations and Names

Following East Asian practice, East Asian surnames precede given names. However, for East Asian authors whose works are published in English and/or who are based outside of East Asia, the Western style is used, with given names preceding surnames. To avoid any confusion, surnames in the Notes on Contributors are given in capital letters.

Acknowledgements

We are extremely grateful to the many people that helped to make this book possible. First, thank you to all the authors that contributed to this book, and for their enormous patience and support. The editorial team of Routledge and Isabella Vitti have guided us with incredible displays of patience and support. Also, it would not have been possible to complete this book without the painstaking copyediting of Francesca Simkin. In this book, five articles were translated from Japanese to English with professional and excellent skills and knowledge by Maiko Behr, Laurence Mann, Midori Oka, and Sara Sumpter.

Also, we are grateful for the many opportunities we had to discuss and exchange ideas with excellent scholars during the previous symposia and conferences that became the foundation of the anthology (given names precede surnames, alphabetical order of surname): Rosina Buckland, Timothy Clark, Maki Fukuoka, Christine Guth, Yōko Hayashi, Charlotte Horlyck, Misato Ido, Atsuko Ishikawa, Maki Kaneko, Hiroko Katō, Ji-young Kim, Angus Lockyer, Akira Matsuda, Shane McCausland, Malcom McNeill, Naoyuki Kinoshita, Younjung Oh, Rhiannon Paget, Seung Yeong Sang, Erin Schoneveld, Timon Screech, Yasuko Tsuchikane, and Bert Winther-Tamaki.

This book began from a symposium and conferences held in London; and we therefore extend our sincerest and warmest thanks to the Sainsbury Institute for the Study of Japanese Arts and Cultures, and all the staff, particularly to Simon Kaner, Mami Mizutori, Akira Hirano, Sue Womack, and Kawai Masatomo. Similarly, our sincere gratitude is extended to the School of Oriental and African Studies, and in particular the Japan Research Centre that have supported the organising of conferences.

Finally, this book has been generously supported by the benevolence of the Kajima Foundation for the Arts, Japan, the Sainsbury Institute for the Study of Japanese Arts and Cultures, and the University of East Anglia.

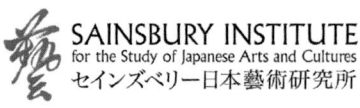
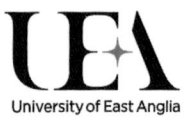

Introduction

Eriko Tomizawa-Kay and Toshio Watanabe[1]

In this volume, we are aiming to provide a range of contributions that explore the issue of transnationality in East Asian art, revealing both connections and disjunctions. This book is neither a textbook nor a survey of East Asian art, but we hope that the volume as a whole will showcase the integrated richness of East Asian art history.

This book project began with two conferences that Eriko Tomizawa-Kay organized in 2013 and 2015. The first took place at the School of Oriental and African Studies (SOAS) in London. It was called *New Boundaries in Modern Japanese Art History: Extending Geographical, Temporal and Generic Paradigms* and reviewed the conventional concept of Japanese/East Asian art history, which has fragmented the history of art in various ways, and tried to determine what kind of methodology should be used to re-construct an overall Asian art history. It also provided a forum for Kinoshita Naoyuki, Kitazawa Noriyuki, and Satō Dōshin, the three art historians who together revolutionized the methodology of examining modern Japanese art, to come together for the first time at a conference and discuss these issues.

The excitement created by this conference led to a second one, again organized by Tomizawa-Kay at SOAS: *Deconstructing Boundaries: Is 'East Asian Art History' Possible?*, which took place in 2015. The aim of this conference was to gain insights into the changing boundaries and concepts of 'art' in Japan and East Asia, focusing especially on the exchanges and dialogues that took place among artists from Japan and other East Asian nations. The papers presented challenged the existing geographic, temporal, and generic paradigms that currently frame the art history of East Asia. Questions included the relationship between artistic production and political discourse, and the role cultural legacies played in the artistic development of East Asia at large. At this conference, debate about the deconstruction of boundaries within East Asian art was expanded to include scholars of Chinese and Korean art history.

Our book is very much the outcome of these debates, but is not a conference proceedings publication. All contributors who were conference participants were asked to be explicit in their engagement with the theme of East Asian art history, while a number of new contributors were also invited in order to create a balance, which would together assist in our overall aim of providing clarifications on the transnationality of East Asian art.

The Terms

For this kind of debate, it is vital to be clear about terms: what they mean, how they are used, by whom, for whom, where, and when. Dictionaries or thesauri provide initial assistance, but terms can adopt subtle variations in different contexts and circumstances. What we are trying to find here are interpretations and clarifications of terms appropriate for the context of transnational East Asian art history.

First, let us consider the term 'transnational'. Here we would like to contrast three terms: the national, the international, and the transnational. The national is the core concept and centres on clearly defined borders between nations, such that the other two terms are dependent on this definition. The international has three main meanings: first, something which is not national or is outside the national, such as 'international waters', which does not belong to any nation; second, where more than one nation comes together, such as when the United Nations is described as an international organization because it consists of multiple nations (but the individual identities of each nation are still firmly preserved). Then we have the third definition of the international, which is rather confusingly the same as the transnational and used more or less interchangeably with it. What, then, is meant by 'transnational'? The transnational goes 'beyond' the national, i.e. trans - national. This term has the least clear border.

In order to understand what the term 'transnational' means, we first need to acknowledge the temporariness of the definitions of these terms. They are historically contingent. When in 2004 Toshio Watanabe and his colleagues set up the Research Centre for Transnational Art, Identity and Nation (TrAIN) at the University of the Arts London, 'transnational' was neither a commonly used nor well understood term. Whenever TrAIN was mentioned, the usual first question was, 'What do you mean by *transnational*?' The term wasn't common currency as it is now.

The point is not that this term was completely unknown in 2004, but that it was *relatively* unknown. If it were totally unknown, we would not have used it as part of the research centre's name. In publications on international relations and economics, this term seems to have been used more frequently in the past than within other disciplines. The *Compact Oxford English Dictionary* (2nd ed. 1991) includes an early example of its use in 1921, to be found in *The Fruits of Victory* by Norman Angell that was published by W. Collins & Sons. This anti-war creed by the future Nobel laureate uses not only 'trans-national' (63) but even 'trans-nationalism' (300). By 2018, this term becomes not only common but downright fashionable. Most stands at the bookfair of the 2018 Association for Asian Studies conference in Washington DC seem to have had at least one book that included 'transnational' in its title. This is an astonishing change to have taken place within just the decade and a half since 2004. What we are trying to emphasize here is the rapid change in the wider understanding of this term and not any changes in its actual meaning.

The Transnational

So what does the term 'transnational' actually mean? Around 2004 the standard answer we gave at TrAIN was that it was about messiness and porous borders. This answer still stands today. Another key factor is that the flow across these porous borders goes both ways.

When we were setting up the research centre, what we wanted to avoid was being constrained by an East/West rhetoric. Edward Said's *Orientalism* (1978) was based on Foucauldian ideas of unequal power relationships in art, and revolutionized our debate. However, we felt that the concept of 'non-Western' art still fell under the constraint of West-as-norm and we wanted to avoid this. We also wanted to have the freedom to discuss North/South or East/East issues, and indeed TrAIN member Yuko Kikuchi developed the notion of Oriental Orientalism.[2] For us at the time the term 'transnational' provided something freer and did not detract from the gains made by the postcolonial debate. We also felt that the notion of 'transnational' could add to this debate by going beyond the term of 'hybridity'. A hybrid C consisting of elements A and B still has the constraint of being defined by A and B, whereas we felt the term 'transnational' offered greater freedom and flexibility. The use of the term 'transnational' did not preclude the interrogation of unequal power relationships, which we still considered an important aspect of research into the transnational; the important point was that the investigation of power relationships was not the whole story, but only part of it.

Debate inside and outside the TrAIN Research Centre showed the complexities arising from a term shifting its meaning over time. Now, nobody seems to ask, 'What do you mean by *transnational*?' Indeed, some scholars have started avoiding the term 'transnational' altogether. Why is this? One of the reasons is that international companies are now sometimes referred to as 'transnational companies'. In other words, the terms 'international' and 'transnational' have, in practice, become interchangeable. The problem is that 'transnational' thus became associated with the neo-liberal flow of capital. Another stopping point is the question of how the transnational can avoid perpetuating the neocolonial. These are the kinds of issues that gave this term a negative nuance for some.

The National

Another constraint that the term 'transnational' labours under is that it is bound by the definition of what is 'national'. The history of study on the 'national' has been dominated by the topic of nationalism, which is a notoriously complex one. The scholarly debate on nationalism reached its most active point during the 1980s and 90s, but has since shown signs of splintering and even stagnating.

One of the early but most illuminating essays on nationalism was the talk given by Ernest Renan at the Sorbonne in 1882.[3] Renan is usually regarded as a conservative thinker, but in this piece he presciently broaches most of the important issues that appear in later debates on nationalism. For example, Renan is against confusing the definition of a nation with dynasty, geography, language, race, religion, or even a community of interest. His argument against defining it by race is succinct and convincing, namely, that 'there is no pure race'.[4] He also correctly notes that '[n]ations . . . are something fairly new in history',[5] and shrewdly observes that '[f]orgetting . . . is a crucial factor in the creation of a nation'.[6] In this lecture he also predicts the formation of the European Union. However, his solution of bringing in the term *patrie* as a kind of *deus ex machina* does not quite work, and even in his clear-sighted analysis the question of 'what is a nation' remains elusive.

There are three points we wish to take from Renan's argument as useful for our debate. First, we agree with all the points he raises regarding what a nation is *not*, including race and ethnicity. We also agree with him that the meaning of what a nation is turns out to be highly volatile; and third, we concur that the notion of a nation is largely a modern concept, which means it would not be applicable to either the Roman or Han periods, for example.

One important lesson that Edward Said and other like-minded scholars have taught us is that a scholar cannot be neutral; pure objectivity in scholarship is not obtainable. However, what we can do is to strive for objectivity, and in order to do so we need to recognize our own subjectivity. As the meaning of 'transnational' is heavily dependent on how the 'national' is defined, it is essential to explain where we stand in the nationalism debate. The following is necessarily, however, a rather shorthand version of our assessment of this debate.

We are against what sociologists call the primordialist interpretation of nation as something natural and ancient. Here national identities are quite rigidly fixed along ethnic lines and each ethnic group is seen as a separate entity. Also, we question the ethno-symbolist interpretation spearheaded by Anthony Smith, as we feel the emphasis on ethnicity could be problematic, as in general we seem to be heading for more ethnically diverse nationhood across the world. Smith is perhaps the scholar who made the greatest contribution to nationalism studies, but his introduction of the term *ethnie* is in our view not helpful, as it simply does not have currency outside the specialized field of nationalism studies. His theory does not work, in other words, in a similar way to how Renan's *patrie* does not work. We also believe that the positions taken by some of the modernists, such as Ernest Gellner, are almost too clear-cut. Our own position is a kind of modified modernist one, whereby we agree that a nation is largely a modern phenomenon with some clearly definable characteristics, acknowledging that it has its own volatility and temporariness.

We agree that the notion of a nation is a not an *a priori* one, but has its own time-limited nature. Nevertheless, it also has some clearly definable features, such as its unitary nature with clear borders. Shiga Shigetaka's 1894 book, *Nihon fūkeiron* (A discourse on Japanese landscape), brilliantly argues the new—for its time—notion of Japan as a modern nation. Shiga is not interested in regional differences within Japan, but tries to identify the characteristics of the Japanese landscape as a whole, a kind of wilful homogenization of all Japanese landscapes. Because of this, borders become very important and he shows great interest in such places. Shiga was actually instrumental in securing Minami Torishima (Marcus Island) in the South Pacific for Japan against the American interest. Border disputes between Japan and China, or Japan and Korea, often about tiny insignificant islands, are frequently based on precisely this issue of the significance of borders for the definition of what counts as the national.

Clearly, how the national is defined affects how the transnational gets defined. In our context, this draws attention to two further points. First, as the national is regarded as modern, so the transnational must also be defined as a modern phenomenon. For example, strictly speaking, the treasures of the Shōsōin, discussed by Itakura Masaaki in Chapter 2, or those of the Higashiyama Gomotsu, discussed by Shimao Arata in Chapter 1, are significant cases of transcultural rather than transnational collections. They are both evidence of the intricate interactions between the Chinese and Japanese cultures and can be seen as a type of very weighty prehistory to the later transnational relationships of our modern times.

The second point is the relationship between the term 'transnational' and national borders. What we are discussing here are cultural borders, including art's. National borders become porous through transnational activities. The transnational flows go both ways and affect the national characteristics of both cultures, and if these flows are happening at these contact zones of multiple nations, the transnational characteristics of this phenomenon become even more pronounced. The transnational movements through these national borders give culture many different shades against the monotone of the national. The essays in this volume demonstrate this in a number of ways.

The Transcultural, the Global, and Other Related Terms

There are quite a number of related terms that occupy adjacent territories to the transnational. These include transcultural, global, glocal, cross-cultural, cosmopolitan, multicultural, multinational, universal, world, and so on. We will confine our discussion here to just three of them: transcultural, world, and global. The term 'transcultural' has a much wider applicability than the transnational, as it is not defined by modernity or any other time span. For example, we could use it when we wish to assert that the Tang period in China was one of the most transcultural in the history of East Asian art. The relationship between transcultural and the transnational is that the latter is a subcategory of the former. The transnational is a transcultural phenomenon, but specific only to the modern period, and in addition should relate to national issues. The term transcultural has a much wider remit and is less historically bound by the concept of the national, whereas the transnational has a much narrower focus. However, the importance of transnational studies is that they open up a new way of tackling the dominance of nationally defined issues of our times. This volume is an attempt at broadening the debate from a nationally confined art history to a transnational one.

The other widely used term is 'global'. This term is at times used interchangeably with 'world'. However, as Hans Belting has pointed out, '"world art" and "global art" today have very different meanings'.[7] According to Belting, 'world art' was 'an old idea . . . [and] includes art from every possible provenance and at the same time excluded it from Western mainstream art.'[8] This is quite similar to how the phrase 'world music' is used to indicate non-mainstream music from places outside Euro-America. Belting narrows down the meaning of 'global art' considerably. For him, global art is 'contemporary and in spirit postcolonial'.[9] We largely agree with this analysis, but also want to acknowledge that there are attempts at establishing world art history where the contemporary and the postcolonial are included, and forms of global art history that are not just about the contemporary and the postcolonial, but include older art as well.

The issue with some past attempts at world art history is that they did not evidence any transnational analysis. Non-Western national art, such as Chinese, Japanese, or Korean art, was merely added to the list of Western ones. This bears similarities to the case of the second definition of the international, discussed above, where it was simply a United Nations-type gathering of the national, where each nation's identity was clearly defined and not threatened.

'Global art history' could similarly harbour the same danger as that described for some cases of 'world art history'. One great advantage of the term 'global' is that it lacks the suggestion of a centre, and thus makes it easier to avoid Euro-centrism. This non-hierarchical notion is very useful and could be deployed profitably. However, it has also become rather overused and some scholars have become allergic to it. For us, the term 'global' contains the danger of homogenization and rootlessness. For example, art critics sometimes use the term negatively when describing biennale-hopping artists as global, thus indicating their lack of cultural identity and supporting communities.

Authenticity, Identity, and Value

When we are investigating the transnationality of an artist or work of art, we also need to look into the issues of authenticity, identity, and value. Let us first examine the term 'authenticity'. Dictionary definitions vary, but usually include terms such as 'genuine', 'true' or 'faithful'. When we are examining whether a work of art is authentic or not, we do indeed need to consider whether it is genuine, true, or faithful—but to what? This could be to the artist's identity. If the artist is true to his/her identity, the work would be authentic; if not, it would be inauthentic.

This all sounds quite simple, but it is not necessarily. If the identity itself is questionable or judged to be insignificant, however authentic a work of art is to that identity, the value of the work would also be judged as questionable or insignificant. Therefore, authenticity itself can be dependent on identity. Furthermore, both authenticity and identity can only be judged through a specific value system. Using a different value system, the judgement of a specific work of art would be likely to change.

Watanabe has previously explored this issue by introducing the concept of a 'value system circle'.[10] For example, a London audience from the 1840s would not be able to appreciate the grunting of a *nagauta* singer, while an Edo audience from the same period would struggle to appreciate a loudly belted opera soprano. This is because the two value system circles of music in London and Edo had nothing in common. However, through the introduction of military bands in Japan and the travelling Japanese performers in the West during the second half of the 19th century, the two value system circles started to overlap. It is like a Venn diagram, where circle A is blue and circle B is yellow, but when they overlap the intersection becomes green. Because of this overlapping, the whole of circles A and B also change, however small the overlap.

This could also be applied to our volume here. The three value circles—China, Korea and Japan—overlapped to a greater or lesser extent throughout history, unlike the musical example above. However, this became exceptionally intense between the mid-19th and mid-20th centuries. Not just artists and collectors, but also many other people from these countries criss-crossed the whole of East Asia. The colours of the three Venn diagram circles became very mixed. We could represent national art history as the uniformly coloured circles in our Venn diagram analogy and the transnational art history as the messily coloured intersections. Which of the two represents reality? Which gives the most authentic picture of our art history? We hope the contributions in this volume will assist you in finding answers to these questions.

East Asian Art History

We titled this volume *East Asian Art History in a Transnational Context* with the aim of emphasizing the transnational aspect of this study. That is what the editors wish readers to take away after reading it. As argued above, we define the term 'transnational' as largely modern and therefore we have prioritized East Asian art of the modern period. We prefer to use 'East Asia' rather than 'Far East', as 'Far East' indicates far east of Europe and is thus contaminated by Euro-centrism. In some quarters, 'North

East Asia' is finding favour, as being slightly more precise, though not yet commonly used among the general public. 'Sinophone' or 'Sinosphere' have also found favour within some scholarly communities, and they have their attractions when discussing cultural matters, but within transnational studies, we still have to keep the national in mind and the above two terms would at times not quite overlap with our focus on the national/transnational. We feel those terms are not quite the same as East Asia.

But then what do we mean by 'East Asia'? We are aware that there is much discussion about this topic. Some include Mongolia, parts of South East Asia, and even parts of East Russia. However, for the purpose of this volume we have focused on China, Japan, and Korea. Nevertheless, transnational studies scholars love to prowl around border territories. Fascinating material is provided by places which are situated between nations, have been forced to assume different national identities, or have divided loyalties, something unacceptable to nationalists of whatever colour. In our context, Ryūkyū/Okinawa provides exactly such a transnational case and we have included this within our remit.

A danger we are aware of in talking about East Asian art history is that the discussion could run into exactly the same kind of problems that many national art histories have done. We could, for example, be accused of seeing this East Asian region simply as a bigger but still unitary entity with clear borders. We could also get into border skirmishes with art historians of South East Asia or South Asia. However, the big difference between transnational art history and national art history or even nationalist art history (yes, we have some powerful ones for example in Japan) is that transnational art history refuses to draw clear borders between territories, whether national or regional.

Another significant aspect of this volume needs to be mentioned, which is the fact that we have put substantial emphasis on the role Japan played in the story of the transnational in East Asia. In the modern period, Japan certainly played a central role in East Asia, particularly in the field of art, but we did not wish to present the role played by Japan as the story of how Japan dealt with the outside world; that would be a different volume. Within the cross-currents of transnational interactions, Japan was not always the active agent, even if it had, at times, an oppressive presence. We are sure that interactions between China and Korea also provide fertile ground for exploration, but again that would be a different book.

While trying to find an appropriate cover illustration, we stumbled across the woodblock print *Hakua (Soshū shoken)* (White walls [Impressions of Suzhou]) by Onchi Kōshiro from 1940. This print was based on Onchi's trip to China in the spring of 1939. Onchi revolutionized the traditional medium of woodblock print in Japan and dragged it into the modern age. The composition shows strong elements of the international abstract art movement, but this work is also part of the story of Japanese colonialism. And yet the mysterious female figure, only partially visible, is wearing a blue *qipao* (symbolic of Chinese modernity of the 1930s) with fashionable Western-style shoes and seems to be serenely gazing at an artwork or a latticed window, which we cannot decipher. It is, in other words, a perfectly transnational piece of work of art from East Asia.

Overview of This Volume

This volume is divided into three parts: I. Constructing the Idea of East Asian Art; II. New Ways of Looking at Others; and III. Translation of Art within East Asia.

Part I opens with Shimao Arata's 'Reconsidering the History of East Asian Painting: Painting from China and Chinese-style Painting in Japan'. In this seminal essay, Shimao argues that the notion of 'East Asian Art History' should not be understood from the perspective of art being produced in three separate entities—China, Korea, and Japan—but rather should be viewed within a single organic system. Grouping paintings from different countries into one category is a major step in the process of 'Deconstructing Boundaries'. The case of Muromachi-period *kara-e* provides an avenue for thinking about this perspective. Shimao argues that when looking at this *kara-e* we must assume that there existed at least 'three Chinas'—that is, the world of Chinese painting that was external to Japan, the (imagined) world of Chinese painting that developed in Japan from paintings that had been imported from the continent, and the world of Chinese-style paintings that was made within Japan itself. Shimao sheds light on the numerous structures bound together as nodes in a network that gives rise to unions of 'artists', 'style', and 'content', and argues that this generative system is the very foundation of 'East Asian painting history'.

With a similar focus to Shimao, Itakura Masaaki has conducted extensive research on the Shōsōin treasure, held at the Tōdaiji temple in Nara. The Shōsōin treasure is a large and venerable collection of cultural objects made in East and West Asia. In his essay, 'The Imperial Treasures of the Shōsōin and the Collections of the Tang Emperors', Itakura points out that the collection, seen by some as a 7th-century time-capsule and a symbolic terminus of the ancient Silk Road, has drawn international attention despite representing only a fraction of the items listed in the catalogues, due to the large number of items removed and lost from the collection over successive generations. By revealing how the objects were collected, Itakura demonstrates that this treasure house was deliberately based on the collections of Tang-dynasty emperors; Emperor Shōmu is known to have collected the works of Wang Xizhi, loved by the emperors of the Tang dynasty, and carefully stored his collection in Tōdaiji as cherished treasures. But calligraphy by Wang and certain of the collection's screen paintings were removed by successive statesmen up through the Heian period. The collection of artefacts accumulated as a result of Emperor Shōmu's admiration of the Chinese emperors' collections was thus partially 'consumed' by Heian-period emperors. As a result, however, the remaining pieces of brilliant craftsmanship are now held in greater admiration and the importance of the Shōsōin's treasure has changed significantly through the process.

Satō Dōshin's 'Overcoming Modernity: Towards a Concept of "East Asian Art History"' offers the opportunity to consider whether it is possible to talk of an East Asian art history. Satō provides a nuanced examination of how institutional frameworks have influenced our ideas about art, art history, and art historiography. There is a reason why the East adopted this nationalistic approach, which does not reflect the reality of Asian art history. It springs from the collapse of the Great Chinese Empire in the 19th century, when satellite countries gained independence, and a strong sense of nationalism led them to rewrite history in isolation from their regional neighbours. A divided Asia thus divided up the presentation of art history, too. The question of whether or not we can re-construct East Asian art history as such therefore depends on whether we can overcome the political legacy of the Modern Age. Satō's essay aims to explain why today the concept of 'art' and the category of 'East Asian art history' remain as they are, and where they can be situated in recent art history. Having conducted extensive research on the major state museums of both East Asia and the West, which highlighted a clear difference in the way that art was selected and displayed in Europe and Asia, Satō concludes that this difference stems both from geographical divides and different concepts of art. Based on this, he discusses the possibility of establishing a new category of East Asian art history, which would represent a radical break—away from the modern age and towards a completely new era.

In Part II, 'New Ways of Looking at Others', four essays explore the art produced in the 20th century, taking various views on the colonial and post-war periods in East Asia: the perception of Japanese art by East Asian artists; the re-evaluation of East Asian art from an external viewpoint which created a renewed self-identity and tradition; and the new perspective of political and social taboos surrounding art and media. Miura Atsushi's 'The Triangle of Modern Japanese *Yōga*: Paris, Tokyo, and East Asia' offers a reappraisal of the historical significance and aesthetic characteristics of these developments. Miura discusses the new framework of *yōga* (Western-style painting) and demonstrates, within the domestic and East Asian contexts, how *yōga* was directly affected by European art. His reading of the historical significance and aesthetic characteristics of these developments proved them to be more than merely Orientalist paintings. He emphasizes new frameworks in which *yōga* painters, who had been affected by Western painting when it became established in East Asian countries (notably Taiwan, Korea, and Manchuria) in the first half of 20th century, copied Western styles but with the themes and motifs of East Asia; from this were created hybrid paintings that mingled the West, Japan, and other locales in East Asia. Those works are a far more complicated phenomenon than Western modern Orientalist painting, and Miura therefore argues that it cannot be understood without precise analysis of the politics and plasticity of painting.

Shin Minj-ong's essay, '"Marginal Man" Pai Un-soung (1900–1978): His European Experience, His Views, and His Art' takes up the case study of Japan-trained Korean *yōga* painter Pai Un-soung during the Japanese colonial period. Shin explores the artist's ambivalent identity as a marginal man who practised art in three regions: the West, Korea, and Japan. Shin connects Pai's activities in Europe with his ideology, and also illuminates the relationship between his Oriental-style paintings and his experiences in Europe. Eriko Tomizawa-Kay's essay, 'Reinventing Localism, Tradition, and Identity: The Role of Modern Okinawan Painting (1930s–1960s)', shifts attention to the hitherto neglected topic of *nihonga* and *yōga* in Okinawa during the pre- and post-war periods. Tomizawa-Kay looks at the complexity of Okinawan history, including the political situation between Japan and the United States, and explores how and why Okinawan artists sought to generate tradition and identity, especially after the 1945 Battle of Okinawa. Tomizawa-Kay examines empirical case studies of how wartime art in Okinawa was integral to the expression of political ideas in relation to national identity, regional struggles, and reflective 'othering'. Her essay aims to explore linkages and disconnects between issues and their socio-political framings in modern paintings and painters in Okinawa.

Miura, Shin, and Tomizawa-Kay's essays suggest that we need to avoid placing modern East Asian paintings within an over-simplistic conceptual framework, within a limited perspective such as the Western Orientalist view or colonial-influence point of view, but instead should explain their significance by placing them in different temporal and geographical contexts, elaborating on their connections to their historical, social, and political environments.

Kitazawa Noriaki's essay, 'The Evolution and Modernization of the Sculpture Genre in East Asia', explains how the modernization of sculpture was conducted on two levels: national and individual. At the national level, monumental bronze statues (*dōzō*) were at first seen as representative of the absolutist reign of the emperor. Quickly, the nation emerged as a major client for monumental statues. Kitazawa argues that while sculptural arts were beginning to dominate the psyche of Japanese society's monument representation, sculpture began to attain its own representational logic. It was to become a medium through which Japanese society could embrace the emerging philosophy of individualism and 'self'. The next essay, Adachi Gen's 'War and Pornography in East Asia', sheds light on Japanese pornography produced from 1931 to 1945, along with examples from Korea and China. Adachi focuses on pornographic images because those of the mid-20th century represent a neglected territory of Japanese art history, unlike *shunga* (erotic images often produced by *ukiyo-e* artists) of the Edo period, which are a renowned form of Japanese art. Adachi explores how human desires expressed themselves in an austere society and enquires into the role of images during times of hardship in modern East Asia.

Part III, 'Translation of Art within East Asia', examines the intercultural relationship between China, Korea, and Japan in terms of art in the 20th century. Essays by Aida Yuen Wong and Tamaki Maeda investigate the historicity specific to modern literati culture as it accrued significance through Sino-Japanese interchange. Aida Yuen Wong's 'Chinese Seal Carving in Modern Japan: Qian Shoutie's Relationship with Hashimoto Kansetsu' examines the seals made by Qian Shoutie—who has been largely overlooked by both Chinese and Japanese scholarship—for Kansetsu and a number of other Japanese figures. Wong's essay uses widely varied and scattered sources to piece together a story of two men caught on opposite sides of an epochal conflict while continuing to support each other's creativity.

Tamaki Maeda's '"National Painting" Unbound: Modernizing Ink Painting in the Sino-Japanese Art World' examines how Japan provided inspiration for China's national painting, by focusing on the widely acclaimed painter Fu Baoshi. This essay dovetails with Wong's and provides insights into the transformation of Fu's art from literati painting to modern ink painting, as he participated in the milieu of Sino-Japanese cultural interchanges. Maeda's critical analysis of Fu's painting and writing reveals how his ink painting transcended the national boundaries of China and Japan, as well as the aesthetic categories of Chan (Zen) and literati art.

Roh Junia's 'Korean Lacquerwork Craftsmen Who Went to Japan: Change and Innovation in Korean Lacquerwork During the Colonial Period' discusses the hitherto neglected lacquerwork craftsmen. Roh's essay examines how the style of Korean mother-of-pearl works dramatically changed thanks to a new tool, the fretsaw, which the artisans who went to Toyama in the early 1920s discovered there. It also discusses how the *geonchil* technique (J: kanshitsu, literally 'dry lacquer'), which had disappeared after the end of the Goryeo dynasty in the late 14th century, was reintroduced to and spread in Korea during the Japanese colonial period.

Liu Yu-jen's 'The Concept of Art in the *Meishu Congshu*: From Foreign Loan to National Tradition' complements Kitazawa's discussion about the process by which institutions surrounding fine art were built. Liu analyses the divergence of the newly imported concept of *meishu* from the traditional Chinese 'art' classification, and shows how endeavours such as the *Meishu Congshu* ('Book collection on *meishu*'), sought to naturalize this imported concept and endow it with an aura of tradition and authenticity in its new Chinese setting.

Notes

1 The preliminary section up to the section 'East Asian Art History' is written by Toshio Watanabe and the section 'Overview of This Volume' by Eriko Tomizawa-Kay. Watanabe would like to thank his colleagues and students for the enriching debates we had on the transnational over the years. This is for him a kind of interim report on the subject.
2 Yuko Kikuchi, *Japanese Modernisation and Mingei Theory: Cultural Nationalism and Oriental Orientalism* (New York and London: Routledge Curzon, 2004).
3 Ernest Renan, 'Qu'est-ce qu'une nation?', *Oeuvres completes de Ernest Renan* (Paris: Calmann-Lévy, 1947), vol. 1, pp. 887–907.
4 Homi K. Bhabha, *Nation and Narration* (London and New York: Routledge, 1990), p. 14. Translation by Martin Thom.
5 Ibid., p. 9.
6 Ibid., p. 11.
7 Hans Belting, 'From World Art to Global Art: View on a New Panorama', *The Challenge of the Object*, 33rd Congress of the International Committee of the History of Art, Congress Proceedings (Nuremberg: Germanisches National Museum, 2013), pp. 1511–1515; p. 1511.
8 Ibid.
9 Ibid.
10 Toshio Watanabe, 'Art Historical Canon and the Transnational', *The Challenge of the Object*, 33rd Congress of the International Committee of the History of Art, Congress Proceedings (Nuremberg: Germanisches National Museum, 2013), pp. 1505–1506.

Part I
Constructing the Idea of East Asian Art

1 Reconsidering the History of East Asian Painting
Painting from China vs. Chinese-style Painting in Japan

Shimao Arata

Introduction

It goes without saying that a wide variety of issues, both theoretical and practical, are embedded in the question at the core of this volume, namely, is 'East Asian Art History' possible? In the field of Japanese history, an 'East Asian perspective' has been advocated for some time, but what seems to have started with the relatively simple idea of looking more broadly at the relationships between Japan, China, and Korea has, in current discourse, having faced the tide of postmodernism, become rife with complexity and even contradiction.

The current view of the issue originated in the critique of discourses founded on histories based in the narratives of individual countries defined by national borders and the illusion of the nation-state. Consequently, it has become necessary to think in terms of a more dynamic model of cultural domains that have ambiguous borders and that expand and contract even as their peoples intermingle. If we are to apply this theory consistently, the only way to talk about these various overlapping, interconnected regions of the world is in terms of a 'Global History'.

On the other hand, the false conception that modern learning itself has the capacity to systematically describe various spheres of human activity has fallen away, while at the same time the self-righteousness of macrohistories that look down on the world from the perspective of a god-like figure is also being criticized. If we take this concept still further, it becomes clear that any theory or method of historical description is no more than a single paradigm. Even setting aside this idea momentarily, there is no way that we can deny cultural pluralism and the microhistories that document defined territories in detail. Indeed, sorting out the theoretical relationship between the part and the whole, and popularising such a method of research, are not simple matters.

There are various different arguments for an East Asian art history, but ultimately we must look at the region not in terms of the three 'countries' of China, Korea, and Japan as discrete elements, but rather must view the whole as a single organic system. In this essay, I would like to examine the example of Muromachi-era *kara-e*—literally, 'Tang pictures'—as a case study for considering the issues at play in such an approach.

'Chinese Paintings' and the Higashiyama Gomotsu Treasures

The challenges in thinking about a history of East Asian painting are clearly apparent in my own field of specialization, art of the Muromachi period (15th–16th centuries). As is widely known, Chinese paintings from the Southern Song to Yuan dynasties entered Japan in large numbers during the Kamakura and Nanbokuchō periods

(13th–14th centuries). In the Muromachi period, major works were brought under the control of the most powerful men of the day, the Ashikaga shoguns, who worked out various systems for display and organization of their collections. Thus, in one sense, these works from China took on a leading role in Japanese art circles and at the same time gradually came to set the standard for Japanese painters. As a result, they have come to be viewed in two separate contexts, that of Chinese painting history and that of Japanese painting history. Unsurprisingly, differences arise between the two viewpoints.

These differences have been exemplified in past exhibitions that have featured these paintings. For example, Itakura Masaaki, author of one of the essays in this volume, organized two exhibitions: *Southern Song Painting: Elegant and Noble in Soul* at the Nezu Museum in Tokyo in 2004, and *Aesthetic Perfection: The Higashiyama Gomotsu Collection Assembled by the Ashikaga Shoguns in the 14th to 15th Centuries* at the Mitsui Memorial Museum in Tokyo in 2014. In the former, Southern Song paintings in Japanese collections were clearly presented as Chinese paintings, while in the latter, the emphasis was placed on the context in which the artworks were collected, displayed, and seen in Japan as a part of a category of Chinese-style paintings known as *kara-e*. As demonstrated in the very wording of the titles of the two exhibitions, the same Chinese paintings could be understood from two distinct angles—that is, as either Chinese or Japanese—through the choice of the term 'Southern Song Painting' or the name 'Higashiyama Gomotsu' (as the Ashikaga shogunal collection was known). Formation of a broader East Asian painting history is not necessarily as simple as joining these two together, however. First, let us examine the situation from the Japanese perspective.

The Three Chinas

In the Muromachi period, both Chinese paintings that had come to Japan and Japanese paintings produced to emulate them were known by the same term, *kara-e*. These existed in contradistinction to Japanese-style paintings known as *yamato-e*, and China itself was of course external to both of these types (Figure 1.1). In short, a framework had come into existence comprised of: (a) Chinese-produced *kara-e* and Japanese-produced *kara-e* internal to Japan, and (b) China itself and other Chinese paintings external to Japan. To better understand this situation, we need to further expand our thinking to account for three Chinas: (1) the world of Chinese painting external to Japan, (2) the world of Chinese painting that was brought to and developed within Japan, and (3) the world of Chinese-style paintings that were produced in Japan.

Once we merge the latter two together as *kara-e*, we are able to look at this situation in two different ways. One is the conventional view of Chinese painting vs. Japanese painting, and the other is Chinese painting vs. *kara-e*. Taken literally, *kara* refers to China as a physical place, but in the case of *kara-e*, it no longer indicates the geographic place of origin of these paintings. In a sense, the term *kara-e*, which encompasses paintings that were made in both China and Japan, represents the very embodiment of the concept of 'deconstructing boundaries' that was at the heart of the symposium (SOAS, London, 2015) that inspired this publication. I believe that thinking in terms of dualities of meaning—or perhaps even a semi-lattice kind of relationship—involving the 'local' and 'global' is essential to the consideration of a history of East Asian painting. For example, as Itakura Masaaki's study of the perspective taken by the Ming-dynasty literati painter Jin Shi from Ningbo demonstrates, we are beginning to see discussions

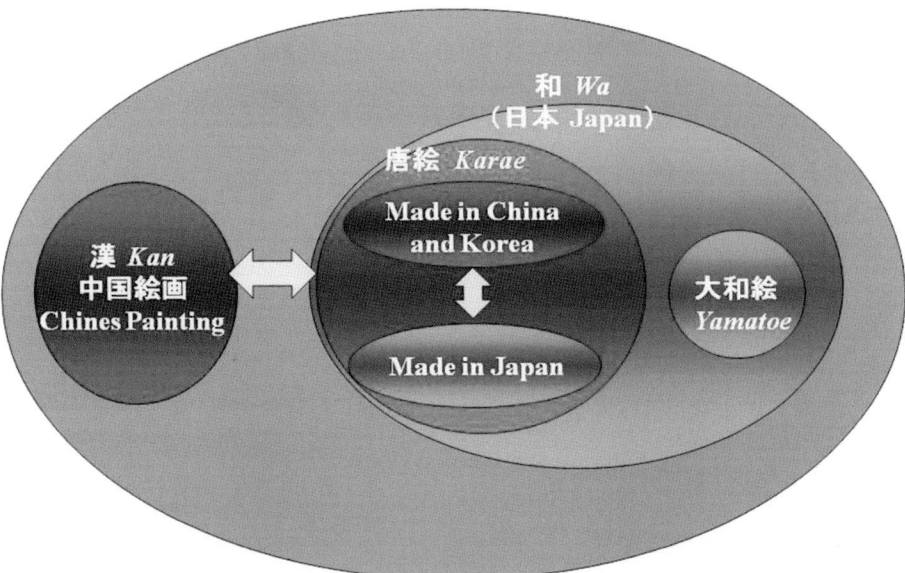

Figure 1.1 Framework of *Kara-e*, *Yamato-e*, and Chinese painting

of local perceptions of East Asia as a broader entity.¹ To clarify this argument, I would now like to reexamine the basic definition of *kara-e*.

It goes without saying that the Chinese paintings that made their way to Japan represented a small fraction of what existed in China itself. The *Gomotsu on'e mokuroku* (Catalogue of the masterworks in the shogunal collection), starting from the time of the third Kamakura shogun Ashikaga Yoshimitsu (1358–1408) onward, lists about 300 paintings, most of them by just thirty Song- and Yuan-dynasty Chinese painters.² Although these thirty individuals were not the only Chinese painters whose artworks had been brought to Japan at the time, the total, including those not listed here, was still probably only around fifty major artists.

The *Kundaikan sōchō ki* (Manual of the attendant of the shogunal collection) provides a list of about 150 names of Chinese painters that was produced in consultation with the Yuan-dynasty painting history *Tuhui baojian* (Precious mirror of painting). It included the names of painters such as Li Cheng and Guo Xi, whose paintings had never been seen but whose names were known from Chinese painting histories, literature, or other written sources.³ As Shih Shou-chien has pointed out, this transmission of *kara-e* through text was also significant, and by this time had enabled an image of Chinese painters external to Japan, including some who were 'yet unseen'.⁴

As for the situation in China itself, *Tuhui baojian* names 1,500 painters, starting with Cao Buxing of the Wu dynasty and continuing through the Yuan dynasty. One thousand names appear from the Song and Yuan dynasties alone. This is just one example of a written source, but even a rough calculation shows China having fifty times the number of painters listed in the *Gomotsu on'e mokuroku*, and ten times the number cited in the *Kundaikan sōchō ki*.

18   Shimao Arata

The difference between Chinese paintings and *kara-e* produced in China does not stop at such quantitative measurements. It is true that the works recorded in the *Gomotsu on'e mokuroku* were a subset of Chinese painting, but if we look at them in terms of cultural history, they do not seem to reflect the general state of painting in mainland China.

For one, there are differences in the range of artists and the numbers of paintings they produced. For example, in terms of the number of paintings, Japanese records document more than one hundred paintings by the Southern Song Zen painter Muqi; he is followed by the Southern Song court painter Liang Kai, with just under thirty paintings. However, Muqi was not a major figure in mainstream painting histories in China and, though he was well known, Liang Kai was not particularly exceptional among the imperial painters of his day. Their dominance in Japan, on the other hand, reflects the unique circumstances of transmission resulting from the fact that it was primarily Zen monks who were bringing the paintings from China to Japan. Muqi was a disciple of the Chinese high priest Wuzhun Shifan, who was also popular among Japanese Zen monks, and although he was an imperial painter, Liang Kai also produced many monochromatic Zen-style ink paintings and had close personal associations with Zen monks. Such factors increased their local popularity within Japan.

Kara-e and Chinese Paintings

Knowing this, if we take an additional look at the artists mentioned in the *Gomotsu on'e mokuroku*, we see notable figures such as Emperor Huizong and Li Gonglin of the Northern Song dynasty or the academic painters Ma Yuan and Xia Gui of the Southern Song dynasty (who were famous in China as well), but we also find the names of Buddhist painters, such as Zhang Sigong, or Zen- and Buddhist-style painters, such as Yuehu and Men Wuguan, who do not appear in Chinese official painting histories. The latter artists most certainly entered Japan in the context of Zen Buddhism, and with some of them it is questionable whether their names were recorded correctly or even if they actually existed at all. However, it is evident that certain individuals whose names have not survived in Chinese painting histories have been preserved in the *kara-e* tradition and from that position have contributed to the larger history of East Asian painting.

There are also considerable incongruities between the ways that certain artists were perceived in Japan and China. The painting *Peach Blossom and Dove* (private collection), understood to be the work of Huizong, bears a date in his characteristic 'slender gold' calligraphic style, but the painting itself is in the imperial court academy style and bears no connection to the painting style demonstrated in Huizong's *Four Seasons Landscapes* (Konchi'in and Kuonji collections). Li Gonglin, who in China is known for monochrome black ink sketches, is known in Japan almost exclusively as a painter of Buddhist subjects, and the term 'Li Longmian (Gonglin) style' apparently referred primarily to the painting style of his arhat paintings. Also, in Japan it was erroneously believed that high priests who, like Wuzhun Shifan, wrote inscriptions in the upper sections of paintings, actually painted the pictures as well.

Neither could the manner in which these 'Chinese things' were displayed—known as *karamono-kazari*—be by any stretch considered to have replicated precisely the way things were done in China. Figure 1.2 represents the basic decorations of the main room of the south-facing gathering pavilion (*kaisho*) at the palace of the sixth shogun, Ashikaga Yoshinori, based on a reconstruction by Miyagami Shigetaka.[5] As illustrated here, the standard mode for featuring paintings in the central display space was the triptych format.

Reconsidering the History of East Asian Painting 19

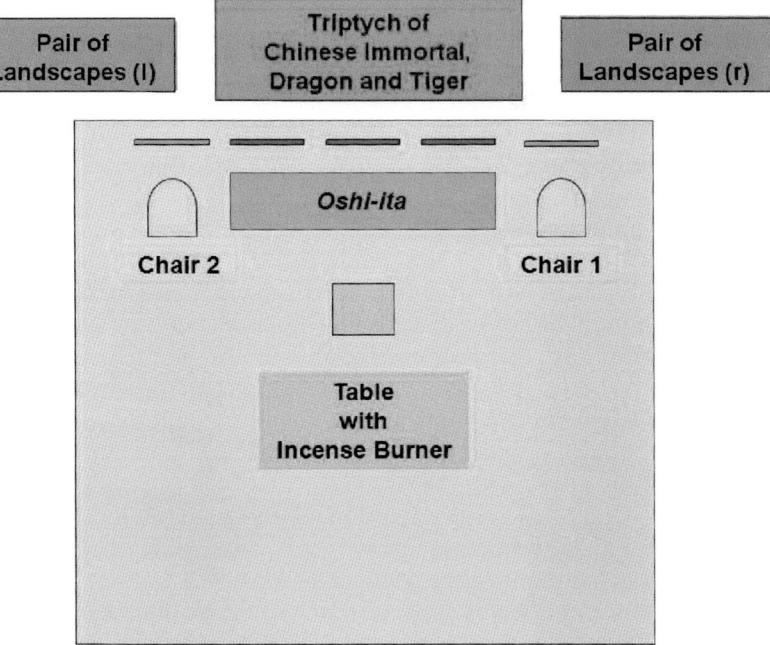

Figure 1.2 Image of *Karamono Kazari* of the main room

However, the triptych was not a standard format for the display of secular paintings in China. Rather, it was originally a format for displaying Buddhist paintings, and more specifically was adopted from Zen temple practice. In order to allow for display in this triptych format, hanging scrolls that were produced as separate, discrete works were frequently matched up into sets of three. The *Gomotsu on'e mokuroku*, for example, lists many such sets, including a *guanyin* (Kannon) by Liang Kai flanked on both sides with monkeys by Muqi. The *mitsugusoku* set of implements—censer, candlesticks, and flower vase—placed in front of this central feature is also a format that was adopted from Buddhist temples. On the other hand, the chairs placed at the right and left with landscape paintings hanging behind them is reminiscent of displays seen at Chinese scholars' residences. The whole is a vague mix of a Buddhist temple-style setting and a literati-style setting.

It was the third shogun, Ashikaga Yoshimitsu, who laid the foundation for this sophisticated mode of *karamono* display. Yoshimitsu created a structure at the shogunal residence called a *kaisho*, which doubled as a space both for holding events and receiving guests, and the interior of this *kaisho* is where he would lavishly display the Chinese items from his collection during formal ceremonial events. Surrounded by monks who had studied abroad, Yoshimitsu was by no means ignorant of the latest news from China, but rather than attempting to recreate Chinese modes exactly, he chose to devise a new world of *kara-e* and *karamono* display that drew upon the authority of the Chinese imperial collection as a means of reaffirming his own power.[6]

This approach remained fundamentally unchanged throughout the Muromachi period. For example, in 1479 (Bunmei 13), Ōuchi Masahiro, daimyo of the western province of Suō (Yamaguchi), presented the shogun with a total of thirty-two Chinese painting scrolls in ten sets, including triptychs and other groupings.[7] The painters found on that list remain within the scope of the *Gomotsu on'e mokuroku* and include Muqi, Ma Yuan, Yan Hui, and Yuehu, suggesting that little interest had arisen in contemporary Ming-era painting. Furthermore, Yoshimasa's particular favourite among these was a painting of *guanyin* by Ma Yuan. Although Ma Yuan painted subjects such as the *Patriarchs of the Zen Sect* (Tenryūji, Tokyo National Museum), and others, Buddhist paintings like those of *guanyin* were not typical of the basic repertoire of academy painters. Here too, painting choice was being guided by a value system foreign to the artworks' country of origin.

Looking back, 200 years had already passed since the fall of the Southern Song dynasty and in that time a variety of different paintings had continued to be brought in, including some dubbed with attributions like 'Yuan[-era] Muqi' and 'Ming[-era] Xia Gui' and others that are clearly what we, from a modern perspective, would call fakes. With the addition of such works, the world of *kara-e* came to include a considerable variety of Chinese paintings, and the 'made in China' component of *kara-e* changed and grew incrementally along with the times.

Drawing on this world of *kara-e* produced in China as a base, Japanese painters also began to produce works in the Chinese mode. As is widely known, for these Japanese artists it was desirable to paint in the manner of known Chinese painters, and their works were frequently identified as such, resulting in the popularization of terms such as 'priestly style (Muqi style)', 'Liang Kai style', 'Ma Yuan style', and 'Xia Gui style'. As just touched upon, the Chinese-made *kara-e* that these Japanese painters had access to included quite a few attributed works and fakes that had been repudiated by Chinese art historical research or otherwise consigned to oblivion. As works that contributed to the birth of Japanese-produced *kara-e*, however, they retain a particular significance when we speak of East Asian painting history.

Viewed in this way, in the context of cultural history, it is clear that we cannot define Chinese paintings in Japan as simply the areas of overlap between Chinese painting and *kara-e*. The Chinese paintings in Japan were not a foregone product of Chinese painting history, but rather themselves gave form to a unique world of *kara-e*. I would therefore argue that to view the world of Chinese *kara-e* as the result of a direct reception history of Chinese painting in Japan is not appropriate, and in fact, that there is a need to reassess the transmission of the Chinese paintings instead in the context of a 'generative history' of *kara-e* in Japan that results in the three Chinas that we examined at the outset. In this sense, Chinese paintings existed not solely as a physical entity outside of Japan, but also in part as an imagined China that existed inside of Japan as well. Consequently, the Japanese 'local' spans both the internal *kara-e* made in China as well as the Japanese imagining of the world of Chinese painting outside its borders.

The Formation of the 'Xia Gui-style' Landscape Scroll

The phenomenon of *kara-e* may be considered unique to Japan, but a similar kind of thing in principle frequently happened within China as well. As an example, let us look at aspects of the transmission of landscape scrolls by the Southern Song-dynasty academic painter Xia Gui. This artist is a particularly interesting example because his style was also widely adopted in *kara-e* in the Muromachi period and his popularity can be considered an East Asian phenomenon. While scholarly opinions about the authenticity of certain attributions to Xia Gui sometimes differ, in the context of Chinese painting history he is generally credited with the works *Pure and Remote Views of Mountains and Streams* (The National Palace Museum, Figure 1.3) and *Twelve Views of Landscape* (The Nelson-Atkins Museum of Art, Yale University Art Gallery).

A number of painted scrolls, including *kara-e*, are believed to be derived from these works. For example, the iconography of the Freer Gallery of Art's *Grand View of Rivers and Mountains* (Figure 1.4) is the same as that of *Pure and Remote Views of Mountains and Streams*. However, it is not attributed to Xia Gui, but bears the signature of another equally regarded Southern Song academic painter, Ma Yuan, and is dated 1192 (Shaoxi 3). In its details, it vaguely resembles the Southern Song academic painting style, but the mountains and rocks are clearly imbued with the modelling sensibilities of the Ming-dynasty Zhe School in their composition, which is based on a distinctive combination of verticals, horizontals, and forty-five-degree diagonal lines. The buildings are accented with ochre pigment, while the mountains and tree leaves are tinted blue, and reds and blues are applied to the robes of the incidental figures in the landscape. In this, too, it differs from the *Pure and Remote Views* scroll, which is painted solely in black ink. Of course, this scroll is not actually by Ma Yuan, and is believed to be a Ming-dynasty work that preserves the iconography of the earlier work but ascribes to it a different painting style and artist.

Holdings at the Liaoning Provincial Museum and Guangzhou Museum of Art also include a group of landscape scrolls that share the same iconography as these scrolls and are believed to have been produced in the Ming dynasty.[8] These are items 6 through 9 of the list appearing in Note 8. A portion of their iconography replicates sections of the *Pure and Remote Views* and *Twelve Views* landscape scrolls and many elements seem to be derived from those works, but the overall scenic composition is

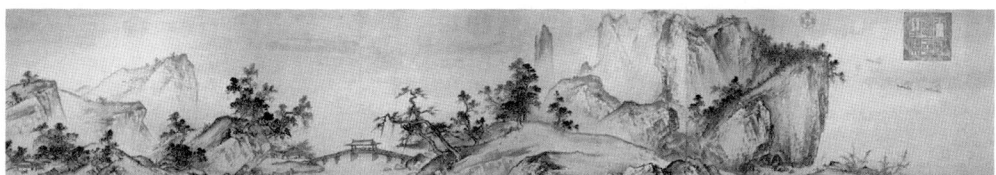

Figure 1.3 Xia Gui, *Pure and Remote Views of Mountains and Streams* (detail), Southern Song dynasty. Ink on paper, 46.5 × 889.1 cm

The National Palace Museum, Taipei

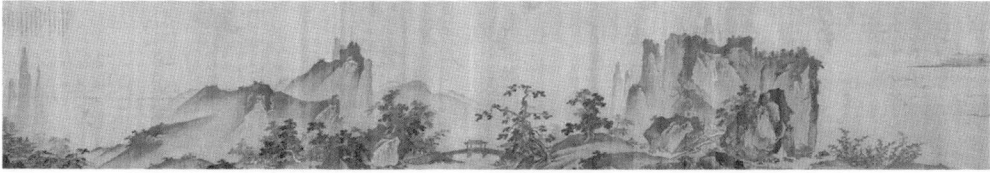

Figure 1.4 [Signed] Ma Yuan, *Grand View of Rivers and Mountains* (detail), Ming dynasty. Ink and light colour on silk, 64.2 × 1276.4 cm

Freer Gallery of Art and Arthur M. Sackler Gallery

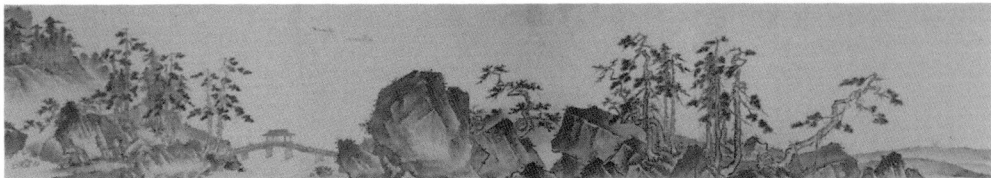

Figure 1.5 [Signed] Dai Jin, *High Mountains and Flowing Rivers* (detail), Ming dynasty. Ink and light colour on paper, 50 × 2073 cm
Guangzhou Museum of Art

different. They also range widely in style and artist. For example, the *Long Landscape* (Figure 1.5), from the Guangzhou Museum of Art, bears the signature and seals of the early Ming academic painter Dai Jin and indeed exhibits a painting style associated with the Zhe School, with colours such as blues and ochres applied in areas of the rocks and mountains. *Superior Views of One Thousand Cliffs*, in the Liaoning Provincial Museum collection, bears the signature and seals of Ma Yuan, but the style, as expected, shows the influence of the Zhe School. Meanwhile, its *Rivers and Mountains for Ten Thousand Miles* is painted in a softer monochromatic style that follows in Xia Gui's tradition. Even within this group of paintings that shares the same subject imagery, issues of painter and painting style are intricately entangled. This complexity makes it difficult to give this group a name, but for expediency, I will refer to it as the 'Dai Jin lineage'.

From Authenticism to a Generative Model

In this way, artist, iconography, and style become complex issues among Ming-dynasty landscape scrolls that carry on the Xia Gui style, and a similar phenomenon to *kara-e* starts to appear in Chinese paintings within China. When trying to describe this situation, the methodology of authenticism, which valorizes a history of painting based on the primacy of authenticity of artist attribution and degrees of proximity to it, ceases to function. As far as contributing to the research of the real Xia Gui of the Southern Song, the Freer Gallery of Art scroll is of little use besides as a reference for reconstructing the lost portions of the *Pure and Remote Views of Mountains and Streams* scroll; nor does it offer any significant insights into the Southern Song Ma Yuan.

However, it is precisely because there was a space for works like this to come into being in the Ming dynasty that this painting scroll exists. This scroll has a postscript signed Jin Shan (1368–1432) and dated 1421 (Yongle 19) that tells a grandiose tale of production and provenance. Jin Shan served the emperors Xianzong and Renzong and became a 'Scholar of Great Learning' at the Imperial Wenyuan Library and a High Official of the Ministry of Confucian Rites. According to the postscript, this illustrated scroll was presented to 'the emperor' in 1380 (Hongwu 13), the year that the treacherous chancellor Hu Weiyong was executed. In this same year, the future Emperor Yongle was installed as the Prince of Yan based in Beiping (Beijing), where he was presented with this 'Ma Yuan masterpiece' that had been secretly treasured at the Yuan court. The year the postscript was written, 1421 (Yongle 19), was the year just after the Ming capital was moved to Beijing (the Northern Metropolis). Emperor

Yongle, rejoicing upon returning to this city after so many years away, held a great banquet and is said to have pointed out this painting scroll to his crowd of retainers. In short, this was a masterwork that commemorated the return of the capital to the place where Yongle had first embarked upon the path to becoming emperor.

As noted earlier, this illustrated scroll is believed to be a Ming-dynasty work, not a masterpiece by Ma Yuan that had been removed from the Southern Song capital of Hangzhou by the Yuan court. However, the support of the painting consists of a single continuous piece of silk measuring more than ten metres in length. Although it is not of exceptionally high quality, there is no doubt that it must have been a commissioned piece. This 'cherished possession of Emperor Yongle' draws its iconography from Xia Gui, bears the name of Ma Yuan, and is presented in the form of a high-quality painting on a single roll of silk. Regardless of the authenticity of the artist or the truth of the magnificent imperial provenance story, when this painting was produced, it was understood that Xia Gui's iconography was typical of Ma Yuan, and the Zhe School style was recognized as Southern Song-style Ma Yuan. In such works, we see a 'generative model' in which artist, style, and iconography associations became attached to paintings in different forms from the Southern Song works.

This is also a matter of historical consciousness—of how Xia Gui and Ma Yuan were perceived in the Ming dynasty—but when we try to generalize to include the Muromachi-era *kara-e* paintings that did not seem to demonstrate much awareness of Chinese painting history, it seems best to understand the attributive process instead more loosely as different impressions of the painting world held by certain groups of people.

Naturally, these impressions differed depending on place and time. There is no way that people in any one region could have known of all the paintings that existed in East Asia or its history, and their awareness of past painting traditions would certainly have varied as well. For example, within Muromachi period Japan, there would have been differences between Kyoto and Yamaguchi, just as in Ming-dynasty China between

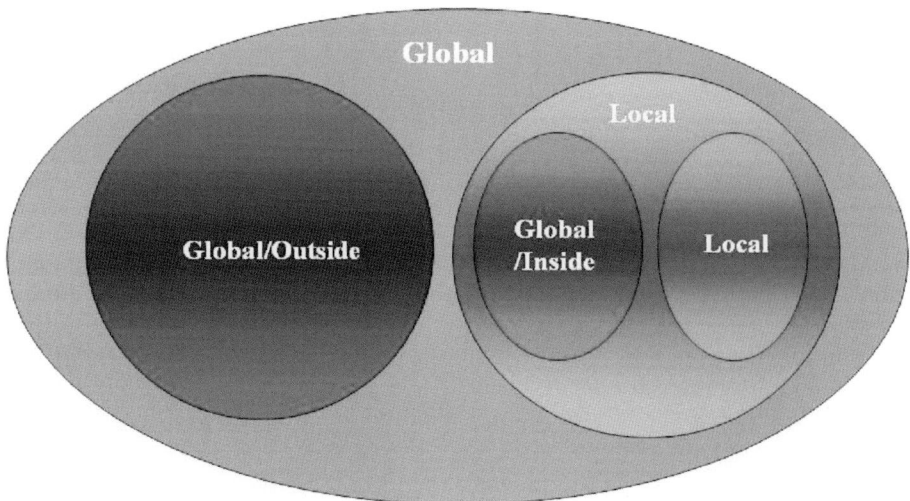

Figure 1.6 Framework of 'global' and 'local'

24 *Shimao Arata*

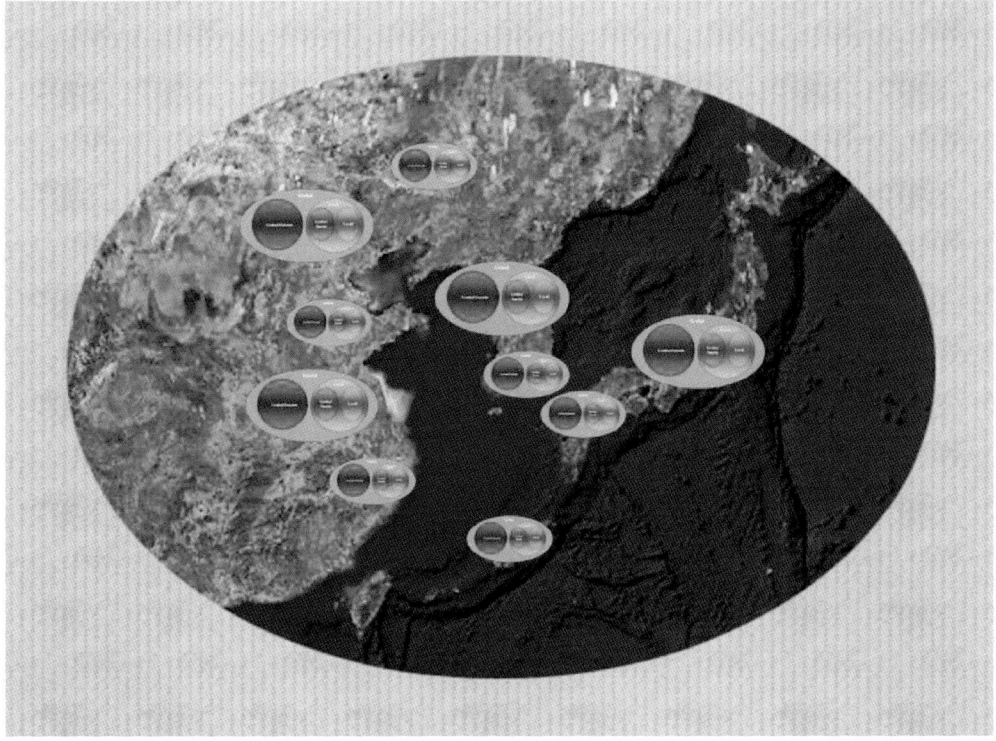

Figure 1.7 Networks of external connection

Beijing and Suzhou. If we simplify things dramatically down to the binary of 'global' vs. 'local', each location (i.e. each 'local') has its own distinctive internal image of the global that does not match up with the actual 'external global' (Figure 1.6). In a broader sense, this framework would have existed separately in various regions, and as they formed networks of connection they changed with time (Figure 1.7). And as regions connect or remain separate, their individual powers of influence over the painting world are necessarily continually shifting.

It is through these interconnections that the relationship between the concepts of 'artist', 'style', and 'iconography' that we looked at earlier begins to be born. When trying to understand this phenomenon, the perspective of authenticism always somehow insists on identifying an 'original', with statements like, 'The *Four Season Landscapes* attributed to Huizong of the Northern Song was *actually* by an academy painter of the Southern Song'. Alternatively, viewed in terms of a chronological 'succession model', we might encounter comments such as: 'Scrolls by Xia Gui of the Southern Song were passed down in the Ming dynasty and engendered a range of variants.' However, those variants—as will be demonstrated again later—go beyond the scope of a tree diagram model consisting of one original and its derivatives. I therefore believe that the term 'generative model' is a more appropriate description. This would allow for comments such as: 'A painting system from somewhere in Ming-dynasty China gave rise to a landscape scroll by Ma Yuan depicting iconography from Xia Gui rendered in Zhe

School style.' In the same way, when Muromachi period *kara-e*, which is a subsystem of East Asian painting history, produces a four-seasons landscape scroll bearing the name of Huizong, it does not constitute an erroneous attribution to a particular Chinese painter or a mistaken understanding of either history or the difference between Japan and China; rather, it represents a certain vocabulary that was created around Muromachi period *kara-e*. It is of course in some ways a simplification, but I believe it is possible to see East Asian painting history as a generative system that is constantly forging ever-changing relationships between artist, style, and content (iconography). In this sense, what is being generated is not just the artwork itself, but also an image or understanding of the painting world that includes a historical awareness that prompted its creation, or the systems of display and appreciation that we saw with the *kaisho* spaces, or even concepts of monetary worth. In that sense, the generative model is a type of value system that should be analysed in terms of its structure and how it works.

The Generative Power of *kara-e* and the Limits of a Name-Based History of Painting

Let us think about the Xia Gui style in Muromachi period *kara-e* from this perspective, then. Take, for example, Geiami, an artist who served under Ashikaga Yoshimasa and was responsible for the management of his collection of Chinese objects. In this role he had free access to a landscape painting in the shogunal collection known as the 'nation's best Xia Gui' that he adapted into a pair of six-panel folding screens with landscapes of the four seasons.[9] Although these screens do not survive, we can surmise much about the artist's approach from his sole surviving work, *Viewing Waterfall* (1480, Nezu Museum) (Figure 1.8). In this long vertical hanging scroll, Geiami depicts a cascade of water framed within a grotto similar to the type that was found in the 'Dai Jin lineage' scrolls, and sure enough, applies here and there some touches of the blue and ochre pigments that were used in Ming-dynasty painted handscrolls. However, the iconographic details of a hut behind the waterfall and the monk walking towards it are his own unique additions. Xia Gui's handscrolls consisted of multiple scenes that made it easy to extract individual motifs and reconfigure them in different ways. This is another reason why they gave birth to a diversity of arrangements, but Geiami took these images and translated them into different formats, producing hanging scrolls and folding screens.[10] As a result, classifications by format, such as 'Xia Gui-style handscroll' and 'Xia Gui-style hanging scroll' were no longer meaningful distinctions.

Here, we run up against the issue of clarifying the nature of the illustrated scroll that served as the original model for the Xia Gui-style scrolls, particularly the 'nation's best Xia Gui', but there does not seem to be an identifiable equivalent from among the Xia Gui-style painted handscrolls made in China that we know of today. Four Xia Gui-style scroll paintings from the Muromachi period are known: Sesshū's *Long Landscape Scroll* (Mōri Museum) (Plate 1) and *Small Landscape Scroll*, Geiai's *Landscape* (Agency for Cultural Affairs), and Isshi Kii's *Landscape* (Kyoto National Museum); however, all of these Xia Gui-style landscapes created within the context of *kara-e* are coloured. They present the distinctive blue and ochre of the rocks that also appeared in Ming-dynasty painted scrolls and in some parts there is also colour on the clothing of the figures, as in the Freer Ma Yuan-signed scroll painting. As a result, it would be natural to think that Xia Gui's original painted scrolls from which these *kara-e* drew

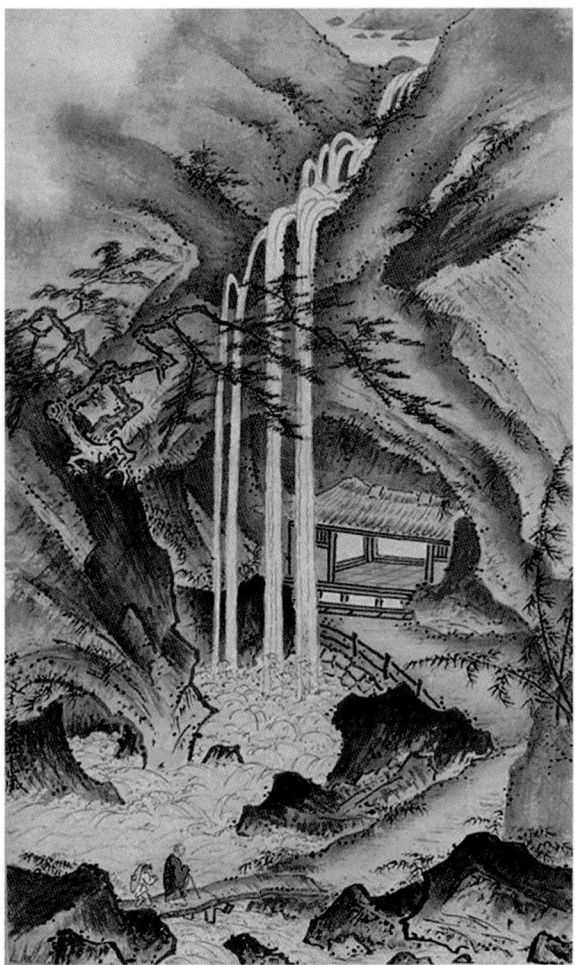

Figure 1.8 Geiami, *Viewing Waterfall* (detail), 1486 (Muromachi period). Ink and light colour on silk, 106.0 × 30.3 cm
Nezu Museum

also had colour, but this feature is not evident in the 'country's best' Xia Gui scroll or other known Southern Song works by Xia Gui.

In terms of iconography, the issue is fairly complex, so I will just very simply touch on the scenes of the waterfall in a grotto and the shore with willows. The 'waterfall in a grotto' scene seems to have been recognized as a symbolic motif that was representative of Xia Gui's painted scrolls, as in the earlier example of Geiami's extracting it for his *Viewing Waterfall* (Figure 1.8). It can be found in both Sesshū's *Small Landscape Scroll* and Geiai's *Landscape*, all with a bridge in front of the waterfall. This scene does not appear in Southern Song Xia Gui paintings, and though there is a large, impressive waterfall in the 'Dai Jin lineage' scroll (Figure 1.9), it does not have the bridge that appears in the *kara-e*

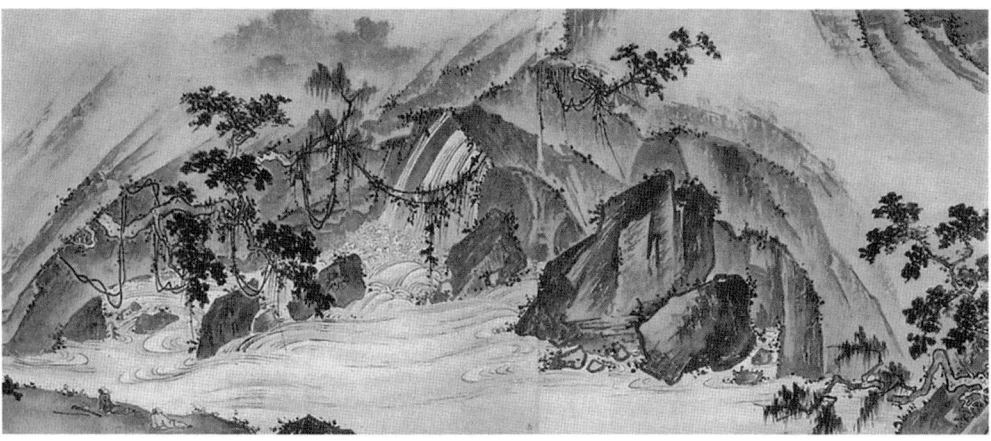

Figure 1.9 [Signed] Dai Jin, *High Mountains and Flowing Rivers* (detail), Ming dynasty. Ink and light colour on paper, 50 × 2073 cm
Guangzhou Museum of Art

paintings. Therefore, we can assume that the painting that *kara-e* took as their original iconographic model was not one of the 'Dai Jin lineage' scrolls, but some other version.

The 'shore with willows' motif appears in Sesshū's *Small Landscape*, Geiai's *Landscape*, and Isshi's *Landscape*, but cannot be found either in Southern Song Xia Gui scrolls or the 'Dai Jin lineage' scrolls. The scene also appears at the beginning of Sesshū's copy of a landscape scroll with Xia Gui's signature and seals (formerly Kobayashi Hideo collection) as well as in the *Eight Views of Landscape* attributed to Oguri Sōtan (Kyushu National Museum), which is almost identical in subject matter, so it is clear that *kara-e* were referencing the Xia Gui original.[11] At the same time, the 'waterfall in a grotto' in this scroll differs significantly from both the 'Dai Jin lineage' scrolls and the Japanese *kara-e* versions.

What becomes clear from this is that (1) a 'Chinese Xia Gui-style illustrated handscroll' different from those that are presently identified as 'Chinese paintings' must have made its way to Japan, and (2) none of the known *kara-e* versions of Xia Gui-style landscape scrolls share the same iconography and style. Starting with the high point of Sesshū's *Long Landscape Scroll*, a variety of different arrangements were added, which, taken together, created a complex 'Xia Gui mode' from a network of artists, content, and styles. As for the 'nation's best' Xia Gui scroll, (1) it was probably coloured, and (2) as such, it is difficult to consider it in the same lineage as the *Pure and Remote Views of Mountains and Streams* or *Twelve Views of Landscape*, so (3) at the present time, it is not possible to identify a work that fits this description perfectly, and we know that new theories and further study are necessary to be able to reconstruct its iconography.[12]

To recapitulate, the situation of *kara-e* and the creation of a painting history cannot be adequately illustrated by the model of an evolutionary tree comprised of an original and variants, and, although it is based on the illusion of a Southern Song Xia Gui, that is not something real to which one can retrace the steps. These are not images that

28   *Shimao Arata*

are direct successors of Xia Gui's manner; rather, they are examples that demonstrate the generative power of East Asian painting history. Through these painted scrolls attributed to Xia Gui and their 'copies', the boundaries between *kara-e* made in China and *kara-e* made in Japan become continuous. Then, if we look at East Asian painting history as a generative system, it becomes impossible to separate the two clearly, and the distinction between made in China and made in Japan loses its significance.

As an additional note, this kind of situation makes using art historical descriptors based on an artist's name a risky undertaking. Conventional East Asian painting history draws on a biographical tradition that discusses style and form based on an artist's name. However, within the constantly developing network of artist-content-style that we have now seen, the full range of aspects that define an artist's 'name' becomes continually less and less clear. The 'Xia Gui' whom we have just examined in the context of *kara-e* is more than the painter who actually lived in the Southern Song period. Indeed, it is probably better to say that the name is almost a kind of label that is attached to works and was thus a type of abstracted historical concept. What is important is that painting 'in the name of Xia Gui' was the driving force behind the functioning of the generative system of *kara-e*. There is a need to distinguish this 'Xia Gui' from the Xia Gui who actually existed in the Southern Song, as well as from Xia Gui as an emblematic banner of a particular style or iconography. This is not a particularly new issue, but there still seems to be a need for clarification in order to make sense of the story being told.

Conclusion: The *Long Landscape* Scroll and the Yamaguchi Local Sphere

Using Sesshū's 1486 *Long Landscape Scroll* (Plate 1) as an example, I would like to close by touching on Sesshū's local sphere of Yamaguchi. The *Long Landscape* is a very long Xia Gui-style painted handscroll measuring 40 centimetres in height and 16 metres in length that Sesshū painted when he was sixty-seven years old. Throughout its length, it is studded with his full lexicon of landscape motifs integrated amidst the four seasons. We know the intent behind the painting, which was created for presentation to the local lord, Ōuchi Masahiro. Around this time, the Ōuchi were the most powerful daimyo in the western provinces, and 1486 was a commemorative year marking the establishment of a provincial administrative system complete with religious rituals. It is easy to imagine that this impressively long handscroll presented at this time to his lord was layered with references to the 'nation's best' Xia Gui from the shogunal collection. The *Long Landscape Scroll* draws upon the layering of the authority of the Chinese emperor, which is embedded in the 'nation's best' Xia Gui, with the authority of the Japanese shogunal family who used it and assumes that identity for itself. Here, we can see the operations of a local system that is conscious of its place *between* China and Japan, but that from the perspective of this manuscript itself is its own local sphere.

This multilayered framework is reflected in the question of this scroll's artist and style as well. Sesshū creates the painting under the name of Xia Gui—or, to put it differently, under two names. In so doing, he creates parallels between the relationship of the shogun (and by extension the Chinese emperor) to the Ōuchi as well as between Xia Gui and Sesshū, resulting in the aforementioned multilayered character of the *Long*

Landscape Scroll. For this reason, the content of the scroll also has to follow that of Xia Gui's 'nation's best' scroll. In that case, the authority of the Ashikaga shogun becomes layered onto the scroll and the Ōuchi have to assert their own identity in relation to this. The *Long Landscape* takes the motifs of certain rocks and trees from Xia Gui-style works, but the clear Sesshū manner of both the iconography and style, which surpasses the original arrangement, indicates a kind of 'Yamaguchi pride' and at the same time asserts Sesshū's own individual identity. The *Long Landscape Scroll* was a product of the generative model of Yamaguchi *kara-e*, which further served to elevate Sesshū as an artist.

Describing the generative effects of this kind of ever-changing network, woven from shared yet distinct value systems existing in the East Asian region, is an immense but fascinating task that will surely take more than my own lifetime. For now, in conclusion, I would like to add one more comment about the distinctive nature of art history. The fact that the region (node) of Yamaguchi in Japan rises to prominence within East Asian painting history of the latter 15th century is without question specifically because of the monk painter named Sesshū. If Sesshū had not lived there, this city in western Japan would surely never have drawn the attention that it has. However, Sesshū was only one painter. Yes, he was a monk painter who represented this location, and his paintings reflect the circumstances of painting production in Yamaguchi; however, this does not mean that they reproduce the state of *kara-e* in Yamaguchi in its entirety. What is reflected in his paintings is basically the world he saw, including his unique circumstance of having travelled to Ming China. Painting history differs from legal history or war history in that the fundamental data it is based upon can essentially be classified as 'microhistory'. Therefore, I hope that when we talk about East Asian painting history, we take care to maintain an attentive gaze towards the act of painting itself and not become trapped in the pitfalls of the 'big history' that can be so problematic.

(Translated by Maiko Behr)

Notes

1 Itakura Masaaki, 'Jūgo seiki ninpō bunjin ga mita higashi ajia kaiga: Kin Jiki o rei ni' [East Asian painting as seen by the 15th-century Ningbo literati: the example of Jin Shi], *Bijutsushi ronsō* 27 (2011): 51–76.
2 The following thirty Chinese painters were listed in the *Gomotsu on'e mokuroku*: Mu Xi, Liang Kai, Ma Yuan, Xia Gui, Emperor Huizong, Yu Jian, Long Mian (Li Gonglin), Yu Shan, Fangru (Zhang Fangru), Ma Lin, Li Anzhong, Li Di, Ke Shan, Yue Hu, Shun Ju (Qian Xuan), Sigong (Zhang Sigong), Abbot Wuzhun (Wuzhun Shifan), Ting Hui, Wang Hui, Yao Qing, Zhao Chang, Junze (Sun Junze), Mo Jie (Wang Wei), Zhi Weng, Xu Xi, Cao Fuxing, Shijin Jushi, Ya Zi, Yan Hui, and Men Wuguan.
3 The number of Chinese painters named in the *Kundaikan sōchōki* differs depending on the copy, but on average it has about 150 names. The Tōhoku University version has the most, with 177.
4 Shih Shou-chien, 'Ka Bungen kara Sesshū e: *Tokai hōkan* to 14-, 15-seiki higashi ajia ni okeru sansuiga no rekishiteki rikai no keisei' [From Xia Wenyan to Sesshū: *Tuhui baojian* and the historical understanding and formation of landscape painting in 14th- and 15th-century East Asia], trans. Uematsu Mizuki, *Bijutsu kenkyū* 403 (2011): 1–37.
5 Miyagami Shigetaka, 'Kaisho to kazari' [*Kaisho* and display], in *Sadō shūkin* 12 (Tokyo: Shōgakukan, 1985), 77–81. See also 'Kaisho kara chanoyu zashiki e' [From *kaisho* to tea room display] in *Sadō shūkin* 7 (Tokyo: Shogakukan, 1984), 50–59, and Shimao Arata, 'Kaisho

to karamono: Muromachi jidai zenki no kenryoku hyōshō sōchi to sono kinō' [*Kaisho* and *karamono*: symbols of authority and their function in the early Muromachi period], in *Shirīzu toshi, kenchiku, rekishi 4: Chūsei no bunka to ba* [City, Architecture, History Series 4: Space and culture in medieval Japan] (Tokyo: Tōkyō Daigaku Shuppankai, 2006), pp. 123–155.

6 Hata Yasunori, 'Muromachi jidai no nansō intaiga ni taisuru ninshiki o megutte: Ashikaga shogun-ke no Ka Kei to Ryō Kai no gakan o chūshin ni' [Attitudes toward Southern Song-dynasty academic painting in the Muromachi period: an examination of painted handscrolls by Xia Gui and Liang Kai in the Ashikaga shogunal collection], *Bijutsushi* 156 (2004): 427–443.

7 *Chikamoto nikki* [Diary of Ninagawa Chikamoto], entry of July 10, 1841 (Bunmei 13).

8 If we include fragmentary works, the number of painted scrolls originating from Xia Gui that are known today is quite large. The list below enumerates the main ones that I draw from for the present essay. Attributed works are not specifically marked as such.

1	Xia Gui	*Pure and Remote Views of Mountains and Streams*	Ink on paper	National Palace Museum
2	Ma Yuan	*Grand View of Rivers and Mountains*	Ink and light colour on silk	Freer Gallery of Art
3	Xia Gui	*Rivers and Mountains without End*	Ink on paper	National Museum of History (Taipei)
4	Xia Gui	*Twelve Views of Landscape*	Ink on silk	The Nelson-Atkins Museum of Art
5	Xia Gui	*Twelve Views of Landscape*	Ink on silk	Yale University Art Gallery
6	Dai Jin	*Long Landscape*	Ink and light colour on paper	Guangzhou Museum of Art
7	Xia Gui	*Rivers and Mountains for Ten Thousand Miles*	Ink on silk	Liaoning Provincial Museum
8	Xia Gui	*Rivers and Mountains with no End*	Ink and light colour on silk	Liaoning Provincial Museum
9	Ma Yuan	*Superior Views of One Thousand Cliffs*	Ink and light colour on silk	Liaoning Provincial Museum
10	Copied by Sesshū	*Landscape by Xia Gui*	Ink and light colour on paper	Ex Kobayashi Hideo Collection
11	Sōtan	*Eight Views of Landscape*	Ink and light colour on paper	Kyushu National Museum
12	Sesshū	*Long Landscape Scroll*	Ink and light colour on paper	Mōri Museum
13	Sesshū	*Short Landscape Scroll*	Ink and light colour on paper	Kyoto National Museum
14	Geiai	*Landscape*	Ink and light colour on paper	Agency for Cultural Affairs, Government of Japan
15	Isshi	*Landscape*	Ink and light colour on paper	Kyoto National Museum

9 Shōjū Ryūtō, 'Byōbuga ki' [Record of screen paintings], in *Gozan bungaku shinshū*, vol. 4, *Tokubi chōheisō* 1. See Tsukahara Akira, 'Shōjū Ryūtō *Byōbuga ki* ni okeru Geiami hitsu shiki sansui zu byōbu ni tsuite' [On Geiami's *Screens with Landscapes of the Four Seasons* in Shōjū Ryūtō's *Record of Screen Paintings*], *Bijutsushi kenkyū* 27 (2000): 105–125.

10 There are similar examples in China as well. For example, the subject of *Talking with a Guest under a Pine Cliff*, attributed to Xia Gui (National Palace Museum), is extracted from the left half of the Dai Jin lineage work *Waterfall in a Grotto*.

11 The former is a second-level or later copy of the copy made by Sesshū. Both have colour and titles inscribed on each landscape scene, just like the *Twelve Views of Landscape* scrolls. In terms of the iconography, it shares some of the same scenes as appear in the Southern Song Xia Gui paintings and the 'Dai Jin lineage' scroll, but it also differs from them in many respects. We know at least that this iconographic element was shared by Kyoto and Yamaguchi. See Shimao Arata, 'Futatsu no Ka Kei–yō sansui zukan' [Two Xia Gui–style landscape scrolls], *Bijutsu kenkyū* 367 (1997): 42–53.
12 Hu Zhimin is currently conducting a detailed analysis of this issue, and will surely be clarifying it in her doctoral dissertation.

Bibliography

Hata Yasunori. 'Muromachi jidai no nansō intaiga ni taisuru ninshiki o megutte: Ashikaga shogun-ke no Ka Kei to Ryō Kai no gakan o chūshin ni' [Attitudes toward Southern Song-dynasty academic painting in the Muromachi period: an examination of painted handscrolls by Xia Gui and Liang Kai in the Ashikaga shogunal collection]. *Bijutsushi* 156 (2004): 427–443.
Itakura Masaaki. 'Jūgo seiki neiha bunjin ga mita higashi ajia kaiga: Kin Jiki o rei ni' [East Asian painting as seen by the 15th-century Ningbo literati: the example of Jin Shi]. *Bijutsushi ronsō* 27 (2011): 51–76.
Miyagami Shigetaka. 'Kaisho kara chanoyu zashiki e' [From *kaisho* to tea room]. *Sadō shūkin* 7 (Tokyo: Shogakukan, 1984): 50–59.
———. 'Kaisho to kazari' [*Kaisho* and display]. *Sadō shūkin* 12 (Tokyo: Shōgakukan, 1985): 77–81.
Ninagawa Chikamoto. *Chikamoto nikki* [Diary of Ninagawa Chikamoto], edited by Tsuboi Kumezō and Kusaka Hiroshi. Tokyo: Yoshikawa Hanshichi, 1902.
Shih Shou-chien. 'Ka Bungen kara Sesshū e: *Tokai hōkan* to 14-, 15-seiki higashi ajia ni okeru sansuiga no rekishiteki rikai no keisei' [From Xia Wenyan to Sesshū: *Tuhui baojian* and the historical understanding and formation of landscape painting in 14th- and 15th-century East Asia], translated by Uematsu Mizuki. *Bijutsu kenkyū* 403 (2011): 1–37.
Shimao Arata. 'Futatsu no Ka Kei–yō sansui zukan' [Two Xia Gui–style landscape scrolls]. *Bijutsu kenkyū* 367 (1997): 42–53.
———. 'Kaisho to karamono: Muromachi jidai zenki no kenryoku hyōshō sōchi to sono kinō' [*Kaisho* and *karamono*: symbols of authority and their function in the early Muromachi period]. *Shirīzu toshi, kenchiku, rekishi 4: Chūsei no bunka to ba* [City, Architecture, History Series 4: Space and culture in medieval Japan]. Tokyo: Tōkyō Daigaku Shuppankai, 2006.
Shōjū Ryūtō. 'Byōbuga ki' [Record of screen paintings]. *Tokubi chōheisō* 1. Reproduced in Tamamura Takeji, *Gozan bungaku shinshū* vol. 4 (1970, no. 7).
Tsukahara Akira, 'Shōjū Ryūtō *Byōbuga ki* ni okeru Geiami hitsu shiki sansui zu byōbu ni tsuite' [On Geiami's *Screens with Landscapes of the Four Seasons* in Shōjū Ryūtō's *Record of Screen Paintings*]. *Bijutsushi kenkyū* 27 (2000): 105–125.

2 The Imperial Treasures of the Shōsōin and the Collections of the Tang Emperors

Itakura Masaaki

It is well known that Chinese art consistently served as a major driving force for premodern Japanese art. A survey of the relationship between the two, however, shows that Japanese art never merely followed contemporaneous Chinese trends. Often it was receptive to, and opted for, art from many centuries past. The independence displayed in the Japanese selection of continental art models indicates the continued survival of set ideas about art that persisted from ancient times to the modern era. The collection of *karamono*—objects imported from China—was not undertaken simply for the love of art. It held significance as a means of both directing art trends of the period and seizing control of the prestige goods (*ishinzai*) that symbolized power and authority.[1] The Shōsōin in Nara is the first example of an imperial collection of *karamono* collected by the statesmen and officials of Japan. Catalogues of its earliest inventory are still extant, and objects that were collected and then passed down through the generations can thus be recognized.[2]

The Establishment and Social Standing of the Shōsōin

The Shōsōin collection is generally believed to have been formed after the death of Emperor Shōmu (701–756, r. 724–749), when a bequest of objects was offered to the Shōsōin of Tōdaiji Temple by Shōmu's wife, Empress Kōmyō (701–760). Over time, two ideas about the collection have developed in the public imagination: that the collection includes art and craft objects emblematic of the Tenpyō era's admiration for the international Tang court, and that those works have been transmitted to the present day by imperial decree, like a kind of time capsule. Even now this belief plays a role in the romanticization of the Tenpyō era (729–750) in fantasies about China and the Silk Road. In actuality, there were multiple motives behind the donation of objects to the collection in the period before the establishment of the Shōsōin. And intriguingly, scholars have identified a considerable number of objects that were removed and replaced shortly after the Shōsōin collection's establishment.

The opportunity to establish the Shōsōin collection first came on the 21st day of the 6th month of Tenpyō-shōhō 8 (756), the 49th-day anniversary of the death of Emperor Shōmu. On that day, Empress Dowager Kōmyō presented a bequest of over 600 objects and sixty types of medicine to the Great Buddha of Tōdaiji in prayer for the repose of the emperor's soul in the next world. The contents of this bequest are known from

The Imperial Treasures of the Shōsōin   33

the *Kokka chinpō chō* (Catalogue of state treasures) (Plate 2) and the *Shuju yaku chō* (Catalogue of medicines). The list in the *Kokka chinpō chō* is as follows:[3]

1. nine monk stoles (*onkesa*)
2. cabinet (*zushi*)—red lacquer keyaki-wood cabinet (*sekishitsu-bun kanboku zushi*)—containing votive objects (*osamemono*):

    - calligraphy of the emperors and empresses—*Miscellany* (*Zasshū*) by Emperor Shōmu; *The Classic of Filial Piety* (Ch: *Xiaojing*, J: *Kōkyō*) by Empress Genshō (683–748, r. 715–724);[4] *Dhūta Monastery Stele Inscription* (Ch: *Toutuosi beiwen*, J: *Zudaji hiben*), *A Collection of Letters in the Style of the Du Family* (Ch: *Dujia licheng*, J: *Toka rissei*), and *Essay on General Yueyi* (Ch: *Yueyi lun*, J: *Gakkiron*) by Empress Kōmyō
    - joint offerings of Emperor Shōmu and Empress Kōmyō
    - calligraphy—copy of original works by Wang Xizhi, twenty volumes
    - short sword (*shōtō*)
    - three kimono sashes (*obi*) with accompanying ornamental knives (*o-tōshi*) and bags (*fukuro*)
    - three ceremonial batons (*shaku*)
    - six scales (*shaku*)
    - 100 counters (*sanshi*)
    - two rhinoceros-horn (*saikaku*) sake cups
    - 116 *sugoroku* dice (two unfinished)[5]
    - 169 *sugoroku* pieces
    - twelve ornamental shell tools (*baiketsu*)
    - rhinoceros-horn vanity case (storing seven Buddhist rosaries [*nenju*])
    - two small knives of Tang China manufacture
    - hundred-colour spool of thread (*hyaku sakuru*)
    - four *shakuhachi* (flutes)

3. red lacquer *keyaki*-wood cabinet containing votive objects:

    - rhinoceros horn (one chunk, three slivers)
    - sixteen white stone ornamental curtain anchors (*shiroishi chinshi*)
    - four silver lacquer containers for chess pieces (*gin-heidatsu gōsu*)

4. musical instruments:

    - two ancient Japanese zithers (*wakin*)
    - two Japanese zithers (*kin*)
    - two *biwa*
    - five-string *biwa* (*gogen biwa*)
    - Chinese lute (Ch: *ruanxian*, J: *genkan*)
    - Chinese zither (Ch: *zheng*, J: *sō*)
    - ancient Chinese zither (Ch: *se*, J: *shitsu*)
    - Chinese bamboo flute (Ch: *xiao*, J: *shō*)
    - Japanese panpipes (*shō*)
    - ancient Japanese flute (*u*)

- transverse flute (*ōjaku*)
- *shakuhachi*
- two ancient Korean zithers (*Shiragi kin*)

5. gaming equipment

- rosewood chess board with inlaid design (*mokuga shitan no go kyoku*)
- rosewood *sugoroku* board with inlaid design (*mokuga shitan no sugoroku kyoku*)

6. weapons

- 100 long swords (*taitō*)
- 100+ bows (*yumi*) in three distinctive colours
- 100 arrows (*ya*)
- 100 helmets (*kabuto*)

7. incense (*zensenkō*)[6]
8. twenty mirrors (*kagami*) and a lacquered bottle (*shokkohei*)
9. 100 folding screens (*byōbu*)
10. assorted furnishings

- large pillow (*ōmakura*)
- two cushions (*shoku*)
- elbow rest (*kyōshoku*)
- two beds (*shō*)

The items on this list give a basic sense of the scope of the Shōsōin collection—from Emperor Shōmu's personal belongings to paintings and calligraphy, craftworks, and weapons.

The *Byōbu kasen tō chō* (Catalogue of folding screens and patterned rugs) records that, less than a month later—on the 26th day of the 7th month—various folding screens bearing calligraphy by the hand of Ouyang Xun (557–641, J: Ōyō Jun) and Wang Xizhi (303–361, J: Ō Gishi) were added to the collection, along with flower-patterned rugs (*kasen*), woven-silk shoes (*sengai*), spherical incense burners (*ginkunro*), chopsticks (*hashi*), and incense holders (*gōshi*). These were combined with the previous donation, and it is probably at this point that the first stage of the Shōsōin's establishment was completed.

One era name change and a little less than two years later, on the 1st day of the 6th month of Tenpyō-hōji 2 (758), a copy of *Daishō Ō shinseki sho* (The calligraphy of Wang Xizhi and Wang Xianzhi) was donated to the collection. The *Daishō Ō Shinseki chō* (Catalogue of the calligraphy of Wang Xizhi and Wang Xianzhi) (Figure 2.1) notes that this scroll 'was transmitted from generation to generation and was a source of great pleasure to our late emperor'. It is described as follows: 'Copy of *Daishō Ō shinseki sho*. One scroll. Yellow paper. Facing side: *Dai Ō sho* (Calligraphy of Wang Xizhi). Nine lines; seventy-seven characters. Backing side: *Shō Ō sho* (Calligraphy of Wang Xianzhi). Ten lines. Ninety-nine characters'. This calligraphy, by father and son Wang Xizhi and Wang Xianzhi (J: Ō Kenshi, 344–386), was used as a model by Emperor Shōmu but for some reason had been omitted from the original bequest. In fact, it was discovered in a box of clothing during a reorganization.

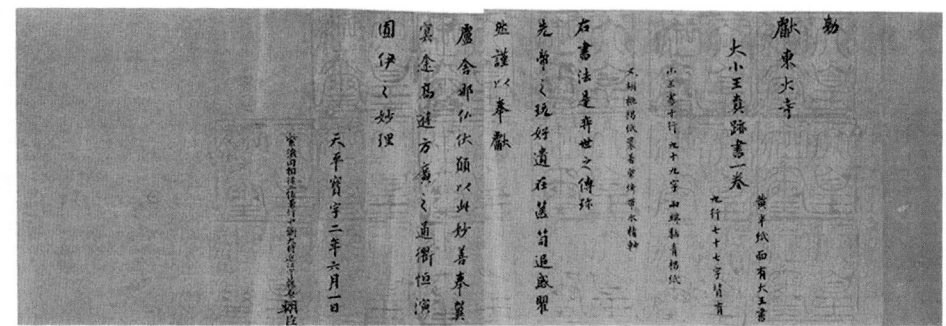

Figure 2.1 Catalogue of the Calligraphy of Wang Xizhi and Wang Xianzhi (Daishō Ō Shinseki chō), 758. Ink on paper, 27.5 × 88 cm
Collection of the Shōsōin, North Warehouse

The *Fujiwara-kō shinseki byōbu chō* (Catalogue of the folding screens of the Fujiwara lords) records that four months later, on the 1st day of the 10th month, Empress Dowager Kōmyō had a pair of six-panel folding screens made using samples of calligraphy by her father, Fujiwara Fuhito (659–720), and offered them to the Great Buddha of Tōdaiji on the occasion of the anniversary of her father's death. Both the *Kokka chinpō chō* and *Shuju yaku chō* record that the objects from these various donations were collected and deposited in the storehouse (*shōsō*) of Tōdaiji. Following these offerings, Buddhist ritual objects (such as those used during the eye-opening ceremony [*kaigen kuyō*] for the Great Buddha)[7] were added to the collection, and then, in Tenryaku 4 (950), objects from Tōdaiji's Kensakuin storehouse—the so-called uncatalogued treasures (*chōgai hōmotsu*)—were moved to the southern storehouse and the so-called Shōsōin Treasures (*Shōsōin hōmotsu*) were formed.

Buddhism, which served as a protector of the realm, fulfilled the role of a state religion. The Shōsōin collection was not, therefore, created merely on behalf of Emperor Shōmu—a fact that is made clear in the *Kokka chinpō chō*, which records the following: 'Through an offering on behalf of the abdicated emperor [Shōmu], treasures of the state were sacrificed and deposited in Tōdaiji as a prayer [for the nation]'. The act of offering these objects must therefore first be understood in a Buddhist context. The actions of the Buddhist emperors of Liang China, like Emperor Wu (personal name: Xiao Yan, 464–549, r. 502–549), who renounced their worldly treasures to become priests and emulated the offerings made by the ancient Indian ruler, Ashoka (d. 232 BCE), who was lauded as a Chakravartin—or ideal—king, can be thought of as forming the background context for these offerings.[8] Emperor Tenji (626–672, r. 662–671) made offerings at Hōkōji (Asukadera) in Tenji 10 (671) and Emperor Tenmu (ca. 631–686, r. 673–686) made them in Tenmu 14 (685). Additionally, in Yōrō 6 (722), sacred texts like the *Flower Garland Sutra* (Sk: *Avataṃsaka Sūtra*, J: *Kegon-kyō*) were copied and offered—along with banners for the Kanjō and Dōjō ceremonies—for the deceased Empress Genmei (661–721, r. 707–715) at various temples in and around the capital. Empress Dowager Kōmyō divided her offerings between the eighteen principal temples and shrines of Nara, including Hōryūji and Konkōmyōji. The Shōsōin was only one of these. In that respect, even the contents of imperial treasure collections functioned as relics connected to Buddhism. In addition, the later inclusion of Buddhist ritual objects, such as those used during the eye-opening ceremony for the Great Buddha of Tōdaiji, coincided with this objective.

A comparison between the extant objects in the Shōsōin collection and early catalogues like the *Kokka chinpō chō* shows that a large number of objects left the collection without passing through the formal 'removal' procedures. The fact that a separate catalogue was prepared for the medicines in the collection suggests that there was always an expectation that they would be retrieved and put to practical use. Indeed, during Kōmyō's lifetime, the medicines were used almost immediately following their presentation to the Shōsōin.[9] Weapons, meanwhile, were treated as a special case, ready to be handed out immediately in the event of potential conflict.[10] In the Heian period, beginning with Emperor Saga (786–842, r. 809–823), any calligraphy, folding screens, and musical instruments that were owned, or actively used, by the emperors are recorded as having been left to the collection. In the midst of this coming and going of objects, there is a fairly substantial number of objects whose return to the collection cannot be confirmed. From this we can infer that by the Nara (710–794) and Heian periods (794–1185) many objects that had left the collection had not found their way back.

From the time of Fujiwara no Michinaga (966–1028), the right to view the treasures of the Shōsōin became tied to the exercise of power by high-ranking officials. The fact that Muromachi period (1336–1573) shoguns like Ashikaga Yoshimitsu (1358–1408, r. 1368–1394), Yoshinori (1394–1441, r. 1428–1441), and Yoshimasa (1436–1490, r. 1449–1473), as well as later military commanders like Oda Nobunaga (1534–1582), also assumed such privileges highlights their significance as emblems of authority. The historical position of the objects in the present-day Shōsōin collection must be considered in terms of this process.

The Shōsōin's Lost Painting and Calligraphy Collection

An array of paintings and calligraphy that cannot be placed in a Buddhist context as reliquary objects also made up a significant part of the Shōsōin collection.[11] Artists and calligraphers represented in the collection include the Eastern Jin (265–420) calligraphers Wang Xizhi and Wang Xianzhi, and the early Tang (618–907) calligrapher Ouyang Xun. The *Kokka chinpō chō* lists twenty volumes of *Tō-Shin u shogun Ō Gishi no shohō* (Calligraphy copybook of the Eastern Jin General of the Right Wang Xizhi):

- *Tō-Shin u shogun Ō Gishi no sōsho*. Cursive script. Volume one. Twenty lines. Yellow paper. Rosewood frame. Blue characters. Light indigo silk wrapper.
- *Tō-Shin u shogun Ō Gishi no sōsho*. Cursive script. Volume two. Fifty lines. Red paper. Rosewood frame. Blue characters. Light indigo silk wrapper.
- *Tō-Shin u shogun Ō Gishi no sōsho*. Cursive script. Volume ten. Twenty-five lines. Yellow paper. Rosewood frame. Blue characters. Light indigo silk wrapper.
- *Tō-Shin u shogun Ō Gishi no sōsho*. Cursive script. Volumes fifty-one to fifty-six.
- *Tō-Shin u shogun Ō Gishi no sōsho*. Cursive script. Volumes fifty-eight to sixty.
- *Tō-Shin u shogun Ō Gishi no sensho*. Accordion book. Volume one. Twenty lines. Yellow paper. Rosewood frame. Woodbine-pattern brocade on blue ground. Light indigo silk wrapper.

This is to say that out of an original sixty volumes, only twenty—including volumes 1–10, 51–56, and 58–60, and a *sensho* (folding fan accordion book)—were initially presented.

The *Byōbu kasen tō chō* notes the inclusion of two six-panel folding screens, *Ōyō Jun shinseki byōbu* (Calligraphy of Ouyang Xun) and *Ō Gishi rinsho byōbu* (Copy of the calligraphy of Wang Xizhi), while the *Daishō Ō shinseki chō*, as I mentioned above, notes the inclusion of a *Daishō Ō shinseki sho* scroll. However, there is not a single example of any of these works of calligraphy in the present-day Shōsōin collection. The monk Dōkyō (700–772) first borrowed the *Ōyō Jun shinseki* folding screen in Tenpyō-hōji 6 (762) and returned it two years later. This screen was borrowed again during the Enryaku era (782–806). After Enryaku 12 (793), however, there is no record of it returning. Next, in Ten'ō 1 (781), the *Daishō Ō shinseki sho* scroll and the twenty *Ō Gishi no shohō* scrolls were taken to the imperial palace. Twelve of these scrolls were returned six days later. In Ten'ō 2 (782), one additional scroll was returned; in Enryaku 3 (784), the final eight were returned. In Kōnin 11 (820), after they were once more taken out of the collection, the scrolls were not returned. Expressed differently, we can surmise that these objects made their exodus during the Heian period after they were taken out of the Shōsōin collection by members of the imperial court.

Objects that might possibly have been part of the original Shōsōin collection include early Tang dynasty copies of Wang Xizhi's *Letter on the Disturbances* (Ch: *Sang luan tie*, J: *Sō ran jō*) (Imperial Household Collection, Tokyo) (Figure 2.2) and *Letter to Kong* (Ch: *Kong shizhong tie*, J: *Kō jichū jō*) (Maeda Ikutokutai Foundation) and a copy of the *Thousand Character Classic in Cursive Script* (Ch: *Zhencao qianziwen*, J: *Shinsō senjimon*) (private collection) by the Sui dynasty (581–618) calligrapher Zhiyong (dates unknown). Both the *Letter on the Disturbances* and the *Letter to Kong* are stamped with red, square-shaped colophons that read 'By imperial decree in the Enryaku era [*Enryaku chokujō*]'—Enryaku meaning during the reign

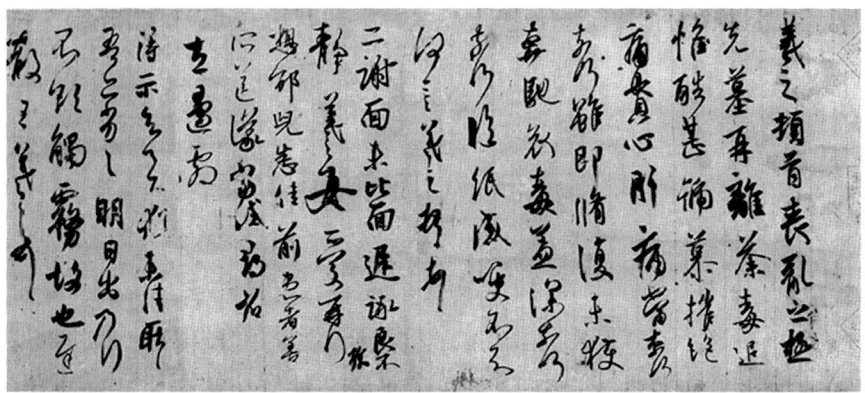

Figure 2.2 Wang Xizhi, *Letter on the Disturbances* (Ch: *Sang luan tie*, J: *Sō ran jō*), Tang dynasty copy, 7th century. Ink on paper mounted on bamboo paper, 26.2 × 58.4 cm
Collection of the Imperial Household Agency

of Emperor Kanmu (737–806, r. 781–806). Meanwhile, there are blank sheets of paper in the *Ō Gishi no shohō* set that correspond to the seventh volume, which is recorded as having been removed. Additionally, a copy of *Sister's Arrival* (Ch: *Meizhi tie*, J: *Maishi jō*) was rediscovered by Nagoya Akira and purchased by the Kyushu National Museum in 2015, while a piece called the *Letter on Important News* (Ch: *Dabao tie*, J: *Daihō jō*) (private collection) was introduced to the public at a 2013 Tokyo National Museum exhibition on the works of Wang Xizhi. The condition of their paper was compared with works like the *Letter on the Disturbances* and found to be a match, making it highly likely that these works originated in the Shōsōin collection.[12] The Edo period scholar Motoori Norinaga (1730–1801) hypothesized that the characters for Xizhi were read as *teshi* (meaning *te no shi*, master of calligraphy) and used in the composition of poetry in the *Manyōshū* (Collection of ten thousand leaves; 8th century). Scholars agree that Wang Xizhi's existence permeated Japanese culture from the time of the *Manyōshū*, and his is the oldest name of a Chinese artist to appear in the literary records of Japan.

It is said that when Jianzhen (J: Ganjin, 688–763) came to Japan, he, too, brought examples of calligraphy by Wang Xizhi and Wang Xianzhi. An entry from the *Fusō ryakki* (A concise history of Japan) for Tenpyō-shōhō 6 (754) records that 'the monk Jianzhen arrived on Tsukushi [present-day Kyushu] in Dazaifu with a book of calligraphy by General of the Right Wang [Xizhi]'. Ōmi no Mifune's (722–785) biography of Jianzhen, *Tō daiwajō tōseiden* (A record of the eastern expedition of the Tang monk [Jianzhen]; 779), records that in Tenpyō-shōhō 5 (753), when Jianzhen arrived in Japan and went to the imperial palace, he had with him a book of running-script calligraphy by Wang Xizhi and three books of calligraphy by Wang Xianzhi. It would therefore not be an exaggeration to say that Wang Xizhi is the artist who initiated Japanese appreciation for Chinese painting and calligraphy.[13]

This collection, which was put together by the emperors of Japan, was surely created with a strong awareness of the art collections of the Tang dynasty emperors. Though it was a collection of paintings and calligraphy, calligraphy books took precedence while the painting collection was focused on large-format screens—a reflection of Tang dynasty collections.[14] It is thought that these imperial collections became prominent from the time of the fashion-orientated Liang dynasty (502–587) onwards, but up until the Tang dynasty their focus was on books of calligraphy. Emperor Taizong of Tang (598–649, r. 626–649) set out to find the most desirable paintings and calligraphy after inheriting the Sui dynasty collection. According to Zhang Yanyuan's (815–876) *Lidai minghua ji* (Famous paintings through history), Taizong gathered objects as clouds gather in the sky. Notably, in Jōgan 13 (639), Taizong issued an imperial command for the collection of all of Wang Xizhi's works, and at great cost collected as many as 3,000 superb examples from all over the country. Moreover, when compiling a history of the Jin dynasty, Taizong wrote a biography of Wang Xizhi, and when the emperor died his last wish was for his copy of the *Lanting xu* (J: *Rantei jō*; Preface to the poems from the Orchid Pavilion), which he had obtained with great difficulty, to be entombed with him. The three masters of the early Tang dynasty, Yu Shinan (J: Gu Seinan, 558–638), Ouyang Xun, and Chu Suiliang (J: Cho Suiryō, 596–658), who flourished under the rule of Taizong, often studied the works of Wang Xizhi. As can be seen from the presence of Wang Xizhi, Wang Xianzhi, and Ouyang Xun in the Shōsōin collection, there was a marked awareness of Tang Taizong's love for Wang Xizhi.

As for the paintings in the Shōsōin collection (other than decorations affixed to industrial art objects), we find records for numerous folding screens, beginning with the *Gyo byōbu ichihyaku jō* (List of one hundred folding screens) record in the *Kokka chinpō chō*.[15] Using this list as a basis, we can say that the painting collection was centred on large-format works. A breakdown of the *Gyo byōbu ichihaku jō* reveals the following: twenty-one picture screens (*ga byōbu*), three screens of beauties under trees (*torige byōbu*), one screen depicting birds (*toriga byōbu*), sixty-five with clamp-resist dye fabric patterns (*kyōkechi*), and ten with wax-drawn dye fabric patterns (*rōkechi*). A closer look at the twenty-one picture screens reveals the following:[16]

- *Sansui ga byōbu* (Landscape) or *Landscape of Mount Penglai (Hōrai)*, pair of six-panel folding screens
- *Kuni zu byōbu* (Regional map) or *Map of China*, six-panel folding screen
- *Daitō kinseirō mae kanraku zu byōbu* (Merriments in front of the Qinzheng building of the Great Tang Empire), or *Sangaku Entertainments*, six-panel folding screen[17]
- *Daitō koyō kyūden ga byōbu* (The palace of the Great Tang Empire in an antique style) or *Equestrian Games at the Old Tang Palace*, six-panel folding screen
- *Daitō koyō kyūden ga byōbu* or *Chinese Palaces in an Antique Style*, six-panel folding screen
- *Koyō sansui ga byōbu* (Landscape in an antique style), six-panel folding screen
- *Koyō honzō ga byōbu* (Medicinal plants in an antique style) or *Medicinal Plants*, pair of six-panel folding screens
- *Shijo ga byōbu* (Women and children) or *Equestrian Games at the Old Tang Palace*, six-panel folding screen
- *Kojin ga byōbu* (Portraits of the ancients) or *Ancient Chinese People*, pair of six-panel folding screens
- *Maiba byōbu* (Dancing horses), six-panel folding screen
- *Shijo ga byōbu* or *Chinese Woman*, six-panel folding screen
- *Koyō kyūden ga byōbu* (Imperial palaces in an antique style) or *Chinese Palaces in an Antique Style*, six-panel folding screen
- *Soga yoasobi byōbu* (Night amusements in monochrome), pair of six-panel folding screens
- *Sansui ga byōbu* or *Lakeside Mansions*, six-panel folding screen
- *Kudara ga byōbu* (Scenes from ancient China and Korea) or *Tendai Buddhist Views*, six-panel folding screen
- *Kojin kyūden byōbu* (Palaces of the ancients) or *Chinese Palaces in an Antique Style*, six-panel folding screen
- *Kojin ga byōbu* or *Ancient Chinese People*, six-panel folding screen

Of these, items that are now lost include: a pair of six-panel screens depicting a mountain landscape with Daoist immortals, referred to as a *Sansui ga byōbu*; a six-panel screen depicting a group of foreigners, referred to as a *Shijo ga byōbu*; the six-panel screen referred to as the *Daitō kinseirō mae kanraku zu byōbu*; both sets of the six-panel screens referred to as *Daitō koyō kyūden ga byōbu*; and a six-panel screen depicting the palaces and famous places of China and Korea, referred to as the *Kudara ga byōbu*. Furthermore, the names of the artists of these folding-screen paintings are not recorded at all, from which we can surmise that painters did not receive the same treatment as calligraphers. Given that so many objects are no longer extant, however, it can be difficult to determine their point of origin. However, because of the use of feathers from a native Japanese mountain bird and the reverse of some scrap paper that provides certain clues, scholars believe that the *Torige ryūjo zu byōbu* (Beauties beneath trees) (Plate 3) were produced in Japan between 752 and 756. All of the extant folding screens have been found to be of Japanese origin. Thus it seems likely that the objects listed in *Gyo byōbu ichihaku jō* were meant to be offerings.[18]

Looking at the art world of Tang China, there are several turning points in the 8th century that overlap with one another.[19] Interest in the experiment of splashed ink (*hatsuboku*) began with the intelligentsia of the Jiangnan region. Favoured materials shifted from polychrome colour to monochrome ink, while subject matter shifted from Daoist-Buddhist figures and portraits of people to landscapes and bird-and-flower pictures. Furthermore, a great change took place in terms of the space of appreciation, from large-format pictures affixed to immovable properties (wall paintings) to small-format pictures packaged as movable properties (hanging scrolls and hand scrolls). Painters of the Tang dynasty, like those who appear in works such as Zhang Yanyuan's *Lidai minghua ji*, are thought to have brushed their paintings on the walls of temples, mansions, and palaces in the capital cities of Chang'an and Luoyang.

Regardless, there are no examples of folding screens that have been passed down from the Tang dynasty or earlier. In recent years, however, successive archaeological excavations have uncovered numerous folding screens and walls painted to look like folding screens.[20] From the high Tang dynasty (first half of the 8th century) onwards, during the middle and the late Tang periods, folding screens became a big craze. In 1989, an archaeological excavation of the Wei family tomb (high-to-middle Tang dynasty), located in the village of Nanliwangcun, Chang'an, in Shaanxi Province, found a painting of a six-panel folding screen containing the 'beauties beneath trees' motif on the southern portion of the west wall. In one panel, a woman is depicted standing under the trees with an attendant, and the basic composition resembles the *Torige ryūjo zu byōbu* in the Shōsōin collection.[21] From the resemblance of both figures we can determine that the folding screen in the Shōsōin, which recent scientific investigations confirm to be a Japanese production, transmits a pictorial style popular in the Tang dynasty capital of Chang'an.[22]

The origin of the 'beauties beneath trees' motif has been traced as far as India, where it was a symbol of sacredness, but its significance has been considerably refined since its removal from its original context. What this tells us is that even though there is an extreme theory that the figure in the *Torige* folding screen in the Shōsōin is meant to be Empress Kōmyō depicted in a Tenpyō-era romance, that cannot be true. At the same time, the theory that the figures in the painted folding screen on the west wall of the Wei family tomb are depictions of the grave owners is also negated by the existence of the folding screen in the Shōsōin. In contrast to transmittable objects, it is thought that folding-screen paintings on the walls of tombs were intended to be appreciated by the occupants of those tombs, and their subject matter is therefore subject to certain limitations. The production of the 'beauties beneath trees' motif is one that recalls the image of an immortal (Ch: *sheng xian*, J: *shōsen*) and its choice for depiction inside a tomb can be considered in terms of that meaning.[23]

On the other hand, however, since the tomb was thought to function as a true home for the deceased (Ch: *mu ru zhenzhai*), where they hoped to continue their daily existence in the afterlife, tomb paintings faithfully reproduced the daily activities of the real world above ground. As archaeological objects, Tang dynasty folding screen wall paintings provide a means to reconstruct and interrogate the presently expanding history of Tang dynasty painting and therefore demand serious consideration. In addition to depictions of people, the subject matter of folding-screen wall paintings from this period extended to landscapes and bird-and-flower scenes that had no apparent relation to thoughts on the nature of life and death—a fact that suggests they directly reflected trends from the world of art. In this case, it is the 'beauties under trees' motif itself that has been handed down through successive generations. It is thought that many such objects were produced during the Tang dynasty and that the wall paintings of the tombs were simply copying those popular motifs. In mapping out the genealogy of *bijinga* (picture of beautiful women), these screens should be placed at the start.[24]

Some noteworthy paintings have been discovered by mapping the 'beauties under trees' motif in this way. In 2014, a folding-screen painting depicting a nobleman under trees was discovered on the west wall of the tomb of Han Xiu (672–739) and his wife (d. 784) in Guoxinzhuang, Xi'an (Figure 2.3).[25] Although the subject of the painting is a young man, in terms of its composition and arrangement it is the closest match to the Shōsōin screens to have been discovered. As the burial occurred in Kaiyuan 28 (740), the painting cannot but bring to mind the reign of Emperor Xuanzong (685–762, r. 712–756). The tomb of Han Xiu and his wife includes another painting; on the eastern portion of the northern wall there is a painting of a landscape screen (*sansui zu tsuitate*) that greatly resembles scenes of musicians riding elephants that are found on the plectrum guard paintings (*kanbachi-e*) of stringed instruments (Figure 2.4).[26] This screen is depicted within a frame and can clearly be considered an independent work (Figure 2.5). This is a complex use of spatial organization that is not seen in earlier extant works, and it therefore marks an important discovery in the development of landscape painting in East Asia at that time.

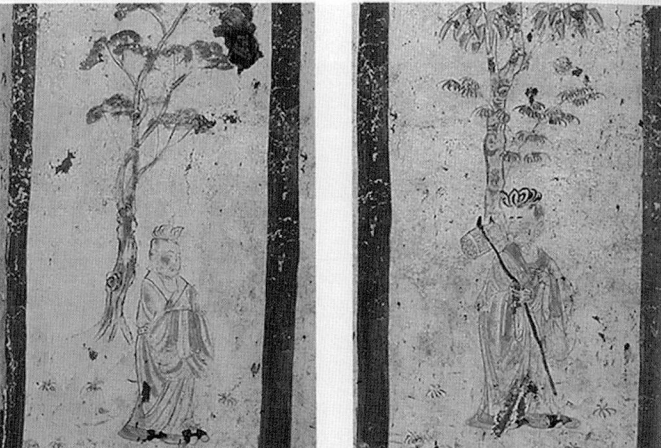

Figure 2.3 Juka kōshi zu byōbu (Nobleman under the trees), ca. 740.
Screen of *Shuxia Gaoshi tu* (Nobleman under the trees), ca. 740. Guoxinzhuang, Xi'an

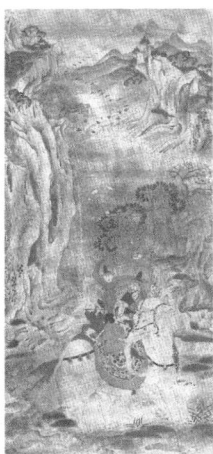

Figure 2.4 Musicians Riding Elephants (Kizō sōgaku zu), Tang dynasty (713~766).
Biwa plectrum guard painting, sappanwood dye and mother-of-pearl inlay on maple wood, 97.0 × 40.5 cm
Collection of the Shōsōin, South Warehouse

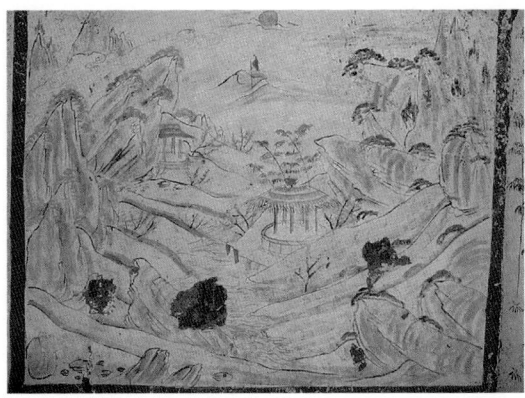

Figure 2.5 Landscape (Sansui zu tsuitate), ca. 740
Standing screen painting on the north wall of the Tomb of Han Xiu and His Wife, Guoxinzhuang, Xi'an

For Emperor Shōmu, the paintings that were offered to the Shōsōin were a reflection of the paintings that were representative of Emperor Xuanzong's reign—a contemporaneous world for which Shōmu had great admiration—and should be regarded as having been appreciated on those grounds. When looking at the paintings and calligraphy donated to the Shōsōin, it is clear that there exists a gap between the calligraphy books and the paintings. In contrast to the copybooks, which include the works of Wang Xizhi and Wang Xianzhi that were heralded as 'classics' even during the Tang dynasty, as well as works by the early Tang master Ouyang Xun, the paintings were folding-screen furnishings produced in Japan by unnamed artists and symbolized the prototypical designs favoured during the reign of Emperor Xuanzong (or the most up-to-date impressions of them). Judging from this, it ought to be clear that the Shōsōin collection, rather than reflecting the latest trends in Chinese art, instead reflected the aesthetic sensibilities of the Tang emperors while also incorporating developments in the history of Chinese painting and calligraphy.

Consequently, the Heian period emperors used the Shōsōin imperial treasures as a symbol of the former glory of the great Tang empire to appropriate the authority of the Tang emperors for themselves. As I mentioned above, the calligraphy of Wang Xizhi and Wang Xianzhi was frequently borrowed from the collection. Scholars have hypothesized that twenty volumes of the *Tō-Shin u shogun Ō Gishi no shohō* were sold to the court in Kōnin 11 (820) and used by Emperor Saga as a copybook. Additionally, thirty-six pairs of folding screens and sixteen white stone ornamental curtain anchors left the collection in the 9th month of Kōnin 5 (814) when they were offered for sale. The price was equivalent to 624 *kan* 600 *mon*.[27] The following thirty-six screens left the collection:

- *Landscape of Mount Penglai* (pair of six-panel folding screens known as *Sansui ga byōbu*)
- *Sangaku Entertainments* (six-panel folding screen known as *Daitō kinseirō mae kanraku zu byōbu*)
- *Map of China* (six-panel folding screen known as *Kuni zu byōbu*)
- *Medicinal Plants* (pair of six-panel folding screens known as *Koyō honzō ga byōbu*)
- *Night Amusements in Monochrome* (pair of six-panel folding screens known as *Soga yoasobi byōbu*)
- three six-panel folding screens called *Chinese Palaces in an Antique Style* (known as *Daitō koyō kyūden ga byōbu*, *Koyō kyūden ga byōbu*, and *Kojin kyūden byōbu*, respectively)
- two six-panel folding screens called *Equestrian Games at the Old Tang Palace* (known as *Daitō koyō kyūden ga byōbu* and *Shijo ga byōbu*, respectively)
- *Lakeside Mansions* (six-panel folding screen known as *Sansui ga byōbu*)
- *Tendai Views* (six-panel folding screen known as *Kudara ga byōbu*)
- one pair of six-panel folding screens and an additional six-panel folding screen called *Ancient Chinese People* (both known as *Kojin ga byōbu*)
- *Chinese Women* (six-panel folding screen known as *Shijo ga byōbu*)
- *Landscape in an Antique Style* (six-panel folding screen known as *Koyō sansui ga byōbu*)
- *Dancing Horses* (six-panel folding screen known as *Maiba byōbu*)

In short, the sale included all twenty-one of the aforementioned picture screens, four calligraphy screens, one flying banner (Ch: *feibo*, J: *hihaku*) screen, and ten of the clamp-resist dye patterned screens. They were sold to the court by Tōdaiji Temple and are thought to have been purchased by Emperor Saga, not just to recover the contents of a specific offering but also to endow the imperial court with the aesthetic character of the Great Tang Empire. According to records of both minor and major damage, the picture screens had considerable visible damage and, at the time, were handled like old paintings. In that sense, they perhaps conveyed a sense of nostalgia for the court's former grandeur.

The Heian period Treasure House

In the Heian period, imported *karamono* were highly prized. From the 10th century on, '*karamono* viewing' by the emperor involved not just looking at objects but also distributing them to royal members of the imperial court—who included empress dowagers, empresses, royal consorts, crown princes, regents, and advisors. For members of the imperial court, who were sustained by these gift-giving relationships, the possession of *karamono* had a direct impact on their political authority.

Treasures and valuable books related to the emperor were kept in the warehouses and libraries of the inner palace (*daidairi*).[28] Inherited treasures (*rekidai hōmotsu*) were stored in the Giyōden Palace, and traditional treasures of the imperial family (*kōrei no gyobutsu*) in the Ryōkiden Palace. Imperial treasures were also stored in the Keihōbō and Ranrinbō storehouses, which were located just outside the inner palace's northern walls. For example, an entry from Fujiwara no Yukinari's (972–1027) diary, *Gonki*, for the 8th day of the 6th month of Kankō 8 (1011) records that he borrowed a number of calligraphy samples from the stores of the Giyōden—including cursive script versions of the *Thousand Character Classic* (Ch: *Qianziwen*, J: *Senjimon*) and *Fragrance of Heaven* (Ch: *Xiang yi tian*) by Zhang Zhi (d. 192 CE) and regular script versions of the *Essay on General Yueyi*, *Yellow Court Classic* (Ch: *Huang ting jing*, J: *Kōtei gyō*), *Classic of History* (Ch: *Shangshu*, J: *Shōsho*), and *Luo River Diagram* (Ch: *Hetu*, J: *Kato*) by Wang Xizhi—and used them as copybooks. It is possible that these samples of Wang Xizhi's calligraphy had been removed from the Shōsōin before being placed in the storehouses of the inner palace.

On the other hand, treasures and books related to deceased (or retired) emperors were moved, after their rule, to storehouses on the premises of imperial retirement palaces or to the storehouses of temples with which they had close relationships. The Shōsōin itself can be considered an early example of this process. In the early Heian period, Emperor Saga stored books, written records, and treasured objects in the storehouse of the Reizei Palace that he built after his abdication. In Shōhei 1 (931), just before Emperor Uda (867–931, r. 887–897) died, his treasures were stored in the Endōin—the scripture storehouse—of Ninnaji Temple. Initially, this collection was strictly managed by court and temple officials. Later, it came to be known as the Ninnaji Treasure House.[29] In the mid-Heian period, the Fujiwara regents—who at that time were the real agents of power in the imperial government—stored their treasures in the Uji Treasure House of the Byōdōin, which was built by Fujiwara no Yorimichi (992–1074).[30] Many rarities were stored there, and due to the various legends that sprung up around them, they became known as royal symbols. During the era of the retired emperors (*insei ki*), Retired Emperor Toba (1103–1156, r. 1107–1123) built a storehouse—known as the Shōkōmyōin—at his retirement villa, the Toba Palace, in emulation of this practice. Retired Emperor Go-Shirakawa (1127–1192, r. 1155–1158) also built a treasure house—the Renge'ōin (present-day Sanjūsangendō Temple)—on a corner of his Hōjūji-dono retirement villa.[31] The Uji Treasure House and the Renge'ōin Treasure House both became legendary for their continuing collection of masterpieces during the medieval period and thereafter.[32]

Rare objects, around which legends formed or that became otherwise renowned, took on a symbolic existence, and the secretive nature of these treasure houses contributed to their growing influence. Meanwhile, however, scripture storehouses did not just safeguard sacred texts. They also functioned as spaces where sacred texts were viewed, transcribed, taught, and, to a certain extent, disseminated. By doing so, these spaces safeguarded the texts' purpose.[33] This practice of viewing, transcribing, and teaching sacred texts ultimately came to take place at Tōdaiji's Shōgozō. It was inside these treasure houses that sections of the sutras were scrupulously examined, and this framework helped to secure these sacred texts' purpose. The Shōsōin and Shōgozō of Tōdaiji can thus be regarded as shouldering this responsibility. This state of affairs was ultimately to change alongside the later influx of Song dynasty (960–1276) culture, and in that change we perceive the transformation of a medieval collection.

(Translated by Sara Sumpter)

Notes

1 For more on what constitutes the category of *karamono*, see *Karamono to Higashi-Ajia: hakusaihin wo meguru bunka kōryūshi* [Karamono and East Asia: imported objects in the history of cultural exchange], *Ajia yūgaku* [Asian Studies] 147, ed. Kawazoe Fusae and Minagawa Masaki (Tokyo: Bensei Shuppan, 2011); Charlotte von Verscheur, *Mono ga kataru Nihon taigai kōekishi: 7–16 seiki* [The object speaks: a history of Japanese foreign trade, 7th–16th centuries], trans. Kōchi Haruhito (Tokyo: Fujiwara Shoten, 2011); and Kawazoe Fusae, *Karamono no bunkashi: hakuraihin kara mita Nihon* [A cultural history of Karamono: Japan as seen through imported objects] (Tokyo: Iwanami Shoten, 2014).

2 Recent publications on the topic of the objects in the Shōsōin include: Sugimoto Kazuki, 'Tō no bunbutsu to Shōsōin' [Tang dynasty objects and the Shōsōin], *Kodai wo kangaeru: Tō to Nihon* [Considering ancient times: Tang China and Japan], ed. Ikeda On (Tokyo: Yoshikawa Kōbunkan, 1992), *Shōsōin: rekishi to hōmotsu* [The Shōsōin: history and treasures], *Chūkō shinsho* 1967 (Tokyo: Chūō Kōron Shinsha, 2008), and *Shōsōin hōmotsu no sekai* [The world of the Shōsōin treasures] (Tokyo: Yamakawa Shuppansha, 2010); Hashimoto Yoshi- hiko, *Shōsōin no rekishi* [The history of the Shōsōin] (Tokyo: Yoshikawa Kōbunkan, 1997); Yoneda Yūsuke, *Shōsōin hōmotsu no rekishi to hozon* [The history and preservation of the Shōsōin treasures] (Tokyo: Yoshikawa Kōbunkan, 1998), *Shōsōin to Nihon bunka* [The Shōsōin and Japanese culture] (Tokyo: Yoshikawa Kōbunkan, 1998), and *Shōsōin hōmotsu to Heian jidai: wafūka he no michi* [The Shōsōin treasures and the Heian period: towards a Japanese style] (Kyoto: Tankōsha, 2000); Nara National Museum, ed., *Shōsōin hōmotsu ni manabu* [Learning about the Shōsōin treasures] (Kyoto: Shinbunkaku Shuppan, 2008) and *Shōsōin hōmotsu ni manabu* 2 [Learning about the Shōsōin treasures 2] (Kyoto: Shin- bunkaku Shuppan, 2012); and Iida Takehiko, 'Higashi-Ajia no naka no Shōsōin hōmotsu' [The Shōsōin treasures in East Asia], *Nihon kodai kōryūshi nyūmon* [An introduction to ancient Japanese cultural exchange] (Tokyo: Bensei Shuppan, 2017).

3 Kita Keita, 'Kenmotsu chō kanken' [An opinion on the catalogue of offerings], *Shōsōin kiyō* 30 (2008).

4 Empress Genshō was the paternal aunt of Emperor Shōmu.

5 Sugoroku is a game similar to modern-day backgammon.

6 *Zensenkō* is a type of aloeswood (or agarwood).

7 The eye-opening ceremony is a consecration ritual held during the dedication of a new Bud- dha figure. In this ceremony, the eyes of the figure are painted in, thus activating the Buddha nature within the figure and transforming it into a true manifestation of the Buddha himself.

8 Inamoto Yasuo, 'Shōsōin hōmotsu no keisei to fuse no jissen' [The formation of the Shōsōin treasures and the practice of offering], *Higashi Ajia no naka no Nihon bijutsu* [Japanese art in East Asia], *Nihon bijutsu zenshū* [The complete works of Japanese art] 6, ed. Itakura Masaaki et al. (Tokyo: Shōgakkan, 2015).

9 Yoneda Kaisuke, *Shōsōin no kōyaku: zaishitsu chōsa kara hozon e* [Incense in the Shōsōin: from survey to preservation] (Kyoto: Shibunkaku Shuppan, 2015).

10 Kondō Yoshikazu, *Nihon kodai no bugu: 'Kokka chinpō chō' to Shōsōin no kijō* [Ancient Japanese armour: the *Kokka chinpō chō* and objects in the Shōsōin] (Kyoto: Shibunkaku Shuppan, 2014).

11 Yoneda Yusuke, *Shōsōin to Nihon bunka* [The Shōsōin and Japanese culture]. Tokyo: Yoshikawa Kōbunkan, 1998.
12 *Tokubetsuten 'Shosei Ō Gishi': Nicchū kokkō seijōka 40-shūnen, Tōkyō Kokuritsu Hakubutsukan 140-shūnen* [Special exhibition *The Calligrapher Wang Xizhi*: Celebrating the 40th anniversary of the normalization of Sino-Japanese relations and the 140th anniversary of the Tokyo National Museum], ed. Tokyo National Museum (Tokyo: Mainichi Shinbunsha, 2013).
13 Itakura Masaaki, 'Higashi-Ajia ni okeru Rantei kyokusui utage no tenkai' [The development of the iconography of the Orchid Pavilion banquet in East Asia], *Bijutsushi ronsō* 29 (2013).
14 Lotar Ledderose, 'Chūgoku kōtei no shūshū bijutsuhin' [The art collection of the Chinese Emperor], trans. Saitō Minoru, in *Geijutsu to minzoku* [Art and the people], *Geijutsugaku kenkyū sōsho* [Art Studies Series], ed. Yamamoto Masao (Tokyo: Tamagawa Daigaku Shuppanbu, 1984); Liang Jiang, *Zhongguo mei shu jian zang shi gao gao* [An enquiry into the history of the Chinese art collection] (Beijing: Wenwu chubanshe, 2009); Tsukamoto Maromitsu, 'Kangi Rokuchō kara Zui, Tō no bunbutsu shūzō to bunbutsukan no hensen' [Object collecting from the Han, Wei, and Six Dynasties to the Sui and Tang and changing perceptions of cultural objects], *Hokusō kaigashi no seiritsu* [The establishment of a Northern Song painting history] (Tokyo: Chūō Kōron Bijutsu Shuppan, 2016).
15 Matsushita Takaaki, 'Kenmotsu chō ga byōbu nitsuite' [On the painted folding screens in the catalogue of offerings], *Shōsōin no kaiga* [Paintings in the Shōsōin], ed. Shōsōin Jimusho (Nara: Nihon Keizai Shinbunsha, 1968); Matsushima Junsei, 'Shōsōin no byōbu nitsuite' [On the folding screens in the Shōsōin], *Kunaichō shoryōbu kiyō* 28 (1976).
16 Matsushima Junsei, 'Shōsōin no byōbu nitsuite' [On the folding screens in the Shōsōin].
17 *Sangaku* is an ancient form of Chinese entertainment similar to a modern-day circus.
18 Nagaoka Ryūsaku, 'Renge zō sekai to Shōsōin no byōbu' [The lotus-world theory and folding screens in the Shōsōin], *Kinōron: tsukuru, tsukau, tsutaeru* [Function theory: making, using, and transmitting], *Bukkyō bijutsu ronshū* [Essays on Buddhist art] 5 (Tokyo: Chikurinsha, 2014).
19 Itakura Masaaki, 'Tō jidai kaiga ni kan suru fukugenteki kōsatsu: byōbu hekiga ni chūshin shite' [A reconstructive enquiry into Tang dynasty paintings: on folding screen wall paintings], *Kaen zasshū: Nara Kokuritsu Hakubutsukan kiyō* 13 (2011).
20 Itakura Masaaki, 'Tō baka hekiga ni egakareta byōbu ga' [Folding screens painted on the walls of Tang dynasty tombs]', *Bijutsushi ronsō* 18 (2002).
21 Zhao Liguang and Wang Jiugang, 'Chang'an xian Naliwangcun Tang bihua mu' [The Tang dynasty mural painting at the Naliwang Village, Chang'an County], *Weibo* 4 (1989); Saitō Ryūichi, 'Shijo zu byōbu' [Folding screens depicting women], *Daitō ōchō josei no bi* [Women in art of the great Tang dynasty], ed. Osaka City Museum of Art (Nagoya: Chūnichi Shinbunsha, 2004).
22 Akiyama Terukazu, '*Torige ryūjo zu* no shimai-tachi: juka bijin zu no keifu' [The *Torige ryūjo zu* folding screen and its sisters: a genealogy of the 'beauties beneath trees' motif], *MUSEUM* 104 (1959); Itakura, 'Tō baka hekiga ni egakareta byōbu ga'; Sugaya Fuminori, 'Zhencangyuan pingfeng hemushi bihua pingfeng', *Su Bai xiansheng bazhi hua dan jinian wenji, shang* [Collected essays in celebration of Mr Subai's eighty-first birthday, Volume One] (Beijing: Wenwe Chubanshe, 2002); Tsai Shin-yu, 'Cong riben "niaomao linü" pingfeng kao Tang zhao "meinü pingfeng" bihua zhi yuanliu' [On the origin of the Tang dynasty mural painting 'Screen of Beauties' from the Japanese screen 'Beauties Under Trees'], *Shuhua yishu xuekan* 7 (2009); Zhang Le, *Zhongri meishu guanlianxing yanjiu: Zhengcangyuan cang 'Niaomao linü pingfeng' xinjie* [A study of the relationship between Chinese and Japanese art: a new interpretation of the screen 'Beauties Under Trees' from the collection of Shōsōin] (Beijing: Zhongguo Wenshi Chubanshe, 2014). Also noteworthy is the existence of silver lacquer folding screens. See Tōno Haruyuki, 'Kentōshi no bunkateki yakuwari' [The cultural role of the Japanese envoys to China], *Kentōshi to Shōsōin* [Japanese envoys and the Shōsōin] (Tokyo: Iwanami Shoten, 1992).
23 Doi Yoshiko, 'Kodai Chūgoku ni okeru jumoku to jinbutsu zu' [Images of people and foliage in ancient China], *Kodai Chūgoku kōko, bunka ronsō* [Essays on ancient Chinese thought and culture] (Tokyo: Gensōsha, 1995); Taniguchi Kōsei, '*Torige ryūjo byōbu* to Tō baka hekiga juka jinbutsu zu byōbu' [The *Torige ryūjo byōbu* and 'beauties beneath trees' folding

24 Huang Peijie, *Tangdai gongbi shinühua yanjiu* [Tang dynasty painting of court ladies in the Gongbi style] (Tianjin: Tianjin Renmin Meishu Chubanshe, 2007); Pai Shih-ming, 'Shengshi wenhua biaoxiang: sheng tang shiqi "zinühua" zhi chuxian jiqi meishushi yiyi zhi jiedu' [Cultural expressions of a prosperous world: decoding the appearance and art historical significance of 'paintings of children and ladies' in 8th-century China], *Yishushi yanjiu* 9 (2007); Li Jie, *Le shi yu gou miao: Tang dai shiguo renwu xianke de huihua fenggexue yanjiu* [A study on the pictorial styles of figural drawings on Tang dynasty stone-chambered tombs] (Beijing: Renmin Meishu Chubanshe, 2012).
25 '"Tang Han Xiu mu chutu bihua xue shuyan taohui" jiyao' [A synopsis of the International Symposium on the Tang Dynasty Mural Paintings in the Tomb of Han Xiu], *Kaogu yu wenwu* (June 2014); Zheng Yan, 'Tang Han Xiu mu shanshui tu chuyi' [On the images of landscape in the Tang dynasty mural painting at Han Xiu tomb], *Gugong bowu yuan yuan kan* 181 (May 2015); Liu Daiyun, 'Han Xiu mu chutu shanshui tu de kaogu xue guancha' [Some archaeological observations on the landscape images at Han Xiu tomb], *Wenbo* (June 2015).
26 Ge Chengyong, "Chuxiao Richu: Tang dai shanshui hua de jiaodian jiyi: Han Xiu mu chutu shanshui bihua yu riben chuanshi pipa shanshui hua huzheng' [The Sun Rises at Dawn: a study on the one-point perspective in Tang dynasty landscape painting—a comparative perspective on the landscape painting at Han Xiu tomb and *biwa* painting in Japan], *Meishu yanjiu* (May 2015).
27 *Shōsōin gyobutsu suitō bunsho* [Dispersal records for the Shōsōin collection] 10, *Dai Nihon komonjo, 25 furoku* (Tokyo: Shiryōhensanjo), pp. 61–62.
28 Tajima Isao, 'Tenjaku no denrai to bunko: kodai, chūsei no tennōke yukari no bunko, hōzō wo chūshin ni' [Inherited writings and literary collections: books and treasures of the ancient and mediaeval imperial family], *Rekishi to sozai* [History and subjects], ed. Ishigami Eiichi, *Nihon no jidai-shi* [Japanese epochal history] 30 (Tokyo: Yoshikawa Kōbunkan, 2004); 'Tennōke yukari no bunko, hōzō no "Mokuroku gakuteki kenkyū" no seika to kadai' [Challenges and results from the *Scholarly Study of Inventories* related to the books and treasures of the imperial family], *Setsuwa bungaku kenkyū* 41 (2006); 'Chūsei tennōke no bunko, hōzō no hensen' [The books and treasures of the medieval imperial family in transition], *Kinri, kuge bunko kenkyū* [A study of the library of the imperial court and palace] 2 (Kyoto: Shinbunkaku Shuppan, 2006).
29 Ōtsuki Yōko, '"Ninnaji omuro gomotsu jitsuroku" no hōmotsu' [Treasures in the *Ninnaji omuro gomotsu jitsuroku*], *Nihon kodai chūsei no bukkyō to higashi-Ajia* [Ancient and medieval Japanese Buddhism and East Asia], ed. Harada Masatoshi (Osaka: Kansai Daigaku Shuppanbu, 2014).
30 Tanaka Takako, 'Uji no hōzō: chūsei ni okeru hōzō no imi' [Treasures of Uji: the significance of treasures in the medieval period], *Gehō to aihō no chūsei* [The outer path and the medieval path of love] (Tokyo: Sunagoya Shobō, 1993).
31 Suzuki Hisao, 'Toba rikyū Shōkōmyōin no kyōzō' [The Shōkōmyōin Scripture House at the Toba Palace], *Heiankyō rekishi kenkyū* [A study of the history of the Heian capital] (Kyoto: Sugiyama Shinzō Sensei Beiju Kinen Ronshū Kankōkai, 1993); Tanahashi Mitsuo, *Go-Shirakawa hōō* [Retired Emperor Go-Shirakawa] (Tokyo: Kōdansha, 1995); Takei Akio, 'Jiin no hōzō (kyōzō) to insei no bunka' [Temple and shrine treasure houses (scripture houses) and the culture of the Insei era], *Nihon kodai bukkyō no bunkashi* [A culture history of ancient Japanese Buddhism] (Tokyo: Yoshikawa Kōbunkan, 1998); Mikawa Kei, 'Go-Shirakawa insei to bunka, gaikō: Renge'ō-in hōzō wo megutte' [Culture, diplomacy, and the government of Go-Shirakawa: regarding the Renge'o-in Treasure House], *Ritsumei bungaku* 624 (2012); Itō Daisuke, 'Kyūtei geinō toshite no kaiga: Kamakura jidai no sezoku kaiga' [Painting as courtly entertainment: popular paintings of the Kamakura period], *Chiten no manazashi, ōchōbi no saikōchiku* [Looking at imperial rule, reconstructing dynastic art], *Tennō no bijutsushi* [Imperial art history] 2 (Tokyo: Yoshikawa Kōbunkan, 2017).

32 Takahashi Kazuki, 'Chūsei seiritsuki ni okeru ōken no hōi to zono rekishiteki seikaku' [Royal treasures in the nascent medieval period and their historical character], *Chūseijin no takaramono: kura ga awarasu kenryoku to tomi* [Treasures of the medieval period: the wealth and political power of storehouses], ed. Ono Masatoshi, Gomi Fumihiko, and Hagihara Mitsuo (Tokyo: Kōshi Shoin, 2011); Hatanaka Ayako, 'Atsumeru, osameru, mederu: Nihon kodai ni okeru "hakubutsukan"-teki na mono' [Collecting, dedicating, admiring: 'museum'-like spaces in ancient Japan], *Sekai no shūshū: Ajia wo meguru hakubutsukan hakurankai, kaigai ryokō* [Collecting the world: museums, exhibitions, and travel abroad in Asia], ed. Fukui Norihiko (Tokyo: Yamakawa Shuppansha, 2014).

33 Kamikawa Michio, 'Insei to shingon mikkyō' [The Insei government and Shingon esotericism], *Nihon chūsei bukkyō keiseishi ron* [A historical treatise on the development of Buddhism in medieval Japan] (Tokyo: Azekura Shobō, 2007); Abe Yasurō, 'Shūkyō tekisuto toshite no kyōzō to mokuroku' [Inventories and scripture houses as religious text], *Chūsei Nihon no shūkyō tekusuto taikei* [The religious text system of medieval Japan] (Nagoya: Nagoya Daigaku Shuppankai, 2013).

Bibliography

Anonymous. '"Tang Han Xiu mu chutu bihua xue shuyan taohui" jiyao' [A synopsis of the International Symposium on the Tang Dynasty Mural Paintings in the Tomb of Han Xiu]. Kaogu yu wenwu (June 2014).

Abe Yasurō. *Chūsei Nihon no shūkyō tekusuto taikei* [The religious text system of mediaeval Japan]. Nagoya: Nagoya Daigaku Shuppankai, 2013.

Akiyama Terukazu. 'Torige ryūjo zu no shimai-tachi: juka bijin zu no keifu' [The Torige ryūjo zu folding screen and its sisters: a genealogy of the 'beauties beneath trees' motif]. *MUSEUM* 104 (1959).

Doi Yoshiko. *Kodai Chūgoku kōko, bunka ronsō* [Essays on ancient Chinese thought and culture]. Tokyo: Gensōsha, 1995.

Ge Chengyong. 'Chuxiao Richu: Tang dai shanshui hua de jiaodian jiyi: Han Xiu mu chutu shanshui bihua yu riben chuanshi pipa shanshui hua huzheng' [The Sun Rises at Dawn: a study on the one-point perspective in Tang dynasty landscape painting—a comparative perspective on the landscape painting at Han Xiu tomb and biwa painting in Japan]. *Meishu yanjiu* (May 2015).

Hashimoto Yoshihiko. *Shōsōin no rekishi* [The history of the Shōsōin]. Tokyo: Yoshikawa Kōbunkan, 1997.

Hatanaka Ayako. 'Atsumeru, osameru, mederu: Nihon kodai ni okeru "hakubutsukan"-teki na mono' [Collecting, dedicating, admiring: 'museum'-like spaces in ancient Japan]. In *Sekai no shūshū: Ajia wo meguru hakubutsukan hakurankai, kaigai ryokō* [Collecting the world: museums, exhibitions, and travel abroad in Asia], edited by Fukui Norihiko. Tokyo: Yamakawa Shuppansha, 2014.

Huang Peijie. *Tangdai gongbi shinühua yanjiu* [Tang dynasty painting of court ladies in the Gongbi style]. Tianjin: Tianjin Renmin Meishu Chubanshe, 2007.

Iida Takehiko. 'Higashi-Ajia no naka no Shōsōin hōmotsu' [The Shōsōin treasures in East Asia]. In *Nihon kodai kōryūshi nyūmon* [An introduction to ancient Japanese cultural exchange], edited by Suzuki Yasutami, Kaneko Shūichi, Tanaka Fumio, and Lee Sungsi. Tokyo: Bensei Shuppan, 2017.

Inamoto Yasuo. 'Shōsōin hōmotsu no keisei to fuse no jissen' [The formation of the Shōsōin treasures and the practice of offering]. In *Higashi Ajia no naka no Nihon bijutsu* [Japanese art in East Asia]. Nihon bijutsu zenshū [The complete works of Japanese art] 6, edited by Itakura Masaaki et al. Tokyo: Shōgakkan, 2015.

Itakura Masaaki. 'Tō baka hekiga ni egakareta byōbu ga' [Folding screens painted on the walls of Tang dynasty tombs]. *Bijutsushi ronsō* 18 (2002).

———. 'Tō jidai kaiga ni kan suru fukugenteki kōsatsu: byōbu hekiga ni chūmoku shite' [A reconstructive enquiry into Tang dynasty paintings: on folding-screen wall paintings]. *Kaen zasshū: Nara Kokuritsu Hakubutsukan kiyō* 13 (2011).

———. 'Higashi-Ajia ni okeru Rantei kyokusui utage no tenkai' [The development of the iconography of the Orchid Pavilion banquet in East Asia]. *Bijutsushi ronsō* 29 (2013).

Itō Daisuke. 'Kyūtei geinō toshite no kaiga: Kamakura jidai no sezoku kaiga' [Painting as courtly entertainment: popular paintings of the Kamakura period]. *Chiten no manazashi, ōchōbi no saikōchiku* [Looking at imperial rule, reconstructing dynastic art]. Tennō no bijutsushi [Imperial art history] 2. Tokyo: Yoshikawa Kōbunkan, 2017.

Kamikawa Michio. *Nihon chūsei bukkyō keiseishi ron* [A historical treatise on the development of Buddhism in medieval Japan]. Tokyo: Azekura Shobō, 2007.

Kawazoe Fusae and Minagawa Masaki, eds. Karamono to Higashi-Ajia: hakusaihin wo meguru bunka kōryūshi [Karamono and East Asia: imported objects in the history of cultural exchange]. *Ajia yūgaku* [Asian Studies] 147. Tokyo: Bensei Shuppan, 2011.

Kawazoe Fusae. *Karamono no bunkashi: hakuraihin kara mita Nihon* [A cultural history of Karamono: Japan as seen through imported objects]. Tokyo: Iwanami Shoten, 2014.

Kita Keita. 'Kenmotsu chō kanken' [An opinion on the catalogue of offerings]. *Shōsōin kiyō* 30 (2008).

Kondō Yoshikazu. *Nihon kodai no bugu: 'Kokka chinpō chō' to Shōsōin no kijō* [Ancient Japanese armour: the Kokka chinpō chō and objects in the Shōsōin]. Kyoto: Shibunkaku Shuppan, 2014.

Ledderose, Lotar. 'Chūgoku kōtei no shūshū bijutsuhin' [The art collection of the Chinese Emperor], translated by Saitō Minoru. In *Geijutsu to minzoku* [Art and the people], Geijutsugaku kenkyū sōsho [Art Studies Series], edited by Yamamoto Masao. Tokyo: Tamagawa Daigaku Shuppanbu, 1984.

Li Jie. *Le shi yu gou miao: Tang dai shiguo renwu xianke de huihua fenggexue yanjiu* [A study on the pictorial styles of figural drawings on Tang dynasty stone-chambered tombs]. Beijing: Renmin Meishu Chubanshe, 2012.

Liang Jiang. *Zhongguo mei shu jian zang shi gao gao* [An enquiry into the history of the Chinese art collection]. Beijing: Wenwu chubanshe, 2009.

Liu Daiyun. 'Han Xiu mu chutu shanshui tu de kaogu xue guancha' [Some archaeological observations on the landscape images at Han Xiu tomb]. *Wenbo* (June 2015).

Matsushima Junsei. 'Shōsōin no byōbu nitsuite' [On the folding screens in the Shōsōin], *Kunaichō shoryōbu kiyō* 28 (1976).

Matsushita Takaaki. 'Kenmotsu chō ga byōbu nitsuite' [On the painted folding screens in the catalogue of offerings]. In *Shōsōin no kaiga* [Paintings in the Shōsōin], edited by Shōsōin Jimusho. Nara: Nihon Keizai Shinbunsha, 1968.

Mikawa Kei. 'Go-Shirakawa insei to bunka, gaikō: Renge'ō-in hōzō wo megutte' [Culture, diplomacy, and the government of Go-Shirakawa: regarding the Renge'o-in Treasure House]. *Ritsumei bungaku* 624 (2012).

Nagaoka Ryūsaku. 'Renge zō sekai to Shōsōin no byōbu' [The lotus-world theory and folding screens in the Shōsōin]. In *Kinōron: tsukuru, tsukau, tsutaeru* [Function theory: making, using, and transmitting], *Bukkyō bijutsu ronshū* [Essays on Buddhist art] 5, edited by Nagaoka Ryūsaku. Tokyo: Chikurinsha, 2014.

Nara National Museum, ed. *Shōsōin hōmotsu ni manabu* [Learning about the Shōsōin treasures]. Kyoto: Shinbunkaku Shuppan, 2008.

———, ed. *Shōsōin hōmotsu ni manabu* 2 [Learning about the Shōsōin treasures 2]. Kyoto: Shinbunkaku Shuppan, 2012.

Ōtsuki Yōko. '"Ninnaji omuro gomotsu jitsuroku" no hōmotsu' [Treasures in the Ninnaji omuro gomotsu jitsuroku]. In *Nihon kodai chūsei no bukkyō to higashi-Ajia* [Ancient and medieval Japanese Buddhism and East Asia], edited by Harada Masatoshi. Osaka: Kansai Daigaku Shuppanbu, 2014.

Pai Shih-ming. 'Shengshi wenhua biaoxiang: sheng tang shiqi "zinühua" zhi chuxian jiqi meishushi yiyi zhi jiedu' [Cultural expressions of a prosperous world: decoding the appearance and art historical significance of 'paintings of children and ladies' in 8th-century China]. *Yishushi yanjiu* 9 (2007).

Saitō Ryūichi. 'Shijo zu byōbu' [Folding screens depicting women]. In *Daitō ōchō josei no bi* [Women in art of the great Tang dynasty], edited by Osaka City Museum of Art. Nagoya: Chūnichi Shinbunsha, 2004.

Sugaya Fuminori. 'Zhencangyuan pingfeng hemushi bihua pingfeng'. *Su Bai xiansheng bazhi hua dan jinian wenji, shang* [Collected essays in celebration of Mr Subai's eighty-first birthday, Volume One]. Beijing: Wenwe Chubanshe, 2002.

Sugimoto Kazuki. 'Tō no bunbutsu to Shōsōin' [Tang dynasty objects and the Shōsōin]. In *Kodai wo kangaeru: Tō to Nihon* [Considering ancient times: Tang China and Japan], edited by Ikeda On. Tokyo: Yoshikawa Kōbunkan, 1992.

———. *Shōsōin: rekishi to hōmotsu* [The Shōsōin: history and treasures]. Chūkō shinsho 1967. Tokyo: Chūō Kōron Shinsha, 2008.

———. *Shōsōin hōmotsu no sekai* [The world of the Shōsōin treasures]. Tokyo: Yamakawa Shuppansha, 2010.

Suzuki Hisao. 'Toba rikyū Shōkōmyōin no kyōzō' [The Shōkōmyōin Scripture House at the Toba Palace]. In *Heiankyō rekishi kenkyū* [A study of the history of the Heian capital], edited by Sugiyama Shinzō sensei beiju kinen ronshū kankō kai. Kyoto: Sugiyama Shinzō Sensei Beiju Kinen Ronshū Kankōkai, 1993.

Tajima Isao. 'Tenjaku no denrai to bunko: kodai, chūsei no tennōke yukari no bunko, hōzō wo chūshin ni' [Inherited writings and literary collections: books and treasures of the ancient and mediaeval imperial family]. In *Rekishi to sozai* [History and subjects], edited by Ishigami Eiichi. Nihon no jidai-shi [Japanese epochal history] 30. Tokyo: Yoshikawa Kōbunkan, 2004.

———. 'Chūsei tennōke no bunko, hōzō no hensen' [The books and treasures of the mediaeval imperial family in transition]. In *Kinri, kuge bunko kenkyū* [A study of the library of the imperial court and palace] 2, edited by Tajima Isao. Kyoto: Shinbunkaku Shuppan, 2006.

———. 'Tennōke yukari no bunko, hōzō no "Mokuroku gakuteki kenkyū" no seika to kadai' [Challenges and results from the Scholarly Study of Inventories related to the books and treasures of the imperial family]. *Setsuwa bungaku kenkyū* 41 (2006).

Takahashi Kazuki. 'Chūsei seiritsuki ni okeru ōken no hōi to zono rekishiteki seikaku' [Royal treasures in the nascent medieval period and their historical character]. In *Chūseijin no takaramono: kura ga awarasu kenryoku to tomi* [Treasures of the medieval period: the wealth and political power of storehouses], edited by Ono Masatoshi, Gomi Fumihiko, and Hagihara Mitsuo. Tokyo: Kōshi Shoin, 2011.

Takei Akio. 'Jiin no hōzō (kyōzō) to insei no bunka' [Temple and shrine treasure houses (scripture houses) and the culture of the Insei era]. *Nihon kodai bukkyō no bunkashi* [A culture history of ancient Japanese Buddhism]. Tokyo: Yoshikawa Kōbunkan, 1998.

Tanahashi Mitsuo. *Go-Shirakawa hōō* [Retired Emperor Go-Shirakawa]. Tokyo: Kōdansha, 1995.

Tanaka Takako. '*Gehō to aihō no chūsei* [The outer path and the mediaeval path of love]. Tokyo: Sunagoya Shobō, 1993.

Taniguchi Kōsei. 'Torige ryūjo byōbu to Tō baka hekiga juka jinbutsu zu byōbu' [The Torige ryūjo byōbu and 'beauties beneath trees' folding screens in Tang dynasty tomb paintings]. In *Dai-66-kai Shōsōin ten: Tennō Kōgō Ryōheika sanji kinen* [The 66th Shōsōin exhibition: in honour of their majesties, the Emperor and Empress's eightieth birthday], edited by Nara kokuritsu hakubutsukan. Nara: Nara kokuritsu hakubutsukan, 2014.

Tokyo National Museum, ed. *Tokubetsuten 'Shosei Ō Gishi': Nitchū kokkō seijōka 40-shūnen, Tōkyō Kokuritsu Hakubutsukan 140-shūnen* [Special exhibition The Calligrapher Wang Xizhi: Celebrating the 40th anniversary of the normalization of Sino-Japanese relations and the 140th anniversary of the Tokyo National Museum]. Tokyo: Mainichi Shinbunsha, 2013.

Tokyo teikoku daigaku bungakubu shiryō hensanjo, ed. *Shōsōin gyobutsu suitō bunsho* [Dispersal records for the Shōsōin collection] 10. Dai Nihon komonjo [Historical texts of Japan], 25 furoku [Supplementary volumes]. Tokyo: Shiryōhensanjo. 1969.

Tōno Haruyuki. *Kentōshi to Shōsōin* [Japanese envoys and the Shōsōin]. Tokyo: Iwanami Shoten, 1992.

Tsai Shin-yu. 'Cong riben "niaomao linü" pingfeng kao Tang zhao "meinü pingfeng" bihua zhi yuanliu' [On the origin of the Tang dynasty mural painting 'Screen of Beauties' from the Japanese screen 'Beauties Under Trees']. *Shuhua yishu xuekan* 7 (2009).

Tsukamoto Maromitsu. *Hokusō kaigashi no seiritsu* [The establishment of a Northern Song painting history]. Tokyo: Chūō Kōron Bijutsu Shuppan, 2016.

Verscheur, Charlotte von. *Mono ga kataru Nihon taigai kōekishi: 7–16 seiki* [The object speaks: a history of Japanese foreign trade, 7th–16th centuries], translated by Kōchi Haruhito. Tokyo: Fujiwara Shoten, 2011.

Yoneda Kaisuke. *Shōsōin no kōyaku: zaishitsu chōsa kara hozon e* [Incense in the Shōsōin: from survey to preservation]. Kyoto: Shibunkaku Shuppan, 2015.

Yoneda Yūsuke. *Shōsōin hōmotsu no rekishi to hozon* [The history and preservation of the Shōsōin treasures]. Tokyo: Yoshikawa Kōbunkan, 1998.

———. *Shōsōin to Nihon bunka* [The Shōsōin and Japanese culture]. Tokyo: Yoshikawa Kōbunkan, 1998.

———. *Shōsōin hōmotsu to Heian jidai: wafūka he no michi* [The Shōsōin treasures and the Heian period: towards a Japanese style]. Kyoto: Tankōsha, 2000.

Zhang Le. *Zhongri meishu guanlianxing yanjiu: Zhengcangyuan cang 'Niaomao linü pingfeng' xinjie* [A study of the relationship between Chinese and Japanese art: a new interpretation of the screen 'Beauties Under Trees' from the collection of Shōsōin]. Beijing: Zhongguo Wenshi Chubanshe, 2014.

Zhao Liguang and Wang Jiugang. 'Chang'an xian Naliwangcun Tang bihua mu' [The Tang dynasty mural painting at the Naliwang Village, Chang'an County]. *Weibo* 4 (1989).

Zheng Yan. 'Tang Han Xiu mu shanshui tu chuyi' [On the images of landscape in the Tang dynasty mural painting at Han Xiu tomb]. *Gugong bowu yuan yuan kan* 181 (May 2015).

3 Overcoming Modernity
Towards a Concept of 'East Asian Art History'

Satō Dōshin

Introduction

I would first like to comment on the meaning and objectives implied in the title of this essay, 'Overcoming Modernity: Towards a Concept of "East Asian Art History"'.

For the past twenty years, I have been systematically researching the topics of 'art', 'art history', and 'art historiography' with a view to understanding the current state of the field and to deliberate on its historiography.[1] I was originally interested in the gap in perception between Japan and the West regarding Japanese art history. Then more recently, in the last ten years or so, I have been comparing exhibits that in effect constitute art history in the West and East Asia, and the differences in their geographic boundaries and the underlying reasons for such frameworks. This essay will consider how the latter relates to 'overcoming modernity' in terms of an 'East Asian art history' and its significance and potential.

I will return to this topic later, but in the various national galleries of the West, we are familiar with chronological displays of art—the Middle Ages beginning with Germany and France, the Renaissance with Italy, the 17th century with the Netherlands, and the 18th to 19th centuries focused around France and England—which, in essence, are exhibits of European art history. Within such chronologies there is naturally an emphasis on a nation's own art, but countries essentially agree upon these narratives of 'European art history' and one's own nation's art is placed within them.

On the other hand, in the national museums of East Asia, exhibits are focused around the art histories of the nation in which they are located, whether in Taiwan, China, Korea, or Japan. Despite the fact that the art of Buddhism, Confucianism, Daoism, and ink paintings were actually historically widespread across regions, they are compartmentalized according to the boundaries of contemporary nation states. 'East Asian art history' of the East Asian nations, therefore, does not represent a regionally shared history.[2]

Let us consider the broader frameworks for these identities—the shared art history of Europe that spans nations, versus the individual nation-based art histories of East Asia. It can broadly be stated that the European structure for art history is dependent on the Christian religion, while the nation-based forms of art history in East Asia rely on the political structures of nationhood.

However, underpinning the establishment of 'art history' in East Asia that does not reflect the actual history of art is the post-19th-century collapse of a Sinocentric Asia; in its wake the East Asian nations constructed their own histories anchored around nationalism. In other words, for East Asia to overcome its own modernity within this divide between history and reality, and establish an 'East Asian art history' based upon actuality, the question of whether this legacy of modernity can be overcome becomes an important criterion for this narrative. But what sort of identity should support this regional art history? If past notions of ethnocentrism, hegemony, power, political dogma, or pan-Asiatic ideologies are to be avoided, what alternative concepts and methodologies remain?

I myself make no claim to have answers to such questions, and the search seems daunting considering the perpetual flux of East–West relations, but I will expound upon them in light of the current context.

Systematic research of 'art history'

My research on the institutional frameworks of 'art' began with a simple quest regarding the concept of 'Japanese art history'. In 1985–1986, when I conducted a survey of modern Japanese art collections in the United States, I realized that 'Japanese art' was focused around *ukiyo-e* and decorative arts and that it differed greatly from what constituted Japanese art and Japanese art history in Japan. Unless collections were influenced by personal connections or other one-off circumstances, there were virtually no works by artists considered to be the great masters of Japanese modern painting, which was a shock for a scholar of modern Japanese art history such as myself. This tendency more or less parallels the Japanese art collections of Europe.

No-one can argue the universal question of taste, and in any case that is not the problem. When considering historicity, the issue could not simply be dismissed in this manner since the 'art', 'art history', and 'art historiography' of Japan always sought to mimic the West. Thus began my quest for how this gap came to be; what was important was to discover the reasons that led to this development and to understand how we came to the 'now', the present based on differing historical viewpoints.[3]

Since Kitazawa Noriaki proposed the theory of the 'systemization of fine art', in *Me no Shinden* (1989),[4] I have also been researching Japanese 'art', 'art history', and 'historiography' based on the premise that the concept of art itself was a Western transplant that became schematized in Japan.[5] My conclusion deriving from that theory is the premise for this essay, namely that 'Japanese art history' as a modern concept is actually looking back to the past of 'art', 'art history', and 'art historiography', and similarly that the 'East Asian art history' of Japan actually reflects the past of 'East Asia'. The forms that these take in present-day Japan are in fact an interpretation of history according to the logics that shaped the modern era of Japan. On the other hand, given that 'Japanese art history' was created as a self-portrait of Japonisme, and 'East Asian art history' was created in the era of modern Japanese anti-Asian policies, it seems that a review of 'East Asian art history' should not take a nativist approach, but rather should be examined within a broader historical and geographical world map and as a theory of connectivity.

Frameworks of 'Art History'—Exhibits in the East and West

Up until that point, I had only considered 'Japanese art history' and 'East Asian art history' within the Japanese context. Both were modelled after 'Western art history', yet I eventually realized there were significant differences in framework and structures from those in the West. The pivotal moment was when I was in Europe in 2000. During a two-month stay in Germany, I visited galleries every weekend both in that nation and in neighbouring countries. Initially I was just seeking out famous works in each place, but eventually came to the realization that 'art history' was being exhibited quite differently from in Japan.[6]

Until then, I had never questioned how the Japanese national museums and their museum exhibits presented 'Japanese art history'. However, in Europe, the Louvre in Paris did not present 'French art history' and the National Gallery in London was far from displaying only 'British art history'. State-run large-scale museums featured chronological exhibits—focusing, as I mentioned above, on Germany and France for the Middle Ages, Italy for the Renaissance, the Netherlands for the 17th century, and France for the 18th and 19th centuries. The various countries fundamentally all shared and exhibited the same basic 'European art history'.

In the Louvre, masterpieces such as the Venus de Milo are showcased on the first floor, while the higher floors feature works from Ancient Egypt, Greece, and Rome, all the way through to 19th-century European art. The collections of the Kunsthistorisches Museum in Vienna, originally formed under the Habsburgs, serve to represent a comprehensive 'art history', as exhibit rooms luxuriously display works by the master artists they patronized. These kinds of exhibits of 'European art history' can also be seen at the Hermitage in St Petersburg and at the National Gallery in Washington, D.C.

Let us now turn to the exhibits of the national museums in East Asia. At the Tokyo National Museum, there are no references to the fact that this is a display of 'Japanese art history'; the museum presents hybridized displays according to genre and time period. Similarly, at the National Museum of Korea, composite displays are arranged by genre and dynastic history, and the exhibits are centred around its own nation's art history. At the National Palace Museum in Taipei, exhibits favour genre but are arranged according to time periods, and the numerous masterpieces present a 'Chinese art history'. The Palace Museum in Beijing also prioritizes genre and presents a chronological 'Chinese art history' housed within its famed architectural compound, the Forbidden City.

In these ways, the museums of East Asia—in Taiwan, China, Korea, and Japan—take a cross section of a chronological history according to current political boundaries, and exhibit an art history focused around their own nations. It is hard to imagine a display of 'East Asian art history' that parallels 'European art history' by exhibiting, for example, various works from China, Korea, or Japan to represent different time periods.

This realization left me with an uneasy feeling. As I feared, the questions it raised led to the problems of religion and politics. I would like to point out that in the following discussion, I do not claim that any one of the differing viewpoints is the correct one.

Historical Identity in 'Art History'

I began comparing the exhibits of 'art history' at the national level because I believe that these represent the accepted histories by each nation and that this would therefore help us understand their underlying historical identities. Allow me to explain briefly the conceptual underpinnings and historical identities that underscore the entirely different art history frameworks between the East and West.[7]

Despite the European Union comprising almost thirty member countries including some of the formerly communist Eastern European states, the fact that Islamic Turkey has not been approved for membership reveals that what supports the unity of Europe has been the shared sense of identity based on the history and culture of nations espousing Christianity. Perhaps nowhere is this shared identity more apparent than in the exhibits of 'European art history' around Europe. I think we can safely assert that the common denominator that transcends the current political boundaries of the nation states is Christianity, and that religion is the largest supporter of the historical identity in creating 'European art history'.

On the other hand, in East Asia, where the exhibits of 'art history' are focused on each nation state and their independent histories, the question becomes what are the underlying identities of these nation states. When considering the historical issues of identity, one can conclude that the most important factor supporting the current nation states and their art histories would not be the plurality of religions, but ethnocentrism in South Korea, North Korea, and Japan, and Sinocentric values in China and Taiwan (Figure 3.1).[8]

Since ethnocentrism in Japan is related to its past aggressions, few people continue to assert this notion; however, the persistence of this inner conscience lies within the duelling facets of ethnocentrism. In short, the national art histories of East Asia are not based on religion but on the ethnocentric and Sinocentric values which lie at the core

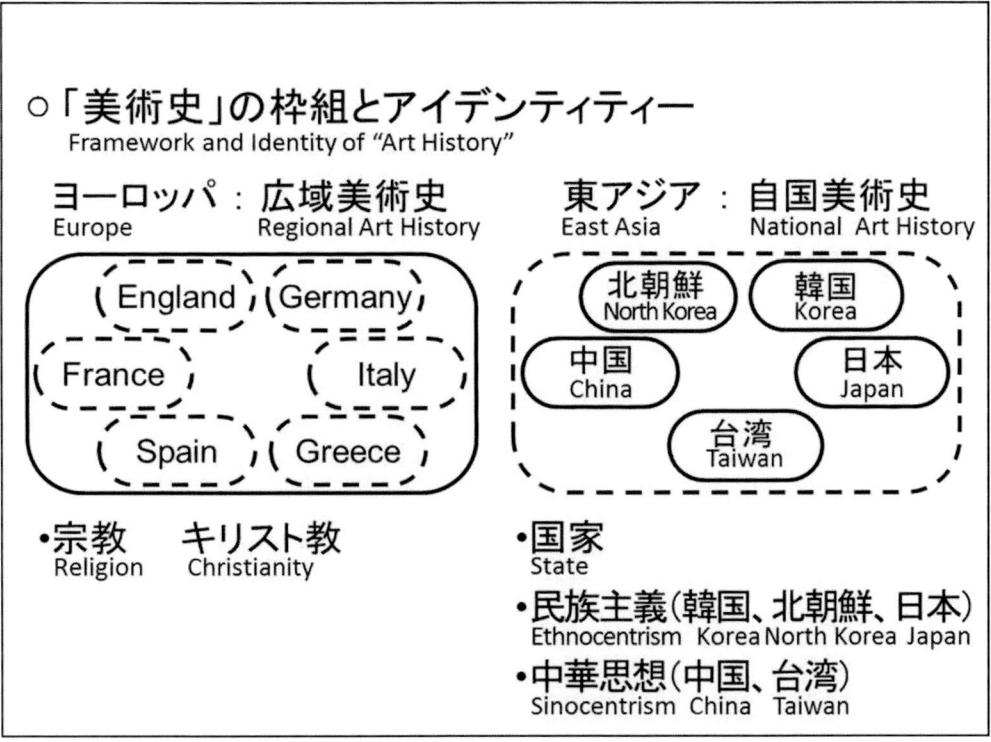

Figure 3.1 Framework and identity of 'art history'

of the present-day nation states. However, when considering the relationship between the nation-based art histories and state borders in East Asia, one must consider not only the historical identities but also the direct and realistic challenges of the East–West binary as a source of contemporary identity.

The Logic of the History Writers: Society and National Borders

This is a deeply political issue, and I do not intend to broach arguments for or against any political or ideological perspective. The goal, instead, is to confirm that history gets written within the framework of the accepted logic of an era or society, rather than based on historical realities that give rise to different historical perspectives.

Taking Japan as an example, what became clear from the research on institutional frameworks since the 1990s is that 'Japanese art history', which should have paralleled history, changed in tandem with the political transition from the nationalism of the modern era to the current democratic societal order. Pre-war 'Japanese art history' was the product of an ideology that sought to expand nationalistic influences as a demonstration of cultural supremacy. Following World War II, these ideologies transformed drastically to a 'History of Japanese beauty' to symbolize the freedom and peace of a new Japan. This stark metamorphosis, which poses a challenge to academic realities, demonstrates that the perception of 'history' and its truths is contingent. Similar types of systematic research into institutional theories that were conducted worldwide since the 1990s accepted the collapse of the East–West divide and set forth to search for a new world vision and historicity. However, in terms of East Asia, this East–West binary still persists.

The East–West divide is a modern phenomenon, but of interest is how a nation's history can be open to interpretation depending on the differences in societal structures. In the case of Japan, the variances in historicity occurred along a timeline from the modern to the contemporary, but the question remains whether this trajectory was paralleled in the East Asian nations of North and South Korea, China, and Taiwan. Another important issue when considering national art histories based on current national frameworks is that they may not necessarily correspond with those of past dynastic or imperial borders. (Of course, regions colonized by Japan in the modern era will not be considered as parts of Japan.)

Take for example the dispute that arose recently between Korea and China when ancient remains from the Goguryeo dynasty (37 BC to AD 668), which encompassed the Korean peninsula and North Eastern China, were considered for World Heritage Site registration. The fundamental differences surrounding national histories became apparent: Korean representatives argued that they were descendants of the same dynastic race, whereas the Chinese claimed that the region constituted part of their multiracial, multi-dynastic national history, and moreover that it was within the contemporary borders of their state. This was partly due to the fact that the current borders cut across history. The issue is not a simple one that can be solved, for example, by placing the art within a geographic framework rather than a nationalistic art history. The problem is quite the contrary. These are the very reasons that make establishing an 'East Asian art history' as a regional art history problematic—but further challenges remain, namely how widespread should a 'region' be and what parameters should determine them.

The Nature and Boundaries of 'Region'

To avoid being dragged into a maze when tackling geographical definitions and standards, perhaps the most sensible way to delineate territories is simply convenience, but further thought on what constitutes the boundaries of a 'region' are nonetheless warranted. *Tōyō* (East Asia) within a Japanese 'East Asian art history' of the modern era refers to the region extending from the Korean peninsula to China and as far as India. This can perhaps be attributed to the introduction of Buddhism to Japan and associated geographical regions. However, there is no shared concept of the nomenclature *tōyō* and the corresponding region within East Asia. What then are the relationships between the terms *tōyō* and Asia, the Orient, and the East?[9]

There are three dictionary definitions of the term *tōyō* in Japan:

1. The region east of Turkey.
2. Eastern and southern parts of Asia.
3. Japan as referred to by China.

The first refers mainly to Asia and the 'Orient', and in contemporary Japanese, the nuance is close to that of *tōhō* (eastward). The second definition is the one in most common use in Japan today. The third, while still in use in China and Taiwan, does not apply to Japan and therefore is not appropriate. That is because in Japan the term describes a region that includes China, whereas in China it describes Japan alone and does not include China itself. Perhaps within China's world-view—one that historically considered itself at the centre of a world with four other regions—a regional concept of *tōyō* similar to that in Japan fundamentally did not exist.

As a result, the 'East Asian art history' established in Japan may just be the history of a region's art envisaged by a nation on the fringes and not necessarily a shared regional art history. Furthermore, 'Asia', 'the Orient', and 'the East' are fundamentally Eurocentric terms, and regional references may differ depending upon the time period. What this means is that the art history of such regions can in actuality be independent art histories whose geographic borders may not even coincide, and that '*tōyō* art history', 'East Asian art history', 'Asian art history' and 'Oriental art history' become muddled.

This leads to the question of quality, or the nature of the art history in question. Can an approach similar to 'European art history'—that which places Christianity as the common factor in defining borders—be employed? It cannot be as simple as this since there are multiple religions in East Asia and their regional extensions and developments are all different. As regional religions, Confucianism, Buddhism, and Daoism are fairly widespread, but there are no overarching reasons for any of these religions to take priority over other factors (for example, the spread of ink painting, Chinese characters, or literature). With such considerations, the possibility of a regional version of East Asian art history becomes doubtful. Are there no ways to discuss the realities of the interactions that took place?

Overcoming Modernity—Towards an 'East Asian Art History'

From this point onward I will move into the hypothetical realm—since it is not sufficiently realistic or feasible to be called a proposal or plan, perhaps it is best to consider these thoughts as fantastical. Rather than considering various definitions to come up with a framework and conceptual software for such a history—a shared regional art history between East Asian nations based on interactions and historical truths—I will begin with an assumption. The assumption is that this regional art history will be called 'East Asian art history' and will comprise the current national boundaries of China, Taiwan, South Korea, North Korea, and Japan.

Wider Publication of 'National Art Histories'

If in modern and contemporary East Asia, the historical reality of interaction is divided among each of the nation's own domestic art histories, perhaps each cannot be fully aware of the others' established national art histories. Therefore, if translations of nationalist art histories were produced, then each could confirm what structures and perceptions belie them. Each could also identify the interpretative differences of shared historical events. Leaving aside differences, the mutual acknowledgement of the situation would be a first step towards the question of what constitutes a region.

Content and Form of Regional Art Histories

A national history of art takes historic interactions and divides them according to a geographic or horizontal axis to produce a descriptive and developmental history along a chronological timeline. It therefore follows that the mere collection and alignment of each country's national art histories would not amount to any meaningful art history based on interaction or a regional art history. For this reason, the configurations of the content and form should prioritize themes pertinent to a common region, while weaving in each nation's current dispositions and developments (Figure 3.2). For example, the account of a history more closely aligned with actual interactions becomes possible when, as in Point 1 in Figure 3.2, we consider the art related to Buddhism, Confucianism, Daoism, as well as ink paintings. Perhaps a developmental history based on regions becomes possible in those categories of art history.

On the other hand, as with court art versus popular art as seen in Point 2 of Figure 3.2, even if the nature of the actual art differs from nation to nation, when it is possible to locate commonalities then it may be interesting to align the art according to each country's individual situations to create comparative theories. Therefore, the art that developed according to regions can be an interactive history while art that developed independently, as in Point 2 of Figure 3.2, can be treated as a comparative theory. Other theories, or Point 3 in Figure 3.2—those that do not belong in either paradigm—can perhaps be categorized as 'others' of individual national themes that existed within the confines of each nation. A wider perspective, a history rooted in interaction, a comparative approach, and broader knowledge would eventually become necessary in describing those accounts.

Methodology

Since we are speaking of art history, it may be best to discuss it as a formative history. However, of most significance when considering a regional art history is overcoming pre-existing perceptions, interpretations, and discourses, and thinking about whether there can be a shared awareness of those. What needs to be avoided are interpretations

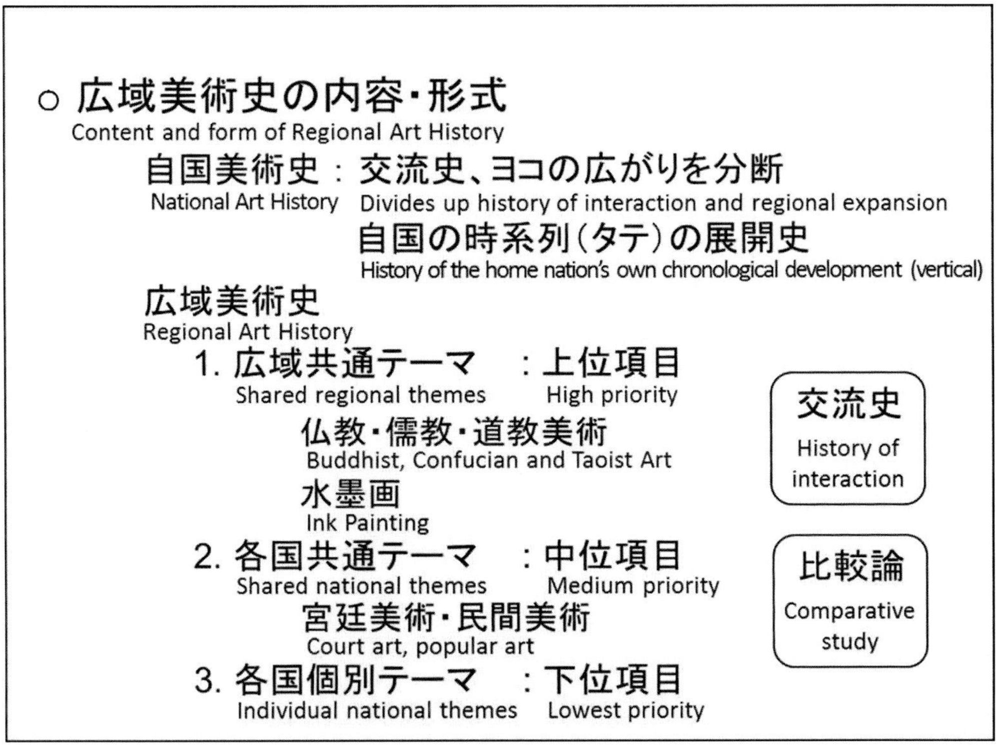

Content and form of Regional Art History

広域美術史の内容・形式
Content and form of Regional Art History

自国美術史：交流史、ヨコの広がりを分断
National Art History Divides up history of interaction and regional expansion

自国の時系列（タテ）の展開史
History of the home nation's own chronological development (vertical)

広域美術史
Regional Art History

1. 広域共通テーマ　：上位項目
   Shared regional themes High priority
   仏教・儒教・道教美術
   Buddhist, Confucian and Taoist Art
   水墨画
   Ink Painting
2. 各国共通テーマ　：中位項目
   Shared national themes Medium priority
   宮廷美術・民間美術
   Court art, popular art
3. 各国個別テーマ　：下位項目
   Individual national themes Lowest priority

交流史 — History of interaction

比較論 — Comparative study

Figure 3.2 Content and form of regional art history

based on ideologies from both the East and West, such as from the point of view of chauvinism, hegemonism, ethnocentrism, or the pan-Asiatic perspective. Perhaps these will be the most difficult obstacles to overcome.

It is said that history is a political tool, and when examining past behaviours, that appears to be all too true as a means of consolidating history. On the other hand, it is my hope that history will be a guidepost for the future. As trite as it may sound, it is necessary to gain an understanding of each other. Interactions including international symposia and the multilateral publication of quality research and texts are an absolute necessity. In addition, exchange students who can gain genuine trans-national experiences would be significant resources for the potential of a future that accepts broader perspectives on regionalities. A great hope for the future lies in the increase of recent foreign students whose research themes go beyond the limits of national borders. Although a regional art history may currently be problematic, with such students ready to embrace new approaches, I am optimistic that there are immediate measures that can be taken by them.

Internationalism and Understanding Others— High Culture and Sub-Culture

I have thus far presented my observations regarding the differences in the structural frameworks of 'art history' in the East and the West, and the possibility of a regional 'East Asian art history'. I have been speaking of a search for an East Asian art history that can overcome the divided views of history towards the dream of mutual understanding. Finally, I would like to depart from 'art history' and make some statements regarding international communication and structures for understanding others.[10]

Since the huge success of the Korean television drama 'Winter Sonata', a Korea-boom in Japan shows no signs of slowing down despite the political and diplomatic challenges between the two nations. Enabling a cultural understanding of Japan abroad is apparently beyond high culture, lying instead in the sub-cultures of *manga* and *anime*. No doubt globalization and information technology play influential roles in these trends, but why is it that sub-culture is able to surpass high culture—that supposedly carries the banners of one's culture—and easily overcome the obstacles of national borders and civilizations? These problems are not to be ignored in the cases of 'art' and 'art history' as high culture.

'Art' and 'art history', as elements of high culture, are often associated with politics, religion, philosophy, aesthetics, history, literature, and music, while sub-cultures are linked with entertainment and daily life. In terms of understanding other cultures, sub-cultures that are rooted in the basic human emotions are undoubtedly superior to high culture. On the other hand, the daily news, whether domestic or international, generally seems to be reported in the following order: politics, diplomacy, the military, economics, industry, culture, and then lifestyle. The focus of political, diplomatic, military, and economic news is on one's nation and its interests, and international news becomes linked to domestic interests as well. This then leads to the news being broadcast in a friendly light when dealing with allies, and with antagonism when concerning those deemed opponents. International topics surrounding culture and lifestyle earn coverage only when there is no other significant news to report. Repeated exposure to such patterns leads viewers to form preconceptions of other nations, influenced by the political, military, and economic news. Furthermore, these preconceptions probably begin to influence our impressions of the people and their lives as well.

However, the actual lives of people and their base emotions are not as different as the political establishments. What is significant here is that whereas sub-cultures closely parallel daily life, high culture connects with politics and diplomacy, history, ideology, and religion. Perhaps it is these links between the elements that characterize nationhood which make it difficult for high culture to break through boundaries. This problem further translates to 'art history', which is part of high culture. Perhaps this tendency is especially pronounced in modern and contemporary East Asia, where history was divided in creating nation-based art histories. On the other hand, it can also be said that the realities of interactions became too divided, and that the reversal of this reality can become a shared trajectory. I believe sub-cultures should continue to be actively and vigorously shared, but if historicity can also be affected by the underlying values, perhaps it is not unreasonable to hope for an optimistic outcome . . .

(Translated by Midori Oka)

Notes

1 Satō Dōshin, *'Nihon bijutsu' tanjō – Kindai nihon no 'kotoba' to senryaku* [The birth of 'Japanese Art': the language and strategy of modern Japan] (Tokyo: Kōdansha sensho mechie 92, 1996), pp. 216–227.
2 Satō Dōshin, *Bijutsu no aidentitii – dareno tame ni nan no tameni* [The identity of beauty: for whom and for what] (Tokyo: Yoshikawa Kōbunkan, 2007), pp. 29–35.
3 Satō, *'Nihon bijutsu' tanjō*, pp. 216–227.

4 Kitazawa Noriaki, *Me no shinden – 'bijutsu' juyōshi nōto* [The temple of the eye: notes on the reception of 'Fine Art'] (Tokyo: Bijutsu shuppansha, 1989), pp. 193–313.
5 Dōshin Satō, *Modern Japanese State and the Meiji State: The Politics of Beauty*, trans. Hiroshi Nara (Los Angeles: Getty Research Institute, 2011), pp. 124–154.
6 Satō, *Bijutsu no aidentiii*, pp. 12–35.
7 Ibid., pp. 36–49.
8 Discussions of ethnocentrism in China (People's Republic of China) and Taiwan (Republic of China) risk leading to the contentious issues around the 'One China' question, which I will not delve into in this essay.
9 Satō, *'Nihon bijutsu' tanjō*, pp. 98–104.
10 Satō, *Bijutsu no aidentitii*, pp. 207–210.

Bibliography

Kitazawa Noriaki. *Me no shinden – 'bijutsu' juyōshi nōto* [The temple of the eye: notes on the reception of 'fine art']. Tokyo: Bijutsu shuppansha, 1989.
Satō Dōshin. *'Nihon bijutsu' tanjō – Kindai nihon no 'kotoba' to senryaku* [The birth of 'Japanese art': the language and strategy of modern Japan]. Tokyo: Kōdansha sensho mechie 92, 1996.
———. *Bijutsu no aidentitii – dareno tame ni nan no tameni* [The identity of beauty: for whom and for what]. Tokyo: Yoshikawa Kōbunkan, 2007.
———. *Modern Japanese State and the Meiji State: The Politics of Beauty*, translated by Hiroshi Nara. Los Angeles: Getty Research Institute, 2011.

Part II
New Ways of Looking at Others

4 The Triangle of Modern Japanese *Yōga*

Paris, Tokyo, and East Asia

Miura Atsushi

For many years, research into the *yōga* (Western-style painting) of modern Japan has been concerned primarily with the circumstances of the art form in the context of Japan itself. There have been attempts to investigate its connections with the various countries in Europe in which many of its pioneering artists studied—in particular, Italy, France, the UK, and Germany—but it is fair to say that, until recently, *yōga*'s links with modern painting in the rest of East Asia have been relatively neglected. Since the 1990s, however, there have been several important exhibitions that engaged with the relationship between modern Japanese *yōga* and East Asia, notably *The Reorganization of the Imperial Academy of Fine Arts in 1935* (Tokyo Metropolitan Teien Art Museum, 1992), *Oil Painting in East Asia – Its Awakening and Development* (Shizuoka Prefectural Museum of Art, 1999), and *Images of East Asia in the Modern Age: How Japanese Modern Art Painted Asia* (Toyota Municipal Museum of Art, 2009).

These exhibitions were structured around two main points of concern relating to the fifty-year period between the end of the First Sino-Japanese War (1894–1895) and the conclusion of the Pacific War in 1945—when Japan annexed Taiwan, Korea, and North-Eastern China (Manchuria) into its territory—and which also included the Russo-Japanese War of 1904–1905. These are, first, how did Japanese *yōga* artists portray East Asian subjects in their paintings, and second, what sort of paintings did artists in the rest of East Asia produce, having digested the artistic achievements of Japanese *yōga*? At the same time, there has been a flourishing of modes of research that analyse and critique the ideology of Japanese *yōga* of this period, under the influence of post-Saidian Orientalist, post-colonial, and gender studies discourses.[1] We have entered an age in which it is untenable to claim that we need only study Japanese *yōga* in the Japanese context.

As an extension of this, the 2014 exhibition *Toward the Modernity: Images of Self & Other in East Asian Art Competitions*, held at the Fukuoka Asian Art Museum, was a revolutionary attempt to consider how modern *yōga* developed in East Asia under Japanese rule (including in Japan) from the end of the 19th century onwards through the lens of the government-sponsored art exhibitions (*kanten*).[2] This was an ambitious experiment to try to command a sweeping view of all of the following at once: the Ministry of Education Art Exhibitions (known as Bunten, 1907–) and the Imperial Fine Arts Academy Exhibitions (Teiten, 1919–; Shinbunten, 1936–) held in Tokyo; the equivalents in Seoul, Korea/Joseon Fine Art Exhibitions (Senten, 1922–1944), in Taipei, Taiwan Fine Art Exhibitions (Taiten, 1927–1936) and, later, Government House Fine Art Exhibitions (Futen, 1938–1943); and in Changchun, Manchurian Fine Art

Exhibitions (Manten, 1938–1945). It is difficult to stress sufficiently the importance of this first real foray into the study of Japanese government art exhibitions in East Asia—which are key to understanding Japan's colonial cultural policies in this period. Without an adequate exploration of both their positive and negative elements, any study that engages with modern East Asian painting is impossible.

This essay explores how to reconfigure our understanding of modern Japanese *yōga* within the grand triangle of France, Japan, and East Asia or, put another way, Paris, Tokyo, and Taipei (or Seoul, or Changchun). It does so with a particular focus on Kuroda Seiki and the *yōga* artists from the Tokyo School of Fine Arts who studied in Western Europe, primarily France. These artists, who went to France to study in the late 19th and early 20th centuries, were to bring Western art back with them to Japan as a normative model to emulate. Later on, however, alongside Japan's move into Asia, these artists formed multifaceted relationships with Taiwan, Korea, and China, visiting locations throughout East Asia to adjudicate at government-sponsored exhibitions, to teach, to paint murals and on private trips (see Table 4.1). They also produced work with a variety of East Asian subjects. Likewise, students from around East Asia poured into the Tokyo School of Fine Art and other private art schools and academies, and studied 'Japanese' *yōga* styles—themselves freshly procured from France. Subsequently, these artists were responsible for the rise of, and advancements in, modern painting in their home countries. While fewer in number, there were also some artists from the rest of East Asia who went directly to France to study, adding further shades of nuance to our triangle.

Table 4.1 Major Japanese modern *yōga* painters: Paris – Tokyo – East Asia
(B: Belgium, C: China, E: Europe, F: France, I: Italy, K: Korea, M: Manchuria T: Taiwan)

山本芳翠 Yamamoto Hōsui (1850–1906). F (1878–87), C (1894, 1903–04)

黒田清輝 Kuroda Seiki (1866–1925). F (1884–93, 1900–01), C (1894)

藤島武二 Fujishima Takeji (1867–1943). F/I (1905–10), T (1933, 1934), K/T (1935), M/C (1937, 1938)

岡田三郎助 Okada Saburōsuke (1869–1939). F (1897–1902), T (1918–19, 1920–21), C (1922), M (1928), E (1930), M (1935)

和田英作 Wada Eisaku (1874–1959). F (1900–03), (1921–22), K (1923)

鹿子木孟郎 Kanokogi Takeshirō (1874–1941). F (1900–04), F (1906–08), F (1915–18), C (1923), C (1937)

満谷国四郎 Mitsutani Kunishirō (1874–1936). F (1900–01), F (1911–14), C/K (1922), C (1923, 1925, 1928), K (1933)

児島虎次郎 Kojima Torajirō (1881–1929). F/B (1908–12), C/K (1917), F/E (1919–21), C (1921), F/E (1922–23), C (1924, 1926)

和田三造 Wada Sanzō (1883–1967). F/E (1909–14), C (1931–32), M (1935), C (1941), M (1943)

安井曾太郎 Yasui Sōtarō (1888–1955). F (1907–14), K (1936), M (1937), M/C (1943, 1944)

梅原龍三郎 Umehara Ryūzaburō (1888–1986). F (1908–13), F (1920–21), C (1929), T (1933, 34, 35, 36), M/C (1939), C (1940, 41, 42, 43)

Were the modern Japanese *yōga* that depicted East Asia under Japanese rule merely 'Orientalist' paintings that projected the relationship of the West vis-à-vis Japan onto that of Japan vis-à-vis East Asia? How should we view the contribution of Japanese *yōga* to the development of modern art in East Asia? To answer these questions, we must now take stock of the triangle that encompassed such a complex network of interactions between Paris, Tokyo, and East Asia in the early 20th century, examine the things that were brought about inside it and the things that changed within its breadth, and reinvestigate their historical importance and aesthetic characteristics.

Kuroda Seiki and Okada Saburōsuke

Kuroda Seiki (1866–1924), who was responsible for establishing *yōga* as an art form in Japan in the modern period, lived in France for a total of ten years. He trained under the tutelage of academic *pleinariste* Raphaël Collin and returned to Japan in 1893 after having been accepted in the Paris Salon. When the First Sino-Japanese War broke out the following summer, Kuroda went to the front as a correspondent for the French newspaper *Le Monde Illustré*, remaining there until February 1895. During this period, he produced many sketches of the battlefields he encountered, but he never turned any of these into history paintings or works of military art.[3] Yamamoto Hōsui (1850–1906), who studied in France earlier than Kuroda, went to the front during both the First Sino-Japanese War and the Russo-Japanese War. He painted scenes of the latter that evoked the military personnel stationed there in a quiet style reminiscent of the Barbizon School as, for example in *Watch under the Moon at Chinese Station (Tōka ton gekka hoshō zu*, 1906).[4] From a historical perspective it is interesting that a Western art department was set up at the Tokyo School of Fine Arts, using money from reparations obtained from the Sino-Japanese War; and, from 1896 onwards, Kuroda gave classes there, rising to the rank of professor in 1898. As Japan, the first regional country to succeed in modernizing and Westernizing, was starting on its path to colonizing East Asia, the need for an institutional marker of cultural and artistic attainment, in the form of a department of Western art in the Tokyo School of Fine Arts, began to be felt.

It is clear that the model for Western art education in the Tokyo School of Fine Art was derived from the Académie Colarossi, where Kuroda received instruction from Raphaël Collin, and the École des Beaux-Arts, where he had sat in on lectures.[5] Viewed from the perspective of our France–Japan–East Asia triangle, we can note that just as Japanese artists had studied in Paris, in the main, students from China, Korea, and Taiwan acquired a working knowledge of Western painting in Tokyo. This, however, was *not* French painting—at most we can say it was 'Western painting', or *yōga*, as received and understood in the Japanese context. The Bunten exhibitions, inaugurated in Tokyo in 1907, were modelled on the Paris Salon. As Japan gained control of East Asia, it transplanted this official system to Korea, Taiwan, and Manchuria, in the form of the Senten, Taiten, and Manten, respectively, as mentioned above. The adjudicators sent to oversee these *kanten* (salons) were, in the main, either professors from or graduates of the Tokyo School of Fine Art. For the first Senten in 1922, for example, the Government-General of Korea requested the secondment of Kuroda Seiki. Since Kuroda was indisposed, Okada Saburōsuke (1869–1939), a protégé of his and also a professor at the School of Fine Arts, was sent to adjudicate instead. Okada is best known for his Raphaël Collin-style nudes, and portraits of beautiful women in kimono.

However, he also painted two murals for Government House in Taiwan, completed in 1921, as well as murals for the General Affairs State Council building in Manchukuo in 1935–36 on the theme of *Gozoku Kyōwa no Heiwagō* (The peaceful abode of the five races in harmony).[6] Finally, he also left a number of paintings of ladies in Chinese dress, and Manchurian landscape scenes, so we must not overlook that he was an artist whose work had strong associations with East Asia.

Fujishima Takeji and Orientalism

As all of this was going on, one Japanese *yōga* artist in particular was very conscious of orientalism; this was Fujishima Takeji (1867–1943). In the travelogue he penned about his visit to Korea in 1913, just after the annexation of the country in 1910, he writes:

> When France captured Algeria, the artists of the time crossed over to that country in droves, and painted its scenery and quotidian life; this became something of a fashion at the time, so that a long string of celebrated painters made it their intention to paint the landscapes, people and wars of that land. In other words, the likes of [Eugène] Delacroix, [Alexandre-Gabriel] Decamps, [Prosper] Marilhat, [Eugène] Fromentin and [Gustave] Guillaumet whipped up a taste for the oriental that was to generate a certain *mode* within artistic circles in France. The fierce light and colour of the Tropics provided the French art world with a stimulus of grand proportions. Now that Korea is annexed to the realm—of course it differs from the example of Algeria—but, in any case, since it has become our territory, just as it is necessary to study, and open up the land, from many angles, we must, at this time, look closely at it from the perspective of art too . . .[7]

Speaking in somewhat orotund terms, we might describe this as modern Japanese *yōga*'s 'Declaration of Orientalism'. Among his peers, Fujishima was relatively late to study abroad. He was taught by Fernand Cormon in Paris from 1905 before moving to Rome in 1907, where, while training under the head of the French Academy, Carolus Duran, he also encountered Italian Renaissance art. During his time in Paris he undoubtedly also saw plenty of the works of 'Delacroix, Decamps, Marilhat, Fromentin and Guillaumet' and other artists' representatives of French Orientalist painting, at the Louvre, the Musée du Luxembourg, the Salon, and elsewhere. When he visited Korea in 1913, it is clear that these memories were revived, causing him to substitute, in his mind, the relationship between Japan and Korea with that of France and Algeria. Interestingly, however, Fujishima notes in his travel writing that he considers the landscape of Korea to resemble Italy—there is a certain commonality in the brightness of the light and picturesque colours—and that Korea, again much like Italy, has nothing of artistic worth in the current age but was possessed of a magnificent body of art in ancient times, the vestiges of this age remaining, to the present, in the garments worn by its people. As Kojima Kaoru explains, he was starting to see a parallel relationship between France and Italy and Japan and Korea.[8]

While there certainly are resemblances between the French Orientalist paintings created as France was colonizing Algeria and the Japanese Orientalist paintings that sought to colonize Taiwan and Korea, we should not overlook a number of important differences. The most glaring differences are, first, that the expression of violence and eroticism was suppressed in Japanese painting as a whole and second, that a

The Triangle of Modern Japanese Yōga   69

large number of art students came from the colonies to study *yōga* in Japan. Another important point of difference, obvious when we consider the history of the reception of Chinese tastes and literature among Japanese literati, is that Japan and the rest of East Asia have in common that they once formed part of the Sinitic cultural bloc. In this latter respect, the oppositional structures built into Western Orientalist art through the division of Christianity in the West and Islam in the East are absent. Fujishima saw Korea as part of a civilization which was, in substance, shared with Japan, not one that was distinctly different from it—an East Asian Italy, and not an Algeria. He was fully aware that Japan and Korea, as well as China and Taiwan, belonged to a single cultural region. It was this, above all, that enabled Japan, with four-character slogans like *nittai yūgō* ('Japan–Taiwan Fusion'), *naisen ittai* ('Homeland-Korea One Body'), and *gozoku kyōwa* ('The Five Races in Harmony'—meaning Japanese, Korean, Manchu, Mongol, and Han), to push forward imperialist policies of cultural assimilation with such ease; however, it also meant that the paintings produced by Japanese artists at this time took on a somewhat different nuance to those of the French Orientalists.[9]

To consider a few examples of Fujishima's work, we can start with a piece entitled *Tōyō-buri* (Orientalism) (Figure 4.1), which the artist himself considered to be a new

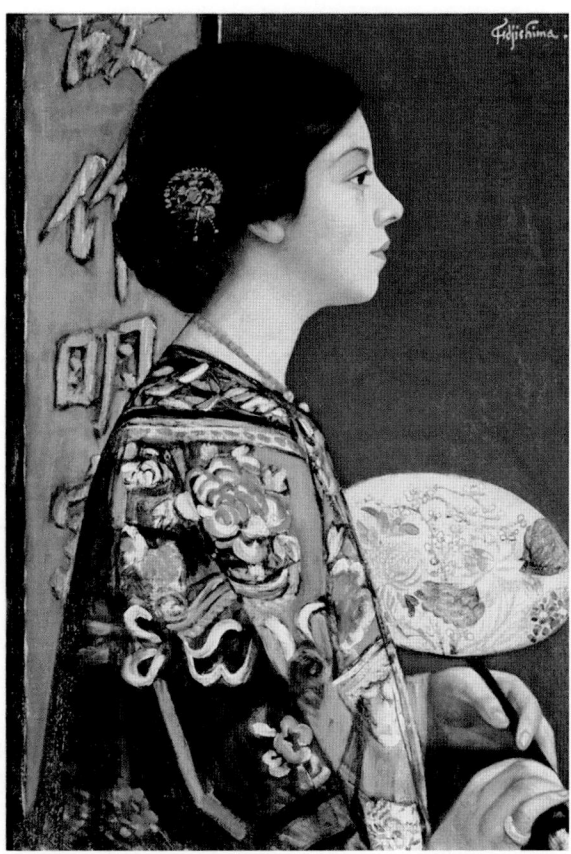

Figure 4.1 Fujishima Takeji, *Orientalism* (Tōyō-buri), 1924. Oil on canvas, 63.7 × 44.0 cm
Private collection

point of departure for him and which was entered in the fifth Teiten exhibition in 1924. It is an impressive piece; a half-figure profile portrait of a woman in Chinese dress (the model was Japanese). According to Fujishima, it originated in his detecting 'a tranquil oriental mentality' in the female profile portraits typical of Renaissance painters like Piero della Francesca.[10] Since he also copied a female portrait by Pisanello in the Louvre (*Portrait of Ginevra d'Este*), it is clear that he had been impressed by this kind of profile depiction of women. Fujishima collected Chinese women's dresses, which he considered fitting to set off the female profile. As he explained:

> It wasn't because I necessarily intended to paint Chinese people. What I was trying to do was to use Japanese women to create a typically oriental beauty. Saying that those Renaissance, oriental-style profiles took me there is sufficient explanation of my muse. I am trying to paint something that makes free use of the materials of Western painting, but that is distant from any scent of the West.[11]

In other words, this painting is a hybrid consisting of an Italian Renaissance portrait, a Japanese model, and Chinese clothing; an aspirational attempt to use media obtained from Western art to fashion a 'typically oriental beauty' common to both China and Japan.[12] Fujishima repeatedly painted women in Mandarin dresses, but the most complete and pared-down example of this is surely *Hōkei* (Orchid, 1926, private collection). Here the model is holding an orchid in her right hand against a backdrop of blue sky with white clouds. The work is the expressive creation of a Japanese painter who saw an oriental mentality in the classicism of the Italian Renaissance and sought to represent oriental beauty through the medium of continental Asian culture. Within this fusion of cultures, the viewer is left slightly uneasy; there is a co-mingling of heterogeneous elements not seen in French Orientalism. While on the one hand this can be seen as a manifestation of Fujishima's artistic ideals, from the perspective of the work's historical context it also indicates that modern Japan, having accomplished the task of Westernization ahead of its neighbours and as the leading power in the Orient, had now succeeded in creating a 'Western' art form of its own, *yōga*.

As will be noted below, between 1933 and 1935, Fujishima would visit Taiwan and be invited to act as adjudicator in the Senten and Taiten salons. Also, in 1937, having been invited to adjudicate at the Manchukuo Fine Arts Exhibition—the precursor of the Manten—Fujishima depicts the sunrise at Dolonnuur (Ch: *Duolun*) in the painting *Mōko no hinode* (*Sunrise in Inner Mongolia*) (Figure 4.2). In doing so, he completed the ten-year task of creating the 1937 work *Kyokujitsu rikugō wo terasu* (*The Rising Sun Shines in the Six Directions*, Imperial Household Agency, Museum of the Imperial Collections), which was to be presented to the Imperial Household. Fujishima wrote the following about *Sunrise in Inner Mongolia*: 'At a time when the national prestige extends far across Manchukuo to distant Mongolia, searching here for the symbol of Japan's shining dignity necessarily takes on deeper levels of meaning.'[13] It is not clear whether Guillaumet's *The Desert* (1867, Musée d'Orsay), which Fujishima had almost certainly seen many years before in Paris, was flickering at the back of his mind when he painted the seemingly boundless tract of Mongol desert, but we can say for sure that the artist was, alongside a sense of duty, aware of the nationalistic significance of the rising sun, gazed at from the westerly-most outpost of the Japanese Empire. Called on

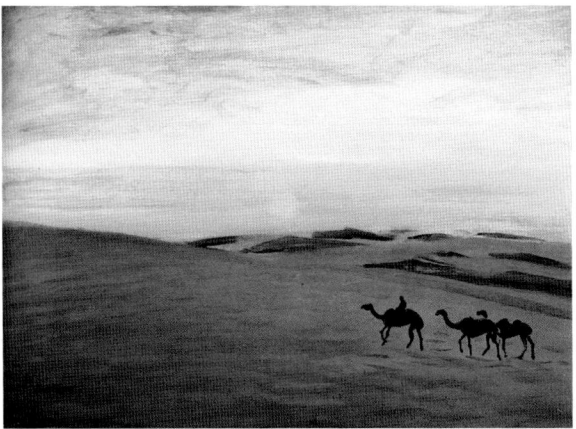

Figure 4.2 Fujishima Takeji, *Sunrise in Inner Mongolia* (Mōko no hi no de), 1937. Oil on canvas, 72.5 × 100.0 cm
Kagoshima Prefectural Museum of Culture, 'Reimeikan'

again in the following year, 1938, to adjudicate at the Manten, Fujishima was without a doubt an artist who played a central role in tying Japanese modern *yōga* to the rest of East Asia.

Kojima Torajirō

Fujishima's penchant for Renaissance-style profiles aside, the notion of distilling oriental beauty into female portraiture was by no means an uncommon one. After returning home to Japan, Kojima Torajirō (1881–1929)—who had resided in Europe, primarily France and Belgium, between 1908 and 1912, and in the process imbibed the style of the Impressionist and Neo-impressionist movements—made his way to China and Korea in search of the nature of oriental beauty. An artist who maintained his relationship with France, continuing to send works to the Paris Salon National, Kojima no doubt had something special in mind when he exhibited the four works *Belle de matin* (pair, 1916 and 1920, Ōhara Museum of Art), *Automne* (Figure 4.3), and *Opéra dynastie Ming, 'Chohannue'* (1918, Ōhara Museum of Art) at the 1920 Salon.[14] In using modish European techniques (albeit in a mix of the Impressionistic and Naturalistic styles taught and approved by the Salon National) to paint women in the national dresses of Japan, Korea, and China—and then displaying those paintings as a set in a Parisian exhibition—Kojima was sending the current which flowed through the triangle of Japanese modern *yōga* back at France.

However, regardless of such an awareness on Kojima's part, there is in these works no tension between heterogeneous elements that cause cultural or artistic friction, as we see in Fujishima's portraiture; on the contrary, they have an easiness of comprehension, an acceptability born of their character—oriental women in a Western painting, no more, no less. More than the common features of oriental civilization, these depictions

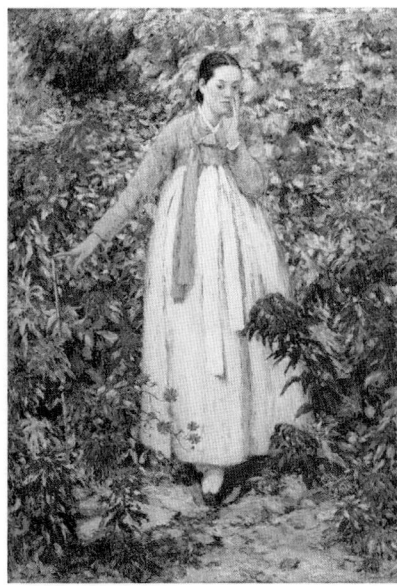

Figure 4.3 Kojima Torajirō, *Autumn* (Aki), 1920. Oil on canvas, 200.0 × 136.0 cm
Centre Pompidou, Musée National d'Art Moderne, Paris

of Japan, Korea, and China through the same eyes tell of the subordination of Eastern culture to that of the West, to the extent that it would not seem strange if they had been painted by a French artist rather than a Japanese one. That these works were indeed held in high esteem in France is clear from the fact that Kojima was made a full member of the Salon de la Société Nationale after the exhibition, and that *Automne* was purchased by the French Government for the sum of 3,000 francs and is now housed in the Musée National d'Art Moderne at the Pompidou Centre. Kojima's portrayals of East Asian women did not undermine the level terrain of Westerners' expectations and, in this sense, they can be understood as an extension of the Orientalist movement, despite the fact that the artist who portrayed Japanese women in this way was himself Japanese.

We can detect a similar sensation in Kuroda Seiki's *Maïko* (Dancing girl, Plate 4), painted after the artist returned to Japan in 1893. This, too, can be seen as the result of a Westernized Japanese artist painting Japanese women through the 'othering' eyes of the French. Kuroda, who had become proficient in Academism in Paris under Raphaël Collin, before adding to his style the composition, colouring, and brush strokes of Impressionism, represented the female dancer from his own country with an elevation that exposes his internalization of Western orientalism.[15] Kojima's female portraits, *Belle de matin* (pair) and *Automne*, can be seen as an extension of this trend, begun by Kuroda.

Yasui Sōtarō

Yasui Sōtarō (1888–1955) and Umehara Ryūzaburō, who belonged to a slightly later generation of artists than Kojima, created their most significant work in response to

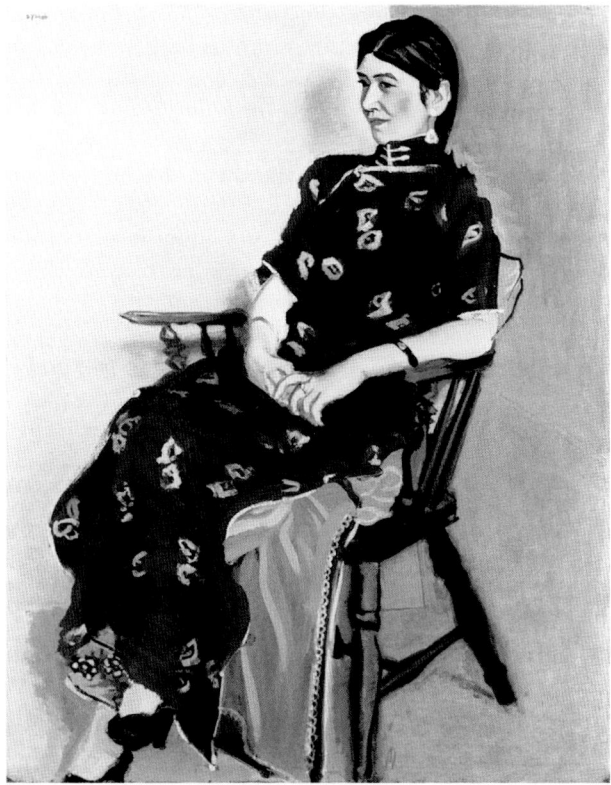

Figure 4.4 Yasui Sōtarō, *A Portrait of Chin-Jung* (Kin'yō), 1934. Oil on canvas, 96.5 × 74.5 cm

The National Museum of Modern Art, Tokyo

their contact with East Asia. When in Paris, Yasui was under the tutelage of Jean-Paul Laurens at the Académie Julian; ultimately however he became drawn to the Impressionist movement and was inspired by the work of Auguste Renoir and Paul Cézanne. On returning to Japan, he went through an exploratory period in which he sought out his own path, eventually arriving at this in 1934 with *Kin'yō* (Portrait of Chin-Jung) (Figure 4.4), displayed at the twenty-first *Nikaten*, to much acclaim. At this point, Yasui was yet to set foot in Korea or Manchuria but, as the 2014 exhibition *Egakareta Chainadoresu* (Painting China dresses) made clear, portraits of ladies in Mandarin dresses were a fashionable theme at the time.[16] The model for Chin-Jung was a Japanese lady, Odagiri Mineko, who was working at the Southern Manchurian Railway Company's 'Yamato Hotel' at the time, and whom Yasui persuaded to model for him while temporarily back in Japan. She liked to wear Chinese dresses and her father (the Consul General at Shanghai) gave her the Chinese-style nickname Chin-Jung (Jinrong). It is certainly possible to interpret the fact that Yasui painted a Japanese woman who lived in Manchuria in Chinese dress in such a way as to conflate it, in an ideological sense, with Imperial Japan's invasion of China.[17] However, this is a somewhat vague stance that can be applied, equally, to all similar portraits of women in Chinese costume, and not something we can imagine the artist being particularly conscious of. Such unintentional political dimensions aside, it is unmistakably the case that aesthetic and formal considerations were also of importance to the artist.

Yasui himself, in an interview, commented on *Portrait of Chin-Jung* as follows:

> I was amazed at the beauty of modern Mandarin dresses. They are very simple in form; and yet there is so much craftsmanship there. The gentle lines that follow the body down are so subtle . . . the model is an acquaintance of mine. She is beautiful and the Mandarin dress suits her well. In order to strengthen the figure, I have made the accompanying objects a little weaker.[18]

What is beguiling Yasui here is not only the beauty of the form and colour of the Chinese dress but also the compatibility of the model's body and the garment, shown in the subtle and gentle lines that trace her contours. In general, the *yōga* artists, on returning from France, struggled with painting figures in Japanese dress, which concealed much of the corporeality they were seeking to express. It is thought that part of the reason that Chinese dress became so popular for female portraiture was that, as in Fujishima's profiles, it accentuated the outline and curves of the body more than Japanese dress did, allowing for better expression of the human body and formal experimentation. As times moved on and artists came to paint women in Western dress, this problem naturally vanished. In *Portrait of Chin-Jung* the space surrounding the subjects and other motifs are kept vague in order to prioritize the expression of a bold and vibrant figure. In the slanted, multi-aspectual expression of space and the tension between spatiality and planarity, we can see the results of the Japanese aesthetic's assimilation of Cézanne's formal sensibilities. This painting, too, is an example of the hybrid fusion to which our cultural triangle gave rise.

Yasui was to visit East Asia for the first time as a judge of the Senten in 1936 and, the following year, in 1937, headed for Xinjing (present-day Changchun) to judge the Manten alongside Fujishima Takeji. The scene of the lamasery in Chengde that he painted on the journey home is his most enduring masterpiece (1937, Eisei Bunko); we can see, therefore, just how significant going to the continent was for this artist. In the rhythmically constructed scene, bright pinks and yellows shine against a backdrop of azure sky, casting the frontality of the building into relief. It is interesting that in the other painting of the lamasery that he made, he tackles it side-on but with, nevertheless, the same planarity and ornamentality in the structure; we can thus say that, in these two works, he established his individual style of landscape painting. However, the fact that he was forced to hasten back to Japan after his stay in Chengde was interrupted by the Marco Polo Bridge Incident drives home that the historical milieu and this artist's activities were not unrelated.

Umehara Ryūzaburō

Umehara Ryūzaburō (1888–1986), who was the same age as Yasui, became enamoured with Renoir's work while studying in Paris and is known for painting voluptuous nudes. His period of trial and error, trying to create a truly Japanese oil painting that was not an imitation of the West, started in 1913 when he returned to Japan and continued through the 1920s. His art matured and he eventually arrived at his own individual style by the 1930s to early 1940s. This, of course, was the period in which Japanese artists were building their closest relationships with the rest of East Asia. While the processes the three artists followed may have been different, Umehara, like Fujishima and Yasui, was ultimately to refine and develop Japanese *yōga* through the medium of Taiwan and China.

Umehara spent time in Taiwan in 1933 and returned in 1934, 1935, and 1936 as a Taiten judge. This was almost exactly the same time as Fujishima, who went there in 1933 and 1934 for leisure, and again in 1935 to judge the Taiten. The two painters spent time with each other while travelling in 1933 and, in 1935, worked together as Taiten judges. During his visit in 1933, Umehara lingered a while in Tainan to paint the Mausoleum to Confucius. He painted the Hall of Bright Ethics in the plot next to the main Hall and the three-storey pagoda in fresh, bright colours and generous brushstrokes, prefiguring his later 'Beijing Period' works (Figure 4.5). What is very interesting indeed is that Fujishima was also taken with the Mausoleum of Confucius in Tainan, and painted it while he was staying there; however, his treatment of the subject is totally different from Umehara's. The choice he made to pay no attention to any of the principal buildings, and instead to paint only the passageways around the perimeter of the site, the gateways, and other very ordinary motifs from a variety of discontinuous viewpoints is quite unusual and rather inexplicable (Figure 4.6). Perhaps this is the difference between Umehara's straightforward, honest perspective and Fujishima's unique and somewhat warped one. Fujishima, liberated from the gaze of the tourist, is searching freely for a subject to suit his artistic interests in order to sculpt a scene that seems almost to deconstruct the hackneyed cardboard cut-out that was Orientalist painting. We occasionally catch a glimpse of these sorts of deviations and aberrations within Japanese modern *yōga* paintings that depict East Asia. These will require further consideration in the future.

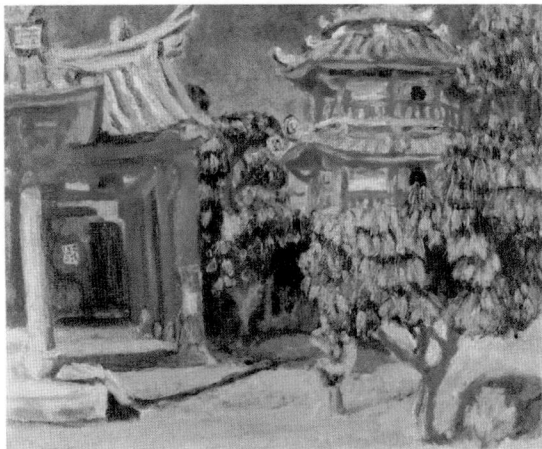

Figure 4.5 Umehara Ryūzaburō, *Scenery of Taiwan* (Taiwan Fūkei), 1933. Oil on canvas, 37.4 × 45.2 cm
Fuchū Art Museum, Tokyo

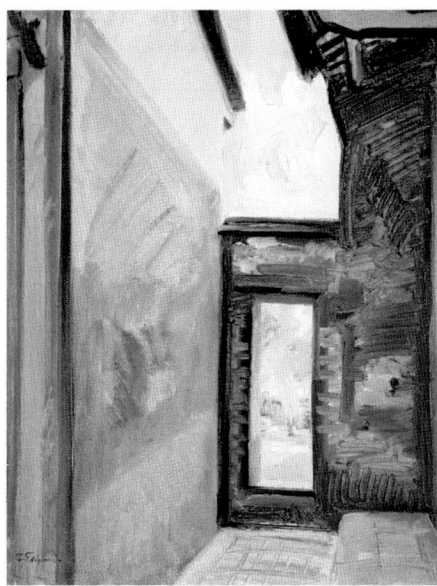

Figure 4.6 Fujishima Takeji, *The Rear Wooden Gate of the Mausoleum of Confucius at Tainan, Taiwan* (Taiwan Tainan Seibyō no Urakido), ca. 1933–1935. Oil on canvas, 53.0 × 40.8 cm

Kitano Museum of Art, Nagano

Let us now consider Umehara and China. Umehara first crossed over to the continent in 1929, at the time of the Shanghai Fine Art Exhibition. However, it was in 1939, after adjudicating the second Manten exhibition, that he stopped over in Beijing and was so moved by its grand and beautiful cityscape that he extended his stay there. Subsequently, from 1940 to 1944, he was to travel there every year, continuing to work. It was during this time that he produced his so-called Beijing Period works, such as *Shikinjō* (The Forbidden City, 1940) (Plate 5) and *Chang-an Streets* (1940, National Museum of Modern Art, Tokyo), which may be considered the pinnacle of his art. In these works he depicts the vista he saw looking down from the fifth floor of the Beijing Hotel, where he was staying at the time. His paintings from this time leave a deep impression on the viewer of their dynamic shapes, rows of vibrant colour, and brush strokes that teem with vitality. In the introduction to his *Diary of Peking*, published in 1973, Umehara recalls this period. He writes: 'There was nothing in the world to resemble those buildings, with their red walls and golden tiles, swimming in a sea of trees. The red lotuses in the park ponds were so beautiful too; I would get up before first light and capture the early dawn without a care to spoil it', confirming that this was his most fulfilling and happy period.[19] As well as scenes of Beijing—the Forbidden City, Chang-an Street, the Temple of Heaven and the like—he was to paint young Chinese ladies and roses displayed in decorative porcelain to create a body of work replete with a feeling of elevation. Of course in reality the Second Sino-Japanese War was being waged in the background; however, Umehara makes no trace of this shadow of war visible in his work.

The factors that combined to create Umehara's Beijing Period masterpieces were multi-layered, just like the cultural triangle itself. This is clearly apparent from the *Diary of Peking*, where he writes: '... from the time the sun sinks away, the air is cool and the vista beautiful in all four directions; it is truly a land of dreams. After dining, I go to the Central Park and take tea beneath the oak. It is like a summer's night on the Champs Elysées, but magnified . . .'[20] There is no doubt, therefore, that Beijing captivated Umehara as a metropolis of oriental civilization to rival Paris in Europe. His experiences studying in France are there, at the base of this artist's expression. And yet, in his interpretation of the Forbidden City, he privileges sculpting the form of the architecture over all else. By way of example, let us compare Umehara's *Forbidden City* with *The Forbidden Palace of Beijing* (1939, private collection), a painting by Guo Bochuan, a Taiwan-born artist resident in Beijing who was friendly with, and influenced by, Umehara.[21] Whereas the latter fills the whole frame with the Palace itself, emphasizing its grandeur and construction, the former paints a scene of Beijing that includes the Palace seen through his own senses and aesthetic palette; the difference is immediately apparent. In Umehara's painting the entire figure of the Palace is indistinct and difficult to grasp. Furthermore, in this period, Umehara blended oil colours with traditional Japanese mineral tints and used Japanese paper called *maniaigami* instead of canvas, making skilful use of not-quite-complete brush marks, such that it seems that he was experimenting with a way to create a kind of technical fusion of East and West (*wayō setchū*). With their amalgam-like interplay of heterogeneity, his Beijing Period works, like *The Forbidden City of Beijing*, constitute the very essence of Japanese *yōga*.

Modern *Yōga* in Taiwan

Unfortunately, there is not space here to fully explore modern painting from the rest of East Asia; however, I would like to present just one parcel of data. Among the 5,799 graduates that the Tokyo School of Fine Art sent out into the world between 1887 and 1952, 103 were from China, eighty-nine from Korea, thirty from Taiwan, and seventeen from other foreign nations.[22] If we were to add to this the students who trained at schools and academies other than the School of Fine Art, the numbers would no doubt grow. Without a doubt, Tokyo was to the artists of East Asia what Paris was to the artists of Japan.

Finally, I would like to make a brief mention of the modern painting of Taiwan, in the context of its relationship with Japan and France. In the story of Taiwan's modern Western art, which set out on new paths during the Japanese Colonial period, the major role played by watercolour artist Ishikawa Kinichirō, who stayed for an extended period in Taiwan as an art teacher at the Taipei Normal School, is of paramount significance. As for artists from Taiwan who studied in Tokyo, there is Chen Chengbo, who was selected for the fifth Teiten, He Delai, who trained under Wada Eisaku and has a firm style, and Li Meishu, a pupil of Okada Saburōsuke, who showed a particular aptitude for female portraiture.[23] Li's knowledge of French painting is evident in the fact that one of his works is clearly an adaptation of a painting by 19th-century naturalism artist Jules Breton. Yan Shuilong, who graduated from the Tokyo School of Fine Art, Yang Sanlang, who studied at the Kansai Academy of Fine Art in Kyoto, Liu Qixiang, a one-time student at Tokyo's Bunka Gakuin Art Department, and Chen Qingfen, who studied under Arishima Ikuma, were four artists among the privileged few who went to study in France in the 1920s and 30s after completing their training in Tokyo. Yan was selected for the 1931 Salon d'automne in Paris. Yang went home having acquired a fierce style of expression that juxtaposes primary colours. Liu, who has a rather out-of-the-ordinary style, gives a hallucinatory touch to scenes of ordinary life through his unique expression of space and modelling of people. In this way, we see that the triangle that encompassed France and Japan existed for Taiwanese artists too.

Concluding notes

As I noted at the outset, research into modern Japanese *yōga* in the context of its relationship with East Asia began properly in the 1990s, and it is only since the 2000s that scholars have started adding breadth and depth to this early work. Looking ahead, there are a number of possible approaches to move this work further along. However, before rushing into analyses and interpretations based on currently established works and sources, it is necessary above all to investigate the works and their historical contexts thoroughly. For a very long time, it was taboo to study the connections between Japan and East Asian modern art during the colonial period, including military art, which this essay did not discuss and which remains to a large extent relatively unknown. The 2014 exhibition, *Toward the Modernity: Images of Self and Other in East Asian Art Competitions*, was an initial opening in this regard—and since then it is heartening to observe that there have been a number of similar events. In Japan, aiming towards the next step in this process, the exhibition *Korean and Japanese Modern Artists in the Korean Peninsula* (Kanagawa Prefectural Museum of Modern Art Hayama, and others) was held in 2015. As for Korea, we have already seen an exhibition in the National Museum of Korea in 2008 that put on public display the 'modern Japanese *yōga*' collected by the (former) Korean Royal Household between 1933 and 1945, the contents of which were later published.[24] The art museums of Taiwan, too, are actively exploring this theme. At the exhibition *Formosa in Formation*, held at the Taipei Fine Arts Museum in 2016, Taiwanese art from the colonial period was put on display alongside closely related works by Japanese artists, and the historical context was revisited, calmly and cogently, from a Taiwanese perspective. Again, in 2014, a new private art gallery called 50Museum was opened in Kaohsiung. The '50' represents the fifty years that passed between 1895 and 1945. In other words, this marked the birth of a museum dedicated to collecting Japanese modern art from the period between the end of the First Sino-Japanese War and the conclusion of the Pacific War, as well as Taiwanese art associated with this. (The main focus is on the decorative arts but there are also some paintings included in the collection.[25]) Setting aside China for the moment, these developments suggest that an environment is being formed in which Japan and other East Asian countries will in the future be able to collaborate in the study of the art of this period.

In the first half of the 20th century, the Japanese artists who went to study in France enthusiastically embraced East Asia as a subject for their art. At the same time, the artists of Korea, Taiwan, and China, influenced by Japan and France, spearheaded the development of modern painting in their own countries, albeit struggling to reconcile this with the distinctive qualities of their surroundings. My proposition in this paper was to try to reinterpret this phenomenon in the context of the triangle of France, Japan, and East Asia—or Paris, Tokyo, and Seoul/Taipei/Changchun. We have seen that this was a distorted triangle, containing complex Orientalist connotations within it; however, it is clear that East Asia played a vital role as the medium within which Western painting was transfigured into Japanese '*yōga*'. We must always remain aware of the need to avoid the over-simplistic conceptual positioning of *yōga* in relation only to Western Orientalist painting, and of the need to consider it in diverse dimensions and contexts. In particular, the study of *yōga* paintings that mix heterogeneous elements produced between 1895 and 1945—and the East Asian art that was born from the study of these—is only just beginning.

(Translated by Laurence Mann)

Notes

1. For example, Yamanashi Emiko, 'Nihon Kindai Yōga ni okeru Orientarizumu' [Orientalism of yōga in modern Japan], in *Kataru Genzai, Katarareru Kako* [Talk now and Past told], ed. Tokyo Kokuritsu Bunkazai Kenkyūsho (Tokyo: Heibonsha, 1999), pp. 81–94; Nishihara Daisuke, 'Kindai Nihon Kaiga no Ajia Hyōshō' [Image of Asia in Modern Japanese paintings], *Nihon Kenkyū* 26 (2002): 185–220; Kojima Kaoru, 'Gaka-tachi no Seiyō Taiken to Ajia e no manazashi' [Painters' experience in the West and Looking at Asia], *Toyota-shi Bijutsukan Kiyō* 3 (2010): 23–32.
2. *Tōkyō, Souru, Taipei, Chōshun: Kanten ni miru Kindai Bijutsu* [Tokyo, Soul, Taipei, Changchun: toward the modernity: images of self & other in East Asian art competitions], exh. cat. (Fukuoka Ajia Bijutsukan, Hyōgo Kenritsu Bijutsukan, Fuchū-shi Bijustukan, 2014).
3. *Seitan 150-nen: Kuroda Seiki – Nihon Kindai Kaiga no Kyoshō* [Kuroda Seiki: master of modern Japanese painting: the 150th anniversary of his birth], exh. cat. (Tokyo: Tōkyō Kokuritsu Hakubutsukan, 2016), pp. 162–165. For information concerning Kuroda Seiki and the First Sino-Japanese War, see the Imperial Household Agency's Museum of the Imperial Collections. Kumamoto Kenjirō, 'Kuroda Seiki to Nisshin Sen'eki' [Kuroda Seiki and Sino-Japanese War], *Bijutsu Kenkyū* 88 (Apr. 1939): 131–141; Yamanashi Emiko, 'Zuhan Kaisetsu Heisei 21-nendo ni kifu sareta Kuroda sakuhin ni tsuite: "Fune" "Shakuyaku" "Nisshin-eki Niryūsan Hōdai Totsugeki Zu" "Rin Seibun Shōzō" Niten' [About work of Kuroda Seiki donated in 2009], *Bijutsu Kenkyū* 402 (Feb. 2011): 106–113.
4. Currently held by the Imperial Household Agency, Museum of the Imperial Collections. *Meiji Bijutsu Saiken IV Kiroku no Geijutsu: Yamamoto Hōsui to sono jidai* [Review of arts in Meiji, IV, the art of record: Yamamoto Hōsui and his era], exh. cat. (Kunaichō Sannomaru Shōzōkan, 2001), pp. 42, 64.
5. For information about the artistic training Kuroda Seiki received in Paris and educational activities with which he was involved after returning to Japan, see Miura Atsushi, 'Kuroda Seiki to Seiyō Bijutsu Kyōiku' [Kuroda Seiki and interacting with Western arts], in *Kōza Nihon Bijutsu-shi* dai 6-kan, ed. Kinoshita Naoyuki (Tokyo: Tokyo Daigaku Shuppankai, 2005), pp. 313–348.
6. For more on these works see Matsumoto Sei'ichi, 'Teikoku no Gadai: Okada Saburōsuke to Kindai Nihon' [Art subject in the imperial nation: Okada Saburōsuke and modern Japan], *Okada Saburōsuke*, exh. cat. (Saga-ken Bijutsukan, 2014), pp. 188–197. The mural *Hagoromo* in the Government-General of Korea (1924) was painted by Wada Sanzō.
7. Fujishima Takeji, 'Chōsen Kankō Shokan' [Comments on sightseeing in Korea], *Bijutsu Shinpō* 13, no. 5 (Mar. 1914), in Fujishima Takeji, *Geijutsu no Esupuri* [Art and Esprit] (Chūō Kōron Bijutsu Shuppan, 1982), pp. 249–250.
8. For further discussion of this issue, see Kojima Kaoru, 'Fujishima Takeji ni okeru "Seiyō" to "Tōyō"' [West and East in Fujishima Takeji], *Bijutsushi-ka Ōi ni Warau: Kōno Motoaki Sensei no tame no Nihon Bijutsushi Ronshū* [The anthology of Japanese art for Prof. Kōno Motoaki] (Tokyo: Buryukke, 2006), pp. 387–406.
9. For more on this notion of 'shared' civilization see Nishihara, 'Kindai Nihon Kaiga no Ajia Hyōshō', pp. 202–208.
10. Fujishima Takeji, 'Ashiato o tadorite (II)' [Trace of footsteps], *Bijutsu Shinron* (May 1930) in Fujishima, *Geijutsu no Esupuri*, pp. 218–219.
11. Ibid., p. 219.

12 For more information on the place of portraits of women in Chinese dress, and related works by Fujishima within modern Japanese *yōga*, see Kojima Kaoru, 'Chūgokufuku no joseizō ni miru Kindai Nihon no aidentiti keisei' [Constructing identity of modern Japan through looking at women wearing Chinese dress], *Jissen Joshi Daigaku Bungakubu Kiyō* 44 (2002): 17–37; Kaizuka Ken, 'Egakareta Chaina-doresu: Chūgoku e no dōkei to yokubō' [Depicted Chinese dress: longing and desire to China], *Egakareta Chaina-doresu: Fujishima Takeji kara Umehara Ryūzaburō made* [Depicted Chinese dress: from Fujishima Takeji to Umehara Ryūzaburō], exh. cat. (Burijisuton Bijutsukan, 2014), pp. 9–20; Kojima Kaoru, 'Fujishima Takeji ni yoru Chūgokufuku no joseizō ni tsuite: "Kōsenbi" o chūshin ni' [About the image of women wearing Chinese dress, in particular for kōsenbi], *Jissen Joshi Daigaku Bigaku Bijutsushigaku* 29 (2015): 1–20.
13 Fujishima Takeji, 'Uchi-Mōko no Hi no De' [Dawn in Mongol], *Tōei* 13, no. 9 (Sept. 1937), see Fujishima, *Geijutsu no Esupuri*, p. 270. For more discussion of these works, see Yamanashi, 'Nihon Kindai Yōga ni okeru Orientarizumu' [Orientalism of yōga in modern Japan], pp. 88–91.
14 *Seitan 130 Kojima Torajirō Ten* [ ], exh. cat. (Ohara Bijutsukan, 2011), pp. 116–119.
15 Nishihara Daisuke referred to this phenomenon as 'Self-Orientalism' (J: *Jiko Orientarizumu*). See Nishihara, 'Kindai Nihon Kaiga no Ajia Hyōshō', pp. 208–215.
16 *Egakareta Chaina-doresu: Fujishima Takeji kara Umehara Ryūzaburō made*. See pp. 9–20 for a discussion of *Chin-Jung*.
17 For example, see Inaga Shigemi, *Kaiga no Rinkai: Kindai Higashi-Ajia Bijutsu-shi no Shikkoku to Meiun* [Image on the edge: a historical survey of East Asian cross-cultural modernity] (Nagoya: Nagoya Daigaku Shuppankyoku, 2014), p. 550.
18 Yasui Sōtarō, 'Shinshū Gadan C Shuppinga no shita-e o miru: "Kin'yō" (Nika) Yasui Sōtarō' [The study of *Chin-Jung* (nika) by Yasui Sōtarō submitted to the exhibition C, Shinshū art circle], *Tōkyō Nichinichi Shinbun*, August 28, 1934.
19 Umehara Ryūzaburō, 'Pekin Nikki' [Beijing diary], *Gashū Pekin Umehara Ryūzaburō Daisanbu* [Collected paintings of Umehara Ryūzaburō, vol. 3] (Tokyo: Kyuryudo, 1973), p. 7.
20 Ibid., p. 154.
21 For a discussion of Guo Bochuan's *Forbidden Palace*, see: *Higashi Ajia no Kindai: Abura-e no Seitan to sono Tenkai*, exh. cat. (Shizuoka: Shizuoka-ken Bijutsukan et al., 1999), pp. 82–83.
22 Yoshida Chizuko, *Kindai Higashi Ajia Bijutsu Ryūgakusei no Kenkyū: Tōkyō Bijutsu Gakkō Ryūgakusei Shiryō* [Study of East Asian overseas students who studied at Tokyo School of Fine Arts] (Tokyo: Yumani Shobō), p. 10.
23 Research on Chen Chengbo is ongoing. As well as a collection of his entire oeuvre, which is currently in publication, the following papers are available: Qiu Hanni, 'Chin Tōha no Kaiga ni mirareru "kokyō" ishiki to aidentiti: "Kagi no machi-hazure" (1926), "Gaitō no natsu kibun" (1927), "Kagi Kōen" (1937) o chūshin toshite' [Consciousness of home and his identity in Chen Chengbo's paintings: 'Outskirts of Jiayi Shi'(1926), 'Summer feeling in street'(1927) 'Jiayi Shi Park (1937)], *Bijutsu-shi Ronsō* (Tokyo: Tokyo Daigaku Daigakuin Jinbun Shakai-kei Kenkyūka, Bungakubu Bijutsu-shi Gakka Kenkyūshitsu Kiyō) 32 (2016): 35–79.
24 *Guglib Jung-ang Bagmulgwan Sojang Ilbon Geundae Misul Seoyanghwa -pyeon* [National Museum of Korea Collection, Japanese modern painting, vol. Western-style painting] (Seoul: Guglib Jung-ang Bagmulgwan, 2010).
25 *Chuancheng zhi Mei Taiwan 50 Meishuguan zang-pin xuancui:* [A consciousness of influence, selections from the Museum 50 of Taiwan] (Kaohsiung: Taiwan 50 Meishuguan, 2016).

Bibliography

Chuancheng zhi Mei Taiwan 50 Meishuguan zang-pin xuancui: [A consciousness of influence, Selections from Museum 50 of Taiwan]. Kaohsiung: Taiwan 50 Meishuguan, 2016.
Fujishima Takeji. 'Chōsen Kankō Shokan' [Comments on sightseeing in Korea]. *Bijutsu Shinpō* 13, no. 5 (Mar. 1914). In Fujishima, *Geijutsu no Esupuri*.

———. 'Ashiato o tadorite (II)' [Trace of footsteps (II)]. *Bijutsu Shinron* (May 1930). In Fujishima, *Geijutsu no Esupuri*, pp. 218–219.

———. 'Uchi-Mōko no Hi no De' [Dawn in Mongolia]. *Tōei* 13, no. 9 (Sept. 1937).

———. *Geijutsu no Esupuri* [The *esprit* of art]. Tokyo: Chūō Kōron Bijutsu Shuppan, 1982.

Guglib Jung-ang Bagmulgwan Sojang Ilbon Geundae Misul Seoyanghwa-pyeon [National Museum of Korea Collection, Japanese modern painting: Western-style painting]. Seoul: Guglib Jung-ang Bagmulgwan, 2010.

Higashi Ajia no Kindai: Abura-e no Seitan to sono Tenkai [Modernism in East Asia: the birth and the development of oil paintings]. Exh. cat. Shizuoka: Shizuoka-ken Bijutsukan, et al., 1999.

Inaga Shigemi. *Kaiga no Rinkai: Kindai Higashi-Ajia Bijutsu-shi no Shikkoku to Meiun* [Image on the edge: a historical survey of East Asian cross-cultural modernity]. Nagoya: Nagoya Daigaku Shuppankyoku, 2014.

Kaizuka Ken. 'Egakareta Chaina-doresu: Chūgoku e no dōkei to yokubō' [Depictions of Chinese dress: longing and desire for China]. *Egakareta Chaina-doresu: Fujishima Takeji kara Umehara Ryūzaburō made* [Depictions of Chinese dress: from Fujishima Takeji to Umehara Ryūzaburō]. Exh. cat. Burijisuton Bijutsukan, 2014.

Kojima Kaoru. 'Chūgokufuku no joseizō ni miru Kindai Nihon no aidentiti keisei' [Constructing identity of modern Japan through women wearing Chinese dress]. *Jissen Joshi Daigaku Bungakubu Kiyō* 44 (2002): 17–37.

Kojima Kaoru. 'Fujishima Takeji ni okeru "Seiyō" to "Tōyō"' [West and East in Fujishima Takeji]. In *Bijutsushi-ka Ōi ni Warau: Kōno Motoaki Sensei no tame no Nihon Bijutsushi Ronshū* [Anthology of Japanese art for Professor Kōno Motoaki], edited by Kōno Motoaki sensei taikan kinen ronbunshū henshū iinkai, 387–406. Tokyo: Buryukke, 2006.

———. 'Gaka-tachi no Seiyō taiken to Ajia e no manazashi' [Painters' experience of the West and looking at Asia]. *Toyota-shi Bijutsukan Kiyō* 3 (2010): 23–32.

———. 'Fujishima Takeji ni yoru Chūgokufuku no joseizō ni tsuite: "Kōsenbi" o chūshin ni' [Fujishima Takeji on images of women wearing Chinese dress, in particularly for *kōsenbi*]. *Jissen Joshi Daigaku Bigaku Bijutsushigaku* 29 (2015): 1–20.

Kumamoto Kenjirō. 'Kuroda Seiki to Nisshin Sen'eki' [Kuroda Seiki and the Sino-Japanese War]. *Bijutsu Kenkyū* 88 (Apr. 1939): 131–141.

Matsumoto Sei'ichi. 'Teikoku no Gadai: Okada Saburōsuke to Kindai Nihon' [Art motifs in the imperial nation: Okada Saburōsuke and modern Japan]. *Okada Saburōsuke*, exh. cat. Saga-ken Bijutsukan, 2014.

Meiji Bijutsu Saiken IV Kiroku no Geijutsu: Yamamoto Hōsui to sono jidai [Review of Meiji arts IV, the art of record: Yamamoto Hōsui and his era]. Exh. cat. Kunaichō Sannomaru Shōzōkan, 2001.

Miura Atsushi. 'Kuroda Seiki to Seiyō Bijutsu Kyōiku' [Kuroda Seiki and his interaction with Western arts]. In *Kōza Nihon Bijutsu-shi* dai 6-kan, edited by Kinoshita Naoyuki, 313–348. Tokyo: Tōkyō Daigaku Shuppankai, 2005.

Nishihara Daisuke. 'Kindai Nihon Kaiga no Ajia Hyōshō' [Images of Asia in modern Japanese painting]. *Nihon Kenkyū* 26 (2002): 185–220.

Qiu Hanni. 'Chin Tōha no Kaiga ni mirareru "kokyō" ishiki to aidentiti: "Kagi no machi-hazure" (1926), "Gaitō no natsu kibun" (1927), "Kagi Kōen" (1937) o chūshin toshite' [Consciousness of home and identity in Chen Chengbo's paintings: *Outskirts of Jiayi Shi* (1926), *Summer feeling in street* (1927) and *Jiayi Shi Park* (1937)], *Bijutsu-shi Ronsō. Tokyo Daigaku Daigakuin Jinbun Shakai-kei Kenkyūka, Bungakubu Bijutsu-shi Gakka Kenkyūshitsu Kiyō* 32 (2016): 35–79.

Seitan 130 Kojima Torajirō Ten. [The 130th-year anniversary of his birth: Kojima Trajirō] Exh. cat. Ohara Bijutsukan, 2011.

Seitan 150-nen: Kuroda Seiki – Nihon Kindai Kaiga no Kyoshō [Kuroda Seiki: master of modern Japanese painting – the 150th anniversary of his birth]. Exh. cat. Tokyo: Tōkyō Kokuritsu Hakubutsukan, 2016.

Tōkyō, Souru, Taipei, Chōshun: Kanten ni miru Kindai Bijutsu [Tokyo, Soul, Taipei, Changchun: towards modernity – images of self and other in East Asian art competitions]. Exh. cat. Fukuoka Ajia Bijutsukan, Hyōgo Kenritsu Bijutsukan, Fuchū-shi Bijutsukan, 2014.

Umehara Ryūzaburō. 'Pekin Nikki' [Beijing diary], *Gashū Pekin Umehara Ryūzaburō Daisanbu* [Collected paintings of Umehara Ryūzaburō, vol. 3]. Tokyo: Kyuryudo, 1973.

Yamanashi Emiko. 'Nihon kindai yōga ni okeru Orientarizumu' [Orientalism of *yōga* in modern Japan]. In *Kataru Genzai, Katarareru Kako: Nihon no Bijutsushigaku hyaku-nen* [The present speaks, the past spoken of: 100 years of Japanese art history], edited by Tokyo Kokuritsu Bunkazai Kenkyūsho. Tokyo: Heibonsha, 1999.

———. 'Zuhan Kaisetsu Heisei 21-nendo ni kifu sareta Kuroda sakuhin ni tsuite: "Fune" "Shakuyaku" "Nisshin-eki Niryūsan Hōdai Totsugeki Zu" "Rin Seibun Shōzō" Niten' [About the work of Kuroda Seiki donated in 2009]. *Bijutsu Kenkyū* 402 (Feb. 2011): 106–113.

Yasui Sōtarō. 'Shinshū Gadan C Shuppinga no shita-e o miru: "Kin'yō" (Nika) Yasui Sōtarō' [Study of *Chin-Jung* ('nika') by Yasui Sōtarō submitted to exhibition C, Shinshū art circle]. *Tōkyō Nichinichi Shinbun*, August 28, 1934.

Yoshida Chizuko. *Kindai Higashi Ajia Bijutsu Ryūgakusei no Kenkyū: Tōkyō Bijutsu Gakkō Ryūgakusei Shiryō* [Study of East Asian overseas students who studied at Tokyo School of Fine Arts]. Tokyo: Yumai shobō, 2009.

5 'Marginal Man' Pai Un-soung (1900–1978)
His European Experience, His Views, and His Art

Shin Min-jong

The Painter Pai Un-soung: Perspective on Korean Modern Art

The concept of a 'broad history of art' that Satō Dōshin discusses in his article 'Overcoming Modernity' is very significant. Satō advocates the need to go beyond a national art history 'that has been forced into each country's own framework' and achieve 'a broad history that reflects the reality of art exchange and sharing'.[1] The gist of his argument is that thinking about the possibilities of a history of art that has overcome national borders is a touchstone that makes possible the 'overcoming of modernity', meaning that it is important to possess an outlook and perspective that enables observation of each other's art from a broad vantage point. Even looking at Korea's modern art history alone, what we refer to as the modern period includes the period of Japanese colonial rule, so it becomes difficult to make sense of it without an understanding of Japanese cultural and colonial policy as well as the movement of people, goods, and ideas across borders during that period. Lee Mi-na advocates the need for this kind of cross-cultural perspective in the catalogue of the 2015 exhibition of Japanese and Korean modern artists held at the Fukuoka Asian Art Museum:

> I think of this exhibition not as something that frames Japanese and Korean modern art simply as belonging to those two countries, but as part of a long process toward positioning it in much more variegated and multi-layered relationships, both within its field of vision—in similar relationships nearby, such as in Taiwan—but also further afield, such as in Britain and India.[2]

Lee's point is that in order to think about Korean modern art, we need to expand our field of inquiry to include East Asia and even Western Europe. A paradigm shift has occurred over the past thirty years whereby Korean modern art has been framed as 'Korean modernity' rather than 'colonial modernity', increasing the need for a comprehensive understanding of the various artists and their works from several perspectives. This cannot be achieved by only studying art institutions and policies. Today, in order to understand the art of one's own country, it is crucial to first grasp the art of other regions and examine their mutual relations.

In response to this kind of problem formulation, this article considers the possibilities of approaching Korean art from multiple perspectives and the validity of an art history that goes beyond national identity and national borders. I use the Korean painter Pai Un-soung as a case study, looking at the complexity of his work and creative activities as well as their liminal characteristics.

Pai Un-soung (1900–1978) was a painter representative of Korean modern art. He was born in Seoul, experienced Japan's 1910 annexation of Korea at age ten, and in 1919 went to Japan and studied economics at Waseda University. In 1922, he went to Germany, where he studied art for five years at the Unified State Schools for Fine and Applied Arts. After this, he was active mainly in Germany (1922–1937) and France (1937–1940). He returned to Korea in 1940 when the war began to gain momentum. Back home, he participated in activities in support of the Japanese Empire, swearing to 'paint for the state' and 'paint in service of the country', but after liberation, with the outbreak of the Korean War resulting from antagonism between left-wing and right-wing ideologies, he crossed over into the north.[3] What stands out when looking at this short biography is the range of locations he experienced as well as the varied ideologies with which he must have come into contact.

The 1920s and 1930s, when Pai was active in Berlin, was a time when almost all Korean Western-style painters studied in Japan. In that context, the fact that Pai went to study the original form in the actual 'home of Western painting', and achieved considerable professional success, makes him an important individual for thinking about Korea's modern art history. He distinguished himself from those who studied in Japan in many ways, not least by displaying work at some of the most prominent public exhibitions in Europe,[4] holding solo exhibitions all over the continent,[5] and by the fact that his work is owned by a number of European art galleries and museums.[6] Most of Pai's contemporaries who studied in Japan were active at the Joseon Art Exhibitions after returning to Korea, with their works being held primarily by art galleries and private collectors inside Korea. Pai's activities were thus very 'international' compared to that of other modern Korean artists, so they must be understood and appraised in a broad geopolitical, historical, and cultural context. At the same time, his art should be understood as a reflection of the social and cultural circumstances of whichever country he was in as well as a product of his individual experiences.

Approaching Pai in his role as the first Korean artist to study in Europe, I attempt an organic understanding of his activities and the art he produced in various locations, paying particular heed to the social and cultural circumstances of those countries at that time. I also look at the connection between Pai's artistic activity and Japan, examining the cultural and artistic exchange between Japan and Korea as well as its political dimension. In sum, I offer a re-interpretation and re-evaluation of Pai by viewing the unique characteristics of his art from multiple vantage points. At the same time, my goal is to present an approach that thinks about Korean modern art in a more flexible way. By rethinking the chronological, ideological, and spatial framework of 'modernity' and 'colony' as well as 'Korea' and 'Asia', I hope to lay a foundation for reorganizing those concepts.

Painting with 'Eastern Lines and Western Colours'

In 1930, Pai graduated from the Unified State Schools for Free and Applied Arts where he had been studying for five years. Having taken his first step as a painter, he made 'Korea' the principal motif of his art. In 1930s Europe, and especially Germany, interest in Far East Asian art was on the rise. Museum collections were formed using cultural artefacts gathered by diplomats and collectors, and related exhibitions were held. With the establishment of research institutions specializing in Asian art, full-fledged research also came to be conducted. For example, *Die Gesellschaft für die ostasiatische Kunst* (Society for East Asian Art), founded in Berlin in 1926, annually organized six or seven regular seminars and conducted research on East Asian art, with the goal of 'spreading and deepening knowledge about East Asian art in the German-speaking world'.[7] It also organized and supported a large number of exhibitions, such as the China Exhibition (1929), Chinese and Japanese Painting Exhibition (1930), the Contemporary Chinese Painting Exhibition (1934), and the Berlin Japanese Ancient Art Exhibition (1939).[8] This shift in the perception of Far East Asian art was one that transformed it from an object of curiosity to one of academic research. However, whereas Chinese and Japanese art had been widely known from the 18th century, the introduction of Korean art to European societies came late and made less of an impact.

In Germany, interest in Korean art rose in the period between the end of the 19th century and the beginning of the 20th, with several collections being formed by individual collectors. Most of these collections were composed of objects acquired on the basis of personal taste or ease of transport rather than artistic value.[9] As a result, most Korean collections in Germany consist of articles such as ceramics or items of daily use. Andre Eckardt (1884–1974) was perhaps the first to spread Korean art in Germany. He endeavoured to consolidate the foundation for Korean art research, writing several

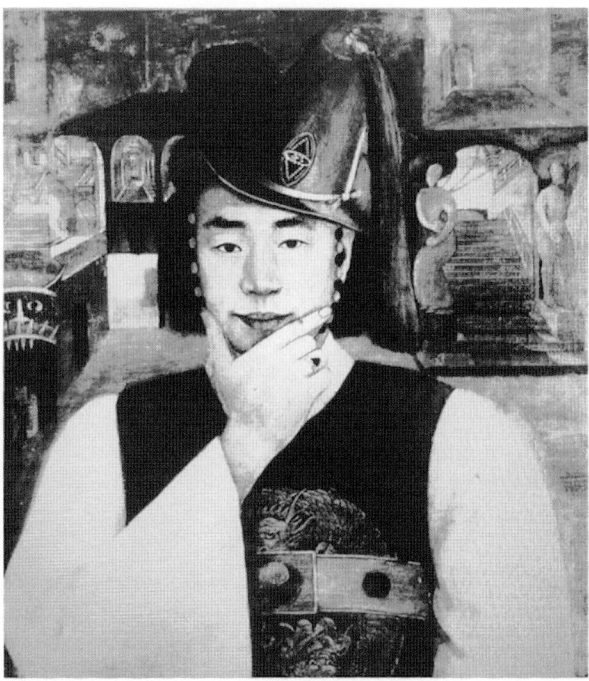

Figure 5.1 Pai Un-soung, *Self-Portrait* (Shaman), 1930s. Oil on canvas, 55 × 45 cm
Ethnologisches Museum, Berlin. Image courtesy Kim Bog-gi Collection of National Museum of Modern and Contemporary Art, Korea, donated by Kim Bog-gi

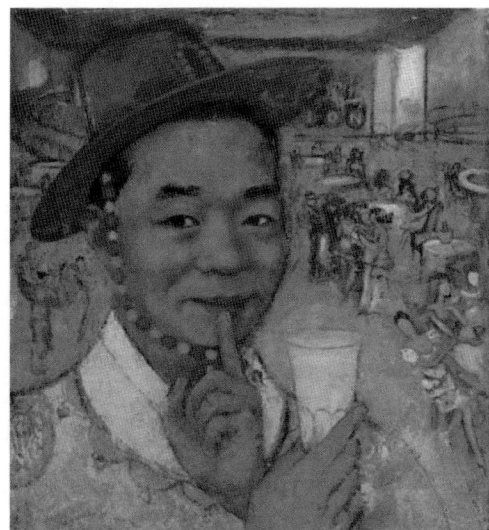

Figure 5.2 Pai Un-soung, *Self-Portrait with Hat*, 1930s. Oil on canvas, 54 × 45 cm
Private collection

articles and an extraordinary book entitled *A History of Korean Art*,[10] as well as giving presentations on Korea at the regular seminars of the Society for East Asian Art.[11] However, there nonetheless existed a very rigid hierarchy among East Asian cultures.

Two Self-Portraits: Pai's Self-Recognition in the Intersection of Different Cultures

In these circumstances, Pai expressed his identity as an 'Asian artist in Europe' by seeking Korean motifs and employing Western techniques to paint with 'Eastern lines and Western colours'. Let us examine two self-portraits that he painted while in Germany, *Self-Portrait (Shaman)* (Figure 5.1) and *Self-Portrait with Hat* (Figure 5.2). The pictures respectively depict Pai dressed as a shaman and a soldier.[12] In the background of the Shaman self-portrait he painted European buildings, and in the hat self-portrait, a typical European dance hall, both contrasting with the human figure.[13] These are paintings depicting a Korean subject using the Western technique of oil painting, thus producing works of art that harmonize and contrast the visual images of East and West. The first thing we can read from such a presentation is Pai's self-perception as 'a Korean self in the midst of Western civilization'. As seen in *Self-Portrait with Hat*, the figure of Pai wearing a folk costume, standing in a European dance hall and holding a glass of champagne, shows the contrast of 'East and West', 'tradition and civilization', and 'spirit and material'. The coupling of such heterogeneous and contradictory images creates tension within the painting.[14] Perhaps this can also be said to reflect the discomfort and sense of foreignness that Pai felt when standing at the intersection of civilizations.

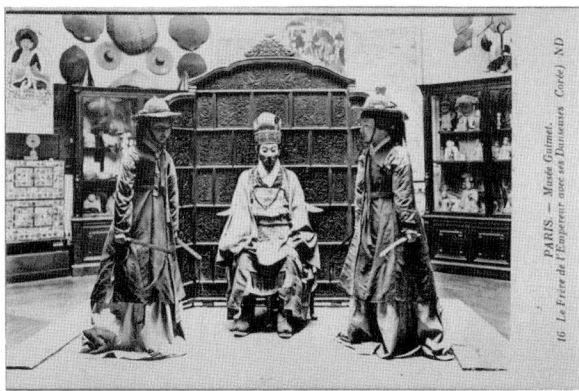

Figure 5.3 View of the Korean Department of the Guimet Museum in the 19th century
Musée nationale des arts asiatiques Guimet, Paris

At the same time, these expressions reveal Pai's interest in the respective civilizations of Korea and Europe. Korean traditional clothing made up a major part of the Korea collections in European museums at the time. For example, the Korea collection at Paris's Guimet Museum contained shaman dresses from early on (Figure 5.3), while the Ethnological Museum of Berlin has held Korean traditional dresses since the late 19th century. Images of various traditional dresses also appear in the genre paintings by Kim Jun-geun (dates unknown, active mainly from the 1880s to early 1900s), held by a number of museums across Europe. It seems that Pai actively borrowed from this material in his own art, presenting unique combinations of a number of outfits.[15] All the while, the European-style backgrounds reveal his interest in Western architecture and spatial expression. The dance hall scene depicted in *Self-Portrait with Hat* is highly vivid, with its details and spatial depth, and reveals a fine command of perspective. Such expression is usually seen in Renaissance paintings and Northern European portraits, hinting at Pai's interest in those traditions. In this way, Pai's self-portraits convey a visual richness by sensitively harmonizing Korean and European subjects and expressive techniques. Furthermore, by presenting himself as an ethnic person, Pai 'others' himself and generates a self-exoticism.

Family Portrait

Family Portrait (Figure 5.4) is Pai's most signature piece and another work whose composition demonstrates the harmony of East and West. This painting is a group portrait featuring seventeen family members posing in a front yard, but as Pai has included himself in the group, it can also be said to be another self-portrait from which we can read his self-perception.

The idea of the family portrait is associated with the Dutch family portrait paintings of the 17th century or the portrait photography of the 19th century. Family portraits began circulating in the mid-19th century as objects symbolizing the model family of

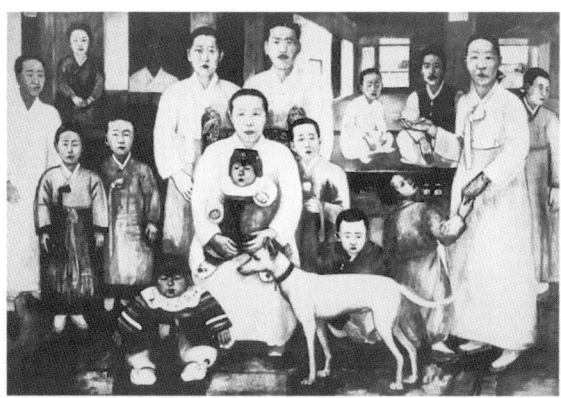

Figure 5.4 Pai Un-soung, *Family Portrait*, 1930–1935. Oil on canvas, 140 × 200 cm

Private collection. Image courtesy Kim Bog-gi Collection of National Museum of Modern and Contemporary Art, Korea, donated by Kim Bog-gi

the bourgeoisie and the patriarchal hierarchy.[16] An article written by a German critic on *Family Portrait*, which notes that 'It is reminiscent of the art of the Dutch old masters', seems to be based on the painting's theme and structure as a family portrait.[17] On the other hand, we can also find various Korean elements within its frame. The appearances and costumes of the family members as well as the composition of the house all reflect traditional Korea. When another critic pointed out that, 'Especially in the unfinished "Family Portrait" we can see the influence of Asian painting', he seems to have had in mind these traditional components.[18]

The significance of Pai's self-inclusion in the painting cannot be understated. It is not uncommon in Western art for painters to include themselves in their paintings. Examples from the Renaissance and Northern European painters include Michelangelo's *The Last Judgment*, Raphael's *The School of Athens*, and *The Sermon of St. John the Baptist* by Pieter Bruegel, who had a strong influence on Pai, as well as French modern painters like Henri de Toulouse-Lautrec and Edouard Manet. Through these 'mini self-portraits', painters expressed their pride and subjectivity as art producers, a sentiment reflective of the period in which they lived. In Pai's case, including himself in a family picture also seems to have been a way to channel his feelings of nostalgia for family and homeland.[19] Pai thus used the ordinary motif of 'the family scene' not only to convey his Korean sensibilities, but also to harmonize Eastern and Western elements of painting.

Pai also attempted expressions of his identity through painting by employing Eastern painting techniques. A contemporary newspaper wrote that 'Mr Pai mainly paints with an oriental brush on woodblocks, rather than on "canvas".'[20] Critics also commented that 'He paints with Chinese ink on a unique kind of paper'[21] and 'This painter's ink portraits draws the interest of European spectators.'[22] We do not know what these paintings looked like since they are no longer extant and there are no images of them. However, we do have photographs that show Pai painting with ink (Figure 5.5).

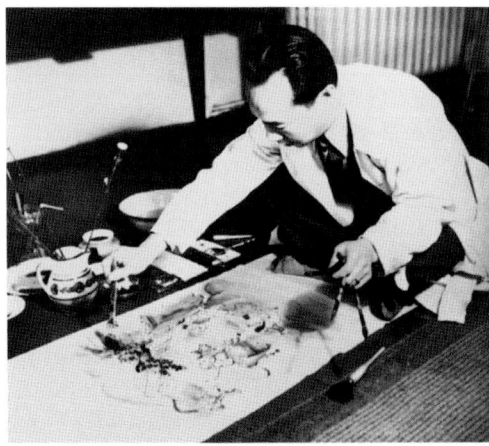

Figure 5.5 Pai Un-soung, painting in Chinese ink in his atelier, 1935

Image courtesy Kim Bog-gi Collection of National Museum of Modern and Contemporary Art, Korea, donated by Kim Bog-gi

As we have seen in these examples, Pai expressed Korean tradition through his motifs and Eastern brush technique, and his internationality through his choice of materials and use of shadows, perspectives, and colours, all the while searching for his own style. It would seem that this kind of 'painting blending East and West' was Pai's ideal form of painting. Upon returning to Korea, he noted in an interview:

> In order to make Western painting completely our own, we cannot limit ourselves to the Western classics. I believe that when it comes to the essence of painting, both the East and the West have something invaluable. If so, I don't think one should forget about the Eastern classics simply because one wants to do Western painting.[23]

As this quotation suggests, Pai felt called to learn the Eastern classics and traditions in order to master Western painting. Perhaps this was Pai's sense of mission. As the first Korean modern artists in Europe, he must constantly have felt both the duty to let Europe know about Korea and the duty to master Western painting.[24]

Pai's 'hybrid art' was created in response to the European demand for unique and exotic Asian images that developed in tandem with the growing interest in Far East Asian art at the time. It was also a manifestation of Pai's racial and ethnic identity as well as the nostalgia he felt for his homeland. As such, Pai's art naturally contained the duality of orientalism and nationalism. Although he managed to break through the massive wall of the European art world by painting with 'Eastern lines and Western colours', he also had to endure his work being referred to dismissively as 'materialist art', which allowed Asia to be consumed simply as images of 'foreign lands'. From this angle, the 'Eastern lines and Western colours' provided Pai's art both with possibilities and limitations, forcing it to straddle the line between East and West to this day.

Pai Un-soung's Activities in Europe and the Japan Connection

Portraits of Prominent Figures: Baron Mitsui and His Works

Among the works painted by Pai in Europe, there is a remarkable woodblock print entitled *Baron Mitsui and His Works* (Plate 6). In contrast to the self-portraits and family portraits mentioned above, which possess a degree of autobiographical character, this work expresses Pai's vision of another person.

The person depicted is Mitsui Takaharu (1900–1983), former board member at Mitsui & Co and Mitsui Mining, and a businessman who invested in international cultural exchange. The painting was commissioned by Mitsui himself, and effectively expresses Mitsui's world with Pai's bold and accurate line drawing.[25] Mitsui himself stands confidently in the centre, his solemnity amplified by his uniform, his seven medals, and the Mitsui family document and sword in his hands. His uniform as a baron of the fifth rank, the medals he earned in Europe, and the painstakingly detailed background all seem to extol the accomplishments of Mitsui and boast of his influence.[26] This was displayed for the first time at Pai's solo exhibition at the Hamburg Museum of Ethnology in 1935,[27] and was appreciated as 'suggesting a new method for contemporary printing by successfully replicating the feel of the person's clothes and skin as well as the medals on a line drawing woodblock print'.[28] It was then selected for exhibitions, including the Second International Exposition of Woodblock Print held in Warsaw in 1936 and the Autumn Fair held in Paris in 1938.

Painting the portraits of powerful individuals like Mitsui was an important part of Pai's work. The reasons were probably not just economic; it was also a way to make connections. New acquaintances would provide new jobs and creative opportunities. As Pai interacted with numerous artists and undertook jobs for diplomats and wealthy Japanese, he also made a name for himself in the German art world.[29] This is how Kurt Runge describes Pai's situation as he was painting the Mitsui portrait:

> For the Mitsui portrait Pae actually used my studio. He must at that time—in 1934/35—probably just have sublet a small room somewhere [. . .]. In order for Mitsui to buy into this, Pae's nametag was attached to the front door. [. . .] Mitsui's impressive full dress uniform then remained between sessions hanging in my closet.[30]

We can see from Runge's anecdote how much effort Pai made to prepare for the sessions with Mitsui. Pai's almost pretentious behaviour is evidence of how much importance he attached to his connection with Mitsui. If, as Runge claims when speaking of Pai, 'all his efforts were aimed at becoming rich', and the foremost goal of Pai's work was money, then his acquaintance with Mitsui must have guaranteed him some financial security. In fact, one of Pai's friends, the dancer Cho Taek-won (1907–1976), recollects that Pai received a large sum, tens of thousands of francs, for the Mitsui portrait, allowing him to purchase a luxury atelier on the Avenue de Saxe in Paris, where the top painters gathered.[31] Not only that, but Mitsui's influence ensured that Pai was given new jobs. As a fellow of the Japanese-German Cultural Society, Mitsui commissioned Pai to produce paintings for the Japanese embassy, and he painted four huge silk scrolls.[32] Besides Mitsui, Pai was also connected with a number of other Japanese men of influence. For example, the Consulate General of Japan was involved in Pai's

1935 solo exhibition at the Hamburg Museum, and indeed it has been documented that almost all of Pai's solo exhibitions in Europe received official support from Japanese authorities.[33]

Baron Mitsui and His Works is one of the few works by Pai that depicts a Japanese person and is basically the only clue we have for understanding the link between his activities in Europe and Japan. It is a truly evocative product of hard work that provides a wealth of information, both with regard to its social and historical significance and to the significance of its design.

Participating in the Publication of the Magazine France-Japon

Pai left Berlin and headed for Paris in 1937, but it would seem that Pai's activities in Paris continued to relate to Japan. Most of the scholarly discussions about his activities in Paris have centred on his Salon selections and solo exhibitions, but I want to focus on activities that require special mention because they have not yet been the subject of scholarly research, namely his involvement with the magazine *France-Japon* and his participation in the Japanese Artist Exhibitions in Paris.

Despite being a man with no connection to Paris, Pai held a solo exhibition at the Charpentier Gallery, said to be the number one gallery in Paris, within just one year of his arrival, something that also caused a stir in Korea. Pai's accomplishment in Paris was so sudden and so big that the Korean media relating the news had to ask, 'For what reason did the Salon de Charpentier lend its gallery to an unknown Easterner?'[34] Let us look at his solo exhibition's invitation letter (Figure 5.6). What is noteworthy here is the phrase 'Sous le patronage du COMITÉ FRANCO-JAPONAIS' ('With the support of the Franco–Japanese Association') in the top half. It indicates that this solo

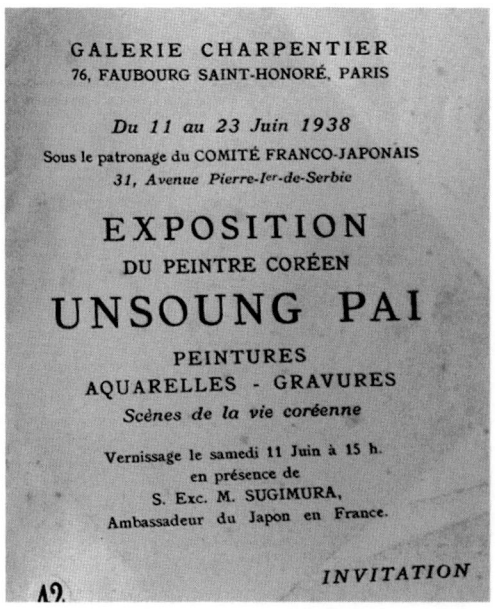

Figure 5.6 Invitation letter to Pai Un-soung's solo exhibition in Paris

exhibition received the support of an influential Japanese organization in Paris at that time.³⁵ It is important to note that this association was a propaganda organization established to repair Japan's image after it had been tarnished in international eyes by the Manchurian Incident (1931) and Japan's withdrawal from the League of Nations (1933), as well as to strengthen the Franco–Japanese relationship. Tsurumi Mitsuzō (1880–1951), who played an important role in the Paris branch of the Franco–Japanese Association, indicated that, 'Because explicit political propaganda has an opposite effect in today's international climate, we shall focus our energies in a cultural and economic direction, adding political propaganda in necessary response to the gradual changing of said climate'.³⁶

We can thus see that the association's cultural and artistic activities were politically motivated at their core. The Franco–Japanese cultural exchange magazine *France-Japon* is usually mentioned as representative of the various cultural activities supported by this association, so it is notable that Pai was involved in the production of this magazine since before his solo exhibition in Paris. Among a total of forty-nine volumes, which had been issued from 1934 to 1940, Pai was the first Korean artist to be the subject of an article. It can be found in *France-Japon* 27 and is entitled 'Exotic Artists in Paris: The Korean Painter Pai Un-soung' (Figure 5.7).³⁷ It seems that there were only a total of seven Korea-related articles during the magazine's six years of publication, and two of them are about Pai.³⁸ Moreover, it is very suggestive that he provided five illustrations between 1938 and 1939 and that his name was listed as a 'co-producer' of the May 1939 issue.³⁹ This suggests that he was continually involved

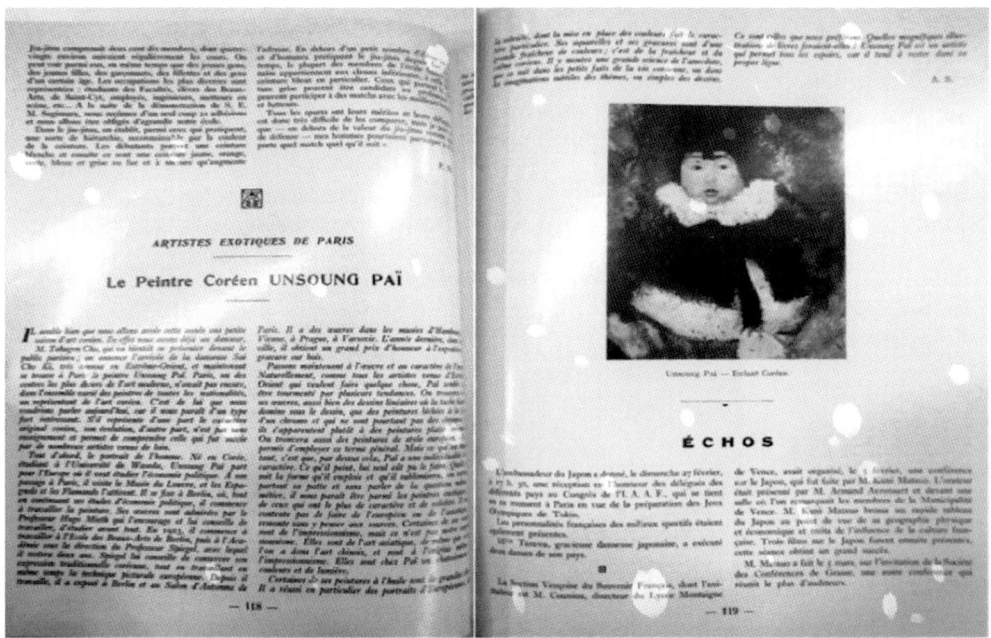

Figure 5.7 Article on Pai Un-soung in *France-Japon* entitled 'The Exotic Artists of Paris: Korean Painter Pai Un-soung' and his illustration, 'Child of Korea'

France-Japon 27 (March 15, 1938)

with this magazine throughout his three-year sojourn in France. Pai recollects that there were about ten Koreans in Paris in the late 1930s, including intellectuals such as the scholar Kim Bong-su and the philosopher Youn Eul-sou (1909–1971).[40] Yet there is no mention of their involvement with the magazine. All we know for sure is that Pai was the only Korean involved over a long period of time, and that two other Koreans wrote articles: Pai's friend Cho Taek-won ('On Korean Dance') and Ri Chai-uk ('On Korean Novels'). Pai and Cho were on friendly terms with some of the Japanese authors at the magazine, so it is possible that their participation was on the basis of a personal connection.[41] Although more research is needed to describe the exact circumstances in which Pai ended up working with the magazine, it is not difficult to imagine that as the production and publication of this magazine was an important part of Japan's policy toward France and cultural propaganda, Pai's involvement secured him opportunities and guaranteed his livelihood as a painter.

The Only Korean Painter in the Japanese Artist Exhibitions in Paris

Participating in the Japanese Artist Exhibitions in Paris (also known as the Second Comprehensive Exhibition) (Figure 5.8) is another example of Pai's activities related to Japan. This was 'the first and most official exhibition', which was founded with the aim of providing Japanese artists in Paris with a regular space to display their work.[42] The

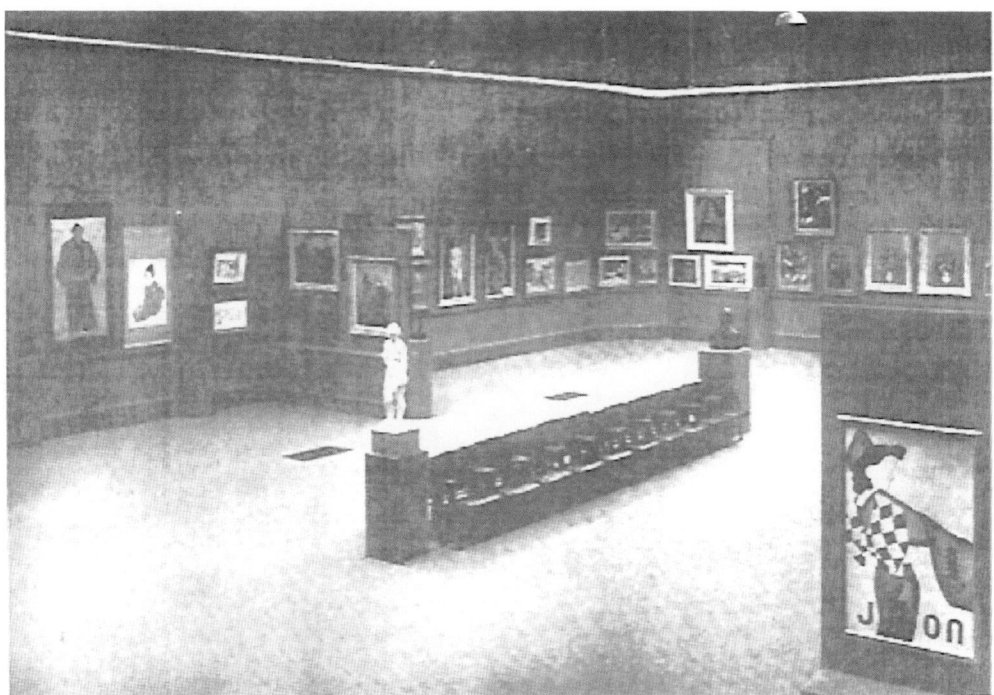

Figure 5.8 Exhibition hall of the Japanese Artist Exhibitions in Paris
 Binokuni 15, no. 8 (August 1939)

exhibition was held twice, first in 1938 and then in 1939, hosted by the Paris Japanese Artists' Association with the support of the Japanese ambassador to France, Sugimura Yōtarō (1884–1939), and the French Minister of Education, Jean Zay (1904–1944).[43] Several articles have been written about these exhibitions based on the information sent back to Japan by Western-painting specialists, including Inokuma Gen'ichirō (1902–1993), Takata Rikizō (1900–1992), and Miyamoto Saburō (1905–1974), all of whom were in Paris at the time, allowing us to get an overall picture. According to these articles, the exhibition was attended by eminent artists of the time, including Okamoto Tarō (1911–1996), Fujita Tsuguharu (1886–1968), and Miyamoto Saburō. Pai is known to have made submissions to the painting and printing divisions for the first exhibition and to the painting division for the second exhibition, and we know in particular that he was on the printing display committee of the first exhibition together with Hasegawa Kiyoshi (1891–1980).[44] Even though these exhibitions had the goal of giving painters the opportunity to display their work, they also aimed to show the French what these painters had accomplished while in Europe. The organisers made the following comment:

> As the organizing art association, we can say that this art exhibition has corrected the ignorant fixed idea among French people that, 'You [Japanese artists] should stop copying Westerners and paint traditional Japanese paintings' and made them understand the necessity of asking 'Why do contemporary Japanese artists study Western artists?'[45]

This comment shows that these exhibitions were meant to showcase the high-calibre Western-style paintings by Japanese painters to the very people of the place where that art style originated. On the international stage at the time, the distinction between Korean and Japanese was not significant; what was more important to Pai was securing opportunities to make and display his work, going beyond the context of ethnicity. Yet considering Japan's position in the international community, it cannot be denied that these exhibitions, just like the activities of the Franco–Japanese Association, oozed political implications. In 1937, one year before the first exhibition, Japan had concluded the Anti-Comintern Pact, and its relationship with France was precarious as the momentum for war was building in Japan with the Second Sino-Japanese War. In such a situation, Ōnaga Hiroyoshi wrote the following when reporting the results of the first exhibition in 1938:

> The art must be splendid. It must be splendid indeed, but if these cultured men can deepen the friendship between Japan and France even slightly, and that shines a ray of bright hope on our native land fighting this holy war, then our goal is half reached.[46]

As can be seen from this comment, these exhibitions also had the purpose of promoting 'friendship between Japan and France' and shining 'a ray of bright hope on our native land fighting this holy war'. We can also see that more importance was attached to the social and diplomatic significance of the artworks than to their visual beauty and appeal. A similar sentiment can be seen in the words of Sugimura Yōtarō, who was an advocate of the exhibitions and their sole financier. Sugimura stated that, 'We must demonstrate to the world that Japan is not only a nation of warriors, but how she is also a nation of artists'.[47] As a man with an interest in literature, sports, and art, this was his expectation of and conviction in art.[48] At the same time, this was a manifestation of the love he felt for his homeland as someone who had lived 'a life of sacrifice for the nation'.[49] He was a person who made acquaintances in all circles, regardless of nationality and profession, from the French Minister of Foreign Affairs to a Korean dancer. It is perhaps not so strange, therefore, that he took an interest in Pai's work and took the time to visit his private showing.[50]

From the above activities, we can see that everything—from the Franco–Japanese Association's support of Pai's solo exhibition, through the publication of *France-Japon*, to the Japanese Artist Exhibitions in Paris—was organically connected within the framework of Japan's cultural projects for state propaganda. Pai did not leave any record concerning these activities, making it difficult to grasp the extent of, and his intentions for, his participation in them. If we consider that the publication of *France-Japon* and the Japanese Artist Exhibitions in Paris also had a strong cultural lustre, then there is nothing odd about Pai wanting to participate in these cultural activities as a painter. Yet if we also consider that these activities were aimed at using culture to influence foreign opinion, then we must conclude that Pai was complicit in the cultural project that was Japan's state propaganda for foreign consumption.[51] As the various media in Korea competed to report on Pai's activities in Europe, why did they leave out information about his Japan-related activities and his Japanese patrons?[52] As Pai refrained from talking about his own ideology, we can only build a picture of his true ideological undercurrents by examining his activities. What is certain here is that because his activities were conducted in the complicated context of the period, his creative work and activities could not but reflect his interpretations of the period's historical and social circumstances.

Searching for New Evaluations and Perspectives

After Pai returned to Korea in 1940, after eighteen years in Europe, he took on the role of leading Korea's modern art world while being active in a number of fields, planning the establishment of an art school and teaching at a university in the faculty of arts.[53] The Korean expectations of a painter who had studied at the 'home of Western painting' must have been very high. Even so, the response to his art in Korea was quite the opposite of what it had been in Europe. For example, while his technique has been viewed in Europe as 'a bit lacking in light and shadow due to unskilled coloring',[54] it was praised in Korea with words like, 'We must pay our respects to his impregnable *matière*'[55] or 'It is precious that the correct method of oil painting has taken hold in his [Pai's] essence.'[56] On the other hand, his Korean material that was popular in Europe received somewhat harsh criticism in Korea. The same critic who had such high praise for his oil-painting technique also commented:

> A bad habit of those oriental painters who have trained in Europe is that they desire fresh individuality and introduce localisms. It is true that tradition and heritage can become weapons in the service of art, but they should be passed on as [illegible characters], so it is an indolent and impatient expediency to apply it directly to materials and styles.[57]

The difference in evaluations between Europe and Korea reveals how the respective art worlds searched for different values in Pai's art. In Europe, Pai is said to have become 'a Korean', even though everyone in Korea wished for him to be 'the West'.[58] Nonetheless, Pai was regarded as a painter who was imbued with the Western artistic canon after returning to Korea. Pai adapted his activities to the needs of the place he was in, and he continued to be evaluated based on that place's standard.

Pai's activities stretched over many regions and were conducted at the various inflection points of that period. Moreover, his art was shaped by the intermingling of each respective social situation and his personal circumstances. Thus, both the evaluation of his activities and art as well as the interpretation of his identity and ideology become fluid. Pai's art is wavering on the borderline between tradition and modernity, East and West, as well as the internationalization of Korean art and the reception of Western art, reflecting the colonial experience that emerged outside of the confines of the Japanese Empire. This is another reason why Pai Un-soung's time in Europe must be reconsidered from the various relevant historical and social vantage points and within a still more diversified and broader context.

Notes

1 Satō Dōshin, 'Kindai no chōkoku' [Overcoming modernity], *Art History Forum* 30 (Seoul: Center for Art Studies, Korea, 2010): 21–22.
2 Lee Mi-na, 'Nikkan kindai bijutsu: nijūsei wo koete' [Japanese and Korean modern art: beyond the dichotomy]. *Nikkan kindai bijutsuka no manazashi, 'chōsen' de egaku* [Korean and Japanese modern artists in the Korean peninsula: 1890s to 1960], exh. cat. (Fukuoka: Fukuoka Asian Art Museum, 2015), p. 280.
3 Kim Mi-geum, *Baeunseongui yuleob chelyusigi hoehwa yeongu* [A study of Pai Un-soung's paintings during his years in Europe (1922–1940)], Master's thesis (Seoul: Hongik University, 2003), pp. 36–37.
4 For example, he was selected for the Autumn Fair (France, 1927), won first prize at the Warsaw International Art Exhibition (Poland, 1936), and exhibited at the National Society of Fine Art (France, 1938 and 1939).
5 Pai held solo exhibitions at the Gurlitt Gallery in Berlin (1930 and 1935), the Hamburg Museum of Ethnology (1935), and the Charpentier Gallery in Paris (1938), among others.
6 For example, *Baron Mitsui and His Works* is housed in the Hamburg Museum for Ethnology, *Self-Portrait (Shaman)* and *Children Spinning a Top* in the Ethnological Museum of Berlin, *Winter Landscape* in the National Gallery in Prague, and *World Tour* in Hrubý Rohozec Castle in the Czech Republic.
7 Yasumatsu Miyuki, '"Higashi ajia" bijutsu no naka no nihon bijutsu: kindai doitsu no "tōa bijutsu kyōkai" no katsudō wo tōshite' [The Japanese art in 'East Asian' art: the Society for East Asian Art in modern Germany]. *Tōyō ishiki: musō to genjitsu no aida: 1887–1953* [East Asian sense: between dreams and reality: 1887–1953], ed. Inaga Shigemi (Kyoto: Minerva shobō, 2012), p. 224.
8 Ibid., pp. 223–250.
9 Maya Stiller, 'Introduction', *Korea Rediscovered! Treasures from German Museums*, exh. cat. (Seoul: Korea Foundation, 2011), pp. 10–11.
10 Eckardt researched Korean art history during his twenty-year stay in Korea that started in 1909. *A History of Korean Art* was published in German and English in 1929. He identified the characteristics of Korean art as 'simplicity' and 'conciseness', praising it as 'a model example of oriental classicism'. See Andre Eckardt, *Geschichte der koreanischen Kunst* [A history of Korean art] (Leipzig: Verlag Karl W. Hiersemann, 1929).
11 There were a total of three presentations on Korean Art: Otto Kümmel, *Chinesische Kunst auf Koreanischem Boden* [Chinese art on Korean soil]; A. Eckardt, *Chinesische und Koreanische Kunst* [Chinese and Korean art] (1928); and A. Eckardt, *Koreanisches Kunstgewerbe*

[Korean craft] (1942). Yet, when compared with China (45 times) and Japan (23 times), this number has to be considered small. See 'Academic Presentations at the Regular Seminars of the Society for East Asian Art (1926–1944)' in Yasumatsu, *Japanese Art in "East Asian" Art*, pp. 247–250.

12 In reality, Pai is mixing a number of Korean traditional clothing styles in these pictures. For example, in *Self-Portrait (Shaman)*, he is wearing a *paksu* hat with Joseon-period military attire; the design on the clothing is that of the king.

13 It is surmised that what is depicted in the background of *Self-Portrait with Hat* is Kadadu Bar (which translates as 'Cockatoo Bar'), one of the biggest dance halls in the Weimar capital of the 1920s and early 1930s. It was known for its exotic interior design that mixed Tahitian and Samoan ornaments and is known to have been frequented by Asian students and businessmen. See Frank Hoffmann, *Berlin Koreans and Pictured Koreans* (Vienna: Praesens, 2015), p. 92.

14 Lee Gwang-pyo, *Geulime naleul damda: hangugui jahwasang ilggi* [Reading Korean self-portraits] (Seoul: Hyeonam-sa, 2016), pp. 88–93.

15 Pai is thought to have referred to various materials when he drew pictures. According to the Korean newspaper, the *Daily Chosun*, Pai had sometimes requested photos of old buildings, genre paintings, and precious artworks of Korea, and did paintings based on these. See 'The Art of Korea Blooms in Foreign Countries', *Chosun Ilbo* [the *Daily Chosun*], January 25, 1936, sec. 2.

16 Harald Olbrich, ed., *Lexikon der Kunst* [Lexicon of art], vol. 1 (Leipzig: Seemann, 1987), p. 126; Marianne Bernhard, *Das Biedermeier* [The Biedermeier] (Dusseldorf: Econ, 1983), p. 64. Cited in Eom Mi-suk, 'Sipgusegi dogilui chogi chosangsajin yeongu' [Research on early portrait photography in 19th-century Germany], *Seoyangmisulsahaghoe nonmunjib* [Collected papers of the association for Western art history] 34 (Seoul: Association for Western Art History, 2011), pp. 19–20.

17 Ernst Sander, 'Das Wert eines Koreanischen Malers' [The value of a Korean painter], *Hamburger Nachrichten* [Hamburg News] 136 (March 21, 1935). Cited in Kim Mi-geum, *A Study of Pai Un-soung's Paintings*, p. 50.

18 M.K.R., 'Ein Koreanischer Künstler in Deutschland' [A Korean artist in Germany], *Hamburger Fremdenblatt* [Hamburg Stranger] 81 (March 22, 1935). Cited in Kim Mi-geum, *A Study of Pai Un-soung's Paintings*, p. 18.

19 See Lee Gu-yeol, "Baeunseongui jaebalgyeon' [Rediscovery of Pai Un-seong], *Pai Un-soung exhibition*, exh. cat. (Seoul: National Museum of Modern and Contemporary Art, 2001), p. 12.

20 'Our Masters on the World's Stage: Mr Pai Un-soung', *Dong-A Ilbo* [the Dong-A Daily News] (January 8, 1939).

21 Herbert Blanken, 'Ein Künstler des Fernen Ostens: Der Koreaner Maler Un-soung Pai' [An artist from the Far East: the Korean painter Pai Un-soung], *Illustrirte Zeitung* (Leipzig, Bd. 187, nr. 4779; October 15, 1936), p. 502. Cited in Kim Mi-geum, *A Study of Pai Un-soung's Paintings*, p. 89.

22 M.R.K., 'A Korean Artist in Germany'. Cited in Kim Mi-geum, *A Study of Pai Un-soung's Paintings*, p. 18.

23 'Baeunseongssiui hwasileul chajaseo' [A visit to Pai Un-soung's atelier], *Chunchu* [The Times] (June 1943), pp. 90–91.

24 It is said that Pai made many efforts to spread knowledge about Korea in Germany, writing about Korea's customs and introducing Korean songs and fairy-tales. See Kim Mi-geum, *A Study of Un-soung Pai's Paintings*, p. 24.

25 Susanne Knödel and Katharina Kosikowski, 'The Korean Collection of the Museum of Ethnology Hamburg', *Korea Rediscovered! Treasures from German Museums*, exh. cat. (Seoul: Korea Foundation, 2011), pp. 96–97.

26 Mitsui Takaharu was granted orders in seven Central and Eastern European countries, including Austria, Hungary, Czechoslovakia, and Poland, for introducing Japanese culture to Europe and stimulating cultural exchange. See Matsushita Denkichi, *Zaibatsu Mitsui no shin kenkyū* [New research on the Mitsui Zaibatsu] (Tokyo: Chūgai Sangyō Chōsakai [Society for the investigation of industry at home and abroad], 1936), p. 53. Cited in Kim Mi-geum, *A Study of Un-soung Pai's Paintings*, p. 54.

27 Knödel and Kosikowski, 'The Korean Collection', pp. 96–97.

28 U.T., 'Un-soung Pai', *Hamburger Anzeiger* [Hamburg Advertisement] 69 (March 22, 1935). Cited in Kim Mi-geum, *A Study of Pai Un-soung's Paintings*, p. 57.
29 Kim Bog-gi, 'Joseonui pungsogeul nolaehan "yuleob misul yuhag ilho"' [The 'number one student to Europe' who celebrated Korean customs], *Art in Culture* (September 1991), p. 95; 'An Asian of Calm and Versatile Talents: interview with Kurt Runge', *Wolgan misul* [The Monthly Art Magazine] 87 (April 1991), p. 65.
30 Kurt Runge, interview (December 6, 1990), Berlin. Cited in Frank Hoffmann, *Berlin Koreans*, p. 97.
31 Cho Taek-won, *Cho Taek-won* (Seoul: Jisik gongjakso, 2015), p. 75.
32 The work was finished in 1937, with two scrolls said to hang on either side of the stairs at the embassy entrance and two more in the drawing room. They were destroyed in a fire during air raids in 1945. See Frank Hoffmann, 'I jaggaleul malhanda: baeunseong, beleullin saenghwal sibyugnyeon ganui baljachwi' [Pae Un-song, the first Korean painter in Europe: traces of his 16 years in Berlin] 87 (April 1991), p. 61; Hoffmann, *Berlin Koreans*, p. 97.
33 The *Hamburger Anzeiger* (March 22, 1935) notes that the Japanese Deputy Consul General invited guests at the exhibition opening to a breakfast at the Uhlenhorster Fährhaus. For further details, see Hoffmann, *Berlin Koreans*, pp. 100–101.
34 'Our masters on the world's stage: Mr. Pai Un-soung', *Dong-A Ilbo* [the Dong-A Daily News] (January 8, 1939).
35 For more about the Franco-Japanese Association, see Wada Keiko, Matsuzaki Sekiko, and Wada Hirofumi, *Mantetsu to nichifutsu bunka kōryūshi* Furansu-Japon [The South Manchuria railway and the Franco-Japanese cultural exchange magazine *France-Japon*] (Tokyo: Yumani shobō, 2012), pp. 7–12.
36 Ibid., p. 10.
37 A.S., 'Artistes Exotiques de Paris: Le Peintre Coréen Un-soung Paï' [The exotic artists of Paris: Korean painter Pai Un-soung], *France-Japon* 27 (March 15, 1938), pp. 118–119.
38 Ibid.; 'Une Exposition à Paris de M. Unsoung Paï' [An exhibition in Paris by Mr Pai Un-soung], *France-Japon* 30 (June 15, 1938), p. 274.
39 (1) 'Enfant Coréen' in no. 27, p. 119; (2) the title page in no. 28; (3) 'Jeux d'enfants Coréens' in no. 28, p. 195; (4) 'Takugen Tchô dans une Danse de Bonze' in no. 30, p. 274; (5) 'Jeux d'enfants coréens en hiver', frontispiece in no. 37.
40 Symposium record, 'Baeglim, pari, baegiuiui jeonhwa sogeseo choegeun gwigughan yangssiui bogogi' [Reports from two who recently returned from the war in Berlin, Paris, and Belgium], *Samchully* [the Whole Land of Korea] 12, no. 10 (December 1, 1940).
41 For example, Cho had a special relationship with contributors like the poet Yamata Kiku and the Japanese ambassador to France, Sugimura Yōtarō. (See Cho, *Cho Taek-won*, pp. 79–94). Moreover, other artist contributors like Satomi Munetsugu and Hamanaka Katsu were fellow participants with Pai at the Japanese Artist Exhibitions in Paris. See Fukui Fine Arts Museum, *Ihōjin tachi no yume: ekoru do pari to pari wo egaita nihonjin* [The foreigners' dream: the École de Paris and the Japanese who drew Paris] exh. cat. (Tokyo: Curators, 2007), p. 140.
42 'Dai ikkai pari nihon bijutsuka tenrankai-hyō' [Review of the first Japanese Artist Exhibitions in Paris], *Binokuni* [the Country of Beauty] 15, no. 3 (March 1939), p. 57.
43 The first exhibition was held on December 17–30, 1938, at the Bernheim–Jeune Gallery in Paris, and the second between June 27 and July 13, 1939 at Charpentier Gallery, also in Paris.
44 Ōnaga Hiroyoshi, 'Pari nihon bijutsuka tenrankai no shōhō wo teni shite' [Acquiring detailed reports about the Japanese artist exhibitions in Paris], *Binokuni* 15, no. 3 (March 1939), pp. 53–59; 'Dai nikai pari nihon bijutsuka tenrankai ni tsuite' [On the second Japanese Artist Exhibitions in Paris], *Binokuni* [the Country of Beauty] 15, no. 8 (August 1939), pp. 28–29.
45 'On the first Japanese Artist Exhibition in Paris', *Binokuni* [the Country of Beauty] 15, no. 3 (March 1939), pp. 54–55.
46 Ōnaga, 'Japanese Artist Exhibitions in Paris', p. 54.
47 'On the Second Japanese Artist Exhibitions in Paris', *Binokuni* [the Country of Beauty] 15, no. 8 (August 1939), p. 28.
48 A.S., 'Hommage à M. Yōtarō Sugimura Ambassadeur du Japon en France' [Hommage to Mr Sugimura Yōtarō Japanese ambassador to France], *France-Japon* 42 (June 1939), p. 320.

49 Ishii Kikoujiro, 'Sur la Mort de S. Exc. M. Yōtarō Sugimura' [On the death of Mr Sugimura Yōtarō], *France-Japon* 42 (June 1939), p. 330.
50 The line 'In the Presence of M. Sugimura' can be found on the letter of invitation to Pai's private showing. See Figure 5.6.
51 For more about the role of *France-Japon* as a foreign propaganda magazine, see Wada Keiko et al., *The South Manchuria Railway*, pp. 89–104.
52 See Hoffmann, *Berlin Koreans*, p. 98.
53 He also served as a judge for the Western painting division at the First Grand Art Exhibition of Korea in 1949, the first president of the Faculty of Arts at Hongik University, and honorary president of Gyeongju Art School. For more on Pai's activities after returning to Korea, see Kim Mi-geum, *A Study of Pai Un-soung's Paintings*, pp. 32–37.
54 M.R.K., 'A Korean Artist in Germany'. Cited in Kim Mi-geum, *A Study of Pai Un-soung's Paintings*, p. 18.
55 Yoon Hee-sun, 'Baeunseongssi gaeinjeonpyeong' [Review of Pai Un-soung's solo exhibition], *Maeil Sinbo* [Daily News] (June 7, 1944).
56 Park Go-seok, 'Yuhwaui jeongtongseong: baeunseongssiui yesul' [The authenticity of oil painting: the art of Pai Un-soung]. *Gyeonghyang Sinmun* [Kyunghyang Daily News] (December 29, 1948).
57 Ibid.
58 Hoffmann, *Berlin Koreans*, p. 100.

Bibliography

A.S. 'Artistes Exotiques de Paris: Le Peintre Coréen Un-soung Paï' [The exotic artists of Paris: Korean painter Pai Un-soung]. *France-Japon* 27 (March 15, 1938).

———. 'Hommage à M. Yōtarō Sugimura Ambassadeur du Japon en France' [Hommage to Mr Sugimura Yōtarō Japanese ambassador to France]. *France-Japon* 42 (June 15, 1939).

Anonymous. 'Une Exposition à Paris de M. Unsoung Paï' [An exhibition in Paris by Mr Pai Un-soung]. *France-Japon* 30 (June 15, 1938).

———. 'Segyee bichna-neun uliui myeong-jang: Baeunseongssi' [Our masters on the world's stage: Mr Pai Un-soung]. *Dong-A Ilbo* [the Dong-A Daily News] (January 8, 1939).

———. 'Dai ikkai pari nihon bijutsuka tenrankai-hyō' [Review of the first Japanese Artist Exhibitions in Paris]. *Binokuni* [the Country of Beauty] 15, no. 3 (March 1, 1939).

———. 'Dai ikkai pari nihon bijutsuka tenrankai' [The first Japanese Artists Exhibitions in Paris]. *Atelier* (March 1, 1939).

———. 'Dai nikai pari nihon bijutsuka tenrankai ni tsuite' [On the second Japanese Artist Exhibitions in Paris]. *Binokuni* [the Country of Beauty] 15, no. 8 (August 1, 1939).

———. 'Baeglim, pari, baegiuiui jeonhwa sogeseo choegeun gwigughan yangssiui bogogi' [Symposium record: reports from two who recently returned from the war in Berlin, Paris, and Belgium]. *Samchully* [the Whole Land of Korea] 12, no. 10 (December 1, 1940).

———. 'Baeunseongssiui hwasileul chajaseo' [A visit to Pai Un-soung's atelier]. *Chunchu* [The Times] (June 1943).

Blanken, Herbert. 'Ein Künstler des Fernen Ostens: Der Koreaner Maler Un-soung Pai' [An artist from the Far East: the Korean painter Pai Un-soung]. *Illustrirte Zeitung* [Illustrated Newspaper] (October 15, 1936).

Cho Taek-won. *Cho Taek-won*. Seoul: Jisik gongjakso, 2015.

Eckardt, André. *Geschichte der koreanischen Kunst* [A history of Korean art]. Leipzig: Verlag Karl W. Hiersemann, 1929.

Eom Mi-suk. 'Sipgusegi dogilui chogi chosangsajin yeongu' [Research on early portrait photography in nineteenth-century Germany]. *Seoyangmisulsahaghoe nonmunjib* [Collected papers of the association for Western art history] 34 (2011): 7–31.

Fukui Fine Arts Museum. *Ihōjin tachi no yume: ekōru do pari to pari o egaita nihonjin* [The foreigners' dream: the École de Paris and the Japanese who drew Paris]. exh. cat. Tokyo: Curators, 2007.

Hoffmann, Frank. 'I jaggaleul malhanda: baeunseong, beleullin saenghwal sibyugnyeon ganui baljachwi' [Pae Un-song, the first Korean painter in Europe: traces of his sixteen years in Berlin]. *Wolgan misul* [The Monthly Art Magazine] 87 (April 1991): 55–62.

———. *Berlin Koreans and pictured Koreans*. Vienna: Praesens, 2015.

Ishii Kikoujiro. 'Sur la Mort de S. Exc. M. Yōtarō Sugimura' [On the death of Mr Sugimura Yōtarō]. *France-Japon* 42 (June 15, 1939): 334.

Kim Bog-gi. 'Cheos yuleob yuhagsaengui saengaewa jagpum' [Pai Un-soung: his life and art as the first Korean artist in Europe]. *Wolgan misul* [The Monthly Art Magazine] 87 (April 1991): 49–54.

———. 'Joseonui pungsogeul nolaehan "yuleob misul yuhag ilho"' [The 'number one student to Europe' who celebrated Korean customs]. *Art in Culture* (September 1991): 87–102.

Kim Mi-geum. *Baeunseongui yuleob chelyusigi hoehwa yeongu* [A study of Pai Un-soung's paintings during his years in Europe (1922–1940)]. Master's thesis. Seoul: Hongik University, 2003.

Knödel, Susanne and Kosikowski, Katharina. 'The Korean Collection of the Museum of Ethnology Hamburg'. *Korea Rediscovered! Treasures from German Museums*. exh. cat. 74–99. Seoul: Korea Foundation, 2011.

Lee Gu-yeol. 'Baeunseongui jaebalgyeon' [Rediscovery of Pai Un-soung]. *Baeunseong jeon* [Pai Un-soung exhibition]. exh. cat. 10–13. Seoul: National Museum of Modern and Contemporary Art, 2001.

Lee Gwang-pyo. *Geulime naleul damda: hangugui jahwasang ilggi* [Reading Korean self-portraits]. Seoul: Hyeonam-sa, 2016.

Lee Gyeong-mo. '1920nyeon-dae-ui yu-leob yu-hag hwa-ga-deul' [The painters who studied in Europe in the 1920s]. *Gyeonghuidaehaggyo hyeondaemisulyeonguso nonmunjib* [Collected papers of the Contemporary Art Research Institute] 4 (2002): 87–120.

Lee Mi-na. 'Nikkan kindai bijutsu: nijūsei o koete' [Japanese and Korean modern art: beyond the dichotomy]. *Nikkan kindai bijutsuka no manazashi, 'chōsen' de egaku* [Korean and Japanese modern artists in the Korean peninsula: 1890s to 1960] exh. cat. 280–284. Fukuoka: Fukuoka Asian Art Museum, 2015.

M.K.R. 'Ein Koreanischer Künstler in Deutschland' [A Korean artist in Germany]. *Hamburger Fremdenblatt* [Hamburg Stranger] 81 (March 22, 1935).

Matsuo Kuninosuke. 'Une exposition des artistes japonais à Paris' [An exhibition of Japanese artists in Paris]. *France-Japon* 36 (December 15, 1938): 566.

Matsushita Denkichi. *Zaibatsu Mitsui no shin kenkyū* [New research on the Mitsui Zaibatsu]. Tokyo: Chūgai Sangyō Chōsakai [Society for the investigation of industry at home and abroad], 1936.

National Museum of Modern and Contemporary Art. *Pai Un-soung Exhibition*. exh. cat. Seoul: The National Museum of Modern and Contemporary Art, 2001.

Ōnaga Hiroyoshi. 'Pari nihon bijutsuka tenrankai no shōhō o teni shite' [Acquiring detailed reports about the Japanese artist exhibitions in Paris]. *Binokuni* 15, no. 3 (March 1, 1939): 53–59.

Park Go-seok. 'Yuhwaui jeongtongseong: baeunseongssiui yesul' [The authenticity of oil painting: the art of Pai Un-soung]. *Gyeonghyang Sinmun* [Kyunghyang Daily News] (December 29, 1948).

Rubinstein, Assia. 'Unsoung Paï'. *Beaux-Arts, The Journal of the Arts* (June 10, 1938).

Runge, Kurt. *Unsoung Pai Erzählt aus seiner Koreanischen Heimat* [Pai Un-soung tells stories of his Korean homeland]. Darmstadt: Kulturbuch Verlag, 1950.

———. 'An Asian of Calm and Versatile Talents: Interview with Kurt Runge'. *Wolgan misul* [The Monthly Art Magazine] 87 (April 1991): 63–67.

Sander, Ernst. 'Das Wert eines Koreanischen Malers' [The value of a Korean painter]. *Hamburger Nachrichten* [Hamburg N ews] 136 (March 21, 1935).

Satō Dōshin. 'Kindai no chōkoku' [Overcoming modernity]. *Art History Forum* 30 (2010): 9–20.

Shin Sang-chel. 'Sibgusegi mal peulangseu bagmulgwan yeogsawa asia kollegsyeon: dongyang yesule daehan saeloun insig' [The historical presentation of Asian arts in France in the 19th century]. *Misulsahag* [Journal of the Korean Association of Art History] 22 (2008): 143–161.

Smoular, Alfred. 'Artistes Exotiques de Paris: Le Peintre Coréen Un-soung Paï' [Exotic artists of Paris: the Korean painter Pai Un-soung], *France-Japon* 27 (March 15, 1938): 118–119.

———. 'Une Exposition à Paris de M. Unsoung Paï' [An exhibition in Paris by Mr Pai Un-soung], *France-Japon* 30 (June 15, 1938): 274.

Stiller, Maya. 'Introduction'. *Korea Rediscovered! Treasures from German Museums*, exh. cat. 9–19. Seoul: Korea Foundation, 2011.

U.T. 'Un-soung Pai.' *Hamburger Anzeiger* [Hamburg Advertisement] 69 (March 22, 1935).

Wada Keiko, Matsuzaki Sekiko, and Wada Hirofumi. *Mantetsu to nichifutsu bunka kōryūshi furansu-japon* [The South Manchuria railway and the Franco-Japanese cultural exchange magazine *France-Japon*]. Tokyo: Yumani shobō, 2012.

Yasumatsu Miyuki. '"Higashi ajia" bijutsu no naka no nihon bijutsu: kindai doitsu no "tōa bijutsu kyōkai" no katsudō o tōshite' [The Japanese art in 'East Asian' art: the Society for East Asian Art in modern Germany]. *Tōyō ishiki: musō to genjitsu no aida: 1887–1953* [East Asian sense: between dreams and reality: 1887–1953], edited by Inaga Shigemi. 223–250. Kyoto: Minerva shobō, 2012.

Yoon Hee-sun. 'Baeunseongssi gaeinjeonpyeong' [Review of Pai Un-soung's solo exhibition]. *Maeil Sinbo* [Daily News] (June 7, 1944).

6 Reinventing Localism, Tradition, and Identity
The Role of Modern Okinawan Painting (1930s–1960s)

Eriko Tomizawa-Kay

Introduction

Located some 400 miles south of mainland Japan, today the Okinawa Islands (Okinawa *shotō*) constitute a local prefectural unit within the Japanese nation state, with the Okinawa people identifying largely as Japanese. However, Okinawa's sociopolitical dynamics are deeply rooted in the history of the Ryūkyū Kingdom, which by the early 15th century had become a tributary state to Ming China, before falling under the dual suzerainty of Japan's Satsuma Domain (which corresponds roughly to present-day Kagoshima prefecture) in 1609. It was only in 1879 that the islands would be formally integrated within the Japanese nation, ushering in a phase of often brutal cultural assimilation. Following Japan's defeat in the Second World War in 1945, Okinawa would be subject to U.S. Occupation and would remain an occupied territory until 1972.

As a result of its colonial history, issues of Okinawan identity, together with the resurrection over the course of the 20th century of Okinawan traditions, have been fraught with complexity. This essay will argue, however, that it is in the visual arts that Okinawans have given expression to some of the most compelling meditations on issues such as nationhood, identity and, in the aftermath of the devastating Battle of Okinawa that ushered in the U.S. Occupation, the experience of trauma that for many would become an integral part of what it meant to be Okinawan.

Okinawan art has a long history of political appropriation. Following the Japanese annexation of the islands in 1879, art policies promoted by the Meiji government were consciously designed to bring Okinawan artistic idioms in line with mainland art movements. This was achieved through art education and the protection of cultural properties in Okinawa, as well as through the participation of Okinawan artists in official art exhibitions in the Japanese metropole. At the same time, however, the tropical Okinawan landscape led to its casting as an exotic 'other' with both mainland and local artists using academic painting idioms to depict a primitive and paradisiac 'southern island'. This exoticizing gaze would characterize Okinawan art until the Second World War, when local artists in particular began to explore their cultural heritage and issues of communal identity on their own terms.

Under the U.S. Occupation, art would be commandeered to peddle a vision of traditional Okinawan culture that pre-dated Japanese assimilation of the islands and implicitly contested Japanese claims of sovereignty. It was only from the 1950s onwards that Okinawan artists increasingly began to challenge these cultural stereotypes and to give expression to the lived experience of Okinawan people both as an occupied nation and victims of a war often passed over in silence.

For this generation of Okinawan artists, the process of creating a sense of local identity and tradition has thus taken place against a troubled backdrop of both pre-war Imperial Japanese colonization and post-war U.S. Occupation. Moreover, tradition itself is necessarily a complex phenomenon. Eric Hobsbawm noted long ago that many '"traditions" which appear or claim to be old are often quite recent in origin and sometimes invented'.[1] This is particularly true for Okinawa. Many supposedly typical features of the Okinawan landscape, for example, such as houses with red roofing tiles adorned with statues of Sīsā (the Okinawan lion), have been consciously constructed in response to the imperative to present a distinct local tradition. [2]

This essay seeks to explore how conflicting political forces have shaped modern Okinawan painting. Through case studies of 20th-century Okinawan artists, it will demonstrate how Okinawan art has been integral to the expression of pre- and post-war attitudes to national identity, reflective 'othering' and, increasingly, regional struggles. It is in this context, it will argue, that Okinawan art merits a significant place within Japanese and, more broadly, East Asian art history.

Art Education in Okinawa: Nihonga and Yōga (1930s to early 1940s)

Following the annexation of Okinawa in 1879, the Meiji government actively promoted an educational policy designed to effect the transformation of the Okinawan people into Japanese subjects. As part of this effort, they would send a number of young and prominent teachers of subjects including painting from mainland Japan to local Okinawan schools.[3] The same assimilationist programme would subsequently be adopted in the colonial education systems of Taiwan and Korea, making Okinawa in this respect a trial ground for proto-colonial policies.

The first wave of Japanese artists to take up roles of colonial educators specialized in *nihonga* (Japanese-style painting). The term *nihonga* was coined around 1880 in a surge of nationalist sentiment in order to distinguish native painting styles from *yōga* (Western-style painting), which had been growing in popularity since the beginning of the Meiji period. *Nihonga*'s proponents saw it as an artistic vehicle for expressing Japan's new national and international self-consciousness.[4] The *nihonga* painter Yamaguchi Zuiu (1868–1933), a pupil of Hirafuku Suian (1844–1890), father of the more famous Hirafuku Hyakusui (1877–1933), would be one of the islands' earliest art instructors. Originally from the mainland, Yamaguchi became an art teacher at an Okinawan secondary school in 1896, and played an important role in the foundation of the first art association (known as the *Tansei-kai*, or Painting Society) for local art teachers.

One of the most acclaimed *nihonga* specialists was Yamada Shinzan (1885–1977), an Okinawan who studied under the painter Kobori Tomoto (1864–1931) at the Tokyo School of Fine Arts (*Tōkyō bijutsu gakkō*). In 1910, Yamada spent a year in China teaching sculpture and design at the *Yi tu xue tang* art school in Beijing. He also began submitting his works to exhibitions organized by the Japan-China Joint Society.[5] By the time he returned from China, he was well established as a *nihonga* painter and remained in Tokyo, only returning to Okinawa after the Second World War. His signature work was the 1924 *Establishment of the Ryūkyū Domain*, depicting Okinawa's brief integration as a feudal domain within the Japanese nation state between 1872 and 1879, a prelude its annexation by the new Meiji government in 1879. The painting, indicative of Shinzan's acceptance in contemporary mainland art circles, was part of a series of works proclaiming the triumphs of the Meiji era created as part of a mural for the Meiji Shrine. Currently held in the collection of the Shōtoku Meiji Shrine Memorial Art Museum in Tokyo, it clearly demonstrates the role of *nihonga* in colonial ideologies.[6]

Shinzan in many ways embodied the early 'Japanization' of Okinawa. His *nihonga* pupils included Kinjō Yasutarō (1911–1999), who specialized in historical genre paintings and paintings of Okinawan women, as well as providing illustrations for Okinawan newspaper serial novels; and Gushiken Seiji (1908–1992), who also trained under Itō Shinsui (1898–1972), a *nihonga* painter known as a painter of beautiful women. Within the space of a few years, however, *nihonga* specialists had largely been replaced by practitioners of *yōga* and it was *yōga* that would become the dominant idiom of modern Okinawan painting. Ōmine Seikan, an Okinawan *yōga* painter, for example, recalled the situation in the early 1930s in the following terms:

> . . . at this time *yōga* was undisputedly dominant in Okinawa, and people who painted *nihonga* were looked down on. There was a notion that Okinawa needed to try to catch up with mainland Japan, and to learn from the West in order to effect its modernization.[7]

There were a number of reasons for *nihonga*'s gradual fall from favour. One was its perceived association with colonialism. This was an issue that Okinawan artists were already grappling with. Up to the Meiji period, Okinawan painters had identified themselves primarily as Ryūkyū and not Japanese artists: representative was Nagamine Sōkyo (1852–1932), who worked with Yamaguchi Zuiu at the *Tansei-kai*. As a result of artistic and cultural relationships between the former Ryūkyū Kingdom and China from the Ming through to the Qing dynasties, however, local Ryūkyū painting had been heavily influenced by Chinese painting styles. Traditional landscape and flower-and-birds paintings owed much to Chinese painters such as the Fuzhou-based Sun Yi (1638–1712) and it was this Chinese idiom that was particularly prized by mainland-Japanese artists during the early Meiji period.[8]

By the early 20th century, however, Okinawan artists had begun to reject traditional Chinese painting styles as symptomatic of the former tributary status of the Ryūkyū Kingdom. It was in the same vein that they would resist the equally tarnished idiom of *nihonga*, which had emerged in the 1880s as part of an effort to formulate a distinctive Japanese painterly idiom in the face of the growing influence of the West. Both Chinese and Japanese painting styles (*nihonga*) became associated in the minds of Okinawan artists with colonial endeavours from which they sought to free themselves. It was against this backdrop that the relative neutrality of Western-style (*yōga*) painting—which simultaneously offered a release from conventional Japanese subjects such as historical figures and depictions of female beauty—recommended itself as a means of forging an indigenous Okinawan art, a vehicle for Okinawan modernity.

Yōga was taught in Okinawan schools for the first time in 1901 by Yamamoto Morinosuke (1877–1928). Yamamoto had studied under the yōga master Kuroda Seiki (1866–1924), who founded the yōga department at the Tokyo School of Fine Arts. Graduating from the school in 1889, Yamamoto became a member of the White Horse Society (Hakuba-kai), before moving to Okinawa where he worked as an art teacher at an Okinawan Prefectural Secondary School from 1900 to 1903.[9] This marked the beginning of the Okinawan yōga movement. In 1922, the Okinawan yōga painter Higa Keijō (1892–1941) would be appointed to Prefectural Number Two Secondary School, becoming instrumental in nurturing talented students such as Nadoyama Aijun (1906–1970) and Ōmine Seikan (1910–1970). Nadoyama was a graduate of the Tokyo School of Fine Arts school and a regular participant at the Ministry of Education Art Exhibitions known as Bunten,[10] while Ōmine was a member of two mainland art societies, the *Shunyō-kai* and *Nika-kai*. Both these painters would become influential Okinawan yōga practitioners.[11]

The Pre-War Period: Exoticism, Nostalgia, and the Colonial Gaze

Up until the Second World War, mainland-Japanese painters had celebrated the Okinawan archipelago as an exotic and, by extension, primitive land, to be captured and redeemed by the colonial gaze. This was powerfully demonstrated in one of the earliest paintings of the Okinawan landscape, executed in 1887 by the yōga painter Yamamoto Hōsui (1850–1906), when he accompanied the then prime minister Itō Hirobumi (1841–1909) on an official visit to Okinawa. This detailed visual record of the new Okinawan territory—its castle and villages with their stone walls and traditional tombs, the unspoiled beauty of its exotic shoreline and luxuriant foliage—was subsequently submitted to the Imperial Household, an act replete with the symbolism of territorial restoration. Paintings could be powerful embodiments of the Japanese colonial gaze. The same relationship between the visual documentation of the landscape and its colonization would be demonstrated throughout Japan's colonies. In 1928, for example, the painter Fujishima Takeji (1867–1943) would paint a sunrise over Mount Niitaka in Taiwan commissioned by the empress dowager for the emperor's study. 'The light of sunrise always reaches any remote place', he wrote. 'This is no different from the fact that the Japanese Empire reaches out widely'.[12] Fujishima would continue painting symbolic sunrises up until his death on the eve of the Second World War.[13]

For mainland-Japanese painters, painting the landscape and local people of Okinawa offered an expedient way to signal control by the Japanese. The 'primitive' Okinawan scenery and local women legitimated their 'othering' as objects of curiosity and exoticism. Indeed, many yōga painters, influenced by their studies abroad and struggling to translate Western subjects into the idiom of the mainland landscape, would turn for inspiration to Okinawa's tropical scenery and the exoticism of its Tsuji pleasure quarter. Fujita Tsuguharu (1886–1968), for example, by this time a celebrated painter in Paris, visited Okinawa in 1938 to sketch its landscapes together with a group of painters including Koiso Ryōhei (1903–1988). During their tour they were guided by the Okinawan yōga painter Haebaru Chōkō (1904–1961).[14]

Fujita would describe Okinawa as 'the Palace of the Dragon King' (*ryūgūjō*) and the Ryūkyū Arc (i.e. the Okinawan island chain) as a 'necklace of black pearls'. Conjuring an imaginary dream-world beneath the sea based on Japanese folktales, Fujita's Okinawa was a fairy-tale land.[15] Oblivious to the complex history of the islands, to the lived experience of the Okinawan people, mainland artists sought simply to reify the land beneath an exoticizing gaze, to uphold it as a symbol of a primitive other. Little coincidence then that already by 1926, a direct route from Osaka to Okinawa had been launched by the Osaka Commercial Ship Company in a move to encourage tourism to the islands.[16] Fujita's own Okinawan-inspired works and essays would subsequently be used for tourism promotions.[17]

One example of Fujita's 'primitivism' is the painting *Grandchildren*, executed during his tour of the islands in 1938 and one of the few Okinawa paintings produced by the artist still extant. The children were modelled on the children of the Okinawan *yōga* painter Haebaru Chōkō, and Fujita was clearly at pains to recreate in the figures a sense of authenticity.[18] Yet his visual rhetoric also spoke powerfully to romantic notions of a spiritual connection to the earth, and an aesthetic idealization of the primitive. The old woman and two young children sit crouched on the scorched red earth so typical of Okinawa, framed by a backdrop of tropical vegetation. Beyond this the bright blue sky, executed in long vertical brushstrokes, radiates upwards. The distinctive physiognomic features (such as the prominent cheekbones and jutting chin of the grandmother), hairstyles, and clothing (the bright semi-figurative designs of *bingata* stencil-dyed cloth) are clear ciphers of foreignness; while the *hajichi* tattoo that encircles the grandmother's wrist like a band, extending arrowlike down over the ridges of fingers that rest lightly on her foot, suggests not simply an exotic 'otherness' but a ritualized connection with the earth. The old woman's steady gaze into an invisible distance, together with the stillness and silence of the monumental figures deliberately captured within a pool of light, suggest an unchanging present, a moment of eternity symbolized in the traditional tortoise-shaped tomb (*kamekō baka*) in the upper right-hand corner (Figure 6.1). This is an essentially primitive landscape, the figures untouched by the artifice of modern civilization, the vegetation both powerful and unruly, the tattoo and the tomb symbols of a spiritual connection with elemental forces lost to modernity. Locked in its own primitivism, Okinawa served as a comforting reminder for mainland viewers of just how far Japan itself had come.

Contemporaries often celebrated the authenticity of Fujita's depictions. The Okinawan poet Yamanokuchi Baku (1903–1963), for example, claimed that, 'only Okinawan people painted by Fujita look like real locals, capable of speaking in the genuine Okinawan dialect'.[19] Yet Fujita's determination to capture a sense of the 'authentic' itself derived from contemporary Western interest in the depiction of 'natives', spearheaded by artists such as Gauguin, that belonged firmly to the romanticizing colonial gaze. In fact, prior to his return to Japan, Fujita had travelled widely, including in Latin America, depicting local peoples, and it seems likely that it was this experience that drew him to the 'foreignness' offered by Okinawan themes.[20]

Authenticity was a double-edged sword: on the one hand honouring the alterity of the subject, on the other satisfying a desire for an exotic or primitive other. Moreover, Fujita would exert an important influence on Okinawan painters. Ōmine Seikan, for example, began depicting the cultural and indigenous heritage of Okinawa, particularly local landscapes of red-roofed houses in the Shuri district as well as tortoise-shaped tombs, because Fujita and Koiso advised him: 'Why not add more Okinawan motifs to your painting?'[21] Another Okinawan *yōga* artist who would succumb to mainland

Reinventing Localism, Tradition, and Identity 107

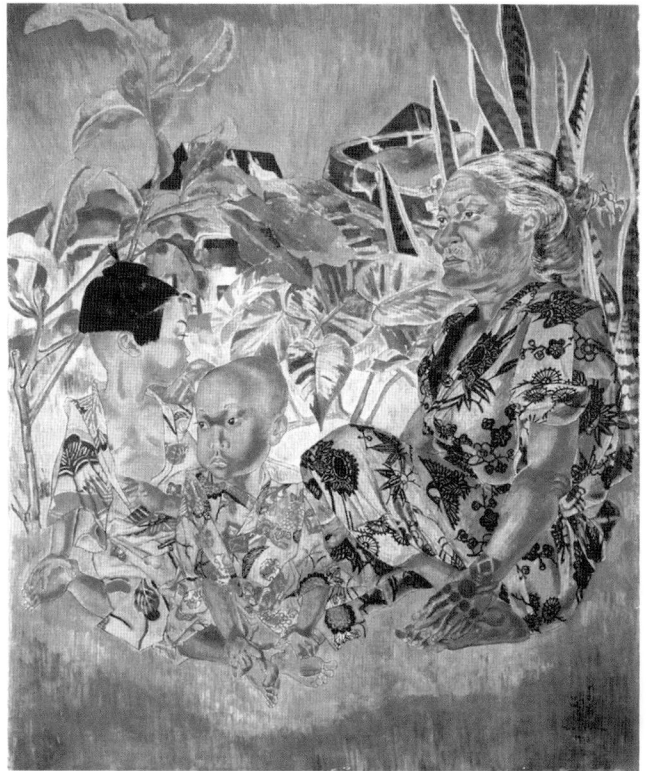

Figure 6.1 Fujita Tsuguharu, *Grandchildren* (Mago), 1938. Oil on canvas, 100.0 × 81.0 cm
Okinawa Prefectural Museum and Art Museum
©Fondation Foujita/ADAGP, Paris and DACS, London 2017.

conceptions of the islands was Nadoyama Aijun. As a young student in 1928, Nadoyama presented his painting *Hot-blooded man in a Southern Country* (*Nangoku no nekketsuji*) at the ninth Imperial Academy of Fine Arts Exhibition,[22] and later, his *In the Ryūkyūan Classical Idiom* (*Ryūkyū kotenchō*) at the 1939 Bunten. Both subjects drew on primitive stereotypes, the hot-blooded savage unconstrained by the burden of civilized society on the one hand, and on the other, the portrayal of a community locked in an imaginary past. Nadoyama would in fact become acclaimed in mainstream Japanese art society as a painter of Okinawan beauties.[23] Inevitably influenced by mainland attitudes to the islands, both Ōmine and Nadoyama would find themselves satisfying a demand for exoticism that ultimately confirmed the Japanese viewer in his or her sense of cultural superiority.

The deliberate invocation of 'local colour' became a requisite of Okinawan art, one that Okinawan painters themselves found expedient to follow. Yet the romanticization of the Okinawan landscape, concomitant with a colonial gaze that presupposed the superior authority of the viewer, carried unsettling political implications. At its most extreme, it recalled the habit of contemporary Korean painters to appeal to the desires of an implicit Japanese viewer by including depictions of *gisaeng (kisaeng)*

(Korean women highly trained in entertainment) in their works. This would subsequently become irrevocably linked with Japan's colonization of Korea and the use of comfort women, as Adachi Gen describes in his paper, 'War and Pornography in East Asia' in the present volume.[24] It also resonated with representations by mainland-Japanese artists of Japan's other East Asian colonies: local women or children in the shadow of masculine figures typically identified as Japanese soldiers. The implicit message—the protection of the weak by the valiant Japanese male—served as an insidious justification for Japan's colonial policies.[25]

Some Okinawan artists resisted the temptation to pander to the mainland gaze, yet few could avoid it altogether. In 1929, the *yōga* painter Haebaru Chōkō organized a joint exhibition with Nadoyama in Okinawa and while his works did not depict obvious Okinawan themes, his use of a vivid, shiny, thick red colour in his still-life paintings (often of southern flora) inevitably called to mind the texture of Okinawan lacquer, a gesture once more to a world of traditional values and local colour. He would also receive an award at the Taiwan Art Exhibition supported by Japanese colonial policies, suggesting that his work was thoroughly in line with mainstream political and artistic values.

Indeed, the discovery of Okinawan wares—such as lacquer and textiles—would become one aspect of the objectifying gaze of the mainland. One of the leaders of the *mingei* (folk craft) movement, the collector and writer Yanagi Muneyoshi (1889–1961), wrote of his visit to Okinawa that, 'for those of us who were looking around the country for traditional crafts, the existence of Okinawa was a wonder . . .', adding, 'Okinawa has remained pure Japan'.[26] For Yanagi, Okinawa once again symbolized that which had been lost in mainland Japan through the process of modernization.[27] In the same vein, the scholar of native Japanese folklore Yanagita Kunio (1875–1962) would celebrate Okinawa as the origin of Japanese culture.[28] Okinawa's reality as a country shackled over centuries by the colonial policies of its neighbours never came into question: it was simply a repository of the past, Japan's own storeroom.

Yanagi exerted a profound influence on the study of Okinawan culture, particularly in the field of *mingei*, and Okinawan folk crafts, like those of Korea, would become highly sought after. Between 1920 and 1945, Okinawan, Korean, Chinese, Manchurian, and Ainu material and Japanese folk culture all gained new status on the mainland as carriers of cultural capital that simultaneously validated the cultural advantage of the collector. It was precisely the perceived peripheral status of these entities that validated them: 'provinciality', Yanagi declared, 'preserves the pure national character'. Folkwares circulated as tokens of tributary nations, testimony to Japan's colonial reach.[29]

The Post-War Period: U.S. Occupation and the Emergence of Political Art

During the war period, renowned painters such as Fujita and Koiso would transform themselves into Japanese imperial war painters, but there is so far no record of Okinawan painters supporting the war in their works. Similarly, there are no extant propaganda paintings of the brutal Battle of Okinawa that ushered in the U.S. Occupation. It may be that by this stage, Japan no longer had the resources to produce propaganda.[30] But it may also suggest a refusal on the part of Okinawan artists to support Japanese aggression.

The Battle of Okinawa was one of the bloodiest battles of the Pacific War, and it left the main island of Okinawa catastrophically damaged. Following Japan's unconditional surrender in August 1945, the U.S. would establish the United States Military Government of the Ryūkyū Islands and proceed to build a number of military bases on the islands. Under U.S. control for the next thirty years, Okinawa would be deliberately cut off from the rest of Japan on the grounds that since it was originally part of the Ryūkyū Kingdom, the Okinawan people were not Japanese. In the eyes of the United States, its segregation therefore represented the liberation of Okinawans who had long suffered under Japan's colonial occupation.[31] The islands would thenceforth become a fortress of anti-communism and a launch pad for U.S. military campaigns, particularly in Korea and Vietnam.

The subsequent promotion of art and culture under the U.S administration can be dismissed, on the one hand, as a merely conciliatory measure. Yet these policies, put in place under the auspices of institutions such as the Okinawa Advisory Council (established in the Higashi Onna district of Ishikawa City in August 1945) and the Art Division of the Department of Culture, nonetheless offered important opportunities for Okinawan artists to develop their own artistic idioms. It was these years that would see the emergence of a modern Okinawan art.

Under the direction of the Department of Culture, artists were encouraged to collect cultural properties, organize entertainment for U.S. soldiers and residents, recreate traditional houses, and organize exhibitions for museums. These activities were guided by U.S. Navy lieutenant commanders. At the same time, the U.S. scholars Willard Hanna and James Watkins were urged to promote and nurture Okinawan traditional cultures.[32] Okinawan painters who were well received before the war—such as the *nihonga* painter Yamada Shinzan, his former pupil Kinjō Yasutarō, and the *yōga* painters Yamamoto Keiichi (1913–1977) and Ōshiro Kōya (1911–1980)—were employed by the government as Art Technical Specialists and were engaged in organizing exhibitions; museums were later established both in Ishikawa and Shuri. Meanwhile, for several years after the war, artists took commissions from U.S. military personnel for portraits, landscape paintings, and Christmas cards, while high demand for souvenir-type painting created important job opportunities, offering a number of painters the possibility of financial stability.[33]

Some might argue that the United States' establishment of democratic society in Okinawa, together with the protection of the arts, was simply part of a strategy to convince Okinawans that the occupation offered them an escape from Japanese militarism.[34] The U.S. military physician, Stanley A. Steinberg, for example, who had close friendships with several painters in the Nishimui art colony, revealed that there was a U.S. Occupational Manual that highlighted U.S. separationist intentions for the islands.[35] The implication was that Okinawan artists had a role to play in buttressing U.S policies. Yet while some artists, such as Ōmine Shinichi (1915–1996)—a bohemian artist who cultivated his own younger art circles—would chafe at what he saw as the failure to develop an independent Okinawan art under the U.S. administration, U.S art initiatives in Okinawa can, on the whole, be considered one of the very few 'silver linings' of the Okinawan occupation during this period.[36]

After the military administration moved to southern Okinawa in 1947, the Arts Division of the Department of Culture was closed. In late 1948, however, a group of painters, including many of the younger generation, moved to Nishimui village where they established an art colony, still sponsored by the U.S. administration but now with greater artistic leeway. The Nishimui colony provided artists with a generous income through commissions from U.S. Navy officers and soldiers; it was also the first modern Okinawan art society to encourage the creativity and development of artists who would go on to become the vanguard of Okinawan art from 1948 to the 1960s. It was here that a modern Okinawan art would first emerge, one that deconstructed colonial tropes of localism and attended to the social and political realities of the Okinawan people.

The first generation of post-war Okinawan artists was comprised of those who had already been active prior to the war, such as Nadoyama Aijun, Yamamoto Keiichi (1913–1998), and ōhiro Kōya (1911–1980). Those who were educated pre-war but active only post-war are regarded as the second generation, most notably Adaniya Masayoshi (1921–1969), Ashimine Kanemasa (1916–1993), Tamanaha Seikichi (1918–1984), Kinjō Yasutarō, and Gushiken Itoku (1912–2009). It was this generation that led the new direction in Okinawan art. Adaniya, Ashimine, and Tamahana had all graduated from the Tokyo School of Fine Arts and served as Japanese soldiers during the war. On their return to Okinawa they were frustrated by the conservative nature of its art and its refusal to engage with political realities. Acutely conscious of the era they were living in, they felt it their responsibility to give new expression to the realities of post-war Okinawan society.

Distinct differences would soon emerge between the work of the pre-war generation, represented by Nadoyama Aijun and Ōmine Seikan, and that of members of the post-war generation such as Adaniya Masayoshi. The pre-war generation had typically adapted mainland academic painting styles to conventional Okinawan motifs such as the exotic landscape, brightly dressed women, and southern flora. In these terms, there was little to distinguish their work from that of near-contemporary mainland painters. Even after the war, Nadoyama continued to paint female figures. Yet while on the one hand these recalled pre-war depictions of Okinawan beauties, in images such as *Nostalgia* (Figure 6.2), the new sombre palette, the wistful gaze, and the strangely

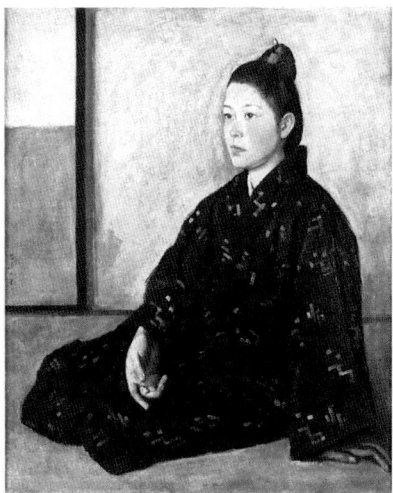

Figure 6.2 Nadoyama Aijun, *Nostalgia* (Kyōshū), 1946. Oil on canvas, 100.3 × 80.2 cm
Okinawa Prefectural Museum and Art Museum

eloquent gesture of the hand resting in the sitter's lap that appears to appeal to the viewer become an expression of nostalgia not for some romanticized past (the colonial gaze) but for an Okinawa that pre-dated the occupation. Similarly, Ōmine continued to paint typical Okinawan landscapes such as tombs, Shuri castle, and red-tiled roofs; these too were motivated not by the desire to appeal to the requirements of mainland audiences, but to archive the monuments of a landscape fast disappearing under the occupation's construction projects.

From the mid-1960s, however, Ōmine began to receive criticism for continually returning to the same subject of landscapes dotted with traditional red-tiled roofs.[37] For those intent on creating a modern art that reflected lived reality, the unchanging subject matter of nostalgic landscapes and beautiful women began to seem naïve, harking back to a mainland academism inseparable from its colonial origins. Modernizing reformers felt that it was their destiny to change the direction of Okinawan art. Ōmine described his own predicament in the following terms: 'After the war, the landscape of Okinawa was irrevocably destroyed. When I tried to depict what once had been a field, there stood abandoned tanks. All had changed. I could no longer find subjects for my paintings, I felt only nothingness.'[38]

It was under these circumstances that he came to paint his *Landscape of Nishihara Village* (1950) (Figure 6.3). During the war, Nishihara village had become home to a Japanese military airfield and the Command Headquarters during the Battle of Okinawa. Nearly half of its residents and an unknown number of soldiers had been killed here during one of the fiercest battles of the war.[39] In his brutalized landscape, Ōmine depicted abandoned U.S. tanks destroyed in the battle in a green field overgrown with weeds. A bright blue sky and fresh green grass indicate that the war is over, but the tiny silhouettes of people and burnt trees in the background become symbols of a haunted past. Ōmine would subsequently travel to the remote Yaeyama Islands in Okinawa and return to his depictions of red-tiled-roof landscapes. But these, he confessed, were expressions of his own 'perception of Yaeyama, namely, of the way Okinawa looked before the war and the commercialization of these islands'.[40] Traditional landscapes on the one hand, they were also poignant expressions of loss.

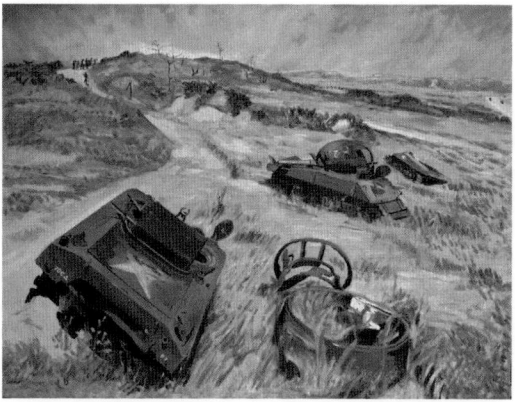

Figure 6.3 Ōmine Seikan, *Landscape of Nishihara Village in 1950* (Nishihara 1950), 1950. Oil on canvas, 91.3 × 117.3 cm
Okinawa Prefectural Museum and Art Museum

The beginnings of Okinawan Modernism

By contrast, the post-war generation of Adaniya and other young painters began to turn to abstract painting as a way to express the new political reality, their sombre palettes a reflection of dark times. Instead of commodifying the physical landscape and fetishizing local crafts, these works become landscapes of the mind, expressions of a heart that had no truck with the colonial gaze. Moreover, aware that pre-war artists had had limited opportunities to display their paintings, the new generation recognized the need for their works to reach larger audiences. Thus in 1949, in response to artists' call for a venue in which to officially exhibit their works, the first Okinawan art competition and exhibition, known as Okiten, was held at the Okinawa Times Publisher in Naha City.[41]

Yet here too, there was a clear boundary between the older generation of Okinawan *yōga* painters—such as Nadoyama and Ōmine, who continued to depict traditional Okinawan landscapes—and the younger generation of Okinawan artists. As a result of disagreements with and frustration towards senior judges (including Nadoyama), in 1950, Ashimine, Tamanaha, and Adaniya, together with Kinjō Yasutarō and Gushiken Itoku, established their own exhibition known as the Five People Exhibition (*goninten*), a chance for artists to display to contemporary audiences works probing the political reality of post-war Okinawa.[42]

The Five People Exhibition itself was short-lived (the group was dissolved in 1954); however, Adaniya, Ashimine, and Tamanaha would subsequently join with Ashitomi Chōshō (1930–) to establish the *Sōtokai* Art Society, which from 1958–1968 would organize study groups and exhibitions to encourage and support a new generation of Okinawan artists.

According to its founders, the Five People Exhibition Group sought to create a modernist aesthetic idiom for Okinawan painting that focused on the expressive potential of formalist concepts such as colour, line, shape, and texture. Earlier landscapes and motifs were no longer strong enough to revive Okinawan art, the group declared: 'the universalism of modernism has been achieved through form and style. The more [artists] want to give eternity to their work, the purer and more stylized its forms must become'.[43] Yet formalism did not deny an engagement with political issues. Adaniya himself believed that a new Okinawan art should be born of careful examination of contemporary society:

> There are many fine examples of Okinawan art: but they belong to an earlier, primitive society. Today, Okinawa belongs within a global community, and this has brought with it both good and bad things. It is impossible to keep past traditions alive blindly, without carefully questioning what we wish to reject, and what we wish to conserve from our history.[44]

Adaniya would play a leading role in the post-war Okinawan art world, and he clearly felt both empathy and resistance to the picturesque representations of Okinawa that formed its artistic heritage. Indeed, it was a legacy he engaged with profoundly, one that he located at the centre both of his artistic practice and the exploration of his own subjecthood:

> Tradition lies at the core of our creativity, it isn't something lurking in the shadows of a world continually looking back on the past . . . The infinite creativity of

human beings is what gives rise to tradition. Creativity requires both freedom and an awareness of one's own identity. Being aware of one's own identity, in turn, means having respect for the customs of the past: but when these customs, in the name of tradition, come to dominate the world of art, this is what I am irrevocably opposed to. For artists today, the most important thing of all is to follow our inner selves. Not to seek meaning in nature, or tradition, or to be influenced by the criticism of others. We must pursue our own path undaunted: and it is in this way that we keep tradition alive.[45]

For Adaniya, the duty of Okinawan artists was to delve within the body of tradition, to interrogate the figments of the art of the past, in order to salvage that which remained relevant to the present. He was advocating not just an intellectual response to the past but an emotional one. For Adaniya in particular, the subjectivity of the artist now lay at the core of the artistic enterprise. His objective, he declared, was to explore the question of Okinawan identity and to create an idiom in which to express it. He would stay loyal to this up until his death in 1967 at the young age of forty-six.

Modernism and the Move towards Abstraction

Post-war Okinawan painters, in particular the Five People Exhibition Group, would become central to the expression of post-war Okinawa: not simply its transformed landscapes, but also the gradual emergence of a new sense of Okinawan identity.

A co-founder of the group was Tamanaha Seikichi (1918–1984) who was both a sculptor, having studied under Ishii Tsuruzō (1887–1973), and a painter. Along with Adaniya and Ashimine he played a leading role in the post-war Okinawan art movement. His *Portrait of an Elderly Mother* (Figure 6.4) shows an elderly woman

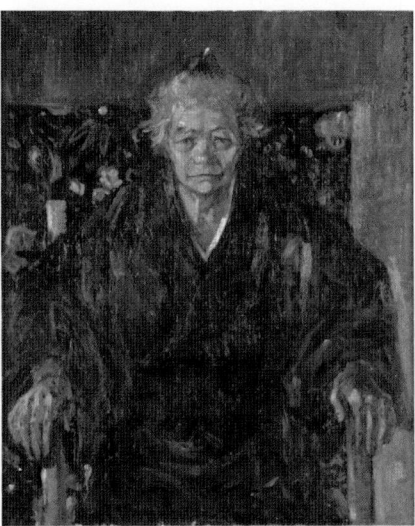

Figure 6.4 Tamanaha Seikichi, *Portrait of an Elderly Mother* (Rōbo-zō), 1954. Oil on canvas, 90.8 × 73.0 cm

Okinawa Prefectural Museum and Art Museum

in traditional Okinawan dress (*Ryūsō*) sitting in front of a *bingata* cloth hanging. The sculpted forms of her face convey not just the experience of age but the ravages of the past. Her large tattooed hands, that seemingly extend beyond the picture plane into reality, are both emphatic emblems of Okinawan tradition and, in their listless drooping, symbols of its disappearance. Set against—indeed largely obscuring, perhaps protecting—the vibrant forms of the traditional cloth that forms the backdrop to the image, the monumental figure appears almost braced in an act of self-defence, a challenge to the viewer seeking to appropriate and objectify a culture that alone gives meaning to her life. The painting was, in many ways, a moving response to Adaniya's call for artists to examine the vital connection between tradition and selfhood.

Like many painters anxious to avoid being 'souvenir' painters for Americans, Tamanaha worked throughout the 1950s to establish his own style.[46] *Portrait of an Elderly Mother*, a depiction of a member of his close family, clearly demonstrates his command of formal techniques, the powerful use of chiaroscuro for the face, the sculpted forms of the seated figure that verge on the abstract; the skin tones highlighted against the sombre hues of the garment and the loose brushwork that animates the still forms. But the power of the image lies in its emotional intensity, an intensity that abruptly forecloses the possibility of its assimilation as a 'traditional portrait' of an Okinawan woman.

Tamanaha's paintings would consistently focus on aspects of traditional Okinawan culture, betraying a continued fascination with the world around him. Yet his distinctive palette—dark reddish browns and deep ultramarine blues—set these works apart from the bright hues of earlier romanticized renditions of the Okinawan landscape, as did the rough application of the paint (often achieved through the use of a pallet knife) that countered any attempt to exoticize his subjects.

Intent on creating a more modernistic idiom, however, and influenced by his friend Adaniya, Tamanaha's paintings would gradually turn to abstraction. His increasingly stylized forms, far from a retreat from reality, served only to reinforce the emotional charge of his works. One particularly powerful example is *Shipwreck* from 1958 (Figure 6.5), in which jagged brown shapes appear to erupt from a dull mirror-like expanse of water, their sharply vectored lines crossing and clashing, refusing, as it were, to accept the erasure of history symbolized in the gradual oblivion of the shipwreck.

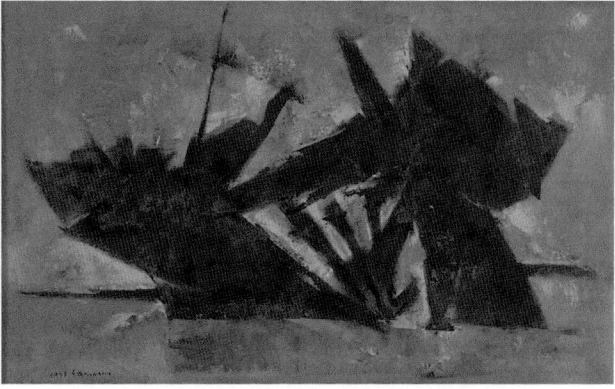

Figure 6.5 Tamanaha Seikichi, *Shipwrecks* (Hasen), 1958. Oil on canvas, 65.6 × 101.0 cm
Okinawa Prefectural Museum and Art Museum

These abstract forms facilitated the expression of the sense of devastation and abiding trauma in the wake of the Battle of Okinawa that literal representation was unable to achieve. He would employ the same strategy in his depiction of typical Okinawan *zushi game* (decorated pottery containers for storing the bones of one's ancestors), in which underlying themes of death and oblivion are reanimated through the savage angles of the abstract forms.

In 1966, Tamanaha wrote an essay published in the *Okinawa Times* entitled 'Path to the Headstone of a Grave' (*Bohyō he no michi*). In the essay he described returning to Okinawa on a U.S. ship, and seeing abandoned navy vessels. It was then, he wrote, that he experienced the emptiness and futility of war and it was this that henceforth informed his art.[47]

The blighted landscape left in the wake of the Battle of Okinawa, and represented in paintings such as *Shipwreck*, fundamentally rejected the romanticizing mainland gaze that had fashioned pre-war Okinawan art. These imageries of destruction became the new subject matter of Okinawan artists who wanted to express not simply what local people were seeing every day, but how it affected them. In his essay, 'About Sculpture' (*Chōkoku ni tsuite*), Tamanaha noted:

> Art is inevitably the conjunction in a single moment of the period, the artist, and the audience. I believe that art cannot exist without an audience, or without reference to its own particular period. Audiences desire not simply art, but art that reflects their own period. Paintings must reflect their period. It is through this that artists and audiences are brought together.[48]

Art was purposed not simply to appeal to the sensibilities of Okinawan people but to shock them into re-interrogating those sensibilities. It was to be a profound meditation not just on the past, but on the future.[49]

Another graduate of the Tokyo School of Fine Arts, Ashimine Kanemasa, studied under *yōga* master Fujishima Takeji (1867–1943). One of his most celebrated works, entitled *I am tired* (1950), was both an expression of Okinawan suffering in the wake of the war, and a sense of its abandonment by Japan. The image depicts a forlorn woman with red lipstick indicating that she is a sex worker, possibly servicing for the U.S. base. The figure is simultaneously the victim of abuse and a victim of betrayal: there is no one to protect her from both political and sexual subjugation. In many ways she was a symbol of Okinawa itself. It was a work that spoke to Ashimine's deep concern for the reality of contemporary life in post-war Okinawa. *Crowd* (1950) returns to the same theme (Figure 6.6). A seated group of young girls with drooping heads occupies the foreground, while in the background U.S. soldiers surround a larger group of women. These works were powerful expressions of contemporary social realities: of uncontested abuse and subjugation.

Over the following years, the situation in Okinawa would begin to change. By the mid-1950s, local opposition to U.S. policies in Okinawa was rising. In July 1955, when people in Ginowan village in the Isahama district had their land confiscated, farmers initiated a series of political demonstrations known as the Beggars' March (*kojiki kōshin*). Later that year, the rape and murder of a six-year-old girl by a 31-year-old American soldier stationed in Kadena Village led to further protests. Notoriously, these were met by the controversial Price Report, which justified the seizure of land from Okinawan citizens. It was at this moment that Okinawans' political awareness reached a peak,

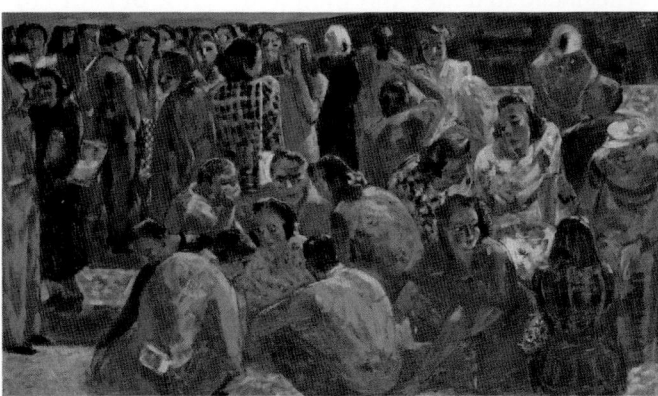

Figure 6.6 Ashimine Kanemasa, *Crowd* (Gunzō), 1950. Oil on canvas, 76.2 × 127.8 cm
Okinawa Prefectural Museum and Art Museum

and a movement began for reunification with Japan. It was over these same years that Okinawan artists produced some of their most politically challenging works.

Of all the second-generation Okinawan artists, the most influential was Adaniya Masayoshi, who had studied design in Tokyo and began oil painting after the war. Initially, under the influence of Fauvism and Cubism he depicted still lives and portraits of family and friends such as *Child Eating* (1951). Much like Tamanaha, however, he would gradually turn to abstract depictions of the contemporary landscape, as he wrestled with how to integrate complex social and political messages, particularly relating to the U.S. military bases, into his works.

Adaniya realized that the realistic and naturalistic idioms of academic painting that had once been used to document the 'primitivism' of Okinawa's landscape was unsuited to the depiction of its now drastically changed society. 'All Okinawan artists with a degree of sensitivity have internalized this question, and in their own different ways have struggled to resolve it,' he wrote.[50] His finest work is considered to be the series, *Tower* (1958) (Plate 7), which depicted the tower in a U.S. military base in terms of slim, barbed vertical lines that extend through and abruptly divide an otherwise empty picture space. The tower itself stands as a scar that dominates and divides the landscape, while the grey blue tones of the background, which consciously elide the traditional bright greens of the flora that characterized earlier landscapes, become simultaneously a metaphor of the erasure of Okinawa's lost cultural heritage. Adaniya would be repeatedly drawn to this motif:

> I was not interested in the U.S. base from a technical or modernist point of view, nor was I interested in depicting it literally. But whenever I thought about Okinawa, this was the vision that came to me. And this is the only way in which I was able to express it.[51]

During the 1960s, Adaniya continued to produce influential paintings of U.S. military bases, using stark geometrical lines to suggest the sense of emptiness that had replaced the former luxuriant landscape. Yet in *Nostalgia* (1965) (Figure 6.7), executed just two years before the artist's death, he looked at the landscape from the other side. Here,

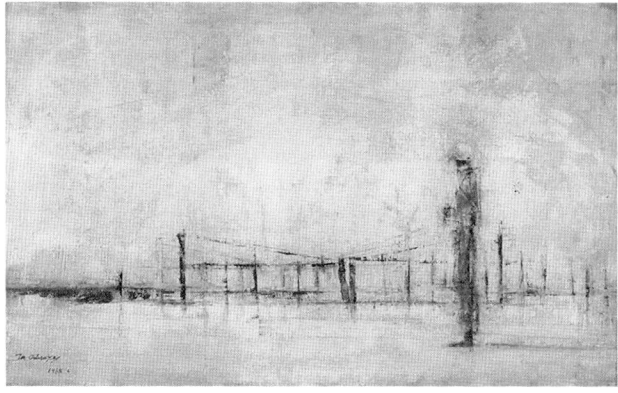

Figure 6.7 Adaniya Masayoshi, *Nostalgia* (Bōkyō), 1965. Oil on canvas, 73.3 × 107.3 cm
Okinawa Prefectural Museum and Art Museum

a U.S. soldier stands alone in front of a wire fence, the only physical feature of a picture space that dissolves into a whitish haze reminiscent of Turner's seascapes (which Adaniya confessed he was particularly drawn to).[52] It was an allusion to the loneliness, and the meaninglessness, of those involved in a war far from their home country. But more than this, it was a moment, perhaps, when Okinawan art began to understand itself in a wider, global context.

Conclusion

The search for a visual idiom to express the socio-political realities of Okinawan identity has been axiomatic to Okinawan art ever since the islands' return to Japanese sovereignty in the early Meiji era. The search has not been easy.

Almost up until the Second World War artists found themselves trapped, both unwittingly and wittingly, within modes of representation commandeered to express the political imperatives of mainland Japan. *Nihonga*, with its overt colonial associations, would be the most pernicious of these idioms, giving rise to works such as Yamada Shinzan's 1924 *Establishment of the Ryūkyū Domain* (1924), which celebrated the achievements of the new Meiji government.

By the early decades of the 20th century, however, as artists consciously moved to break free from the colonial appropriation of art, it was Western-style (*yōga*) painting that would come to dominate Okinawan artistic production. Yet ironically, *yōga* itself was enmeshed in mainland efforts to assimilate Japan to the Western world, to participate, on the world stage, as a progressive nation. It was this that made it such a compelling vehicle for aesthetic movements such as primitivism that romanticized less developed societies as tokens of a spirituality, or a ritualized connection to the earth lost in more developed nations.

It was in this context that mainland practitioners of *yōga*, such as Fujita Tsuguharu, would turn to Okinawa as representative of a lost world of primal energies, an exotic other: a symbol of what Japan itself had not just lost, but what it had left behind. Okinawa was relevant only in so far as it could be exploited as a romanticized token of alterity. It was in this same context that Okinawa's crafts—its distinctive lacquerware and dynamic *bingata* textiles—would garner the attention of mainland collectors and representatives of the *mingei* craft movement, who would celebrate these wares not in their own right but as embodiments of what Japan had once been: symbols of 'pure Japan', 'the origin of Japanese culture'.

Pre-war Okinawan artists such as Nadoyama Aijun and Ōmine Seikan struggled under the contradictions embodied in *yōga* painting, conscious both of the need to meet mainland expectations—to offer up exotic representations of the landscape to satisfy the colonial gaze—and of a duty to express the socio-political realities of contemporary Okinawa. Often their works would be marked by a nostalgia not for a lost paradise (the primitivist enterprise) but for a way of life that pre-dated the islands' colonization. It was not until the post-war generation of artists, however, that colonialist idioms would be finally rejected for a modernist aesthetic that facilitated the expression of Okinawa's dark political reality: in particular the devastation of war and the U.S. occupation.

Over the 20th century, Okinawan art has given witness to the experience of colonialism, war, and occupation. Its shifting idioms offer a testimony of the continued effort of artists to express, in the face of oppression, something of their social and political realities; to create works that give voice to the communal experience of loss and erasure. Their works warrant a place not simply in Okinawan art histories, nor even Japanese art histories. As expressions both of loss, and resistance in the face of some of the most pernicious events of the modern era, they take their place firmly in the context of a global art history.

Notes

1 Eric Hobsbawm, 'Introduction: Invention of Tradition', in *The Invention of Tradition*, ed. Eric Hobsbawn and Terence Ranger (Cambridge: Cambridge University Press, 2000), p. 1.
2 According to Shibuya Ken, 'Traditional landscapes, such as red roofing tiles with statues of an Okinawan lion had been disseminated and formalized only after the disappearance of thatched-roof houses after 1972 when Okinawa was returned to Japan from U.S. control.' Shibuya Ken, 'Anayā, nukiyā, surabuyā: Okinawa "Minka" no hensen' [Changes in Okinawan house architecture], *Ajia Yūgaku* no. 53 *Okinawa bunka no sōzō* [Intriguing ASIA no. 53: creation of Okinawan culture] (Tokyo: Bensei Publishing, 2003): 61–72, p. 70.
3 Terms such as *Hondo* (mainland) or *naichi* (inland/homeland) could be construed as discriminatory but will be used in this chapter, as they are widely used in Okinawa.
4 Eriko Tomizawa-Kay, 'Changes in the Japanese Art Market with the Emergence of the Middle-Class Collector: A Study of Hishida Shunsō (1874–1911)', *Journal of the History of Collections* 28, no. 2 (2016): 261–277, p. 261.
5 Anonymous, 'Yamada Shinzan-den' [Biography of Yamada Shinzan], *Ryūkyū no bunka* [Culture of Ryūkyū] 3 (1973): 123.
6 Anonymous, 'Gendai Okinawa no geijutsuka sono 4—chōkokuka/nihongaka, Yamada Shinzan' [Modern Okinawan Artist no. 4 – Sculptor/nihonga painter, Yamada Shinzan]. *Ryūkyū no bunka* [Culture of Ryūkyū] 3 (1973): 118.
7 Ōmine Seikan, *Watashi no sengoshi* [My history after the war] vol. 3 (Naha: Okinawa Times, 1980), p. 259.
8 Higa Chōken, 'Ryūkyū rekidai gafu, jō' [Biographies of Old Ryūkyūan Painters. Volume 1]. *Bijutsu Kenkyū* [the Journal of Art Studies] 45 (1935): 21–28.
  Higa Chōken, 'Ryūkyū rekidai gafu, ge' [Biographies of Old Ryūkyūan Painters. Volume 2]. *Bijutsu Kenkyū* [the Journal of Art Studies] 48 (1935): 23–34.
9 *Nijusseiki nihon jinmei jiten* [Encyclopaedia of Japanese people in the 20th century] (Nichigai Associates, 2004).

10 An abbreviation of *Monbushō bijutsu tenrankai*.
11 However, according to Nadoyama Aikō, son of Nadoyama Aijun, the latter initially studied at No. 2 Secondary School in Okinawa under Hara Yoshito from Japan, and, after Hara left, under Higa Keijō. Tomiyama Megumi, 'An Interview with Nadoyama Aikō', *Okinawa kenritsu hakubutsukan bijutsukan kiyō* [Bulletin of the Art Museum, Okinawa Prefectural Museum & Art Museum] 6 (2016): 104–116, p. 108.
12 Translation by Toshio Watanabe. In Toshio Watanabe, 'Japanese Landscape Painting and Taiwan: Modernity, Colonialism and National Identity', in *Refracted Modernity: Visual Culture and Identity in Colonial Taiwan*, ed. Yūko Kikuchi (Honolulu: University of Hawai'i Press, 2007), p. 73.
13 Toshio Watanabe discusses *yōga* and colonialism in Taiwan in 'Japanese Landscape Painting and Taiwan: Modernity, Colonialism and National Identity', in *Refracted Modernity: Visual Culture and Identity in Colonial Taiwan*, ed. Yūko Kikuchi (Honolulu: University of Hawai'i Press, 2007), pp. 72–73.
14 Hayashi Yōko, *Fujita Tsuguharu – Sakuhin wo hiraku* [Fujita Tsuguharu, exploring his works] (Nagoya: Nagoya University Press, 2008), p. 407.
15 Fujita Tsuguharu, 'Yume no kuni Ryūkyū (1)–(3)', *Asahi Shinbun*, June 5–7, 1938. Quoted in Hayashi Yōko, *Fujita Tsuguharu – Sakuhin wo hiraku* [Fujita Tsuguharu, exploring his works] (Nagoya: Nagoya University Press, 2008), p. 407.
16 The National Museum of Modern Art, Tokyo, *Okinawa purizumu 1872–2008* [Okinawa Prismed 1872–2008] (Tokyo: The National Museum of Modern Art, Tokyo, 2004), p. 32.
17 Kobayashi Junko, 'Okinawa no bijutsu: genzai made' [Okinawan art: up to the present], in *Bijutsu no nihon kingendaishi—seido, gensetu, zōkei* [Histories of modern and contemporary Japan through art: institutions, discourse, practice], eds. Kitazawa Noriaki, Satō Dōshin, and Mori Hitoshi (Tokyo: Tokyo shuppan, 2014), pp. 402–433, p. 414.
18 Haebaru Chōkō studied at the Nihon Art School and lived in Ikebukuro in Tokyo in the 1930s where he interacted with Yamanokuchi Baku. Further details are discussed in Okinawa Prefectural Museum and Art Museum ed. *Over the Wandering Sea: Artist from Okinawa, Haebaru Chōkō and World War II* (2017) and Itabashi Art Museum and Kyodo News eds. *Ikebukuro Montparnasse and Nishimui Art Village* (2018).
19 Yamanokuchi Baku, 'Mitsutani shi no "gajumaru no kage" to Fujitashi no "Ryūkyū bijin"' [Under the shade of *gajumaru* (banyan) trees' by Mr Mitsutani and 'Ryūkyūn beauties' by Mr Fujita], *Rekitei* no. 6 (1939): 17–21. Also, *Yamanokuchi Baku Zenshu*, vol. 3 (Tokyo: Shichōsha, 1975).
20 Personal correspondence with Japanese art historian Hayashi Yōko. (January 2018). Western attitudes to the 'exoticism' of Latin America are discussed in Kirkpatrick, Gwen. 'The Aesthetics of the Avant-Garde', in *Through the Kaleidoscope: The Experience of Modernity in Latin America*, ed. Vivian Schelling. (London: Verso, 2001), pp. 183–184. See also Kikuchi, Yūko, *Japanese Modernisation and Mingei Theory: Cultural Nationalism and Oriental Orientalism* (London: RoutledgeCurzon, 2004), p. 148.
21 Ōmine Seikan, *Watashi no sengoshi* [My history after the war], vol. 3, p. 263.
22 Known as the Teiten, or *Teikoku Bijutsu-in Tenrankai*.
23 It is known that *yōga* painter Kanayama Heizo (1883–1964) suggested to Nadoyama Aijun to depict Okinawan local colour. Onaga Naoki, 'Jiko hyōgen wo motomete: tukurareta shutai kara no dakkyaku' [Aspiring to self-expression: escape from artificial subjectivity], in *Okinawa bunka no kiseki 1872–2007* [The trace of Okinawan culture 1972–2007], p. 18.
24 See Adachi Gen, 'War and Pornography', in the present volume.
25 Tan'o Yasunori and Kawata Akihisa, *Imēji no naka no sensō* [War in images] (Tokyo: Iwanami shoten, 1996), pp. 37–38.
26 Yanagi Muneyoshi, 'Kōgei no michi' [The way of crafts], in *Yanagi Muneyoshi zenshū* [Collected works of Yanagi Muneyoshi], vol. 8 (Tokyo: Chikuma Shobō, 1981), p. 91.
27 Yakabi Osamu, 'Kindai Okinawa zō no hyōshō to kumikae' [Reconstructing the image of modern Okinawa], in *Okinawa bunka no kiseki 1872–2007* [The trace of Okinawan culture 1972–2007], ed. Okinawa Prefectural Museum & Art Museum (Naha: Okinawa Prefectural Museum & Art Museum, 2007), pp. 36–41.
28 However, Takami Hirotaka suggests that Yanagita thought mainland-Japanese culture was distinct from that of Okinawa in ethnological terms, but felt the need to unite the

people in the Japanese archipelago as a single nation, from an ethnogenesis point of view. Takami Hirotaka, *Yanagita Kunio to Seijō/Okinawa/Kokugakuin* [Yanagita Kunio and the relationship with the Seijō region, Okinawa and Kokugakuin University] (Tokyo: Hanawa Shobō, 2010).

29 Kim Brandt, 'Object of Desire: Japanese Collectors and Colonial Korea', *Positions: East Asia Cultures Critique* 8, no. 3 (Winter 2000): 711–746, p. 740. Also, Yūko Kikuchi discusses the complicit relationship between Japanese cultural nationalism and modern Western Orientalism in the development of *Mingei* theory from its beginnings in the 1910s to the end of the 20th century. Kikuchi, Yūko. *Japanese Modernisation and Mingei Theory: Cultural Nationalism and Oriental Orientalism*. London: RoutledgeCurzon, 2004.

30 Okuma Seisaku, 'Okinwasen to bijutsu' [The Battle of Okinawa and its art], *Bijutsushi kenkyū* no. 26 (2008): 137–158.

31 Sakurazawa Makoto, *Okinawa Gendaishi—Beikokutōchi hondo fukki kara ōru Okinawa made* [Modern Okinawan history: from U.S. occupation, reversion to Japan to 'all Okinawa']. (Tokyo: Chūōshinsho, 2015), p. 8.

32 Hoshi Masahiko, 'Yasutarō to Kashō no gyōseki kara mietekuru mono' [Points which can be seen from the achievements of Yasutarō and Kashō], in *Hōjun no bi wo motomete—Kinjō Yasutarō to Takahata Kashō* [Seeking abundant beauties: Kinjō Yasutarō to Takahata Kashō], ed. Editorial committees of *Hōjun no bi o motomete* (Okinawa: Okinawa Times, 2009), pp. 65–71, p. 66.

33 Onaga Naoki, 'Senryō to bunka' [Occupation and culture], in *Idō to hyōgen: henyōsuru shintai, gengo, bunka* [Translation and expression: changing body, language and culture], ed. Okinawa Prefectural Museum & Art Museum (Naha: Okinawa bunka no mori, 2009), p. 11.

34 The U.S. would subsequently enact a number of soft measures aimed at recreating the distinctive Okinawan cultural identity that decades of Japanese assimilation had sought to erase, in an effort to drive a deep ethnic wedge between the island and the mainland. These measures, aimed at assisting the establishment of democratic government in Okinawa, included societies for the promotion of cultural activities and for the protection of the island's artistic heritage. Office of the Chief of Naval Operations, Navy Department Civil Affairs Handbook, Ryūkyū (Loochoo) Islands OPNAV13–31 (Hawaii: U.S. Office of the Chief of Naval Operations, 1944).

35 Miyagi Etsujirō, 'Amerika bunka to sengo Okinawa' [American culture and post-war Okinawa], in *Sengo okinawa to amerika* [Post-war Okinawa and the United States], ed. Teruya Yoshihiko and Yamazato Katsunori (Naha: Okinawa Times, 1995), pp. 20–21. Also, Stanley A. Steinberg vividly describes his friendship with Okinawan young artists, Tamanaha Seikichi, Ashimine Kanemasa, and Adaniya Masayoshi, in his essay, 'Nishimui Remembered' in *Idō to hyōgen: henyōsuru shintai, gengo, bunka* [Translation and expression: changing body, language, and culture], pp. 106–108.

36 Ōmine Shinichi, 'Sengo kaikoroku' [Memoirs of post-war period], *Ryūkyū no bunka* [Culture of Ryukū] 1 (1972): 121.

37 Makiminato Atsuzō, 'Ōmine Seikan san no koto' [About Mr Ōmine Seikan], *Shinsei Bijutsu* [New birth of art] no. 7 (Urasoe: Shinsei bijustu kyōkai, 1988), p. 52.

38 Nakazato Yasuhiro, 'Ōmine Seikan Gagyō no hensen to akagawara: Ōmine ga motometa fūkeiga to sono rōkarusei ni tsuite' [Ōmine Seikan's changes of works and red roof tiles: his ideal landscape and localism], *Bulletin of the Art Museum, Okinawa Prefectural Museums & Art Museum* 5 (1988): 82–92, p. 85.

39 See the Nishihara official website: www.town.nishihara.okinawa.jp/asset/nishihara_tower.html (accessed October 20, 2017).

40 Naoko Pontillo, 'Memories of My Father, Seikan Ōmine' [Occupation and culture], trans. Roberta Pontillo, in *Idō to hyōgen: henyōsuru shintai, gengo, bunka* [Translation and expression: changing body, language, and culture], pp. 26–28, p. 28.

41 Toyohira Ryōken (Okinawa Times), and painters, Ōshiro Kōya, Ōmine Seikan, Nadoyama Aijun, and Yamamoto Keiichi were engaged as judges for the first Okiten exhibition. Kinjō Yasutarō, Gushiken Itoku, Adaniya Masayoshi, Ashimine Kanesamasa, Tamanaha Seikichi, Yabu Ken, and Ōmine Shinichi, among others—a total of fifteen artists—were invited to exhibit their works without judges. Ōmine Seikan, 'Sengo Okinawa no bijutsu

katsudō' [Art activities in post-war Okinawa], *Ryūkyū no bunka* [Culture of Ryukū] 1 (1972): 115–120, p. 115.
42 Ōshiro Seitoku, 'Nishimui bijutsu mura tuisō' [Memoir of Nishimui art village], *Shinsei Bijutsu* [Shinsei art magazine] 10 (1992): 118–123.
43 Adaniya Masayoshi, 'Okinawa gadan no kongo no mondai' [The Okinawan art world's future problem], *Kyō no ryūkyū* (Today's Ryūkyū) 2, no. 2 (1959), p. 17, reprinted in *Adaniya Masayoshi e to bun* [Adaniya Masayoshi: paintings and essays], ed. Adaniya Masayoshi sakuhinshū kankōkai (1973), p. 20.
44 Ibid.
45 Adaniya Masayoshi. 'Dentō to wa nani ka—Keida Kiichi shi no "Gendai kaiga no dentō sei" wo yonde' [What is tradition? After reading 'Tradition of modern painting' written by Mr Keida Kiichi]. Okinawa Times, 1957, reprinted in *Adaniya Masayoshi e to bun* [Adaniya Masayoshi: paintings and essays], ed. Adaniya Masayoshi sakuhinshū kankōkai (1973), p. 19.
46 His American customer and friend, Stanley Steinburg, said 'Painting souvenirs was not their desire but they were also pleased that they could paint at all. After the American soldiers left, some artists would reveal their mixed feelings. However, it was necessary for them to earn money to support their family.' Tsuchie Makiko, 'Nishimui (1948–1950) he mukatte' [Toward Nishimui (1948–1950)], in *Idō to hyōgen: henyōsuru shintai, gengo, bunka* [Translation and expression: changing body, language and culture], p. 19.
47 Tamanaha Seikichi, 'Bohyō he no michi' [The path to a gravestone], in *Okinawa Times*, 24 April 1966.
48 Tamanaha Seikichi, 'Chōkoku ni tsuite—shutoshite kanshō wo chūsin ni' [About sculpture—mainly for appreciation], in *Okinawa kindai chōkoku no ishizue—Tamanaha Seikichi: Chōkoku to kaiga no kiseki* [Exhibition of Tamanaha Seikichi, pioneer of modern sculpture in Okinawa: a record in sculpture and painting], ed. Okinawa Prefectural Museum & Art Museum (Naha: Okinawa Prefectural Museum & Art Museum, 2012), p. 159.
49 *Okinawa hontō* (Okinawa Main Island) is the focus of this essay; the author uses the term 'Okinawan' for everything that has roots in the Ryūkyū Islands.
50 Adaniya Masayoshi, 'Okinawa gadan to sono shōrai—Geijutsu senshō jushō wo jiten to suru' [Okinawan art world and its future: at the moment of winning the Selected Art Award], *Shin Okinawa Bungaku* [New Okinawan literature] no. 5 (April 1967), reprinted in *Adaniya Masayoshi–Modanizumu no yukue*, pp. 157–168, p. 158. Quoted from Nakazato Isao, 'Colonial Cultural Politics and Aporias', trans. Robin Thompson, in *The Tracks of Okinawan Culture, 1872–2007*, p. 385.
51 Adaniya Masayoshi sakuhinshū kankōkai, ed., *Adaniya Masayoshi e to bun* [Adaniya Masayoshi: paintings and essays], p. 23. First printed in Adaniya Masayoshi, 'Okinawa to Tokyo no kyori – Forumu garō no koten o oete' [A distance between Okinawa and Tokyo: after solo-exhibition at Forum Gallery], *Okinawa Times*, 25–27 December 1963.
52 Adaniya Masayoshi sakuhinshū kankōkai, ed., *Adaniya Masayoshi e to bun* [Adaniya Masayoshi: paintings and essays]. p. 48. First printed in Adaniya Masayoshi, 'Tabi no oboegaki' [Memo for my travel], *Kyō no Ryūkyū* [Today's Ryūkyū] (1961).

Bibliography

Adachi Gen. 'War and Pornography'. In *East Asian Art History in a Transnational Context*, edited by Eriko Tomizawa-Kay and Toshio Watanabe. London: Routledge, 2018.
Adaniya Masayoshi. 'Dentō to wa nani ka—Keida Kiichi shi no "Gendai kaiga no dentōsei" o yonde' [What is tradition? After reading 'Tradition of modern painting' written by Mr Keida Kiichi]. *Okinawa Times*, 1957. Quoted in *Adaniya Masayoshi—e to bun* [Adaniya Masayoshi: his paintings and essays], edited by Adaniya Masayoshi sakuhinshū kankō-kai, 18–19. Naha: Adaniya Masayoshi sakuhinshū kankō-kai, 1973.
———. 'Okinawa gadan no kongo no mondai' [Okinawan art world's future problem]. *Kyō no ryūkyū* [Contemporary Ryūkyū] 2, no. 2 (1959).

———. 'Okinawa to Tokyo no kyori—Fōrumu garō no koten wo oete' [A distance between Okinawa and Tokyo: after solo-exhibition at Forum Gallery]. *Okinawa Times*, December 27, 1963.

———. 'Okinawa gadan no tenbō to sono shōrai—Geijutsu senshō jushō o jiten to suru' [Okinawan art world and its future: at the moment of winning the Selected Art Award]. In *Adaniya Masayoshi–Modanizumu no yukue* [Adaniya Masayoshi: the path of modernism], edited by Okinawa Prefectural Museum & Art Museum, 157–168. Naha: Okinawa bunka no mori, 2011. First published in *Shin Okinawan Bungaku* [New Okinawan literature] no. 5 Spring: Geijutsu senshō tokushū [Special issue for the Selected Art Award]. Okinawa: Okinawa Times, 1967, pp. 136–149.

———. 'Tabi no oboegaki' [Memo for my travel]. *Kyō no Ryūkyū* [Contemporary Ryūkyū]. Naha: Ryūkū rettō beikoku seifu shōgai hōdōkyoku, 1961. Quoted in *Adaniya Masayoshi—Modanizumu no yukue* [Adaniya Masayoshi: the path of modernism], edited by Okinawa Prefectural Museum & Art Museum, 86. Naha: Okinawa bunka no mori, 2011.

Adaniya Masayoshi sakuhinshū kankō-kai, ed. *Adaniya Masayoshi—e to bun* [Adaniya Masayoshi: his paintings and essays]. Naha: Adaniya Masayoshi sakuhinshū kankō-kai, 1973.

Anonymous. 'Yamada Shinzan-den' [Biography of Yamada Shinzan]. *Ryūkyū no bunka* [Culture of Ryūkyū] no. 3 (1973).

Brandt, Kim. 'Object of Desire: Japanese Collectors and Colonial Korea'. *Positions: East Asia Cultures Critique* 8, no. 3 (Winter 2000): 711–746.

Fujita Tsuguharu. 'Yume no kuni Ryūkyū (1)–(3)' [A dream country, Ryūkyū]. *Asahi Shinbun*. June 5–7, 1938.

Hayashi Yōko. *Fujita Tsuguharu sakuhin wo hiraku—tabi, teshigoto, Nihon* [Fujita Tsuguharu's works: travel, handwork and Japan]. Nagoya: Nagoya daigaku shuppankai, 2008.

Higa Chōken. 'Ryūkyū rekidai gafu, jō' [Biographies of Old Ryūkyūan Painters. Volume 1]. *Bijutsu Kenkyū* [the Journal of Art Studies] 45 (1935): 21–28.

———. 'Ryūkyū rekidai gafu, ge' [Biographies of old Ryūkyūan painters. Volume 2]. *Bijutsu Kenkyū* [the Journal of Art Studies] 48 (1935): 23–34.

Hobsbawm, Eric. 'Introduction: Invention of Tradition'. In *The Invention of Tradition*, edited by Eric Hobsbawn and Terence Ranger. Cambridge: Cambridge University Press, First published 1983, Reprinted 2000.

Hoshi Masahiko. 'Yasutarō to Kashō no gyōseki kara mietekuru mono' [Points that can be seen from the achievements of Yasutarō and Kashō]. In *Hōjun no bi o motomete—Kinjō Yasutarō to Takahata Kashō* [Seeking abundant beauties: Kinjō Yasutarō and Takahata Kashō], edited by Henshū Iinkai. Okinawa: Okinawa Times, 2009.

Itabashi Art Museum and Kyodo News eds. *Ikebukuro monparunasu to nishimui bijutsu mura* [Ikebukuro Montparnasse and Nishimui Art Village]. Tokyo: Kyodo News, 2018.

Kikuchi, Yūko. *Japanese Modernisation and Mingei Theory: Cultural Nationalism and Oriental Orientalism*. London: RoutledgeCurzon, 2004.

Kirkpatrick, Gwen. 'The Aesthetics of the Avant-Garde'. In *Through the Kaleidoscope: The Experience of Modernity in Latin America*, edited by Vivian Schelling. London: Verso, 2001.

Kobayashi Junko. 'Okinawa no bijutsu: genzai made' [Okinawan art: up to now]. In *Bijutsu no nihon kingendaishi—seido, gensetu, zōkei* [Histories of modern and contemporary Japan thorough art: institutions, discourse, and practice], edited by Kitazawa Noriaki, Satō Dōshin, and Mori Hitoshi, 402–433. Tokyo: Tōkyō shuppan, 2014.

Makiminato Atsuzō. 'Ōmine Seikan san no koto' [About Mr Ōmine Seikan]. *Shinsei Bijutsu* [Shinsei art magazine] 7 (1988): 52.

Miyagi Etsujirō. 'Amerika bunka to sengo Okinawa' [American culture and post-war Okinawa]. In *Sengo okinwa to amerika* [Post-war Okinawa and the United States of America], edited by Teruya Yoshihiko and Yamazato Katsunori, 20–21. Naha: Okinawa Times, 1995.

Naha-shi bunkakyoku bunka shinkō shitsu ed. *Sengo gojūnen 1945–1995 Okinawa no bijutsu* [The fine arts of Okinawa 1945–1995]. Naha: Naha City, 1995.

Nakazato Isao. 'Colonial Cultural Politics and Aporias', translated by Robin Thompson. In *Okinawa bunka no kiseki 1872–2007* [The trace of Okinawan culture 1972–2007], edited by Okinawa Prefectural Museum & Art Museum, 384–386. Naha: Okinawa Prefectural Museum and Art Museum, 2007.

Nakazato Yasuhiro. 'Ōmine Seikan gagyō no hensen to akagawara—Ōmine ga motometa fūkeiga to sono rōkarusei ni tsuite' [Ōmine Seikan's changes of works and red-roof tiles: his ideal landscape and localism]. *Bulletin of the Art Museum, Okinawa Prefectural Museums & Art Museum* 5 (1988): 82–92.

Namihira Tsuneo. *Kindai higashi asia shi no naka no ryūkyū heigō* [Ryūkyū annexation in modern East Asian history]. Tokyo: Iwanami shoten, 2014.

The National Museum of Modern Art, Tokyo, ed. *Okinawa purizumu 1872–2008* [Okinawa prismed 1872–2008]. Tokyo: The National Museum of Modern Art, 2004.

Nijusseiki nihon jinmei jiten [Encyclopaedia of Japanese people in the 20th century]. Tokyo: Nichigai Associates, 2004.

Nishihara Town official website (www.town.nishihara.okinawa.jp/asset/nishihara_tower.html) (Accessed October 20, 2017).

Office of the Chief of Naval Operations, ed. *Navy Department Civil Affairs Handbook, Ryūkyū (Loochoo) Islands OPNAV13–31*. Hawaii: U.S. Office of the Chief of Naval Operations, 1944.

Okinawaken kankō bunkakyoku bunka shinkō-ka, ed. *Taiheiyō sensō/Okinawasen shūketsu gojusshūnen jigyō: Okinawa kingendai bijutsuka ten—Okinawa sengo bijutsu no nagare (1) modanizumu no keifu* [Projects commemorating the 50th anniversary of the end of Pacific War and the Battle of Okinawa: exhibition of contemporary Okinawan artists—trend of Okinawan post-war arts, series 1, the lineage of Modernism]. Urasoe: Okinawa prefecture, 1995.

Okinawaken kankō bunkakyoku bunka shinkō-ka, ed. *Taiheiyō sensō/Okinawasen shūketsu gojusshūnen jigyō: Okinawa kingendai bijutsuka ten—Okinawa sengo bijutsu no nagare (2) koyūsei he no kodawari* [Projects commemorating the 50th anniversary of the end of Pacific War and the Battle of Okinawa: exhibition of contemporary Okinawan artists—trend of Okinawan post-war arts, series 2, the indigenous character]. Urasoe: Okinawa prefecture, 1995.

Okinawa Prefectural Museum and Art Museum ed. *Hōkōno umi: Tabisuru gaka—Haebaru Chōkō to Taiwan, Okinawa* [Over the wandering sea: artist from Okinawa, Haebaru Choko and World War II], Naha: Okinawa Prefectural Museum and Art Museum, 2017.

Okuma Seisaku. 'Okinwasen to bijutsu' [The Battle of Okinawa and its art]. *Bijutsushi kenkyū* [Study of art history] 46 (2008): 137–158.

Ōmine Seikan. 'Sengo Okinawa no bijutsu katsudō' [Art activities in post-war Okinawa]. *Ryūkyū no bunka* [Culture of Ryukū] 1 (1972): 115–120.

———. *Watashi no sengoshi* [My post-war history] *vol. 3*. Naha: Okinawa Times, 1980.

Ōmine Shinichi. 'Sengo kaikoroku' [Memoirs of post-war period]. *Ryūkyū no bunka* [Culture of Ryukū] 1 (1972): 121.

Onaga Naoki. 'Jiko hyōgen wo motomete: tukurareta shutai kara no dakkyaku' [Aspiring to self-expression: escape from artificial subjectivity]. In *Okinawa bunka no kiseki 1872–2007* [The trace of Okinawan culture 1972–2007], edited by Okinawa Prefectural Museum and Art Museum. Naha: Okinawa Prefectural Museum and Art Museum, 2007.

———. 'Senryō to bunka' [Occupation and culture]. In *Idō to hyōgen: henyōsuru shintai, gengo, bunka* [Translation and expression: changing body, language and culture], edited by Okinawa Prefectural Museum & Art Museum. Naha: Okinawa bunka no mori, 2009.

Ōshiro Seitoku. 'Kaiga ni okeru rōkarizumu to kurima' [Localism and climate in painting]. *Shinsei bijutsu* [Shinsei art magazine] 1 (1982): 11–15.

———. 'Nishimui bijutsu mura tuisō' [Memoir of Nishimui Art Village]. *Shinsei Bijutsu* [Shinsei art magazine] 10 (1992): 118–123.

Ōshiro Tatsuhiro. 'Tsuioku no Adaniya Masayoshi' [Reminiscences of Adaniya Masayoshi]. In *Adaniya Masayoshi Modanizumu no yukue* [Adaniya Masayoshi: the path of modernism], edited by Okinawa Prefectural Museum & Art Museum. Naha: Okinawa bunka no mori, 2011.

Pontillo, Naoko. 'Memories of My Father, Seikan Ōmine', translated by Roberta Pontillo. In *Idō to hyōgen: henyōsuru shintai, gengo, bunka* [Translation and expression: changing body, language and culture], edited by Okinawa Prefectural Museum & Art Museum, 26–28. Naha: Okinawa bunka no mori, 2009.

Ryūkyū daigaku kyōikugakubu bijutsu kōgeika, ed. Ryūkyū daigaku taikan kinen—Ashimine Kanemasa gashū [Paintings of Ashimine Kanemasa in commemoration of his retirement at Ryūkyū University]. Naha: Ashimine Kanemasa, 1982.

Ryūkyū seifuritsu hakubutsukan, ed. Adaniya Masayoshi Isakuten [Retrospective exhibition of Adaniya Masayoshi]. Naha: Ryūkyū seifuritsu hakubutsukan, 1969.

Sakurazawa Makoto. *Okinawa Gendaishi—Beikokutōchi hondo fukki kara ōru Okinawa made* [Modern Okinawan history: from US occupation, the reversion of Okinawa to 'all Okinawa']. Tokyo: Chūōshinsho, 2015.

Satō, Dōshin. *Modern Japanese Art and the Meiji State: The Politics of Beauty*, translated by Nara Hiroshi. Los Angeles: Getty Research Institute, 2011.

Shibuya Ken. 'Anayā, nukiyā, surabuyā—Okinawa 'Minka' no hensen' [Changes in Okinawan house architecture]. In *Ajia Yūgaku* no. 53: *Okinawa bunka no sōzō* [Intriguing ASIA no. 53: Creation of Okinawan culture] (2003): 61–72.

Shin Okinawan Bungaku [New Okinawan literature]—*Geijutsu senshō tokushū* [Special issue for the Selected Art Award], no. 5 Spring. Okinawa: Okinawa Times, 1967.

Steinberg, Stanley A. 'Nishimui Remembered'. In *Idō to hyōgen—henyōsuru shintai, gengo, bunka* [Translation and expression: changing body, language and culture], edited by Okinawa Prefectural Museum & Art Museum, 106–108. Naha: Okinawa bunka no mori, 2009.

Takami Hirotaka. *Yanagita Kunio to Seijō/Okinawa/Kokugakuin* [Yanagita Kunio and the relationship with the Seijō region, Okinawa and Kokugakuin University]. Tokyo: Hanawa Shobō, 2010.

Tamanaha Seikichi. 'Bohyō he no michi' [Way to burial marker]. In *Exhibition of Tamanaha Seikichi, Pioneer of Modern Sculpture in Okinawa: A Record in Sculpture and Painting*, edited by Okinawa Prefectural Museum & Art Museum, 96. Naha: Okinawa Prefectural Museum & Art Museum, 2012. First published in Tamanaha Seikichi, 'Bohyō he no michi' [Way to burial marker], *Okinawa Times*, April 24 1966.

———. Chōkoku ni tsuite—shutoshite kanshō wo chūsin ni [About sculpture: mainly for appreciation]. In *Okinawa kindai chōkoku no ishizue—Tamanaha Seikichi: Chōkoku to kaiga no kiseki* [Exhibition of Tamanaha Seikichi, pioneer of modern sculpture in Okinawa: a record in sculpture and painting], edited by Okinawa Prefectural Museum & Art Museum, 159–160. Naha: Okinawa Prefectural Museum & Art Museum, 2012.

Tan'o Yasunori and Kawata Akihisa. *Imēji no nakano sensō* [War in images]. Tokyo: Iwanami shoten, 1996.

Tinello, Marco. *Seikaishi kara mita Ryūkyū shobun* [Ryūkyū annexation from the view of world history]. *Ryūkyū Library* 30. Ginowan: Gajumaru shorin, 2017.

Tomiyama Megumi. 'An Interview with Nadoyama Aikō'. *Okinawa kenritsu hakubutsukan bijutuskan kiyō* [Bulletin of the Art Museum Okinawa Prefectural Museum & Art Museum] no. 6 (2016): 104–116.

Tomizawa-Kay, Eriko. 'Changes in the Japanese Art Market with the Emergence of the Middle-Class Collector: A Study of Hishida Shunsō (1874–1911)'. *Journal of the History of Collections* 28, no. 2 (2016): 261–277.

Tsuchie Makiko. 'Nishimui (1948–1950) he mukatte' [Toward Nishimui (1948–1950)]. In *Idō to hyōgen: henyōsuru shintai, gengo, bunka* [Translation and expression: changing body, language and culture], edited by Okinawa Prefectural Museum & Art Museum. Naha: Okinawa bunka no mori, 2009.

Watanabe, Toshio. 'Japanese Landscape Painting and Taiwan: Modernity, Colonialism and National Identity'. In *Refracted Modernity: Visual Culture and Identity in Colonial Taiwan*, edited by Kikuchi, Yūko, 67–81. Honolulu: University of Hawai'i Press, 2007.

Yakabi Osamu. 'Kindai Okinawa zō no hyōshō to kumikae' [Reconstructing the image of modern Okinawa]. In *Okinawa bunka no kiseki 1872–2007* [The trace of Okinawan culture 1972–2007], edited by Okinawa Prefectural Museum & Art Museum. Naha: Okinawa Prefectural Museum & Art Museum, 2007.

Yamanokuchi Baku. 'Mitsutani shi no "gajumaru no kage" to Fujita shi no "Ryūkyū bijin"' ['Under the shade of gajumaru tree' by Mr Mitsutani and 'Ryūkyūan Beauty' by Mr Fujita]. *Rekitei* no. 6 (1939): 17–21. Also, in Yamanokuchi Baku Zenshu 3, 22–27. Tokyo: Shichōsha, 1975.

Yanagi Muneyoshi, *Yanagi Muneyoshi Zenshū* [Collected works of Yanagi Muneyoshi], vol. 8. Tokyo: Chikuma Shobō, 1981.

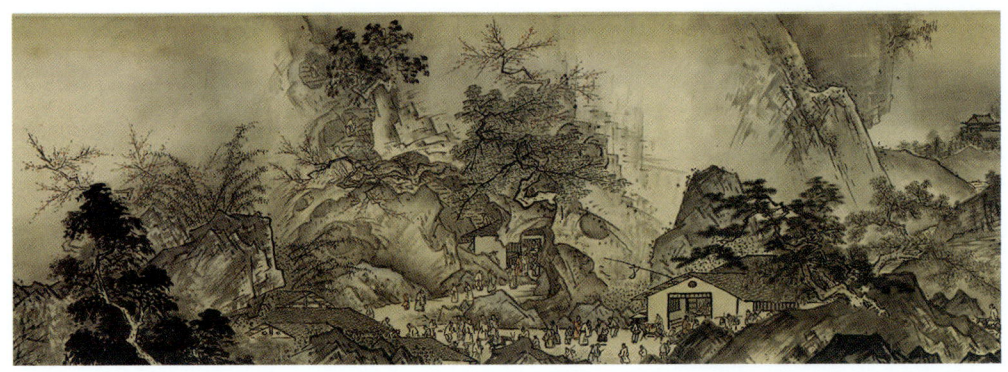

Plate 1 Sesshū, *Long Landscape Scroll* (Sansui chōkan) (detail), 1486 (Muromachi period). Ink and light colour on paper, 39.8 × 1580.2 cm. Mōri Museum

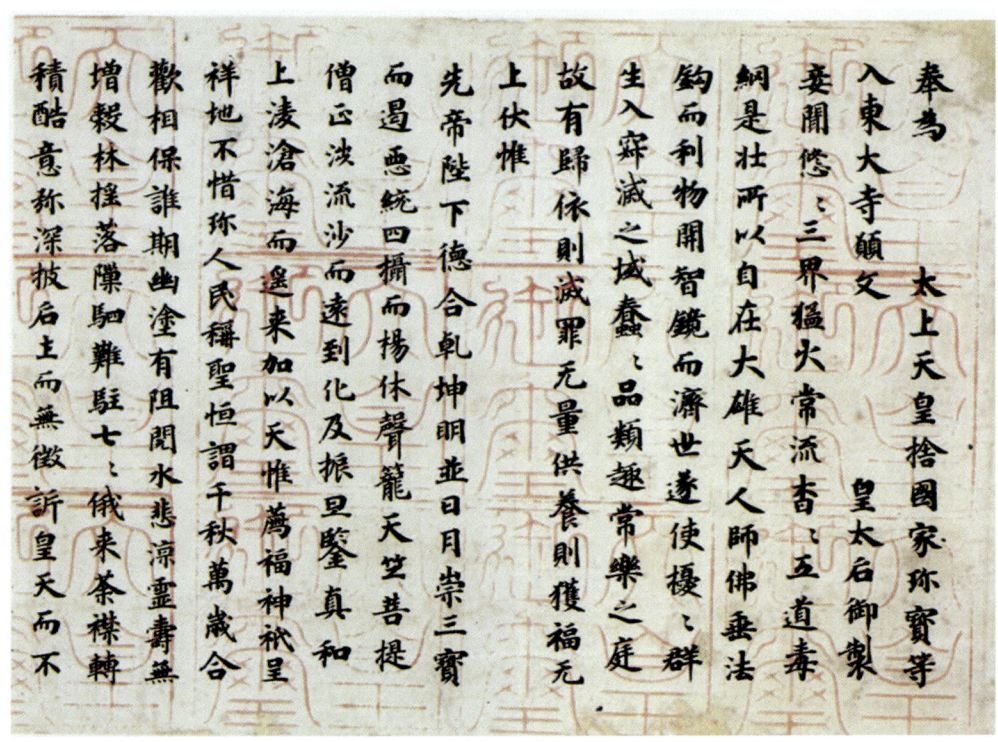

Plate 2 *Catalogue of State Treasures* (Kokka chinpō chō), 756. Ink on paper, 25.9 × 1474.0 cm. Collection of the Shōsōin, North Warehouse

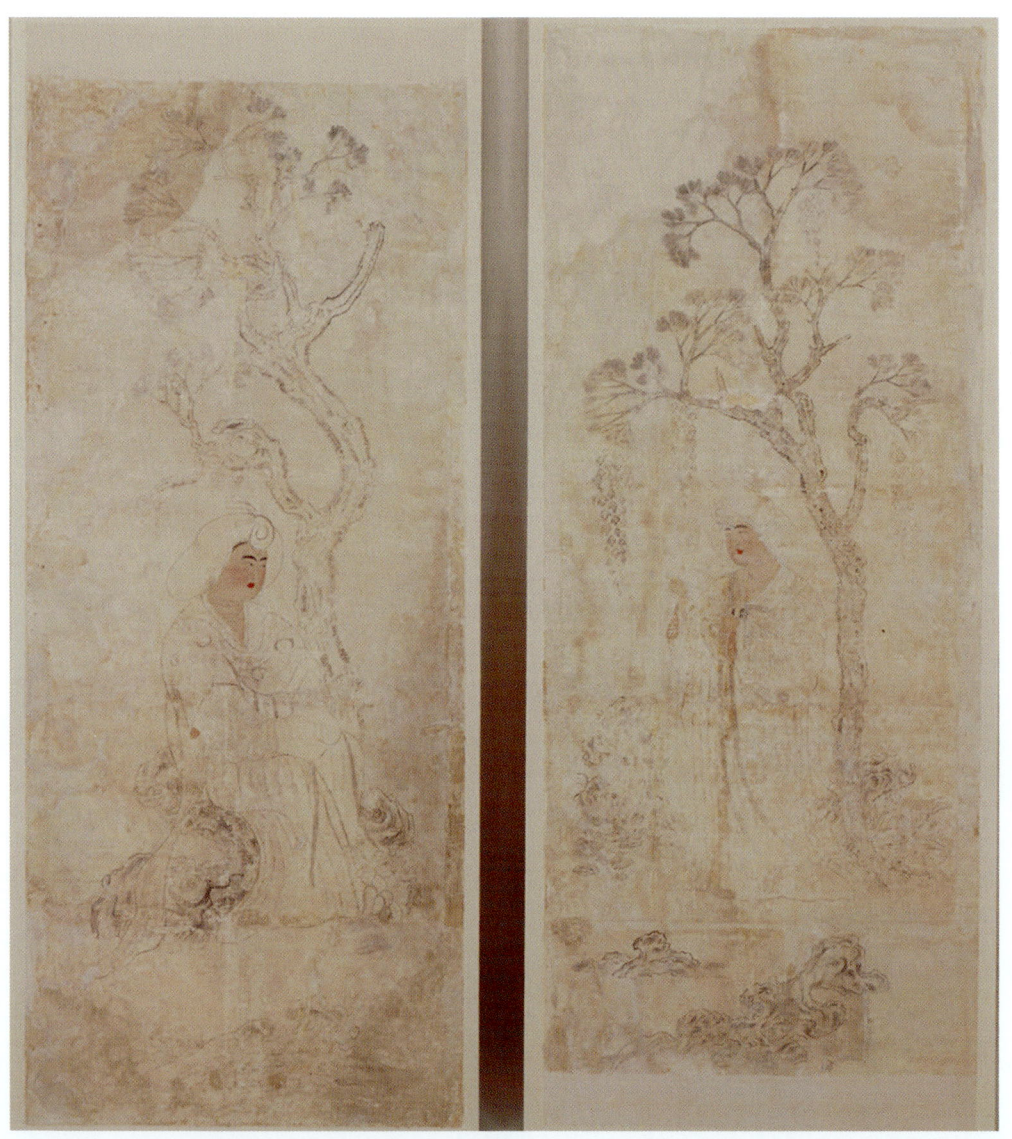

Plate 3 Beauties Beneath Trees, detail (Torige ryūjo zu byōbu), Nara period. Folding screen, polychrome paint on white ground with *yamadori* feathers. 136.0 × 56.0 cm. Collection of the Shōsōin, North Warehouse

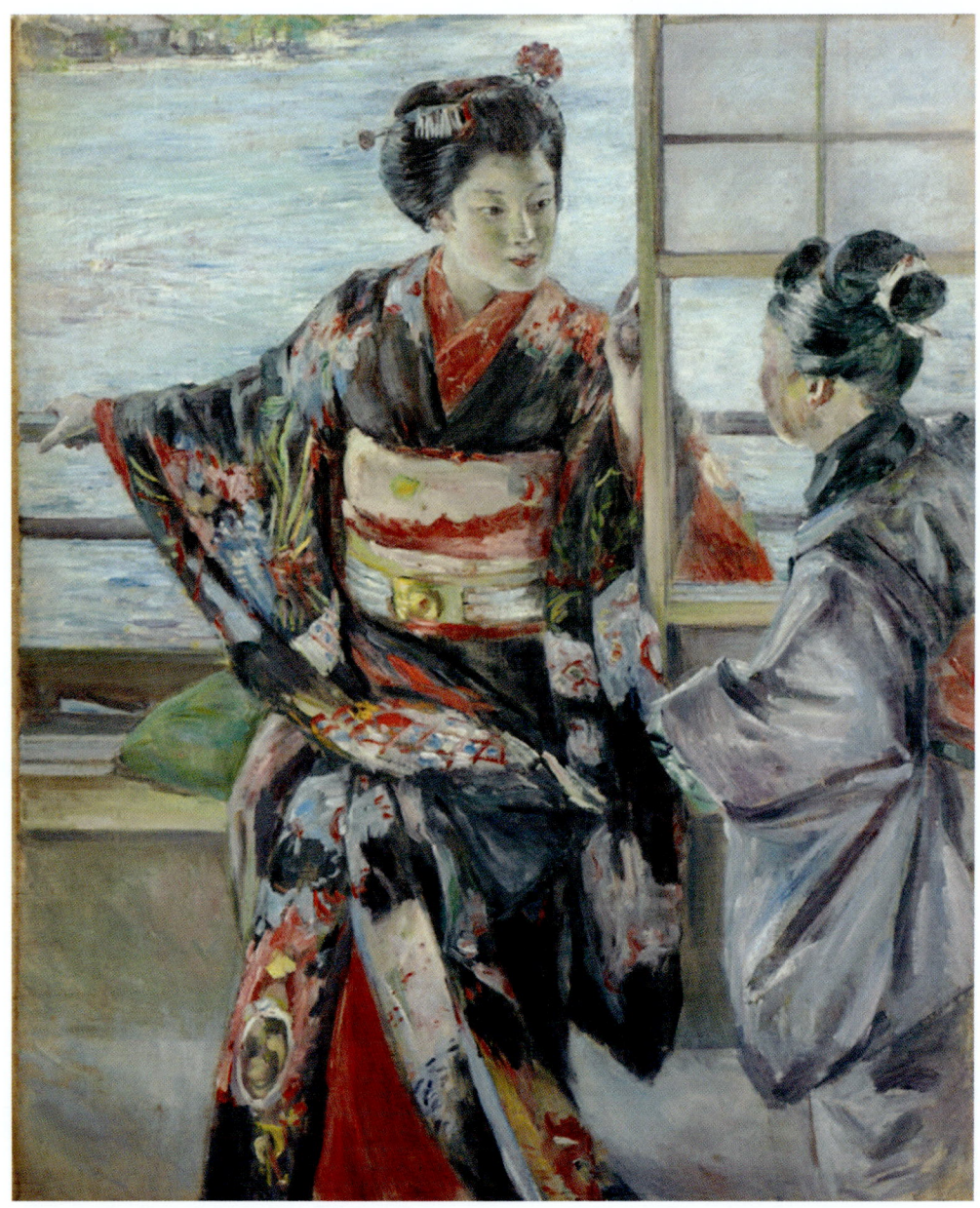

Plate 4 Kuroda Seiki, *Maïko, Dancing Girl* (Maïko), 1893. Oil on canvas, 80.4 × 65.3 cm. Tokyo National Museum

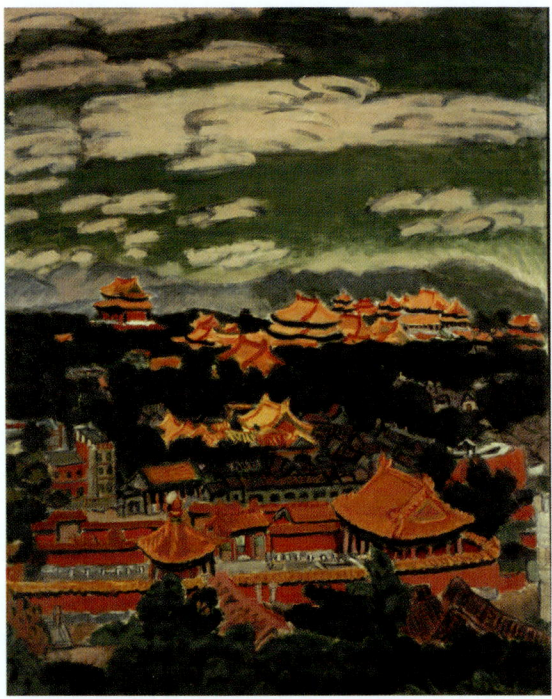

Plate 5 Umehara Ryūzaburō, *Forbidden City* (Shikinjō), 1940. Oil and *iwae-no-gu* (Japanese mineral pigment) on *maniaigami* (traditional Japanese paper), 115.0 × 89.0 cm. Eisei Bunko Museum, Tokyo

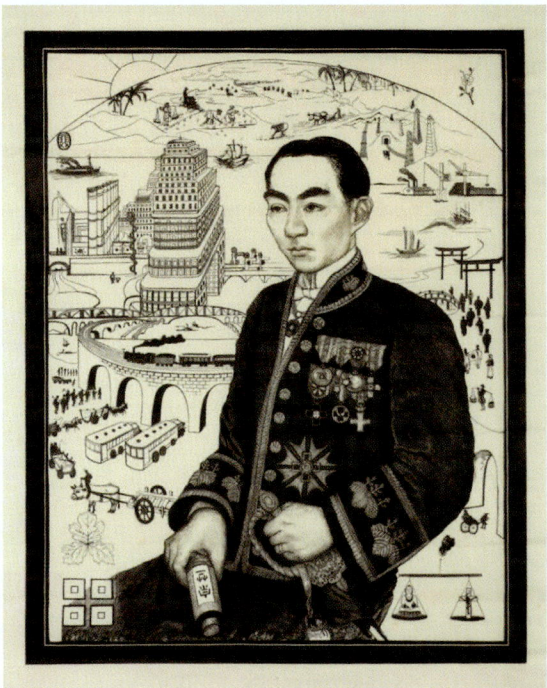

Plate 6 Pai Un-soung, *Baron Mitsui and His Works*, 1935. Woodblock print, 55 × 43 cm. Museum für Völkerkunde, Hamburg. Photo credit: National Research Institute of Cultural Heritage, Korea

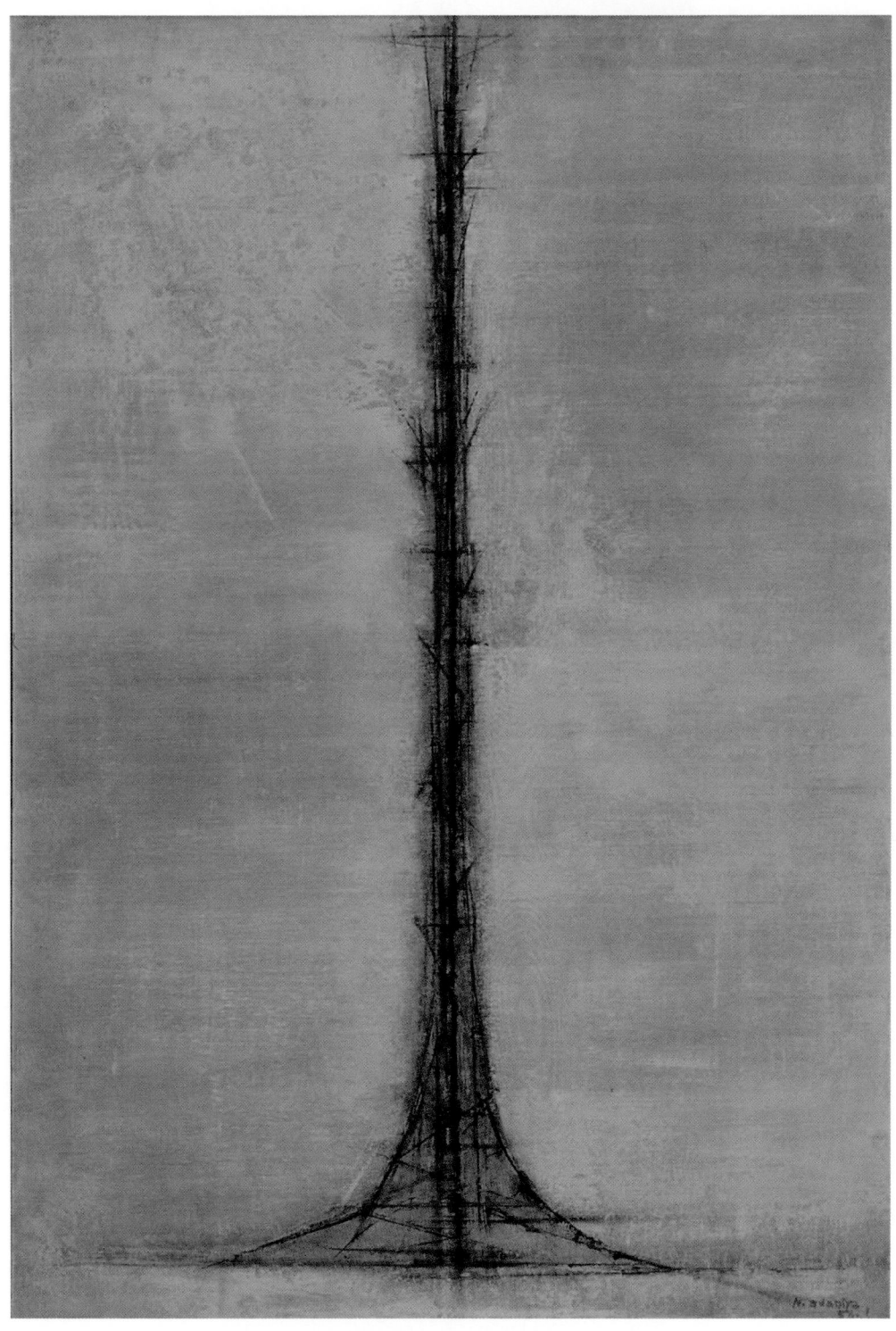

Plate 7 Adaniya Masayoshi, *Tower* (Tō), 1958. Oil and sand on canvas, 91.0 × 61.0 cm. Okinawa Prefectural Museum and Art Museum

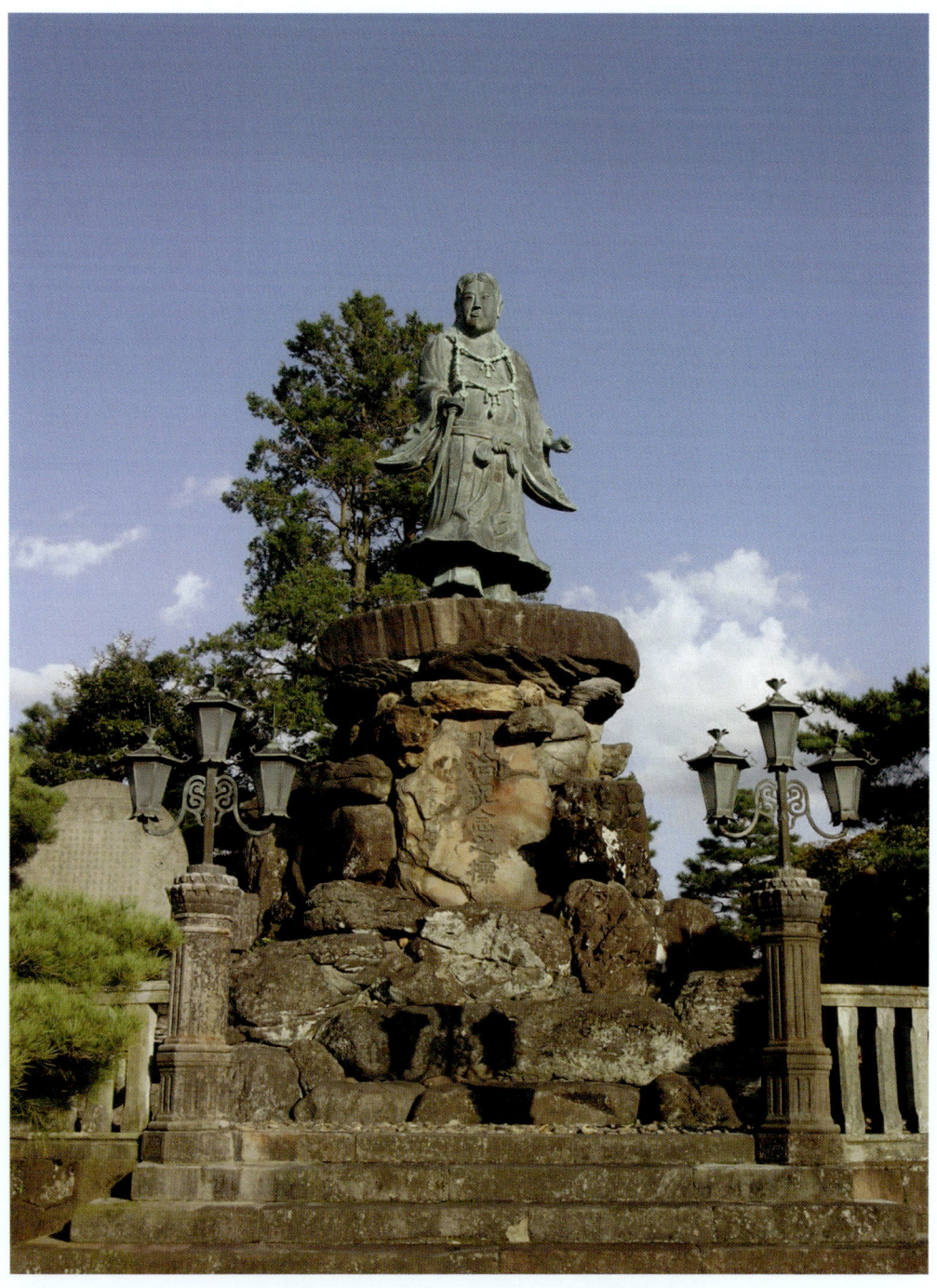

Plate 8 Statue of Prince Yamato Takeru (Meiji kinen no hyō), 1880. Bronze and glass, 554 cm. Kanazawa, Ishikawa Prefecture

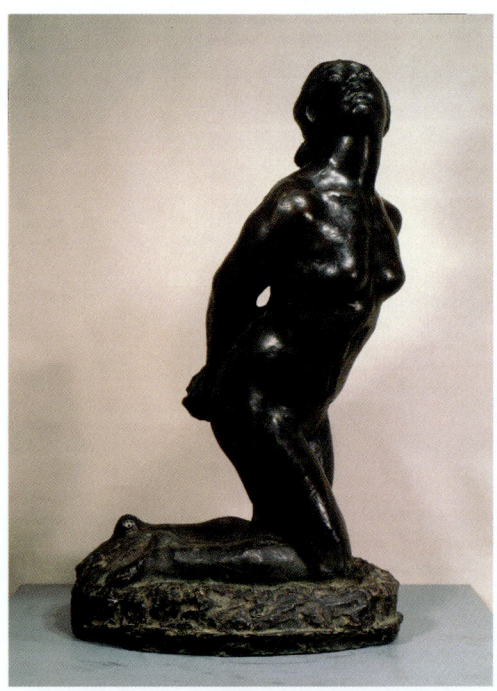

Plate 9 Ogiwara Morie, *Woman* (Onna), 1910. Bronze, 98.5 × 47 × 61 cm. Collection of the National Museum of Modern Art, Tokyo. Photograph courtesy MOMAT/DNPartcom

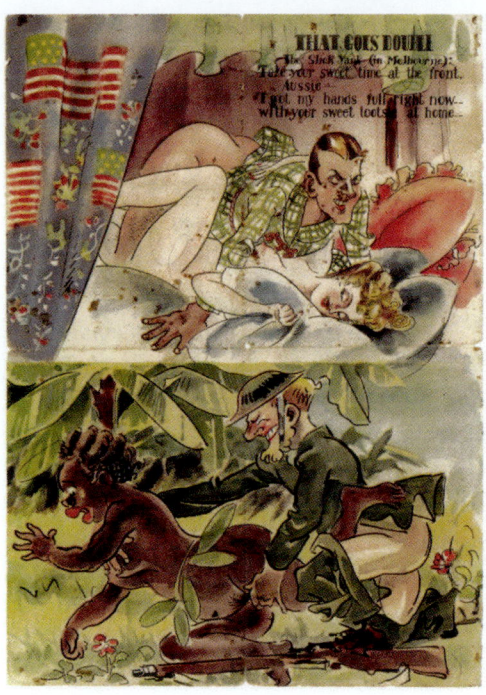

Plate 10 Leaflet entitled 'That Goes Double', made by the Japanese army (Ono Saseo) against the Australian army, ca. 1943. In Ichinose Toshiya, *The Asia-Pacific War Seen in Advertisement Plotter Flyers* (Tokyo: Kashiwa Shobō, 2008), p. 49

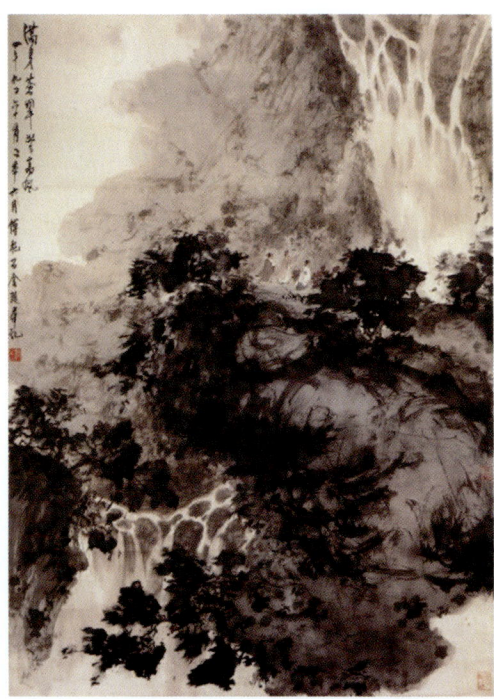

Plate 11 Fu Baoshi, *Landscape* (Manshen cangcui jing gaofeng), 1962. Hanging scroll, ink and colour on paper, 102.8 × 71.6 cm. Fu Family Collection. In Chen Lusheng, et al., *Fu Baoshi quanji*, vol. 4, p. 223

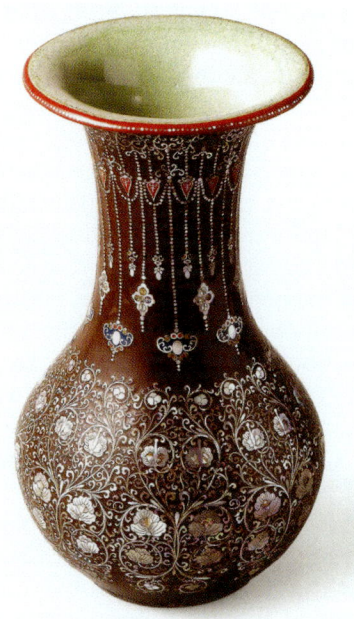

Plate 12 Kim Bong-ryong, *Lacquered Ceramic Vase*. Lacquered celadon, inlaid with mother-of-pearl, 1970, 35.0 × 18.5 cm, Wonju Museum of History

7 The Evolution and Modernization of the Sculpture Genre in East Asia According to the Japanese Example

Kitazawa Noriaki

Introduction

In order to critically examine the current state of sculpture (*chōkoku*) in Japan, it is not enough to trace the history of its development. Before discussing the modernization of sculpture, it is necessary to consider the evolution of sculpture as a genre; up until the Edo period (1603–1868), sculpture as a genre of fine art (*bijutsu*) did not exist in Japan. Both sculpture and fine art are genres that were originally brought to Japan from Europe in the early Meiji period (1868–1912).

No clear idea accompanied the importation of either fine art or sculpture. The terms first appeared as translated words with ambiguous definitions, and a focused concept only took shape around them after that first appearance. Under such circumstances, the deployment of these terms in Western writing and discursive texts naturally had a large impact on their translation. Although pre-Edo period plastic arts (*zōkei*)[1] also influenced the evolution of the concept of these terms, traditional forms largely developed in exclusion from Western sculpture genres or were transformed by the ideas surrounding the newly introduced concepts. From that point on, three-dimensional decorative objects produced in Japan were, to a greater or lesser extent, subject to the pressures imposed by sculpture as a conceptual framework.

Therefore, in order to trace the development of sculpture in Japan, it is necessary to begin with the appearance of the Japanese words that corresponded to terms such as 'fine art' and 'sculpture' that had first emerged in the West. In other words, we must approach the topic from a theory of translation—investigate the process by which the corresponding Japanese terms for 'fine art'—*bijutsu*—and 'sculpture'—*chōkoku*—were introduced and established. Moreover, in addition to the correspondences between Western languages and Japanese, it is necessary to keep in mind the translation networks between countries whose languages use Chinese characters. As I have already compiled a book addressing the process by which Japanese institutions involved in fine art, *bijutsu*, developed, in this essay I would like to explore the equivalent process regarding sculpture.[2] I will therefore focus on sculpture as a genre, with related terms such as 'relief' and 'embossment', perhaps unexpectedly, left out of the discussion.

The thing to note when it comes to the fine arts institutions of modern Japan is that it is relatively easy to trace the process by which genre names—and associated concepts—developed. Essentially, one need look no further than the expositions, exhibitions, and art schools of the Meiji period as a preliminary access point for enquiry. The process by which these institutions were maintained is also the process by which a system of genres formed. Expositions and exhibitions, with their considerable social standing, had tremendous clout and served to speed the publicizing of the fine art and sculpture genres.

As a classification of art, genre is easily influenced by traditional customs and media representation. Consequently, a fundamental ambiguity is difficult to escape. In this essay, I would like to advance a theory that broadly stipulates the fine arts genre as a social system of visual art objects and decorative plastic arts, and the sculpture genre as a category of three-dimensional art that is subordinate to the fine arts genre. Additionally, I will, when appropriate to the context of the discussion, make note of the codes that regulated the sculpture genre, explain the evolution of the canon of classes that formed the genre standard, and consider the hierarchical relationships of other fine arts genres such as painting (*kaiga*) and crafts (*kōgei*).

As noted above, the development of the sculpture genre in modern Japan can be separated into two stages. The importation of the sculpture genre from the West constitutes the first stage. During this stage, the reception of Western sculpture in Japan and then the establishment of Japanese terminology for sculpture as a genre were the focal points. Following the acceptance of sculpture as a genre in this manner, the modernization of sculpture as an expressive art form proceeded apace—with modernization here referring to the adoption of the concept that the purpose of artistic expression is to convey the interiority of human existence and that self-expression is the goal of artistic output. This constitutes the second stage of the development of the sculpture genre in modern Japan.

This essay is organized into three sections, which focus on these stages of development. In the first section, 'A hypothesis on the development of the sculpture genre', I discuss the development conditions of the subordinate genre of sculpture after the concept was brought to Japan via the medium of translation from Western languages. The purpose of this section is to clarify not the modernization of sculpture, but rather the fundamental assumptions underlying the development of a modernized sculpture genre.

In the second section, 'The advent of *chōkoku* as a genre name and the development of the sculpture genre', I trace how the terms used to describe the sculpture genre changed in the modern period and examine the transplantation of the sculpture genre, using the following three events as indices: 1) the appearance of the phrase 'the art of statue-making' (*zō wo tsukuru jutsu*) in a translation, in 1872, of the 1873 Vienna World's Fair exhibition listing of classifications and divisions; 2) the establishment in 1876 of a sculpture course (*chōkoku-gaku*) at the Technical Art School (*Kōbu bijutsu gakkō*); and 3) the shifts in the name given to the sculpture genre at the Domestic Industrial Exposition (*Naikoku kangyō hakurankai*) of Japan from 1877 to 1890, from statuary art (*chōzōjutsu*) to relief carving (*chōru*) to sculpture (*chōkoku*).

In the final section, 'The movement toward the modernization of the sculpture genre', I explore the social establishment and development process of the sculpture genre by means of the following two points: 1) the sculpture training course at the Tokyo School of Fine Arts (*Tōkyō bijutsu gakkō*, est. 1887); 2) the controversy surrounding the inclusion of a sculpture classification at the Ministry of Education Art Exhibition (*Monbushō bijutsu tenrankai*, launched in 1907).

These sections will be followed by a conclusion that sketches out the circumstances surrounding the moment when the sculpture genre finally made the jump to modernization.

A Hypothesis on the Development of the *chōkoku* Genre: The Transplantation of the Term *bijutsu*

The Appearance of the Term bijutsu *and the Absence of a Sculpture Genre*

The term *chōkoku*—typically translated as 'sculpture'—was used even before the Edo period. The word *chōkoku*, due to characteristics stemming from its Chinese origin, can be used as either a verb or a noun. As a result, both the act of carving or engraving (*horikizamu*), and its result, could be denoted by the term *chōkoku*. The act of carving a woodblock (*hangi wo horu*) was popularly referred to as *chōkoku*, but the product—the carving itself (*horimono*)—was also called *chōkoku*. In either case, up to the Edo period, the general idea of *chōkoku* decisively differed from contemporary notions. At that point, both *bijutsu*, the Japanese analogue for 'fine art', and *chōkoku*, had yet to be established.

The Japanese term *bijutsu* made its first appearance when the Japanese government participated in the 1873 Vienna World's Fair. The word was coined during the translation of the exhibition listing of classifications and divisions—published by the Grand Council of State in January 1872—which had been sent by administrators of the Vienna World's Fair (Figure 7.1). It made its way into the Japanese lexicon from there.[3] The term *bijutsu* first appears in section 22. The exhibition listing that was sent

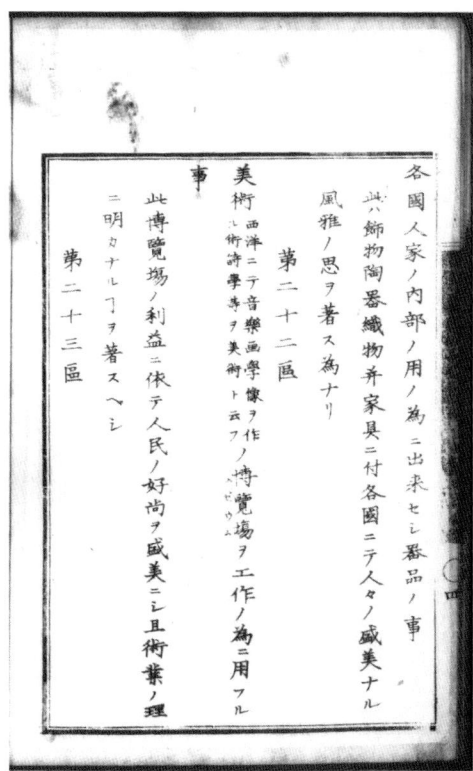

Figure 7.1 Vienna World's Fair exhibition listing of classifications and divisions, January 1872

by the administrators of the Vienna World's Fair was published in three languages: German, English, and French; we therefore cannot know from which language the term *bijutsu* was originally derived. As a matter of convenience, we will use the English text as our example. The text for section 22 reads: 'Group 22. Exhibition showing the organization influence of museums of fine art applied to Industry'.[4]

The first appearance of a corresponding word for 'fine art' in Japanese is *bijutsu*. In the Japanese version of the text, the phrase 'fine art' is immediately explained with the following annotation: 'In the West, things such as music [*ongaku*], painting [*gagaku*], the art of statue-making [i.e. sculpture], and poetics [*shigaku*] are called fine arts [*bijutsu*]' (Figure 7.1).[5] In other words, the passage explains that in the West the category of 'fine arts' includes music, painting, 'sculpture', poetry, and other arts. This is a definition that was appended to the document by Japanese officials; in the English, French, and German versions, this annotation does not appear. The special need for this definition was down to the simple fact that *bijutsu* was an entirely new word. The use of the phrase *zō wo tsukuru jutsu*—'art of statue-making'—in this definition indicates that, at this point, the sculpture genre had not yet been established. I will discuss this in the next section.

The bijutsu *Tidal Wave*

In reading the Vienna World's Fair exhibition listing of classifications and divisions, it is clear from the inclusion of literature and music that *bijutsu* was, at first, a craft whose object was viewer appreciation, with a meaning much like *geijutsu* (art) has today. Today, just as 'fine arts' includes visual arts as well as other fields of art, *bijutsu* means anything from visual arts to plastic arts and is used to describe various mediums. Presently, this narrowing down of meaning to the visual plastic arts has enabled a new usage of *bijutsu* for premodern plastic arts and for the writing of the history of primitive and ancient art. The retroactive adaptation of this term to sculpted objects produced in a period where the word *bijutsu* did not exist can be likened to the impact of a tidal wave. This new concept, which had its origin in 'fine art', flowed through the river of history, swallowing up appropriate art objects, and dragging them to the estuary of the modern era.

Let us consider Buddhist statues as an example. Today, Buddhist statues are often presented as objects for viewing appreciation. However, as the name implies, the statues were originally produced as objects of worship within the Buddhist faith. To treat them as ornamental objects is to subvert their original meaning—to shift their context from a religious one to an artistic one.

Walter Benjamin has offered several compelling comments on this topic. Sculpted objects occupy one of two extremes: they possess cult value (*reihai kachi*) or exhibition value (*tenji kachi*). When the object is involved in magical or religious practices, it inclines towards a cult value. In that case, the object's significance is its presence (G: *vorhanden*, J: *sonzai*). The act of looking upon these objects does not hold great significance. Instead, it is preferable to hide them from sight. As the object is liberated from religious formalities, however, it moves forcefully towards the opposite extreme. In other words, its value standard migrates from a cult value to an exhibition value as modernization occurs and it comes to have importance as something to look at.[6] The fact that Buddhist statues in museums have become objects of appreciation can be taken as evidence in support of Benjamin's argument. Moreover, these shifts are observable regardless of the object's production method.

Takamura Kōun (1852–1934), a sculptor of the early Meiji period, worked in the tradition of the Edo period Buddhist sculptors (*busshi*), but his own son, Takamura Kōtarō (1883–1956), strongly criticized Kōun's statues of Amida (Sk: Amitābha) and Kannon (Sk: Avalokiteśvara), writing that they smacked of coquettish vulgarity.[7] This criticism suggests that the statues' exhibition value had surpassed that of their cult value, as coquettishness indicates an awareness of audience. As this example shows, Buddhist sculptors' sense of value had shifted from a cult value centred in faith to an exhibition value that aims at delight in being seen.

Museums as Spaces for the Perpetual Display of Buddhist Statues

This shifting perception of value, however, had already begun in the Edo period. During this period, the display of Buddhist statues (*kaichō*) was a component of festival activities, when statues that were typically not on view were made available to the public. The display of statues began as a component of religious worship, but it became an element of exhibition-like events (*misemono*) in the Edo period. Museum exhibitions of Buddhist statues were based on these displays—both those that took place at Buddhist temples (*igaichō*) and those that took place outside of the temple setting (*degaichō*)—but the display of these statues in museums as constant exhibits enabled the stripping away of their aura of religiosity.

Generally, the focus of a *kaichō* is the display of hidden Buddhas (*hibutsu*)—a good example of Benjamin's cult-value hypothesis. *Hibutsu* are objects of worship, typically Buddha figures, that are kept hidden from sight. Worshippers have faith in the existence of these Buddha figures that are hidden behind the doors of cabinets or miniature shrines (*zushi*). During *kaichō*, these sacred hidden figures were brought out for public view in a festival setting. With the start of the Meiji period, however, the newly formed state government could, and did, bring their force to bear to compel *kaichō* displays at a nationwide level. They did this mainly through the surveying, conservation, cataloguing, and acquisition of cultural properties. This process began in 1872 with the issuing of an edict to conserve and catalogue cultural properties—an action taken in response to a sense of crisis about the widespread and growing inclination towards newly imported Western values. The focus of this process included the aforementioned Buddhist statues.[8] This edict, which had its roots in the shifting perception of Buddhist statues—from objects with cult value to objects with exhibition value—presupposed the establishment of a museum system.[9]

The climax of the national *kaichō* project was the survey, by Okakura Kakuzō (1862–1913, better known as Okakura Tenshin) and Ernest Fenollosa (1853–1908), of the Guze Kannon, a *hibutsu* in the Yumedono Hall of Hōryūji Temple. In 1890, Okakura gave a lecture at the Tokyo School of Art in which he discussed the moving experience of seeing the face of the Guze Kannon appear when the white cloth that covered it was lowered.[10] Okakura and Fenollosa's lowering of that cloth was nothing short of the process by which the Guze Kannon figure moved from having cult value to exhibition value. It was an act of faith in art that was done without faith in Buddhism. The concept of *bijutsu*, which had begun to be established in the modern era, was thus adapted to the past, and—through that adaptation—the study of the history of art became possible.

Okakura's lecture was the first fully fledged attempt by a Japanese person to engage in the practice of art history. This lecture was ultimately compiled into a published volume, *Kōhon Nihon Teikoku bijutsu ryakushi* (A brief history of the art of Imperial Japan). In 1900, it was published in French as *L'Histoire de l'art du Japon* during the Paris World's Fair. For the first time, the Japanese were able to present a description of Japanese art to the world, and that description was divided into the categories of painting, sculpture, architecture (*kenchiku*), and craft arts (*bijutsuteki kōgei*). It was a description by a Japanese person, but presented in this way—translated into the Western-language origin of the word *bijutsu*—it could only be presented using a Western classification system.

As I noted above, the Japanese sculpture genre developed in tandem with the fine arts genre, and that process—from a historical point of view of the associated institutions—can be understood in terms of the process by which use of the phrase *zō wo tsukuru jutsu* eventually developed into use of the term *chōkoku*. Broadly speaking, the phrase *zō wo tsukuru jutsu* became the term *chōkoku*, and the process by which that term became incorporated into the Japanese lexicon is the process by which the sculpture genre developed.

The Advent of *chōkoku* as a Genre Name and the Development of the Sculpture Genre: From *zō wo tsukuru jutsu* to *chōkoku*

The 1872 Translation of the Vienna World's Fair Exhibition Listing of Classifications and Divisions: The Debut of the Phrase *zō* wo tsukuru jutsu

As I explained above, when the new word *bijutsu* appeared in the translated exhibition listing of the Vienna World's Fair in 1872, an attached explanatory note described sculpture with the phrase *zō wo tsukuru jutsu*. The character for *zō* originally had a meaning akin to 'resemble' or 'look like'—to duplicate its form or call to mind its features, whether in a two-dimensional image or a three-dimensional object.¹¹ Consequently, the meaning of *zō* was not restricted to sculpted figures (*chōzō*). However, because the annotation to the Vienna World's Fair exhibition listing gives *gagaku*—painting and drawing—as the word for two-dimensional *zō*, we can interpret *zō*, in this context, as having a meaning akin to sculpture. On the same page of the exhibition listing of classifications and divisions, *zō wo tsukuru jutsu* is given as the corresponding term for 'sculpture'. Why it is that sculpture, unlike music, painting, and poetics—which were translated into the nouns *ongaku*, *gagaku*, and *shigaku*, respectively—was the only term translated into a noun phrase? It is because a unified sculpture genre—sculpture as a type of fine arts genre—did not exist in Japan at the time?

Indeed, Takamura Kōun, who worked in the style of Edo period Buddhist sculptors, noted in a 1926 interview with *Kokka* magazine that the term *chōkoku* had not existed in the Edo period.¹² Now, as I mentioned earlier, the word *chōkoku* was in use both during the Edo period and before it, but it was typically used to refer to carving and engraving, not to a genre. That is what Kōun was saying.

Kōun continues: 'Carvers and engravers [*chōkokuka*] all had their specialities: Buddhist sculptors carved Buddhist statues; dollmakers [*ningyōshi*] made dolls; carpenters [*horimono daiku*] created ornamental decoration for temples and shrines. No one specialized in the creation of decorative objects [*okimono*].'¹³ The first point to take note of is that Kōun treats sculpture as an *okimono*, or decorative object. The literal interpretation of *okimono* is a sculpted object with a fixed location. This implies an industrial or craftwork ornamentation, which is different from the idea of sculpture as a work of fine art. A decorative object that takes account of its setting runs counter to the standards of sculpture, which are concerned with autonomy and the interiority of experience.

Another notable point is that these statements show that *chōkoku*, as a genre, suppressed the other genres of plastic arts that had been produced up through the Edo period. The *bijutsu* tidal wave pulled those plastic arts that fit comfortably within its categorization from their traditional positions in order to reorganize them under its own name. Furthermore, after this occurred, those things that were difficult to reorganize under the umbrella of the *bijutsu* term were either expelled from the fine arts entirely or relegated to its periphery.

Considering the origin of the phrase *zō wo tsukuru jutsu* in terms of the history of English language studies in Japan, it is likely that it had its origin in the second edition of the *Pocket Dictionary of the English and Japanese Language* (*Eiwa taiyaku shūchin jisho*), which translates 'sculpture' as *zō wo tsukuru jutsu*.[14] Regarded as the first true English–Japanese dictionary in Japan, it is highly probable that this dictionary was consulted for the translation of the World Fair's exhibition listing. In William Lobscheid's *English and Chinese Dictionary*, which was published from 1866 to 1868, 'sculpture' is translated as the art of sculpting (*diaoke zhi yi*).[15] This Chinese expression would have been suitable for a designation of sculpture as a genre, but it was not adopted for the project. Though it is possible to see the impact of Lobscheid's dictionary at this time, it does not appear to have been referenced for the annotation on the Vienna World's Fair exhibition listing.[16] Walter Henry Medhurst's *An English and Japanese and Japanese and English Vocabulary*, which is ranked alongside Lobscheid's dictionary, translates 'sculpture' as *horimono*, written in katakana.[17]

The 1876 Foundation of a 'Sculpture Course' at the Technical Art School

The Technical Art School was initially called the College of Art. It was established as part of the system of industrial education institutions that was run by the Ministry of Industry (*kōbushō*)—whose primary function was to arrange infrastructure in support of Japan's IndustrialRrevolution—and served by Italian professors, who taught sculpture and painting. At this industry-affiliated school, the deployment of *bijutsu*—which referred to various artforms—refined the meaning of plastic art. The sculpture course was called *chōkoku-gaku*, and Vincenzo Ragusa (1843–1927) was its director.[18]

Attaching the character for 'study'—*gaku*—to *chōkoku* gave it a kind of substance, turning it into a legitimate academic course. It could be said that the act of turning *zō wo tsukuru jutsu* into the name of an academic course began the process of sculpture's genrefication. This was not a mere matter of a name, however. Through his enthusiastic leadership, Ragusa endeavoured to transplant the sculpture genre to Japan. His technique generally centred on making copies, mainly from clay but also carved from marble, and he introduced both oil-based clay and pantographs (*kakudaiyō konpasu*). He taught classical European traditions from the age of the Greeks to the modern era through the use of plaster figures and a series of lectures, while also bringing attention to the sculptural value of Nara's Buddhist statues.[19]

This addition of the character for 'study' was a clear opportunity for people who were involved in sculpture production to break away from the apprenticeship system to which they had been tied as mere craftsmen. Though the wielding of paintbrushes fit within the intellectual hierarchy—as demonstrated by the idea that painting and the much-revered art of calligraphy correspond to one another (*shoga icchi*)—the plastic arts were largely considered the job of craftsmen. This distinction is recounted in the Technical Art School section of the *Taisei kiyō* (Bulletin of imperial rule),[20] which notes the inferiority of sculpture relative to painting: 'In our great country, the study of sculpture is the province of lowly workers; it is not a craft that one learns like a European gentleman for the purpose of aggrandizing one's name or garnering success.'[21] This is one of the reasons why a sculpture genre was not established until the Meiji period. Sculpture received the same treatment in Korea. As Kim Youngna has noted, sculpture was traditionally regarded as craftwork and even today has fallen far behind painting in terms of its prestige.[22]

This hierarchical positioning is evident from the secondary placement of sculpture after painting in the organization of academic courses. The predominance of painting was rooted in the Italian concept of *disegno*—a tradition that had bundled painting, sculpture, and architecture together from the time of Giorgio Vasari (1511–1574)—and the leadership of Italian professors at the school must have made this predominance natural. Be that as it may, however, in the year following the school's foundation, the Meiji government, as part of its industry promotion measures, would create a National Industrial Exposition at which the hierarchy of painting over sculpture would be overturned.

Names and Circumstances in Transition at the Domestic Industrial Exposition, 1877–1890: Chōzōjutsu, Chōru, and Chōkoku

The Domestic Industrial Exposition was organized by the Meiji government as one element of its policy to promote industry.[23] The 'National' portion of the title referred to the general rule that participation in the exposition was limited to Japanese citizens. During the inaugural exposition in 1877, the Art Gallery (*bijutsukan*) was built at a pivotal location within the exposition grounds (Figure 7.2). This was the first art museum in Japan. It was referred to as 'The Fine Art Gallery' in English, and—in accordance with that name—displayed only visual art objects. Here, too, the same continuous refining of the term *bijutsu* that was ongoing at the Technical Art School took place, and this happened as a matter of course, given that the exposition was itself an instructional device for encouraging modernization via the visitors' sense of sight.

The term used to denote the sculpture genre at the first Domestic Industrial Exhibition was *chōzōjutsu*, or statuary art. At the second exhibition in 1881, the term *chōru*, or relief carving, was used. And in 1890, at the third exhibition, the organizers settled on *chōkoku*, the term that is still in use today. Of particular interest is the fact that *chōzōjutsu* was a synthesis of the Technical Art School's *chōkoku-gaku* sculpture course and the Vienna World's Fair's exhibition listing translation *zō wo tsukuru jutsu*. It holds onto *chō*—which bears the meaning of 'sculpture' faithfully in mind—at the same time that it adopts *zō*—which references the object of production. Meanwhile, the Technical Art School's use of the character *gaku* (study) in place of *jutsu* (art) can be seen as being in line with the goal of promoting industry. *Chōkoku* does appear in

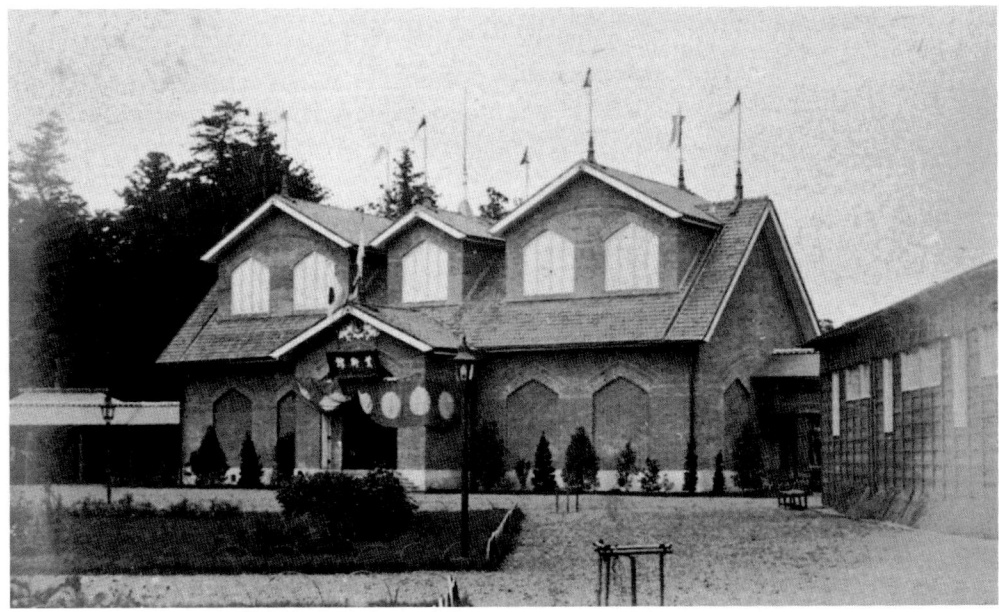

Figure 7.2 Matsuzaki Shinji, *Exterior View of the Fine Art Gallery at the First Domestic Industrial Exposition*, albumen silver print (*kenranshi*), 9.2 × 5.8 cm.

> Collection of the Amagasaki Shiritsu Bunkazai Shūzōko. Reproduced in *Meiji jū-nen naikoku kangyō hakurankai reppin shashin jō* [Photographs of exhibited objects at the Domestic Industrial Exposition in Meiji 10 (1877)], 11.6 × 19.5 × 7.5 cm

the list of classifications and divisions for the first national exposition, but it refers in this instance to the technique used to carve woodblocks for printing.

The most noteworthy aspect of the sculpture genre's role at the Domestic Industrial Exposition is the castling that took place between the chess pieces of painting (king) and sculpture (rook). In other words, sculpture came to occupy painting's position of prominence, and the organizers of the Domestic Industrial Exposition conceived this idea when they had the chance to participate in the Vienna World's Fair, where sculpture was placed ahead of painting in the classifications and divisions ranking.[24] Just as the Technical Art School had learned from Italy, the art department of the Domestic Industrial Exposition patterned themselves on the Vienna World's Fair.

Simple copying alone cannot explain this conversion, however. It was also bound up with national necessity. In centralizing the imperial system known as the feudal shogunate (*bakuhan taisei*), monuments to national figures were required to instil a sense of national unification. Monuments to people were called *dōzō* (lit. bronze statues). With the construction of the 1880 monument *Meiji kinen no hyō* (A symbol of the Meiji Restoration), a statue of the legendary hero Yamato Takeru, in Kanazawa City's Kenrokuen Park (Plate 8), similar monuments honouring national heroes began to be built one after the other. A glance through the Iwakura Mission (*Iwakura shisetsudan*) report, 'A True Account of a Tour of Europe and the United States' (*Beiō kairan jikki*, 1878),[25] shows numerous illustrations of European monuments mounted on pedestals.[26] In other words, the hierarchy of genres was dependent on national needs.

It must be said, however, that setting aside painting and ranking sculpture first on the *bijutsu* classification list is problematic for the visual arts genre. Compared to sculpture, with its grounding in tactile reality, painting not only displays a superiority of visuality, but also—having its basis in traditions originating with Giorgio Vasari—governs the *disegno* fundamentals of the visual arts. In short, the disregarding of the genre's distinctive features in deference to national necessity, when considered in light of artistic modernism, is nothing but a difficulty in need of straightening out—a difficulty that was ultimately overcome during the third Domestic Industrial Exposition. Once more the hierarchy shifted, painting was returned to a place of prominence, and a modernistic reform was contemplated for every genre.

Until the second Domestic Industrial Exposition, the art department had not established a genre of industrial arts. Craft arts had been intermingled with painting and sculpture. For example, the 'statuary art' and 'relief carving' divisions featured vases, incense burners, and sake bottles. If the object involved any carving technique, regardless of what it was, it was treated as sculpture, and the situation was no different when it came to painting. Expressed differently, the craft arts were omnipresent across the varying genres. The chaos inherent in this situation could be viewed as the result of following traditional ideas about what plastic arts encompassed. The decorative plastic arts of the Edo period and earlier were fundamentally incorporated into daily life—ornamentation and all. For that reason, the boundary between industry, with its focus on practical use, and fine art, with its focus on aesthetic quality, was vague.[27]

The third Domestic Industrial Exposition attempted to resolve this situation. An art-industry (*bijutsu kōgyō*) department was established to cover those objects that possessed overlapping elements of both fine and industrial arts, and measures to single out industrial plastic arts were taken. The directors, in turning things back, thus attempted a dissection of painting and sculpture. The settling on *chōkoku* as the name of the genre can also be seen as a component in this modernist dissection. *Zō wo tsukuru jutsu*, *chōkoku-gaku*, and *chōzōjutsu* are, in point of fact, not so much names for a genre as techniques or courses of study. When the suffixes *jutsu* and *gaku* are removed from them, the focus of interest shifts—not to actions or processes, but to the actual plastic arts that have their origin in those actions and processes. This implies that as sculpture became independent from the work of craftsmen and of scholarship, the sculpture genre became a tangible reality. In distilling the phrase *zō wo tsukuru jutsu* down to the word *chōkoku*, the term took on the unique nuance of a genre. Thus, *chōkoku* became the name of the genre, entering the lexicon of art historical terminology, and eventually coming to be limited by traditional convention to three-dimensional sculpted objects.[28]

This advance towards modernization in both *bijutsu* and *chōkoku* mirrored the progress the Japanese made in developing as a modern nation. The year the third Domestic Industrial Exposition opened, 1890, was a year after the proclamation of the Meiji constitution. The first Imperial Diet had been convened, and Japan had fully entered into the Industrial Revolution. To express this another way, the modernism of politics and the modernism of art were synchronised. However, although the project of the third Domestic Industrial Exposition—to fully separate the various art genres from one another—did achieve a certain amount of success as far as paintings were concerned, industrial handicrafts were never fully removed from the sculpture genre. It is thought that the fact that the genre was widely and deeply associated with general craft techniques played a big role in why it was difficult to separate from industrial art objects. At the Domestic Industrial Exposition, paintings and sculpture marched in lockstep, and it was not until the fifth and final exposition that they settled into a modernist classification. Nevertheless, the movement towards a modernist revolution had already begun to be actualized in the years before the third exhibition—with the opening of the Tokyo School of Fine Arts and its academic art course that was organized around the hierarchical ranking of painting, sculpture, and industrial arts.

The Movement Towards the Modernization of the Sculpture Genre

Teaching in the chōkoku Department—the Tokyo School of Fine Arts

The Tokyo School of Fine Arts succeeded the Technical Art School. It was established in 1887 by the Ministry of Education as a national school of art; in 1889, it held its first classes. By this time, the Technical Art School had been closed for six years. One reason for its closure was the rise of cultural nationalism. Cultural nationalism was a common component of the modern nation states that originated in Europe. At the time, in the face of the establishment of a National Diet grounded in a constitution that was intended to arrange the country into a nation-state system, the immediate motivation for the rise of cultural nationalism in Japan stemmed from a need to unite the will of the people. Proceeding from that assumption, the rise of cultural nationalism, as has frequently been pointed out, should not be seen as a reaction to, but rather as an important part of, the move towards Europeanization. In this way, the Tokyo School of Fine Arts began with cultural nationalism as its founding ideology, and led the charge by focusing on the painting, sculpture, and craft arts techniques that had developed up to the end of the Edo period.

After completing a two-year general curriculum course at the school, students advanced into a painting or sculpture specialization course. Of the first students in the specialization course, eight pursued a degree in painting and two in sculpture.[29] Takamura Kōun was the principal instructor of the sculpture courses, and under his leadership students focused primarily on wood carving. The department was known as the *chōkoku-ka*, or sculpture department—an appropriate name given its professor's emphasis on the technique of carving.[30] At that time, however, *chōkoku* was already in the process of being established as the corresponding name for the comprehensive genre of sculpture. In other words, it was also being used to refer to objects that were the product of modelling, which included three-dimensional objects such as clay ceramics, marble carving, and metal casting. If we look at the original plan for the course organization in English, it is easy to see that the course name *chōkoku* was used as a translation for sculpture.[31] The use of *chōkoku* as a comprehensive title for a genre name in the official announcements of the third Domestic Industrial Exposition appeared in the same year that the Tokyo School of Fine Arts was established.[32]

Furthermore, in the year that the third Domestic Industrial Exposition was held, Okakura Tenshin gave a lecture on Japanese art history at the Tokyo School of Fine Arts. Around the same time, the school, in cooperation with the Imperial Gallery of Art, initiated a project to carve wooden blocks for publishing classic texts,[33] and Takamura Kōun had been sent to Nara the previous year for a survey of classical sculptures.³⁴ While the genre name was being defined, a movement to retroactively develop a classical canon specific to the genre was also underway.

As I mentioned above, classes at the Tokyo School of Fine Arts focused on wood carving, but the intention was to concentrate initially on clay modelling. In Ernest Fenollosa's plan, the teaching of clay modelling took place during preparatory courses,³⁵ in which clay materials and modelling tools were prepared.³⁶ Teaching staff for this course consisted of two clay-working artists, Fujita Bunzō (1861–1934), who had taught at the Technical Art School, and Naganuma Moriyoshi (1857–1942), who had taught at the Venice School of Art.³⁷ Kōun himself had a great interest in the production of reproducible images using modelling techniques.³⁸ Before coming to the school to teach, he had collaborated with the metal caster, Ōshima Takajirō (dates unknown), and his son, Katsujirō (1858–1940, better known as Jōun), on the production of wax models.³⁹ Jōun later assumed the leadership of the casting programme at the Tokyo School of Fine Arts and taught wax modelling in the sculpture department.⁴⁰

Clay modelling flourished in the Nara period (710–794) but went out of fashion shortly thereafter. In the Meiji period, it was transplanted from Europe as the latest in three-dimensional image reproduction technology, and Okakura Tenshin, using this importation as the basis of his argument, pointed out the contemporary possibilities of clay modelling and dry lacquer in an 1889 comment published in *Kokka* magazine.⁴¹ Okakura made another important proposal about sculpture in this article—to construct monuments out of bronze—noting: 'The features of the Buddha and Bodhisattva figures of Jōchō (d. 1057) and Annami (dates unknown, late 12th/early 13th century) were possessed of a spirit of service. Should we not apply this approach to the depictions of our most loyal subjects and devoted warriors?'⁴² In accordance with this proposal, the Tokyo School of Fine Arts began taking orders for bronze statues—manufacturing commissioned bronze monuments like the statue of Kusunoki Masashige (1294–1336) at the Imperial Palace in Tokyo and the statue of Saigō Takamori (1828–1877) in Ueno Park (1898; Figure 7.3). The central figure in these projects was Takamura Kōun, who made use of his own skills to create wooden models for these monuments.⁴³ These commissioned works prompted the rapid growth of metal casting technology, and offered a chance to spur the recognition of the artistic significance of metal work to sculpture.

Okakura's two proposals were ultimately to become entwined, as wooden models came to replace clay models. Furthermore, the process of substitution, in a kind of twist, resulted in large changes to the state of wood carving itself. Yonehara Unkai (1869–1925), a student of Kōun's, manufactured a bronze statue of Edward Jenner (1749–1823) to commemorate the hundred-year anniversary of the development of the smallpox vaccine in 1904 (Figure 7.4). This sculpted monument, like those produced by Kōun, was cast using a wooden model (Figure 7.5), and this model was enlarged from a smaller statue using the pantograph method that was brought to Japan by Vincenzo Ragusa. According to Yonehara, the smaller sculpture that was used to create the model was also made of wood.⁴⁴

This method of enlarging the model by means of a pantograph was taken up by wood sculptors because of its convenience, and it became a widely established technique for making wooden sculptures from small-sized clay models as well. The use of this process was not just a matter of convenience, however. Manufacture by means of

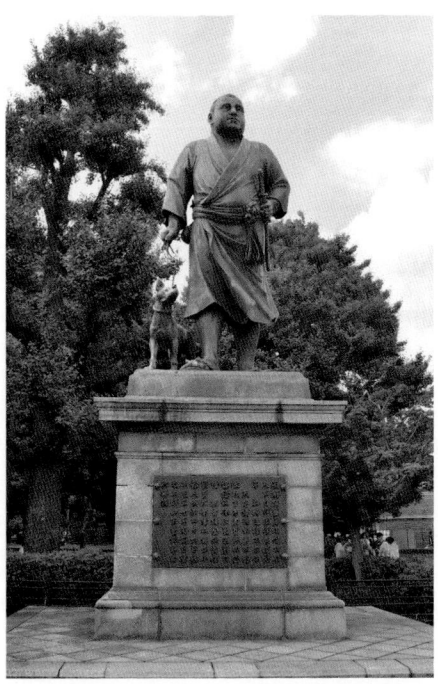

Figure 7.3 Takamura Kōun, Hayashi Biun, and Gotō Sadayuki, *Portrait of Saigō Takamori* (Saigō Takamori zō), 1898. Bronze, 363.6 × 360 cm

Ueno, Tokyo

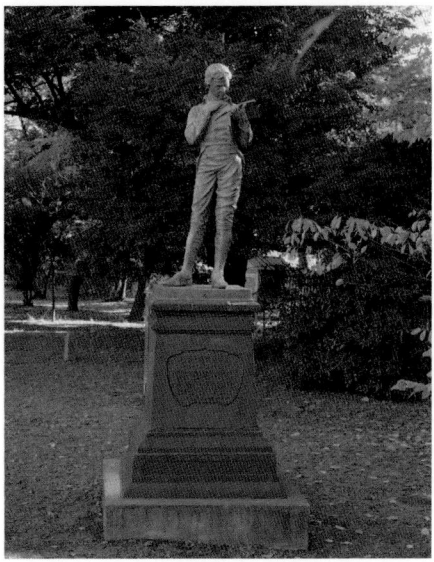

Figure 7.4 Yonehara Unkai, *Portrait of Edward Jenner* (Zenna zō), 1904. Bronze, 180 × 190 cm

Collection of the Tokyo National Museum. Photograph courtesy TNM Image Archives

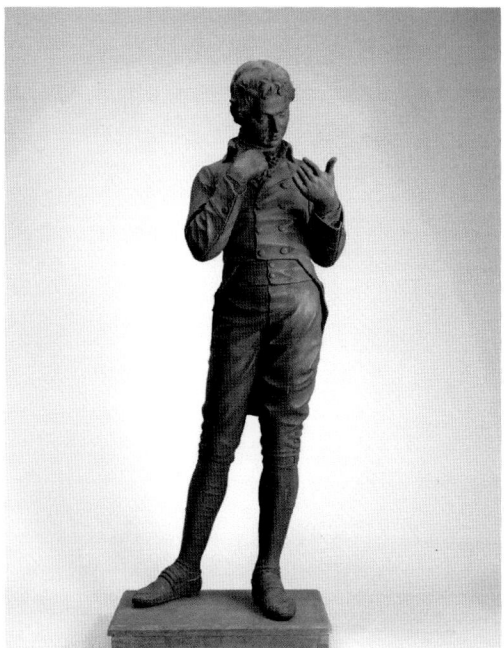

Figure 7.5 Yonehara Unkai, *Portrait of Edward Jenner in Wood* (Zenna kigata), 1897. Wood, height: 183.2 cm

Collection of the Tokyo University of the Arts

clay models brought about major changes in wood sculpting. This is because the clay model, with its continuous curved surfaces, would obscure neither the wood grain nor the characteristic plasticity derived from the sharpness of the chisel. Wood sculpting's dependence on clay modelling was a significant move away from the essentials of carving. Consequently, if one compares this form of wood sculpting with traditional carving techniques, even with the development of new carving techniques, there is no denying that the essence of traditional wood carving had been lost.[45]

Nevertheless, in time, this hollowing gave birth to a work of art that resulted from the mutual osmosis between clay modelling and wood sculpting: Takamura Kōtarō's *Hand* (*Te*; Figure 7.6). This portrait of a hand, which combines mould-casting techniques with an end product that resembles a wooden sculpture, renewed the appeal of carving techniques that had been lost through modelling, and connected modelling techniques to Edo period traditions. The motif of the hand functions as a symbol of the tactile art of sculpture while simultaneously carrying significance as a symbol of Buddhist statuary art. Incidentally, Unkai was a principal member of the Youth Association of Carving and Modelling (*Seinen chōsokai*) that was started by sculpture students at the Tokyo School of Fine Arts in 1898, and this association voiced objections to the status of wood sculpting as the mainstay of the sculpture department. Demanding freedom of technique and materials was an enterprise of the entire school, faculty and students alike.[46] However, though the rallying cry of the association was freedom, their use of the term *chōso*—carving and modelling—indicates that the

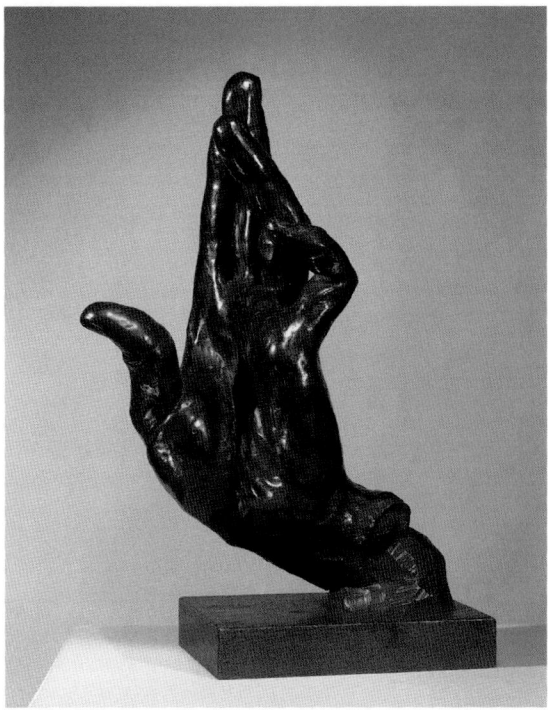

Figure 7.6 Takamura Kōtarō, *Hand* (Te), ca. 1918. Bronze, 38.6 × 14.5 × 28.7 cm
Collection of the National Museum of Modern Art, Tokyo. Photograph courtesy MOMAT/DNPartcom

association's focus was on the introduction of this superb new modelling technology that empowered reproducible plastic arts.

The word *chōso* was coined by Ōmura Seigai (1868–1927), the first graduate of the Tokyo School of Fine Arts sculpture programme, who presented it as a theoretical fulcrum for the Youth Association of Carving and Modelling. For Ōmura, it was absurd to use *chōkoku*, which originally meant to carve, as the genre name since the genre comprised not just objects made from carving but those from modelling as well. With the term *chōso*, and its meaning of carving-plus-modelling, the association advocated 'a substantive general term for the plastic arts'.[47] Ōmura, proceeding from the *chōso* concept, likened carving to the brushstrokes of monochrome ink paintings (*sumi-e*) or Japanese-style paintings (*nihonga*) done in polychrome glue pigment (*nikawa enogu*), which stress the tension arising from the once-in-a-lifetime nature of the work. On the other hand, he compared modelling to the gradual building up of an oil painting through the process of layered painting. Both methods, Ōmura argued, had their advantages and disadvantages. This argument, and the activities of the association founded upon it, had great significance for the cultural nationalism-championing Tokyo School of Fine Arts as a herald of the introduction of modelling. In the year following the formation of the Youth Association of Carving and Modelling, a modelling department (*sozō-ka*) was established.[48]

In the original draft of the association's bylaws, it is worth noting that the following three things were excluded from the list of what counted as sculpture:[49]

1. forms furnished with a practical function
2. objects carved in relief
3. small objects less than 3 cm

We can read this as an assertion that sculpture should, to the very end, have an independent existence as an object of aesthetic appreciation. Three-dimensional plastic arts, as fine art objects, are not meant to be taken in the hand and enjoyed like *netsuke* or *kibutsu* (a receptacle, container, or utensil); they are supposed to have an independent existence that confronts the viewer. For this reason, objects carved or modelled in relief, which rely upon a base of some kind, must also be rejected. This shows the specific state of the sculpture production-appreciation system, but the rules concerning size can be seen as an exclusion of the amulet from Herbert Read's two outermost limits of sculpture art—the amulet and the monument—or, to express it another way, as an inclination towards monumentality.[50] Though these three assertions never went any further than the original draft of the bylaws, and therefore never appeared in the codified rules, they can be seen as indicative of the association's fundamental ideas about sculpture.

As an additional comment on the Tokyo School of Fine Arts, many young men from East Asia who aspired to a career in fine arts studied at this national art school. Kim Bok-jin (1901–1940), whom Youngna Kim has called 'the first modern Korean sculptor', was one such foreign exchange student. In 1922, he and his peers participated in the Korean Art Exhibition (*Chōsen bijutsu tenrankai*), which opened in connection with Japan's colonial policy.[51] Kim Bok-jin studied modelling at the Tokyo School of Fine Arts and was selected to participate in a government-sponsored exhibition in 1924.[52] In China, Jin Xuecheng (dates unknown) was showered with attention after being selected to participate in a government-sponsored exhibition in 1936,[53] while the Taiwan-born Huang Tu-Shui (1895–1930) collected accolades from his multiple invitations to participate in government-sponsored exhibitions.[54] These exhibitions are discussed in the next section.

The 1907 Ministry of Education Art Exhibition and the Establishment of a chōkoku Category

In 1907, the Ministry of Education, in imitation of the French salon system, established an annual art exhibition—the Monbushō bijutsu tenrankai, known as the Bunten for short. From the early Meiji period onward, state-level promotion of art had basically been part of the government's policy to encourage industry. By contrast, the Bunten was the brainchild of the cultural administration. For the authorities of the art world, it was the equivalent of a review in which the power of the state was in the background. For that reason, it served as a gateway to success for artists and became the subject of considerable social attention.

The exhibition was comprised of three groups: Japanese-style paintings, Western-style paintings (*seiyōga*), and sculpture.[55] It is thought that the *chōkoku* sculpture genre was established at the societal level by means of this exhibition. State power, coupled with the authority of the art world, served to impress this word upon the public, and it came to be passed on to subsequent exhibitions, continuing in usage even at the present-day Nitten exhibition.[56] The Bunten's use of *chōkoku* was also emulated at the Korean Art Exhibition.[57] Its competitor, *chōso*, was also in use at this time, but though it appeared at the Tokyo Industrial Exposition (*Tokyo kangyō hakurankai*) in the same year[58] and later at the Manchurian Art Exhibition (*Manshūkoku bijutsu tenrankai*),[59] it has remained a subsidiary term to the present day. A sculpture category was not created for the Taiwan Art Exhibition (*Taiwan bijutsu tenrankai*).[60]

There are two notable points about the Bunten exhibition when it was first established. First, there was no craft arts group. Second, though the paintings were divided into the two categories of 'Japanese' and 'Western-style', this was not done for the sculpture group. In the term *nihonga*, we perceive a kind of expectation that traditional paintings will be made to represent the cultural perspective of the Japanese nation state—a glorification of the visual arts in Japanism, where the idea is to try to make 'Japan' conspicuous in representative painting examples. In sculpture, too, as Ōmura Seigai pointed out in his *chōso* theory, it is not impossible to create an opposition between Japan and the West.[61] However, as we noted in the section above on the Youth Association of Carving and Modelling at the Tokyo School of Fine Arts, the fact that such measures were not taken with sculpture is thought to be due to the fact that the points of conflict—in comparison with painting—are far more obscure.

The absence of crafts can be understood in terms of the modernist purging of the painting and sculpture genres that had become widely recognized by the public during the third Domestic Industrial Exposition, or in other words, as a prolongation of the exclusion of industrialized plastic arts that had begun there. At the third exposition in 1890, craft arts were included in the fine arts category, but at the fourth exposition in 1895, and from that time on, fine arts and craft arts were classified in juxtaposition with one another, as indicated by the use of the group title "Fine Arts' and 'Art Crafts" (*bijutsu oyobi bijutsu kōgei*).[62]

The exclusion of craft arts from the fine arts meant the exclusion of industrial art objects in other genres as well, and, at the same time, the exclusion of crafted plastic arts objects. For sculpture, the start of this discriminating behaviour is found at the Tokyo Industrial Exposition, which was held with the support of the Tokyo Prefectural government in 1907—the same year as the first Bunten. At the exposition, Kitamura Shikai (1871–1927), who exhibited a marble statue in the *chōso* division, destroyed his own statue in protest at the craftsman-like attitude of the awards jury. This incident invited considerable debate and was also widely picked up by the press. In a conversation published by the Asahi Shinbun newspaper, Kitamura—speaking on the source of the unfairness of jury-members giving priority to their own factions—stated, 'It is because there are no people of scholarship among the judges today. There is nobody but people who have worked their way up from nothing, people possessed with what you might call the spirit of craftsmanship.'[63] Kitamura further criticized the people whose participation he saw as the source of inequity and unfairness, saying that people with such craftsman-like attitudes had no sense of technique, no ideals, and no visual discernment. This was unquestionably a modernist's appeal for the autonomy and purity of the fine arts genre.

Since there are no objects with a practical function to be found in the photos of the exhibition catalogue,[64] it is clear that Kitamura's problem was not with industrial art objects themselves but with the craftsman ideal that he associated with plastic arts. In contrast to superior sculpted objects, which smack of centripetal—or inward trending—concepts, decorative ornaments belonging to the category of craftworks, like the objects that are placed in *tokonoma* alcoves, for example, move centrifugally—or outwardly—towards their environments. Kitamura, who learned ivory sculpting and relied upon mass-produced models for his ivory-work and livelihood, was the son of a temple carpenter.[65] It is thought that those circumstances led him to a frustrated desire to divide sculpted arts from industrial arts. Although the exclusion of craft arts at the Bunten can be seen as an acceptance of the rise of the modernism of art, a polemic with far more destructive power than Kitamura's statue-breaking would later come to ripple through the exhibition. The vanguard of this movement was Takamura Kōtarō.

Conclusion: Modern *chōkoku* and the Reception of Rodinism

Takamura Kōtarō published notes from his conversation with Naganuma Moriyoshi under the title 'Gendai bijutsu no yōran jidai' (The cradle of contemporary art) in the July 1936 issue of *Chūō kōron*. In the preface, Kōtarō writes that Naganuma is the artist and the benchmark that avant-gardists (*zen'eisha*) sculpture should surpass. Takamura Kōtarō disavowed them by name, saying that while Technical Art School alumni may be pioneers, they are not worth challenging.[66] This was about sixty years after the opening of the Technical Art School and several years after the end of the Taishō era (1912–1926) avant-garde movement, however. Takamura Kōtarō's severe criticism of the modern Japanese sculpture genre actually begins with a commentary on the early Bunten exhibitions. In 1909, after more than four years in the West as an exchange student, he shook the sculpture world by publishing multiple harsh critiques of the Bunten exhibition one after another. The sculpture genre, in becoming a subject of criticism, had—however imperfectly—been firmly established.

The object of Kitamura Shikai's repudiation was decorative ornaments lacking in ideals. Takamura Kōtarō, too, was searching for the ideals of sculpture—forcefully bringing up the importance of fundamental values and standards to the sculpture genre. However, bronze statues are burdened not just with ideals, but with a national ideology, and they are easily clad in the ideology of the moment via attributes or costumes. Nevertheless, such sycophantic intentions were not the customary ideals that Kōtarō sought. Rather, what was important to him was the antithesis of the ideology of the national perspective, namely, the inner existence of human lives—*la vie*—itself. Kōtarō was searching for a unique ideology within sculpture. A perusal of the Bunten criticism that he was writing at the time shows the term life—*la vie*—appearing everywhere. For example: 'I want life—*la vie*. Simply life—*la vie*. I will never look back on the surplus waste that I have cast aside'.[67] Rather than give shape to that which is external, Kōtarō instead wanted to give birth to that which is internal, as if in a great burst of orogenic mountain-making. He captured that concept with the phrase 'life—*la vie*'. We might say that he was searching for those works that were synchronised with the life of the inner self. Kitamura's assertion was that true art was only possible when it related to the inner self, not when it was related to external factors, like perceived symbols or established ideologies. In other words, he was looking for the modern human perspective in the sculpture genre, and from that perspective Japanese sculpted works of the period were utterly 'lacking in impact, like an overboiled bowl of udon'.[68]

Takamura Kōtarō learned this perspective from Auguste Rodin (1840–1917). Although Kōtarō did not study under Rodin, he had been captivated by Rodin through photographs of his work even before he left to study abroad. Once Kōtarō had the opportunity to encounter Rodin's works in the flesh in New York and Paris, his admiration quickly intensified. He also had decisive exchanges with Ogiwara Morie (1879–1910, better known as Rokuzan) during his time as a foreign exchange student. Ogiwara, one step ahead of Takamura in setting down in Paris, met with Rodin in person and made many studies of his sculptures. Kōtarō was fascinated by these works, and he gave them high praise. Upon their return to Japan, the two men would disseminate Rodinism through the cooperation of tangible works and criticism. In addition to his criticism of the Bunten, Kōtarō translated a compilation of Rodin's observations, *The Words of Rodin* (*Rodin no kotoba*)[69] and published a critical biography of his life.[70] He did not merely inspire Rodinism; through it he brought to Japan the fundamental idea of sculpted art where massive and real forms are realized by creating 'volume'.

Ogiwara, who was again one step ahead in returning to Japan, also worked to promote Rodinism. At the second Bunten exhibition, which opened in 1908, he declared his personal perspective on sculpture, saying, 'It can express a kind of inner power through a single production. It is an expression of life'.[71] When you consider that this discourse developed in the aftermath of the Russo-Japanese War (1904), which left 55,655 dead and 144,352 wounded,[72] it is clear that Ogiwara and Kōtarō's thoughts on 'life'—while a particular product of the impact of Rodin and the West's 'philosophy of life' (*sei no tetsugaku*)—were also rooted in a sense of being in the shadow of the distinctive and pressing concerns of modern Japan.

Ogiwara Morie presented his work on the main stage of the Bunten exhibition. In 1910, he died at the age of thirty, having just completed work on *Woman* (*Onna*; Plate 9)—a sculpture modelled on the woman he had fallen in love with. Ogiwara's friend, the metal caster Yamamoto Azumi (1880–1945), cast the statue—which had been finished in clay—and exhibited it at the fourth Bunten exhibition that same year.[73] The bronze monuments of national heroes that had been constructed throughout the capital city embodied ideologies external to both the art and the artists who created them. By contrast, this bronze statue of a kneeling unnamed woman comes from a fixed place within the artist himself. She assumes an air of upward motion through a surface that unfolds in a spiral. One cannot help but feel that the woman's expression, leaning as if to look up, recalls some heavenly thing or ideal dimension. Ogiwara's *Woman* was a bronze statue inverted from external concerns to internal ones. The *chōkoku* genre had finally arrived at the beginning of its modernization.

As Yashiro Yukio has noted, due to the pantheistic ideological topography in Japan, the focus of plastic arts was not narrowed down to the human figure. Furthermore, the influence of the Buddhist idea that the human body is tainted resulted in representations of the human form that were fainthearted at best.[74] This is a convincing explanation for why the sculpture genre, in which the human form had played a pivotal role since the time of the Greeks, transitioned to a position of inferiority in Japan. The relative rarity of realism was consistent with the state of traditional aesthetic plastic arts, which inclined towards the decorative. Amid such historical and social conditions, the sculpture genre—which makes the human form its foundation—was concerned with surmounting the problems of art. That is to say, it was concerned with the question of an awareness of human existence—with a self-consciousness that embodied the contradiction of both belonging to the world and being in confrontation with it. The woman created by Ogiwara Morie, with her lower legs buried in the earth as she twists her body in an attempt to stand, is an emblem of the drama of such a history of thought. Ogiwara's posthumous works saw completion with the launch of the self-published literary magazine *Shirakaba* (White birch) when Takamura Kōtarō published *Green Sun* (*Ryokushoku no taiyō*) in a year of heightened artistic anarchism. Under the deep black shadows of the colonization of Korea and the High Treason Incident (*Taigyaku jiken*, 1910–1911), modern individuals stood up. *Woman* was created in the midst of this period.

Four years after *Woman* was presented, the first art dictionary was published in Japan. The entry for *chōkoku*—sculpture—includes the following: 'The space of sculpture requires solid space—that is to say, three-dimensionality. It is primarily tactile and at the very least must reproduce that sense of tactility'.[75] The term *chōkoku* had thus acquired a stable position in the fine arts lexicon of Japan. The wording of this entry, however, demonstrates that sculpture, as a genre of visual arts, had a difficult-to-describe dimension. Tactility depends upon a nullification of distance, and for that reason it is difficult for the sculptural arts to fulfil visual art's requirement of distance. *Woman*, for example, is intangible when cut off from the blind tactility of a caress. Expressed another way, sculpture involves complications that render it difficult to incorporate within 'art'; therefore, sculpture was an important opportunity to open new possibilities for the fine arts that had come along on the verge of the modern era. Be that as it may, a fully grasped awareness of this opportunity as a critical perspective on the state of fine arts had to wait for the appearance of the Taishō era avant-garde, but a debate of that topic would be beyond the scope of this essay.

(Translated by Sara Sumpter)

Notes

1 'plastic arts' here refers to objects modelled or carved in clay, wood, stone, or metal.
2 Kitazawa Noriaki, *Me no shinden: 'Bijutsu' juyōshi nōto* [Temple of the eye: notes on the history of the reception of 'fine art'] (Tokyo: Buryukke/Seiunsha, 2010). See also Kenneth Masaki Shima, 'From Temple of the Eye: Notes on the Reception of "Fine Art"', *Josai daigaku kokusai bunka kyōiku senta kiyō* 24 (2010): 228–241.
3 Numerous researchers give Nishi Amane's 'Bimyō gakusetsu' [Theory of elegance] as the first appearance of the term *bijutsu*, but that text did not appear until 1879. See Mori Wataru, 'Nishi Amane *Bimyō gakusetsu* seiritsu toshi no kōshō' [An investigation of the period in which Nishi Amane's *Theory of Elegance* was developed], *Kobungaku* 14, no. 6 (1969).
4 *Universal Exhibition in 1873 in Vienna*, 'Classifications and Divisions' (Gaimushō Archives, Tokyo), p. 4.
5 See 'Ōkoku Ifu hakurankai shuppin kokoroe' [Information on exhibits at the Exposition in Vienna, Austria] (1872), *Bijutsu*, *Nihon kindai shisō taikei* [A survey of modern Japanese thought] 17 (Tokyo: Iwanami Shoten, 1989), p. 404.
6 Walter Benjamin, 'The Work of Art in the Age of Its Technological Reproducibility', trans. Edmund Jephcott et al., in *Walter Benjamin: Selected Writings*, Vol. 3, ed. Howard Eiland and Michael W. Jennings (Cambridge: Belknap Press, 2006), p. 106.
7 Takamura Kōtarō, 'Chichi to kankei' [My relationship with my father], in *Takamura Kōtarō zenshū* [The complete Takamura Kōtarō] 10 (Tokyo: Chikuma Shobo, 1995), p. 229.
8 Entry for May 23, 1871. 'Gofukoku' [Edicts], in *Tokyo kokuritsu hakubutsukan hyakunen-shi: shiryōhen* [A hundred years' history of the Tokyo National Museum: historical documents] (Tokyo: Tokyo Kokuritsu Hakubutsukan, 1973), p. 606.
9 Entry for April 25, 1871. 'Daigaku kengen' [University proposals], in *Tokyo kokuritsu hakubutsukan hyakunen-shi*, pp. 606–607.

10 Okakura Tenshin, *Nihon bijutsushi* [Japanese art history] (Tokyo: Heibonsha, 2001), pp. 57–59.
11 Wang Yun and Shen Xu, *Shuo wen jie zi ju dou, zhong juan* [Explaining characters] (Taipei: Taiwan Shang Wu Yin Shu Guan, 1968), p. 1180.
12 Takamura Kōun, 'Meiji shonen no chōkoku nitsuite' [On early Meiji sculpture], *Kokka* 429 (1926): 229–300.
13 Ibid., 230.
14 *Eiwa taiyaku shūchin jisho—A Pocket Dictionary of the English and Japanese Language* (Tokyo: Kurataya Seiemon, 1869), p. 361. An earlier version of this dictionary, published in 1862, included a listing for 'sculpture' that was translated as *shōzō wo kizamu jutsu* ('the art of portrait-carving').
15 William Lobscheid, *English and Chinese Dictionary, with the Punti and Mandarin Pronunciation*, Part IV (Hong Kong: Daily Press, 1866), p. 1554. In the modern *Pocket Oxford Chinese Dictionary* (Oxford: Oxford University Press, the Commercial Press, 2009), 'sculpture' is translated as *diaoke, diaosu, diaoke pin*, and *diaosu pin*. In the *Pocket Kenkyusha Japanese Dictionary* (Oxford: Oxford University Press, 2003), it is simply translated as *chōkoku*.
16 Morioka Kenji, 'Yakugo keiseiki ni okeru Lobscheid eika jiten no eikyō I' [The influence of Lobscheid's *English and Chinese Dictionary* during the formative stages of translating terms, part 1], *Tokyo Joshi Daigaku fuzoku hikaku bunka kenkyū kiyō* 19 (1965): 68–71; and 'Yakugo keiseiki ni okeru Lobscheid eika jiten no eikyō II' (part 2), *Tokyo Joshi Daigaku fuzoku hikaku bunka kenkyū kiyō* 21 (1966): 114–125.
17 Walter Henry Medhurst, *An English and Japanese and Japanese and English Vocabulary* (Batavia: s.n., 1830), p. 33.
18 'Kōbu bijutsu gakkō sho kisoku' [Various regulations of the Technical Art School], *Bijutsu, Nihon kindai shisō taikei* 17 (Tokyo: Iwanami Shoten, 1989), p. 431.
19 Kaneko Kazuo, *Kindai Nihon bijutsu kyōiku no kenkyū—Meiji, Taishō jidai* [A study of modern Japanese art education: Meiji and Taisho periods] (Tokyo: Chūō Kōron Bijutsu Shuppan, 1999), pp. 140–179.
20 This document was compiled in 1883 by the Minister of the Right, Iwakura Tomomi (1825–1883), and Councilor Yamagata Aritomo (1838–1922).
21 'Kōbu bijutsu gakkō sho kisoku', p. 433. It is not the case, however, that no samurai ever created sculptures. A legend showing the relationship between members of the warrior class and sculpture production remains extant today. There is, for example, Morikawa Kyoriku (1656–1715), a feudal retainer in Hikone—present-day Shiga Prefecture—who was known as both a haiku poet and a painter. When his master, the haiku master Bashō (1644–1694), passed away, Kyoriku carved a cherry tree as a relic of his master. This relic is said to be enshrined in Kyoto's Bashōdō Temple. See Ishimaru Shōun, *Ōmi no gajin-tachi* [Artists of Omi] (Tokyo: Sanburaito Shipman, 1980).
22 Kim Youngna, *20th Century Korean Art* (London: Laurence King, 2006), p. 153.
23 The exposition was held a total of five times: in 1877, 1881, 1890, 1895, and 1903.
24 *Universal Exhibition in 1873 in Vienna*, 'Classifications and Divisions', p. 4.
25 The Iwakura Mission was a Japanese diplomatic mission to Europe and the United States. It took place from 1871 to 1873.
26 *Beiō kairan jiki*, ed. Kume Kunitake (Tokyo: Hakubunsha, 1878).
27 Yashiro Yukio, *Nihon bijutsu no tokushitsu* [Characteristics of Japanese art], 2nd ed. (Tokyo: Iwanami Shoten, 1965), pp. 183–184.
28 It is possible to see the influence of the Paris World's Fair that was held the previous year on the modernist revolution that took place at the third Domestic Industrial Exposition. See Kitazawa Noriaki, *Bijutsu no Poritikusu: 'kōgei' no naritachi wo shōten toshite* [The politics of art: on the development of 'industrial arts'] (Tokyo: Yumani Shobo, 2013), pp. 29–34.
29 Tokyo Geijutsu Daigaku Hyakunen-shi Kankō Iinkairon, *Tokyo bijutsu gakkō hyakunen-shi: Tokyo bijutsu gakkō hen* [A hundred years' history of the Tokyo School of Art: Tokyo School of Art] 1 (Tokyo: Gyosei, 1987), pp. 165–167.
30 Ibid., pp. 112–114.
31 Ibid., pp. 65–66.

32 Dai-san-kai Naikoku Kangyō Hakurankai Jimukyoku, *Dai-san-kai naikoku kangyō hakurankai jimu hōkoku* [Business report of the third Domestic Industrial Exposition] (Tokyo: Nōshōmushō, 1891), pp. 193, 216–217.
33 Tokyo Geijutsu Daigaku Hyakunen-shi, *Tokyo bijutsu gakkō hyakunen-shi* 1, pp. 181–182.
34 Ibid., p. 141.
35 Ibid., p. 431.
36 Ibid., p. 67.
37 Ibid., p. 517.
38 Takamura Kōun, *Kōun kaikodan* [Kōun's reminiscences] (Tokyo: Manrikaku Shobo, 1929), pp. 185–189.
39 Ibid., pp. 189–194.
40 From the reminiscences of Itaya Hazan (1872–1963). See 'Honkō sōritsu tōji kaiko zadankai' [A symposium on recollections of the period when our school was founded], *Tokyo bijutsu gakkō kōyū geppō* 29, no. 42 (April 1931), pp. 30–31.
41 Okakura Tenshin, '"Kokka" hakkan no kotoba' [Comment published in 'Kokka' Magazine], *Okakura Tenshin zenshū* [The complete Okakura Tenshin] 3 (Tokyo: Heibonsha, 1979), p. 46.
42 Ibid.
43 Tokyo Geijutsu Daigaku Hyakunen-shi, *Tokyo bijutsu gakkō hyakunen-shi* 1, pp. 177–181, 222–224, 231–233.
44 Yonehara Unkai, 'Saneki-ka yōsei no konyaku' [Training with carpenters, past and present], *Shoga kottō zashi* 52 (1912): 39.
45 Fujii Motohiko, '"Chōso" no jitsugen: shinhakken no Yonehara Unkai sakuhin niten wo kaishite' [The realization of 'chōso': through two newly discovered works by Yonehara Unkai], *Kindai gasetsu* 18 (2009), p. 39.
46 Tokyo Geijutsu Daigaku Hyakunen-shi, *Tokyo bijutsu gakkō hyakunen-shi* 1, pp. 352–358.
47 Ōmura Seigai, 'Chōso ron' [A theory of chōso], *Kyoto bijutsu kyōkai zasshi* 29 (1894), p. 4.
48 Tokyo Geijutsu Daigaku Hyakunen-shi Kankō Iinkairon, *Tokyo bijutsu gakkō hyakunen-shi: Tokyo bijutsu gakkō ron* [A hundred years' history of the Tokyo School of Art: Tokyo School of Art] 2 (Tokyo: Gyosei, 1992), pp. 6–14.
49 Tokyo Geijutsu Daigaku Hyakunen-shi, *Tokyo bijutsu gakkō hyakunen-shi* 1, p. 354.
50 Herbert Read, *The Art of Sculpture* (Princeton: Princeton University Press, 1969), p. 5.
51 Kim Youngna, *20th Century Korean Art*, pp. 153–154.
52 Yoshida Chizuko, *Kindai higashi-Ajia bijutsu ryūgakusei no kenkyū: Tōkyō bijutsu gakkō ryūgakusei shiryō* [A study of modern East-Asian foreign exchange art students: records of exchange students at the Tokyo School of Art] (Tokyo: Yumani Shobō, 2009), p. 184.
53 Ibid., pp. 54–55.
54 Ibid., p. 209.
55 'Bijutsu tenrankai kitei 2' [Art exhibition regulations], *Kanpō* 7181 (June 8, 1907).
56 'Kōeki shadanhōshin Nitten teikan' ['Nitten' Fine Arts Exhibition articles of incorporation], https://nitten.or.jp/wp-content/uploads/2017/07/teikan_h270529.pdf (accessed May 29, 2015).
57 'Chōsen bijutsu tenrankai kitei' [Regulations of the Korean Art Exhibition], *Kanpō* 2841 (January 24, 1922).
58 Masaki Naohiko, 'Sōsetsu' [General remarks], *Tokyo Kangyō Hakurankai shinsa hōkoku, kan-ichi* [Evaluation report of the Tokyo Industrial Exposition, volume one] (Tokyo: Tokyo-fucho, 1908), p. 171. However, in a later publication, chōso was replaced with chōzō (carved statues), sozō (clay statues), tsuikizō (hammered metal statues), chūzō (cast metal statues), chōhan (block carving), and tenkoku (seal engraving). See 'Shuppin burui mokuroku' [List of exhibit classifications], *Tokyo Kangyō Hakurankai jimu hōkoku, jō* [Business report of the Tokyo Industrial Exposition, Part One] (Tokyo: Tokyo-fucho, 1909).
59 'Manshūkoku Bijutsu Tenrankai kisoku' [Regulations of the Manchurian Art Exhibition], *Seifukōhō* 2771 (August 26, 1943).
60 'Taiwan Bijutsu Tenrankai kitei' [Regulations of the Taiwan Art Exhibition], *Kanpō* 3464 (July 21, 1938). In 1927, a painting-centred exhibition was organized by the Taiwanese Board of Education with the support of the Governor-General's Bureau of Education.

The Taiwanese Board of Education eventually intended to include such categories as *chōso*, *zuan* (design), and industrial arts. In 1938, however, the exhibition was taken over by the Governor-General, organized with national funds, and focused strictly on paintings. See Yen Chuan-ying, *Fūkei shinkō: Taiwan kindai bijutsu bunkendō doku, gekan* [Landscapes of the mind: a bibliography of modern Taiwanese art, part two], trans. Tsuruta Takeyoshi (Taipei: Xiong Shi Tu Shu Gu Gen You Zian Gong Si, 2001), pp. 638–646.
61 Ōmura, 'Chōso ron', pp. 5–6.
62 Kitazawa, *Bijutsu no poritikusu*, p. 21.
63 'Kitamura-shi Shikai-shi no jikiwa' [The personal account of Mr. Kitamura Shikai], *Tokyo Asahi Shinbun*, June 13, 1907.
64 *Tokyo Kangyō Hakurankai bijutsukan shuppin zuroku: seiyōga oyobi chōso no bu* [An illustrated catalogue of exhibits in the art gallery of the Tokyo Industrial Exposition: oil paintings and engraving sections] (Tokyo: Tokyo-fu, 1907).
65 'Kitamura Shikai ryakuden' [A short biography of Kitamura Shikai], in *Shikai yoteki* [The trivialities of Shikai], ed. Kitamura Masanobu (Self-publication, 1929).
66 Naganuma Moriyoshi and Takamura Kōtarō, eds., 'Gendai bijutsu no yōran jidai' [The cradle of contemporary art], *Chūō kōron* (July 1936), p. 214.
67 Takamura Kōtarō, 'Bunten no chōkoku' [Sculpture at the 'Bunten' exhibition], *Takamura Kōtarō zenshū* [The complete Takamura Kōtarō] 6 (Tokyo: Chikuma Shobo, 1957), p. 115.
68 Takamura Kōtarō, 'Dai-san-kai Monbushō tenrankai saigo no ichibetsu' [A last look at the third annual Ministry of Education Art Exhibition], *Takamura Kōtarō zenshū* 6 (Tokyo: Chikuma Shobō, 1957), p. 18.
69 Takamura Kōtarō, ed., *Rodin no kotoba* [Words of Rodin] (Tokyo: Aranda Shobo, 1916); and *Shoku Rodin no kotoba* [Futher words of Rodin] (Tokyo: Sobunkaku, 1920).
70 Takamura Kōtarō, *Ōgiyusuto Rodan* [Auguste Rodin] (Tokyo: Arusu, 1927).
71 Ogiwara Morie, 'Yo ga mitaru tōzai no chōkoku' [Sculpture I have observed, East and West], *Chōkoku shinzui* [The quintessence of sculpture] (Tokyo: Chuō Kōron Bijutsu Shuppan, 1978), p. 32.
72 From the 'statistics' list of the 'Russo-Japanese War by Theme' search function of the Kokuritsu Kōbunshokan Ajia Rekishi Shiryō Sentā website. www.jacar.go.jp/nichiro/keyword06.htm (accessed December 18, 2018).
73 'Bunten hen, ni' [The 'Bunten' exhibition, 2], *Nitten shi* [A history of the 'Nitten' exhibition] 2, edited by Nitten shi henshū iinkai. (Tokyo: Nitten, 1980), p. 166. See also Kitano Susumu, *Azumi to Rokuzan: chūkin shinzui, Yamamoto Azumi* [Azumi and Rokuzan: Yamamoto Azumi and the quintessence of metal casting] (Shuppan Azumino, 1998), pp. 39–42.
74 Yashiro, *Nihon bijutsu no tokushitsu*, p. 225.
75 *Bijutsu jiten* [Dictionary of Art] (Tokyo: Nihon Bijutsu Gakuin, 1914), p. 178.

Bibliography

Anonymous. 'Bijutsu tenrankai kitei 2' [Art exhibition regulations]. *Kanpō* 7181 (June 8, 1907): 202.

———. *Tokyo Kangyō Hakurankai bijutsukan shuppin zuroku: seiyōga oyobi chōso no bu* [An illustrated catalogue of exhibits in the art gallery of the Tokyo Industrial Exposition: oil paintings and engraving sections]. Tokyo: Tōkyō-fu, 1907.

———. 'Shuppin burui mokuroku' [List of exhibit classifications], *Tokyo Kangyō Hakurankai jimu hōkoku, jō* [Business report of the Tokyo Industrial Exposition, Part One]. Tokyo: Tōkyō-fucho, 1909.

———. 'Chōsen bijutsu tenrankai kitei' [Regulations of the Korean Art Exhibition], *Kanpō* 2841 (January 24, 1922): 419–420.

———. 'Taiwan Bijutsu Tenrankai kitei' [Regulations of the Taiwan Art Exhibition], *Kanpō* 3464 (July 21, 1938).

———. 'Manshūkoku Bijutsu Tenrankai kisoku' [Regulations of the Manchurian Art Exhibition]. *Seifukōhō* 2771 (August 26, 1943).

---. 'Bunten hen, ni' [The Bunten exhibition, 2], *Nitten shi* [A history of the 'Nitten' exhibition] 2. Tokyo: Nitten, 1980.

---. 'Kōbu bijutsu gakkō sho kisoku' [Various regulations of the Imperial College of Art]. *Bijutsu, Nihon kindai shisō taikei* 17, edited by Aoki Shigeru and akai Tadayasu. Tokyo: Iwanami Shoten, 1989. p. 431.

---. 'Ōkoku Ifu hakurankai shuppin kokoroe' [Information on exhibits at the Exposition in Vienna, Austria] (1872). *Bijutsu, Nihon kindai shisō taikei* [Fine art. a survey of modern Japanese thought] 17, edited by Aoki Shigeru and Akai Tadayasu. Tokyo: Iwanami Shoten, 1989.

---. 'Kōeki shadanhōshin Nitten teikan' ['Nitten' Fine Arts Exhibition articles of incorporation], https://nitten.or.jp/wp-content/uploads/2017/07/teikan_h270529.pdf. Accessed May 29, 2015.

Benjamin, Walter. 'The Work of Art in the Age of Its Technological Reproducibility', translated by Edmund Jephcott et al. In *Walter Benjamin: Selected Writings*, Vol. 3, edited by Howard Eiland and Michael W. Jennings. Cambridge: Belknap Press, 2006.

Bijutsu jiten [Dictionary of art]. Tokyo: Nihon Bijutsu Gakuin, 1914.

Dai-san-kai Naikoku Kangyō Hakurankai Jimukyoku. *Dai-san-kai naikoku kangyō hakurankai jimu hōkoku* [Business report of the third National Industrial Exposition]. Tokyo: Nōshōmushō, 1891.

Fujii Motohiko. '"Chōso" no jitsugen: shinhakken no Yonehara Unkai sakuhin niten wo kaishite' [The realization of '*chōso*': through two newly discovered works by Yonehara Unkai]. *Kindai gasetsu* 18 (2009): 29–46.

Horii Tatsunosuke, ed. *Eiwa taiyaku shūchin jisho—A Pocket Dictionary of the English and Japanese Language*. Tokyo: Kurataya Seiemon, 1869.

Ishimaru Shōun, *Ōmi no gajin-tachi* [Artists of Omi]. Tokyo: Sanburaito Shipman, 1980.

Itaya Hazan. 'Honkō sōritsu tōji kaiko zadankai' [A symposium on recollections of the period when our school was founded]. *Tōkyō bijutsu gakkō kōyū geppō* 29, no. 42 (April 1931): 30–31.

Kaneko Kazuo. *Kindai Nihon bijutsu kyōiku no kenkyū—Meiji, Taishō jidai* [A study of modern Japanese art education: Meiji and Taisho periods]. Tokyo: Chūō Kōron Bijutsu Shuppan, 1999.

Kim, Youngna. *20th Century Korean Art*. London: Laurence King, 2006.

Kitamura Masanobu. 'Kitamura Shikai ryakuden' [A short biography of Kitamura Shikai]. In *Shikai yoteki* [The trivialities of Shikai], edited by Kitamura Masanobu. Self-publication, 1929.

Kitamura Shikai. 'Kitamura-shi Shikai-shi no jikiwa' [The personal account of Mr Kitamura Shikai], *Tokyo Asahi Shinbun*, June 13, 1907.

Kitano Susumu. *Azumi to Rokuzan: chūkin shinzui, Yamamoto Azumi* [Azumi and Rokuzan: Yamamoto Azumi and the quintessence of metal casting]. Azumino: Shuppan Azumino, 1998.

Kitazawa Noriaki. *Me no shinden: 'Bijutsu' juyōshi nōto* [Temple of the eye: notes on the history of the reception of 'fine art']. Tokyo: Buryukke/Seiunsha, 2010.

---. *Bijutsu no Poritikusu: 'kōgei' no naritachi wo shōten toshite* [The politics of art: on the development of 'industrial arts']. Tokyo: Yumani Shobo, 2013.

Kokuritsu Kōbunshokan Ajia Rekishi Shiryō Sentā website. www.jacar.go.jp/nichiro/keyword06.htm. Accessed July 7, 2017.

Kume Kunitake, ed. *Beiō kairan jiki*. Tokyo: Hakubunsha, 1878.

Lobscheid, William. *English and Chinese Dictionary, with the Punti and Mandarin Pronunciation*, Part IV. Hong Kong: Daily Press, 1866.

Medhurst, Walter Henry. *An English and Japanese and Japanese and English Vocabulary*. Batavia: s.n., 1830.

Mori Agata. 'Nishi Amane *Bimyō gakusetsu* seiritsu nenji no kōshō' [An investigation of the period in which Nishi Amane's *Theory of Elegance* was developed], *Kokubungaku* 14, no. 6 (1969): 206–207.

Morioka Kenji. 'Yakugo keiseiki ni okeru Lobscheid eika jiten no eikyō I' [The influence of Lobscheid's *English and Chinese Dictionary* during the formative stages of translating terms, part 1]. *Tokyo Joshi Daigaku fuzoku hikaku bunka kenkyū kiyō* 19 (1965): 68–71.

———. 'Yakugo keiseiki ni okeru Lobscheid eika jiten no eikyō II' (part 2). *Tokyo Joshi Daigaku fuzoku hikaku bunka kenkyū kiyō* 21 (1966): 114–125.

Naganuma Moriyoshi and Takamura Kōtarō, eds. 'Gendai bijutsu no yōran jidai' [The cradle of contemporary art]. *Chūō kōron* (July 1936): 214–244.

Nasaki Naohiko. 'Sōsetsu' [General remarks]. *Tokyo Kangyō Hakurankai shinsa hōkoku, kan-ichi* [Evaluation report of the Tokyo Industrial Exposition, volume one]. Tokyo: Tōkyō-fucho, 1908.

Ogiwara Morie. 'Yo ga mitaru tōzai no chōkoku' [Sculpture I have observed, East and West]. *Chōkoku shinzui* [The quintessence of sculpture], edited by Miyagawa Torao. Tokyo: Chuō Kōron Bijutsu Shuppan, 1978.

Okakura Tenshin. '"Kokka" hakkan no kotoba' [Comment published in 'Kokka' Magazine]. In *Okakura Tenshin zenshū* [The complete Okakura Tenshin] 3, edited by Kumamoto Kenjirō, Okakura Koshirō, Kinoshita Junji, Kawakita Michiaki, and Hashikawa Bunzō. Tokyo: Heibonsha, 1979.

———. *Nihon bijutsushi* [Japanese art history], edited by Kinoshita Nagahiro. Tokyo: Heibonsha, 2001.

Ōmura Seigai, 'Chōso ron' [A theory of *chōso*]. *Kyoto bijutsu kyōkai zasshi* 29 (1894): 4–9.

Pocket Kenkyusha Japanese Dictionary. Oxford: Oxford University Press, 2003.

Pocket Oxford Chinese Dictionary. Oxford: Oxford University Press, the Commercial Press, 2009.

Read, Herbert. *The Art of Sculpture*. Princeton: Princeton University Press, 1969.

Shima, Kenneth Masaki. 'From Temple of the Eye: Notes on the Reception of "Fine Art"'. *Josai daigaku kokusai bunka kyōiku senta kiyō* 24 (2010): 228–241.

Takamura Kōtarō. *Ōgiyusuto Rodan* [Auguste Rodin]. Tokyo: Arusu, 1927.

———. 'Bunten no chōkoku' [Sculpture at the Bunten exhibition]. *Takamura Kōtarō zenshū* [The complete Takamura Kōtarō] 6 (enlarged edition), edited by Kitagawa Taichi. Tokyo: Chikuma Shobo, 1995.

———. 'Dai-san-kai Monbushō tenrankai saigo no ichibetsu' [A last look at the third annual Ministry of Education Art Exhibition]. *Takamura Kōtarō zenshū* 6 (enlarged edition), edited by Kitagawa Taichi. Tokyo: Chikuma Shobō, 1995.

———. 'Chichi to kankei' [My relationship with my father]. In *Takamura Kōtarō zenshū* [The complete Takamura Kōtarō] 10 (enlarged edition), edited by Kitagawa Taichi. Tokyo: Chikuma Shobo, 1995.

Takamura Kōtarō, ed. *Rodin no kotoba* [Words of Rodin]. Tokyo: Aranda Shobo, 1916.

———, ed. *Shoku Rodin no kotoba* [Further words of Rodin]. Tokyo: Sobunkaku, 1920.

Takamura Kōun. 'Meiji shonen no chōkoku nitsuite' [On early Meiji sculpture]. *Kokka* 429 (1926): 229–300.

———. *Kōun kaikodan* [Kōun's reminiscences]. Tokyo: Manrikaku Shobo, 1929.

Tokyo Geijutsu Daigaku Hyakunen-shi Kankō Iinkairon. *Tokyo bijutsu gakkō hyakunen-shi: Tokyo bijutsu gakkō hen* [A hundred years' history of the Tokyo School of Art: Tokyo School of Art] 1. Tokyo: Gyosei, 1987.

Tokyo Geijutsu Daigaku Hyakunen-shi Kankō Iinkairon. *Tokyo bijutsu gakkō hyakunen-shi: Tokyo bijutsu gakkō ron* [A hundred years' history of the Tokyo School of Art: Tokyo School of Art] 2. Tokyo: Gyosei, 1992.

Tokyo Kokuritsu Hakubutsukan. Entry for April 25, 1871. 'Daigaku kengen' [University proposals]. In *Tokyo kokuritsu hakubutsukan hyakunen-shi* [A hundred years' history of the Tokyo National Museum], edited by Tokyo Kokuritsu Hakubutsukan. Tokyo: Tokyo Kokuritsu Hakubutsukan, 1973.

Tokyo Kokuritsu Hakubutsukan. Entry for May 23, 1871. 'Gofukoku' [Edicts]. In *Tokyo kokuritsu hakubutsukan hyakunen-shi: shiryōhen* [A hundred years' history of the Tokyo National Museum: historical documents], edited by Tokyo Kokuritsu Hakubutsukan. Tokyo: Tokyo Kokuritsu Hakubutsukan, 1973.

Universal Exhibition in 1873 in Vienna, 'Classifications and Divisions'. Gaimushō Archives, Tokyo.

Wang Yun and Shen Xu. *Shuo wen jie zi ju dou, zhong juan* [Explaining texts]. Taipei: Taiwan Shang Wu Yin Shu Guan, 1968.

Yashiro Yukio. *Nihon bijutsu no tokushitsu* [Characteristics of Japanese art], 2nd ed. Tokyo: Iwanami Shoten, 1965.

Yen Chuan-ying. *Fūkei shinkō: Taiwan kindai bijutsu bunkendō doku, gekan* [Landscapes of the mind: a bibliography of modern Taiwanese art, part two], translated by Tsuruta Takeyoshi. Taipei: Xiong Shi Tu Shu Gu Gen You Zian Gong Si, 2001.

Yonehara Unkai. 'Jitsuzai-ka yōsei no konyaku' [Training with carpenters, past and present]. *Shoga kottō zashi* 52 (1912): 38–39.

Yoshida Chizuko. *Kindai higashi-Ajia bijutsu ryūgakusei no kenkyū: Tōkyō bijutsu gakkō ryūgakusei shiryō* [A study of modern East-Asian foreign exchange art students: records of exchange students at the Tokyo School of Art]. Tokyo: Yumani Shobō, 2009.

8 War and Pornography in East Asia[1]

Adachi Gen

Introduction

There can be no doubt that austerity stifled the availability of erotic images in wartime Asia, especially in the era of Japanese militarism from 1931 to 1945.[2] The people, however, respected austerity, as attested by the common slogan, 'I don't want anything until we win the war'.[3] Art in this period was known as 'wartime art', and had the purpose of serving the war effort and the country.[4] Censorship was in force, decadent material banned, and erotic books were absolutely unthinkable.

But was this really true? It seems unlikely that the availability of erotica was entirely suppressed. This paper examines the representations of erotica and pornography in the period of Japanese militarism and war between 1931 and 1945 and gives examples from Korea and China.

In general, 'pornography' is understood as obscene text and images.[5] Here I focus on images from the mid-20th century, a neglected period in the study of Japanese art history. While the *shunga* (erotic images often produced by *ukiyo-e* artists) produced in the Edo period (1603–1868) are a renowned form of Japanese pornography, and Japan is now famous for adult videos, games, comics, and other kinds of pornography, the vast but somewhat obscure pornography produced in mid-20th-century Japan and East Asia is relatively unknown.[6]

Was there any pornography available in wartime East Asia? Most people would say no. For example, a comparison of the decorations on Japanese and U.S. military aircraft shows that the Japanese Mitsubishi A6M 'Zero' planes were not embellished in any way except for the Japanese flag symbol of the rising sun and a vertical stripe; however, U.S. military aircraft were decorated with provocative images of nude or barely clothed women. This was called 'nose art', and was done as unofficial graffiti to easily identify friendly units, a tradition that was not followed by any Asian military.

This difference could simply reflect the cultural differences between Asian and Western countries. However, in 1930s Europe, Nazi Germany also condemned pornography and burned pornographic books and images.[7] Therefore the decision to acknowledge the existence of pornography may actually stem from the differences between totalitarian and individualistic ideologies. The questions then become, 1) under austere totalitarian regimes, what pornographic images survived and were available to the general public? 2) who was making/producing pornographic images at this time? and finally, 3) what did pornography represent at this time?

During the period of Japanese aggression, from the occupation of Korea and China to the end of World War II, there was a marked climate of violence against women in the Japanese military. In both Korea and China, the Japanese military collected young women and put them in 'comfort stations' for the use of soldiers stationed in China and other Asian countries and thus systematized and approved rape. A photograph of a naked woman standing by a bed from around 1943 shows her smiling slightly; however, in reality, a Japanese army sword was being held to her back and she was forced to smile to survive.[8] On the battlefields of Asia and the Pacific Islands, the Japanese were involved in numerous massacres, the taking of sex slaves, and other horrendous acts. Foreign females were seen as nothing more than sex objects; for example, Hamada Chimei, a former soldier, depicted a scene that showed the aftermath of a cruel rape in his print series *Shonenhei Aika* (Elegy of youth soldiers) in 1952. Against the background of a deserted landscape, the print shows a woman's corpse with a stick protruding from her vulva and some soldiers in the distance. Although this image may have been only a symbolic representation or a surreal hallucination of the postwar era, Hamada was drawing on his personal military experiences.

In such a dire situation, why should anyone have cared about the availability of pornography? Further, faced with the reality of the brutal invasions in East Asia, was any art produced at this time that is worthwhile considering as part of art history?

One critical perspective was provided by Susan Sontag in her discussion of the power of images in her book *Regarding the Pain of Others*. Sontag described images that presented the pain of others in the following way: 'The painful, stirring images supply only an initial spark' for thinking about how we are existing '—in ways we might prefer not to imagine'.[9]

Pornographic images could be seen as similar to images of others' pain as they give an insight into the inner sexuality of the person in the image, which many people may prefer not to imagine, much less see. Therefore, questioning the availability of wartime pornography could also reveal a hidden pain. In the following, I examine what this means in the context of available wartime images.

Censorship and Eroticism

Censorship became increasingly stringent during the Fifteen Years' War, as the period from 1931 to 1945 is known in Japan. In the period preceding this, from 1923 to 1930, there was a cultural phenomenon known as 'Eroticism, Grotesque and Nonsense', when a great deal of energy was put into erotic pictures, grotesque exaggerations, and nonsense movies.[10] One notable example was an experimental pornographic photograph taken by the painter Itō Seiu, which was based on an 1885 *ukiyo-e* print by Tsukioka Yoshitoshi of a strung-up and bound pregnant woman. Itō Seiu's picture was published in an exclusive underground magazine, *Hentai shiryō* (Pervert document), in 1925. Following this publication, many other underground magazines emerged, and despite restrictive publishing laws, commercial magazines also published erotic images under the guise of medical science or folklore. To some extent, therefore, whether underground or public, erotic images were allowed during this time. Totalitarian militarism, however, changed everything.

After the defeat of the Japanese in 1945 and the end of World War II, thousands of cheap erotic magazines were published, known as *kasutori* after a nickname for cheap alcohol, and strip shows also appeared in Japan for the first time.[11] This period came to be called 'Nikutai no Kaihō', or the 'liberation of the body', after a phrase taken from Tamura Taijirō's 1947 novel, *Nikutai no Mon* (Gate of the flesh).[12] While this was the beginning of Japanese postwar culture, it nonetheless embodied a substantial legacy of the war.[13]

At the turn of the 20th century there was some acceptance of female nudes as art, even though French cartoonist George Bigot had lampooned the porno-phobia of Japanese people in a caricature in 1895. However, painter Kuroda Seiki's 1893 work, *Morning Toilette*, caused an outcry with many claiming that it was shameless to show a naked body in public;[14] however, it was only later that this image was considered obscene.[15] Even though explicit eroticism or nudes were banned during the Fifteen Years' War, images related to art were to some extent an exception; in reality, however, most artists tended to avoid provoking the authorities or offending public morals through a type of self-regulation.[16]

Under these restrictions, the artist Ōta Saburō published a book in 1934 entitled *Ratai no Shūzoku to Sono Geijutsu* (Customs and art of the nude), which introduced academic research on the nude to ordinary readers.[17] The painter Ishii Hakutei commented that '. . . [Ōta's] writing style is elegant and no matter how close he comes to the border [of pornography], it is very euphemistic and never becomes immoral'.[18] Notwithstanding, the book was largely considered pornographic. Both Ōta and Ishii were well known as strong advocates of portraying nudes in art, and Ōta had co-translated a work of French erotica by Pierre Louÿs in 1896 called *Aphrodite: mœurs antiques* (Aphrodite: ancient morals), which had been banned in Japan in 1928 for immorality, as the nude was not seen as simply art at this time.[19] Presumably Ōta deliberately omitted to clarify the borders between artistic nudes and obscene nudity in *Customs and Art of the Nude*.

Similarly, in the early 1940s, art books from the great Western masters such as Goya and Rubens were also banned because the nudes in these books were thought to hasten a collapse in social morals.[20] Even though art exhibitions became a type of sanctuary for female nude paintings, such paintings gradually disappeared in the early 1940s. In 1941, an unknown cartoonist lampooned the nude statues in the government-sponsored exhibition known as the Kanten, and criticized the nude for being 'art for art's sake' as in the Meiji period fifty years earlier.[21] By 1944, no nude paintings were included in government-sponsored exhibitions, and only sculptors were allowed to make and display female nudes, as these were not considered erotic.[22] Consequently, in this period, pornography was greatly feared, as officialdom was convinced that nudes provoked sexual desire and societal disorder.

Resurrection of an Old Form of Eroticism

Although images of female nudes disappeared, eroticism was still present. An examination of the records at the Department of Security's Home Ministry (*Naimushō Keihokyoku*), which had been officially in charge of censorship, shows the types of eroticism that were banned most frequently. In fact, an old erotica form had been resurrected; geisha district documents that had been widely published and then banned in the 1930s because of the fear of corruption of public morals reappeared in studies of folklore or old literature.[23]

Viewed from the present, it may be difficult to understand why a photo of a geisha in a kimono might be banned; however, when nude images had almost completely disappeared, any implication of prostitution was considered sufficiently erotic to trigger censorship. Of the books about geisha, renowned novelist Nagai Kafū's *Bokutō kitan* (A strange tale from east of the river) stands out. Kimura Shōhachi's simple monochrome drawings in the novel were also considered too erotic, not because they showed a naked body but because of the stirring old-fashioned emotions aroused by a geisha in a kimono.

However, traditional erotic books and magazines did not completely vanish. In a rare case, a small underground pornographic publisher, Sōtai-kai, survived until 1944. Sōtai-kai collected stories of sexual experiences and shared them with those who had provided the stories and also published reproductions of *shunga* from the Edo period. In 1944, however, the publisher, Ogura Seizaburō, who was living in abject poverty, was arrested.[24]

Erotica in Colonial Korea and Wartime China

The strict censorship in Japan also affected the publication of erotic images in Korea, which had been annexed by Japan and was under Japanese control from 1910 to 1945. Traditionally, the East Asian body was hidden under many layers of clothing as it was not considered to be an object for observation. However, in Japanese-occupied Korea, female portraits and pornography arrived with the colonizers.

In 1916, the painter Kim Gwanho graduated from the Tokyo School of Fine Arts (*Tokyo bijutsu gakkō*) with his work *Sunset* and received a special prize in the eighth Bunten (an abbreviation for *Monbushō bijutsu tenrankai*, the Ministry of Education Art Exhibition), a major government-sponsored exhibition held in Tokyo. As this was the first time a Korean had painted a Korean nude, it was big news in Korea; however, no reproductions were allowed in Korean newspapers as the image was considered a risk to public morality.[25] While *Sunset* was considered in the art world as just a nude study, for ordinary Koreans at that time, it was considered pornographic.

The scholar Lee Kyeoungmin noted that in Korea at that time, pornography was almost entirely imported from Japan, and although nude photos were taken in private, Korea did not officially publish any pornographic images during the Japanese occupation. The only pornography available was in Japanese picture books that had been published under the guise of either art or science (while none of these books has survived, newspaper advertisements for them from the 1920s and the 1930s still exist). It used to be said that it was more difficult for Korea to become 'pink' than 'red', suggesting that for Koreans it was more difficult to become a maker of pornography than to become a communist.[26] After the late 1930s, as in Japan, censorship in Korea became even stricter and there were almost no erotic images available until the end of the war.

In my research, however, I uncovered a pornographic photograph from Korea in a book by the sexologist Takahashi Tetsu (Figure 8.1).[27] The picture is overlaid with a one-frame cartoon so cannot be seen in full; however, the importance of this picture is not in the concealment of the figures' genitals but in the couple's faces and gazes. Even though the photograph is pornographic and was made to provoke sexual desire, the faces of the couple express melancholy and suffering, so the image seems to represent the victimhood of colonialism.

Although there was no sanctioned pornography in Korea, at this time the country was known to Japanese men as a place that offered sexual experiences not possible

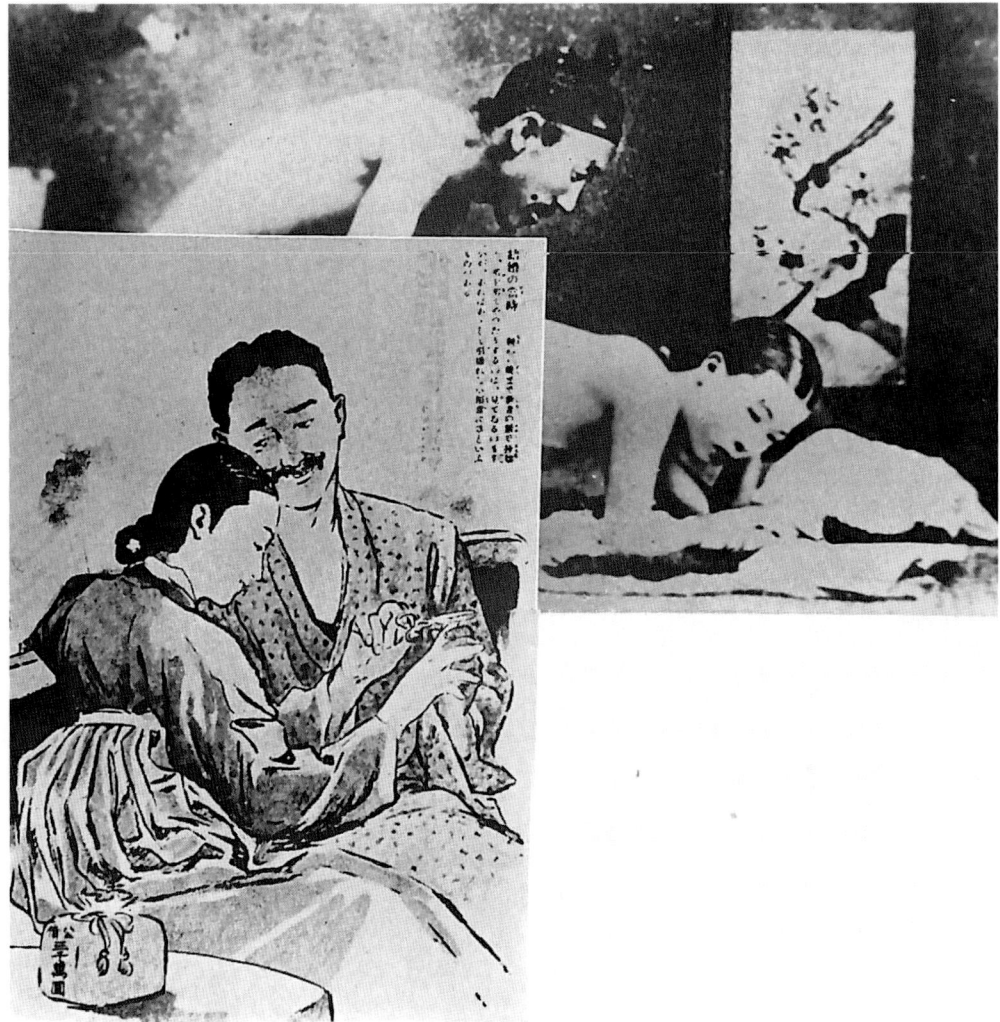

Figure 8.1 A photo of Koreans having sex and a cartoon of a Japanese man and a Korean woman, date unknown

Takahashi Tetsu, *The Graphical History of Sex* (Tokyo: Kuboshoten, 1968), p. 98

in Japan. As a result, the *kisaeng*, or 'Korean dancer', was often used as a motif by Japanese artists because she implied sexuality.[28] The painter Yuasa Ichirō, a follower of Kuroda Seiki, painted the work *Chōsen Fujin* (Korean woman) as a *kisaeng* in 1913–1914. In this work, the woman's hairstyle is oddly Japanese and she shows her naked shoulder without its usual meaning; therefore, it could be interpreted as the result of the colonial view of Korean women.[29]

Korean painters also used *kisaeng* as an important motif of local colour stained by Japanese colour, of which Lee Qoede's *Dancer Taking a Rest* in 1938 was the most notable example. The viewer looks down on a model who is dressed in colourful clothes that flash in the dark room, and she looks up at the viewer with eyes of dignity that seem to hold a mixture of fear and courage. Art historian Kim Hyeshin has claimed that this woman was a reflection of the colonial artist and intellectual and was therefore a self-portrait of the colonial status forced onto Korean females who were viewed as 'others' in the Empire.[30]

In the Republic of China, meanwhile, Shanghai enjoyed prosperity between the two world wars. While Tokyo was still recovering from the Great Kantō Earthquake of 1923, Shanghai was the most exciting global metropolis in East Asia. The historian Lynn Pan has noted that it was exotically Chinese, yet at the same time, familiarly European.[31] In Shanghai, artists adopted both Japanese and Western art in their pornographic stylings.

Magazines for young intellectuals, such as *Shanghai Cartoon* and *Young Companion*, were venues for these progressive artists, providing a space where their urban feelings could be expressed through nude female drawings and photographs. Among these was an image titled *Heroine*, which shows a Western nude female holding a Chinese sword. Art historian Zhang Yingjin explains that this image implied a 'resistance' against the Japanese invasion and the Communist Party through the Chinese characters used in the title. Zhang also discusses the complicated ambivalence of strength and weakness in *Heroine* and comments that the illustration was not just about sexual consumption, but also an image that suggested the multiple discourses of fantasy and public anxiety.[32]

This multiplicity was also seen in photos of a Caucasian nude taken in Manchuria, an area bordering Russia that was occupied by the Japanese army in 1932. In Harbin, one of the largest cities in Manchuria, many Japanese men dreamed of falling in love with a Caucasian woman. Harbin cabaret clubs held strip shows with Russian dancers; there were regular showings of blue films; and according to historian Shimokawa Kōshi, Japanese boys on school trips to Manchuria bought nude photographs as souvenirs. In the nude photographs in Shimokawa's book, it is possible to detect varied feelings of pride and anxiety in the images of the models.[33]

In this period, posters in the 'Shanghai style' were renowned. Pan notes that these posters, in which the women were dressed in the fashions of the day, were made for commercial consumption to represent the new life in Shanghai. Of these fashion artists, Hang Zhiying was the most prominent, with his motifs of the outdoor, sporty woman. At that time, as the government was promoting fitness to bolster the strength of the country, so commercial artists were able to show legs, arms, and torsos without incurring accusations of pornography. In an advertising poster in 1930 for the Great Eastern Dispensary from the Hang Zhiying Studio, a girl in a canoe is slightly revealing one of her breasts.[34] After the Communist Party came to power in 1949, however, such representations were banned and replaced by conventional dogmatic images.

Pornography in the Battlefield

Let us now return to Japan. During the war, there appeared a variety of erotic cartoon propaganda, such as those produced by cartoonist Ono Saseo, which always included a female body and clever and subtle parodic elements.[35] One example of his subversion of ideology was *Big Waves and the Beauty of Health* in 1938. The text at the top right states that 'The big waves of the Japan Sea got angry, saying, "What are you doing in swimsuits during wartime?!"' and the image shows two women in a small boat called 'Zeitaku Maru' or Luxury Boat. However, the image was not meant to incite sympathy for the banning of luxury, nor was it criticizing bourgeois-like women; rather, viewers at that time would have seen the women's bodies as impressive, with their ample, prominent curves.

Ono went to Indonesia in 1941; the fabled place of half-naked women was a paradise for him, even though he was there serving in the Japanese army. *A Market on the Island of Bali* from 1945 shows his love of women's bodies and his independence from authority.[36]

As a military artist, Ono was engaged in psychological attack operations to disturb enemy soldiers. He and his team created leaflets to be distributed on the battlefields in Southeast Asia and the Pacific Islands, among which were many erotic images of housewives betraying their husbands. A leaflet titled 'That Goes Double' was made to disturb the Australian army (Plate 10). In the upper portion there is the image of a wife committing adultery in Melbourne with an American man, and in the lower, a scene of her husband raping a native woman. Historian Ichinose Toshiya claimed that this leaflet was intended to break the alliance between the U.S. army and the Australian army; that is, the image was designed to evoke anxiety and decoupling.[37]

Another leaflet, entitled 'SPRING DANCE', had an image of five small naked women dancing energetically beside their dead husbands' graves. Using such leaflets, the Japanese army attempted to spark anti-war sentiments in their enemies.[38] However, it appears that this propaganda campaign was not successful. Former U.S. sergeant Herbert Friedman wrote that these erotic pictures became collectors' items and tended to raise the morale of American troops.[39]

In any event, the apparent light-heartedness of these images was very different from the gloomy official war paintings that usually depicted fighting male figures.[40] However, these images and light-hearted humour were not a reflection of the Japanese army; rather, they were created to fit with the Japanese perspective of the enemy's culture.

Similarly, in a radio show produced by the Japanese army, the female announcers, who were known as 'Tokyo Rose' by the Americans, spoke in English and played jazz to make the U.S. soldiers feel homesick, and even told the soldiers that their wives back home were committing adultery.[41]

In addition to their titillating or satirical effects, pornographic images had other important uses for the military. The U.S. army, for example, also produced leaflets written in Japanese. Let us look briefly at two propaganda leaflets calling for surrender, one made by the Japanese military and the other by the U.S. military. Both leaflets used nude monochromatic pictures accompanied by text. The Japanese leaflet showed a naked Western woman looking passionate and defiant sitting up and showing her breasts majestically (Figure 8.2),[42] while the U.S. leaflet showed an Asian woman in a kimono mournfully revealing one breast like a poor prostitute (Figure 8.3), with the text in Japanese reading 'Imagine your wife, sister, or daughter looking like this' and on the other side, 'throw down your weapons and surrender without a fight'.[43] The image's pathos was increased by the use of overexposure and contrast. Both images showed considerable insight into their enemy's culture.

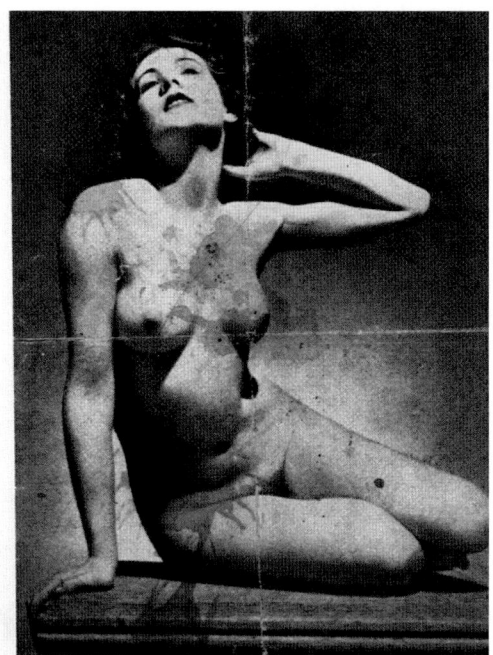

TICKET TO ARMISTICE

USE THIS TICKET, SAVE YOUR LIFE
YOU WILL BE KINDLY TREATED

Follow These Instructions:

1. Come towards our lines waving a white flag.
2. Strap your gun over your left shoulder muzzle down and pointed behind you.
3. Show this ticket to the sentry.
4. Any number of you may surrender with this one ticket.

JAPANESE ARMY HEADQUARTERS

投 降 票

此ノ票ヲ持ツモノハ投降者ナリ
投降者ヲ殺害スルヲ嚴禁ス

大日本軍司令官

Sing your way to Peace pray for Peace

Figure 8.2 Leaflet made by the Japanese army against the U.S. army, ca. 1943

Getty Images

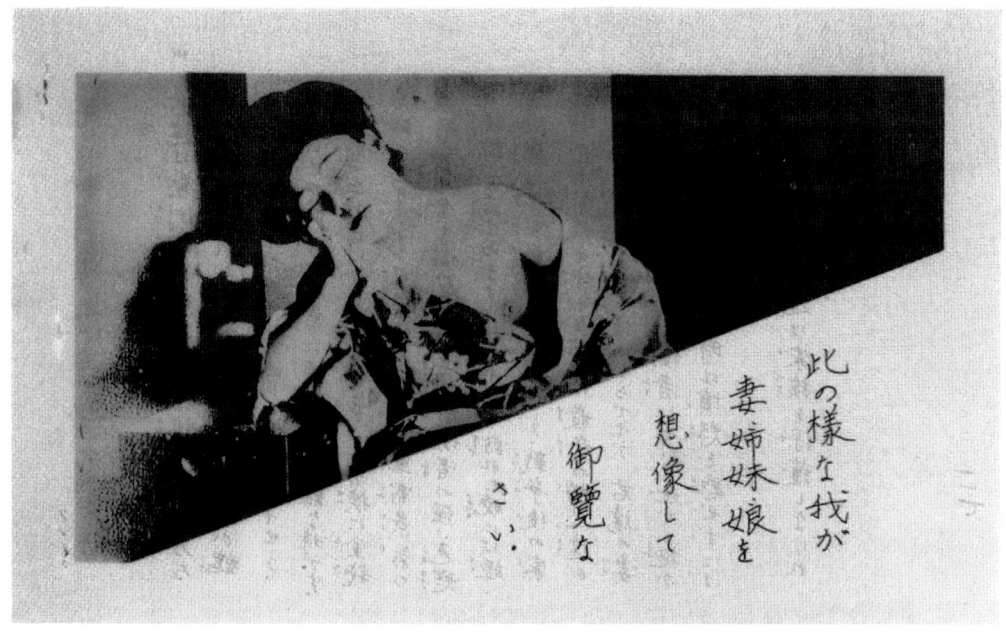

Figure 8.3 Leaflet made by the U.S. army against the Japanese army, ca. 1944

Ichinose Toshiya, *The Asia-Pacific War Seen in Advertisement Plotter Flyers* (Tokyo: Kashiwa Shobō, 2008), p. 51

160 Adachi Gen

In his book *War without Mercy*, historian John Dower examines Asia-Pacific War propaganda and argues that both sides provoked racism through their images.[44] On a further examination of these erotic leaflets made for the battlefield, it can be seen that both sides were also tapping into their opponent's sexuality and cultural values. It could be said, therefore, that the use of pornography led to a sort of mutual understanding.

Eroticism was not the exclusive province of heterosexuals, as a gay, homoerotic culture also existed in the army. In 2014, Dian Hanson compiled a fascinating collection of photographs with commentaries entitled *My Buddy: World War II Laid Bare*.[45] The book includes photos of young soldiers engaging in naked activities, ranging from

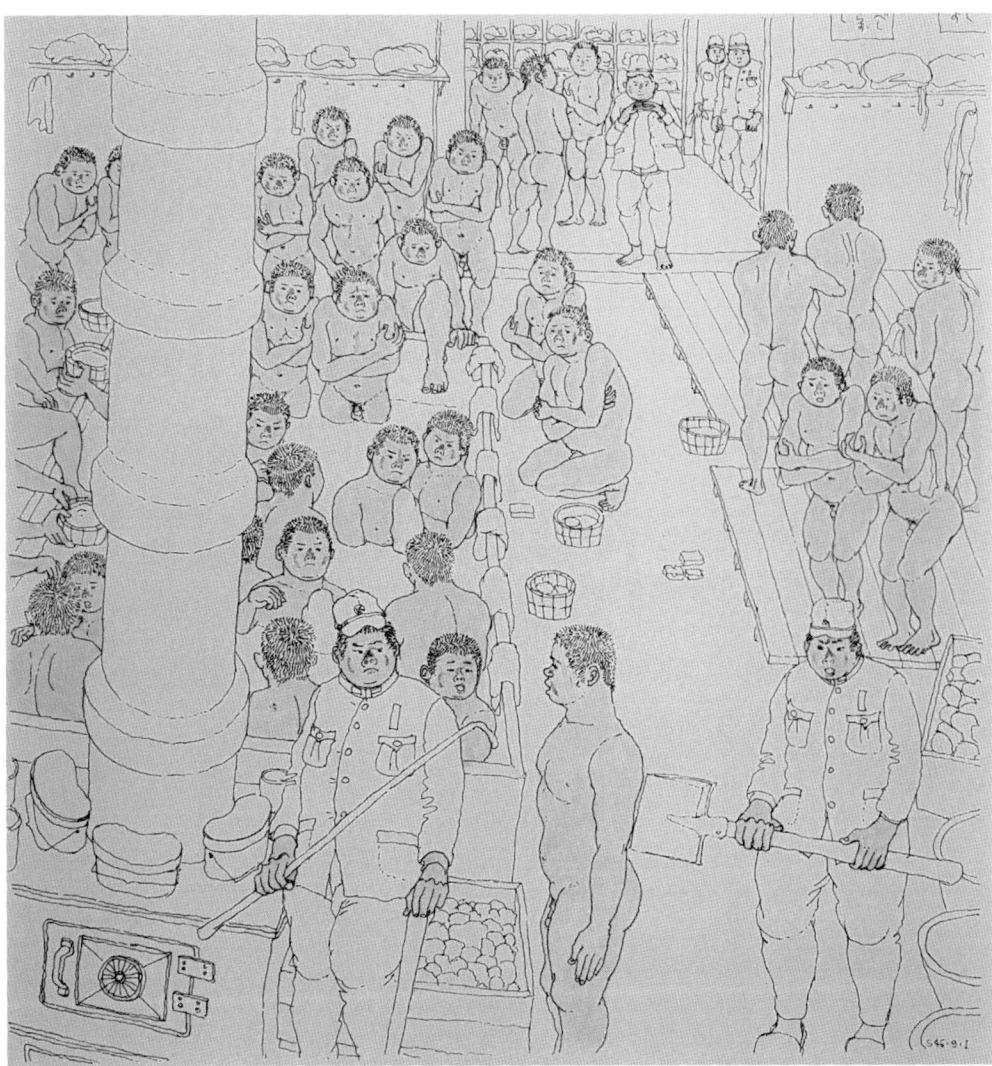

Figure 8.4 Tomita Akihiro (Sasaoka Sakuji), 'Bathing of Soldiers'
A Picture Book of Soldiers (Tokyo: Banchō Shobō, 1972), p. 83

showers and swimming to more playful and tactile interactions. The book also shows illustrations of gay men from *LIFE* magazine at that time.[46] In Japan, macho war paintings were seen as an endorsement of the homoerotic social culture.

Some former soldiers in the Japanese military who experienced the war at first hand subsequently became famous gay illustrators. As they had had no way to express their feelings during wartime, and even had to use pseudonyms after the war to publish their works in gay magazines like *Barazoku* and *Sabu*, they nevertheless managed to express the war experiences that affected them—the hidden history of the postwar Shōwa period.[47]

One gay illustrator, Tomita Akihiro, also known as Sasaoka Sakuji, published *Heitai Gashū* (A picture book of soldiers) in 1972. In a bathing scene, many male nudes are fully depicted, all of whom look alike (Figure 8.4).[48] While this was a clear contrast to U.S. homosexual illustrations in style and colour, both showed a type of paradise. Even though such depictions could have been fictional, it remains true that however tragic the war was, it could also have provided a homosexual fantasy, with some gay illustrations showing a kind of pleasure within a warlike environment.

Such military fantasies can be seen in Ōkawa Tatsuji's untitled illustration from around 1973 that recalls the pain of his army experiences.[49] In the picture, an army boot is hanging from the large penis of a naked man who had been hanged and beaten by a superior officer as a punishment. The naked man's face, however, seems to reflect an inner complicated pleasure. Works of other ex-military gay artists of the same generation also display melancholic faces or moods, a marked contrast to the buoyancy of the U.S. gay graphics. In this way, the Japanese seem to have internalized their pain of war.

Conclusion

Use of pornography during wartime was much more complex than simply stimulating sexual desire. It could even be said that pornography in East Asia played an important role in the wartime history of the region. At the very least, there was a war of survival for nude models, prostitutes, sexual slaves, photographers, illustrators, painters, soldiers, and sexual minorities, a war in the erotic leaflets distributed on the battlefield, and a war of resistance by Korean and Chinese pornographers against Japan. This study of erotic images and pornography shows that there are alternative ways to examine wartime experiences.

Notes

1 This work was supported by a DNP Foundation for Cultural Promotion Graphic Culture Research Grant.
2 During the Manchurian incident of 1931, Japanese troops invaded China; six years later, in 1937, the Marco Polo Bridge was bombed, killing a Chinese general, and thereby initiating the Second Sino-Japanese War. Four years later, in 1941, Japan began the Pacific War against the U.S. Both wars ended in 1945.
3 Gonda Hiromi, ed., *Kokumin Seishin Sōdōin* [Total mobilization of the people's spirit] (Tokyo: Yumani Shobō, 2013).
4 Hariu Ichirō et al., eds., *Sensō to Bijutsu 1937–1945* [Art in wartime Japan 1937–1945] (Tokyo: Kokusho Kankōkai, 2016).
5 The definition of pornography has always been debated. See, for example, Lynn Hunt, ed., *The Invention of Pornography* (New York: Zone Books, 1993).

6 Timothy Clark et al., eds., *Shunga: Sex and Pleasure in Japanese Art* (London: British Museum, 2013); Motohashi Nobuhiro, *Shin AV Jidai* [The new age of adult video] (Tokyo: Bungei Shunjū, 2010); Kawamoto Kōji, *Poruno Zasshi no Shōwa Shi* [A Showa history of pornographic magazines] (Tokyo: Chikuma Shobō, 2011); Motohashi Nobuhiro and Tora Miki, *Ero Hon ōgon Jidai* [The golden age of porn books] (Tokyo: Kawade Shobō, 2015).
7 Kirty Topiwala, ed., *The Institute of Sexology* (London: Wellcome Collection, 2014).
8 Fujita Masao, *Rikugun to Seibyō* [Sexual diseases and the military] (Tokyo: Enishi Shobō, 2015).
9 Susan Sontag, *Regarding the Pain of Others* (New York: Picador, 2003), p. 77.
10 Aramata Hiroshi, *Puroretaria Bungaku wa Monosugoi* [An introduction to proletarian literature] (Tokyo: Heibonsha, 2000); Adachi Gen, *Zenei no Idenshi* [The meme of avant-garde art in Japan: from anarchism to postwar art] (Tokyo: Brücke, 2012).
11 Yamamoto Akira, *Kasutori Zasshi Kenkyū* [A study of Kasutori magazines] (Tokyo: Chūōkōronsha, 1998).
12 Tamura Taijirō, *Nikutai no Akuma* [The demon of the flesh] (Tokyo: Kodansha, 2006).
13 Meguro Museum of Art, ed., *Sengo Bunka no Kiseki 1945–1995* [Japanese culture: the fifty postwar years] (Tokyo: Asahi Shinbun, 1995).
14 Jacqueline Berndt, 'Nationally Naked? The Female Nude in Japanese Oil Painting and Posters', in *Performing 'Nation' Gender Politics in Literature, Theater, and the Visual Arts of China and Japan, 1880–1940*, ed. Barend Haar et al. (Leiden, Boston: Brill, 2008).
15 In the 1930s, there was a public outcry against using nude models in art schools. People thought nudes, especially professional female nude models, were unsuitable because of the country's collapsing morals. Looking overseas at art schools in Hungary and Germany, professional nude models were prohibited in the 1930s because of extreme Catholicism. So Tokyo art schools followed suit. *The Asahi Shinbun*, 'Hungary no Ratai Tsuihō' [Banning nude models in art schools in Hungary], July 5, 1937; 'Doitsu de Shokugyō moderu Kinshi' [Professional models are banned in art schools in Germany], February 23, 1938; 'Ratai Hadaka Bōkoku Ron' [The theory of the naked and nudes destroying the nation], July 28, 1838; Shimokawa Shūji, ed., *Seifūzokushi Nenpyō Taisho Shōwa Hen 1912–1945* [The chronological history of sex and public morals in Japan 1912–1945] (Tokyo: Kawade Shobō, 2009).
16 Kuraya Mika, ed., *Nugu Kaiga: Nihon no Nūdo 1880–1945* [Undressing paintings: Japanese nudes 1880–1945] (Tokyo: The National Museum of Modern Art, Tokyo, 2012).
17 Ōta Saburō, *Ratai no Shūzoku to Sono Geijutsu* [Customs and art of the nude] (Tokyo: Heibonsha, 1934).
18 Ishii Hakutei, 'Ratai no Shūzoku to Sono Geijutsu' [Customs and art of the nude], *Asahi Shinbun*, May 25, 1934.
19 Pierre Louÿs, Ōta Saburō, and Araki Sueo, trans., *Aphrodite: mœurs antiques* [Aphrodite: ancient morals] (Tokyo: Kokusai Bunken Kankōkai, 1928).
20 Jō Ichirō, *Hakkinbon* [Banned books] (Tokyo: Heibonsha, 1999), p. 150; Furusawa Iwami, *Goya 1746–1828* (Tokyo: Goryū Shoin, 1942); Furusawa Iwami, *Rubens 1577–1640* (Tokyo: Goryū Shoin, 1943).
21 Unknown cartoonist, 'Rajin Gunzō' [Nude statues] (Tokyo: Bijutsu Shimpō, November 1941).
22 Hariu, *Sensō to Bijutsu*, pp. 119–123.
23 Naimushō Keihokyoku [Department of Security, The Home Ministry], ed., *Kinshi Tankōbon Mokuroku* [The catalogue of banned books], Vols. 1–3 (Tokyo: Kōhokusha, 1976–1977); *Hakkinbon III* [Banned books III] (Tokyo: Heibonsha, 2002).
24 Jō Ichirō, *Hakkinbon II* [Banned books II] (Tokyo: Heibonsha, 2001); Ogura Michiyo, 'Ogura Seizaburō to Sōtai-kai' [Ogura Seizaburō and the Sōtai-kai], *Ningentankyū* 1, no. 5 (October 1950).
25 Lyang Hon Yeon, 'Kankoku Kaiga no Kindaika to Josei no Hyōgen' [Modernization of paintings in Korea and expression of female figures] (PhD diss., Kyoto Sangyō University, 2014).
26 Lee Kyeoungmin, 'Yokmangkwa kumkgiui ijungju, ero sajinkwa sikminji kumyeol' [Duets of desire and taboo, erotic photos and colonial censorship], *Hwanghae Munhwa* [Yellow sea culture] 58 (2008). (in Korean)

27 Takahashi Tetsu, *Kinsei Kindai 150 Nen Seifūzoku Zushi* [The illustrated history of sex: 150 years from the early modern to modern period], Vol. 2 (Tokyo: Kuboshoten, 1968), p. 98.
28 Onozawa Akane, *Kindai Nihon Shakai to Kōshō Seido Minshū Shi to Kokusai Kankei Shi no Shiten Kara* [Modern Japanese society and the prostitution system: from the point of view of popular history and international relations] (Tokyo: Yoshikawa Kōbunkan, 2010).
29 Lyang, 'Modernization of paintings in Korea'.
30 Kim Hyeshin, 'Shokuminchi Ki Kankoku no Modern Girl to Yūjo' [Modern girls and prostitutes of colonial Korea], *Asia no Josei Shintai ha Ikani Egakaretaka: Shikaku Hyōshō to Sensō no Kioku* [How was the female body in Asia painted? Memory of visual representation and war] (Tokyo: Seikyūsha, 2013).
31 Lynn Pan, *Shanghai Style: Art and Design Between the Wars* (San Francisco: Long River Press, 2008).
32 Zhang Yingjin, 'Artwork, Commodity, Event: Representation of the Female Body in Modern Chinese Pictorials', in *Visual Culture in Shanghai 1850s–1930s*, ed. C. Jason Kuo (Washington, D.C.: New Academia Publishing, 2007), p. 153.
33 Shimokawa Kōshi, *Nihon Ero Shashinshi* [The history of Japanese erotic photography] (Tokyo: Seikyūsha, 1995), pp. 162–163.
34 Pan, *Shanghai Style*, pp. 161–183.
35 Adachi Gen, 'Ono Saseo: Gyakusetsu no Mangaka, Kūdanka' [Ono Saseo: a paradoxical cartoonist and comic chat artist], *Shōwaki Bijutsu Tenrankai no Kenkyū* [Studies of art exhibitions in the Showa era] (Tokyo: Chūō Kōron Shuppan, 2009).
36 Saseo taught Indonesian painters and they respected him for a long time following his departure after the war. His humanistic character helped him to become an exceptional cartoon artist during the war.
37 Ichinose Toshiya, *Senden Bōryaku Bira de Yomu Nicchū Taiheiyō Sensō: Sora o Mau Kami no Bakudan, Dentan Zuroku* [The Asia-Pacific war seen in advertisement plotter flyers: a catalogue of flying paper bombs, Dentan] (Tokyo: Kashiwa Shobō, 2008).
38 Ibid.
39 Herbert Friedman, 'Sex and Psychological Operations', *The Psywarrior*. www.psywarrior.com/sexandprop.html (accessed August 15, 2017).
40 Maki Kaneko, *Mirroring the Japanese Empire: The Male Figure in Yōga Painting 1930–1950* (Leiden, Boston: Brill, 2015).
41 Masayo Duus, *Tokyo Rose* (Tokyo: Bungeishunjū, 1982).
42 *Japanese Armistice Ticket*, courtesy Getty Images.
43 Ichinose, *The Asia-Pacific War*, p. 51.
44 John W. Dower, *War without Mercy* (New York: Random House, 1986), pp. 258–259.
45 Dian Hanson, ed., *My Buddy: World War II Laid Bare* (Cologne: Taschen, 2014).
46 Scotty Bowers, 'No Queens in the Marines', in *My Buddy: World War II Laid Bare*, ed. Hanson, pp. 61–77.
47 Bungaku Itō, *Barazoku no Hitobito* [The people of 'Barazoku'] (Tokyo: Kawadeshobō Shinsha, 2006), pp. 99–132.
48 Tomita Akihiko (also known as Sasaoka Sakuji), *Heitai Gashū* [A picture book of soldiers] (Tokyo: Banchō Shobō, 1971).
49 Tagame Gengorō, ed., *Nihon no Gei Erothikku Āto* [Gay erotic art in Japan], vol. 1 (Tokyo: Pot Publishing, 2003).

Bibliography

Adachi Gen. 'Ono Saseo: Gyakusetsu no Mangaka, Kūdanka' [Ono Saseo: a paradoxical cartoonist and comic chat artist]. *Shōwaki Bijutsu Tenrankai no Kenkyū* [Studies of art exhibitions in the Showa era]. Tokyo: Chuūō Kōron Shuppan, 2009.
———. *Zenei no Idenshi* [The meme of avant-garde art in Japan: from anarchism to postwar art]. Tokyo: Brücke, 2012.
Anonymous. 'Hangarī no Ratai Tsuihō' [Banning nude models in art schools in Hungary]. *Asahi Shinbun*, July 5, 1937.

———. 'Doitsu de Shokugyō model Kinshi' [Professional models are banned in art schools in Germany]. *Asahi Shinbun*, February 23, 1938.

———. 'Ratai Hadaka Bōkoku Ron' [The theory of the naked and nudes destroying the nation]. *Asahi Shinbun*, July 28, 1938.

Anonymous cartoonist. 'Rajin Gunzō' [Nude statues]. Tokyo: Bijutsu Shimpō, November 1941.

Aramata Hiroshi. *Puroretaria Bungaku wa Monosugoi* [An introduction to Proletarian literature]. Tokyo: Heibonsha, 2000.

Berndt, Jacqueline. 'Nationally Naked? The Female Nude in Japanese Oil Painting and Posters'. In *Performing 'Nation': Gender Politics in Literature, Theater, and the Visual Arts of China and Japan, 1880–1940*, edited by Barend Haar. Leiden, Boston: Brill, 2008.

Bowers, Scotty. 'No Queens in the Marines'. In *My Buddy: World War II Laid Bare*, edited by Dian Hanson, 61–77. Cologne: Taschen, 2014.

Clark, Timothy, and Andrew Gerstle, Aki Ishigami, Akiko Yano, eds. *Shunga: Sex and Pleasure in Japanese Art*. London: The British Museum, 2013.

Dower, John W. *War without Mercy*. New York: Random House, 1986.

Duus, Masayo. *Tokyo Rose*. Tokyo: Bungeishunjū, 1982.

Friedman, Herbert. 'Sex and Psychological Operations'. *The Psywarrior*. www.psywarrior.com/sexandprop.html. Accessed August 15, 2017.

Fujita Masao. *Rikugun to Seibyou* [Sexual diseases and the military]. Tokyo: Enishi Shobō, 2015.

Furusawa Iwami. *Goya 1746–1828*. Tokyo: Goryū Shoin, 1942.

———. *Rubens 1577–1640*. Tokyo: Goryū Shoin, 1943.

Gonda Hiromi, ed. *Kokumin Seishin Sōdōin* [Total mobilization of the people's spirit]. Tokyo: Yumani Shobō, 2013.

Hanson, Dian, ed. *My Buddy: World War II Laid Bare*. Cologne: Taschen, 2014.

Hariu Ichirō, and Sawaragi Noi, Kuraya Mika, Kawada Akihisa, Hirase Reita, Ōtani Shōgo, eds. *Sensō to Bijutsu 1937–1945* [Art in wartime Japan 1937–1945]. Tokyo: Kokusho kankōkai, 2016.

Hunt, Lynn, ed. *The Invention of Pornography*. New York: Zone Books, 1993.

Ichinose Toshiya. *Senden Bōryaku Bira de Yomu Nicchū Taiheiyō Sensō: Sora o Mau Kami no Bakudan, Dentan Zuroku* [The Asia-Pacific War seen in advertisement plotter flyers: a catalogue of the flying paper bombs, Dentan]. Tokyo: Kashiwa Shobō, 2008.

Ishii Hakutei. 'Ratai no Shūzoku to Sono Geijutsu' [Customs and art of the nude]. *Asahi Shinbun*, May 25, 1934.

Ito Bungaku. *Barazoku no Hitobito* [The people of 'Barazoku']. Tokyo: Kawadeshobō Shinsha, 2006.

Jō Ichirō. *Hakkinbon* [Banned books]. Tokyo: Heibonsha, 1999.

———. *Hakkinbon II*. Tokyo: Heibonsha, 2001.

———. *Hakkinbon III*. Tokyo: Heibonsha, 2002.

Kaneko Maki. *Mirroring the Japanese Empire: The Male Figure in Yōga Painting 1930–1950*. Leiden, Boston: Brill, 2015.

Kawamoto Koji. *Poruno Zasshi no Shōwa Shi* [A Showa history of porn magazines]. Tokyo: Chikuma Shobō, 2011.

Kim Hyeshin. 'Shokuminchi Ki Kankoku no Modern Girl to Yūjo' [Modern girls and prostitutes of colonial Korea]. In *Ajia no Josei Shintai wa Ikani Egakaretaka: Shikaku Hyōshō to Sensō no Kioku* [How was the female body in Asia painted? Memory of visual representation and war], edited by Kitahara Megumi. Tokyo: Seikyūsha, 2013.

Kuraya Mika, ed. *Nugu Kaiga: Nihon no Nūdo 1880–1945* [Undressing paintings: Japanese nudes 1880–1945]. Tokyo: The National Museum of Modern Art, Tokyo, 2012.

Lee Kyeoungmin. 'Yokmangkwa kumkgiui ijungju, ero sajinkwa sikminji kumyeol' [Duets of desire and taboo, erotic photos and colonial censorship]. *Hwanghae Munhwa* [Hwang Hae Review], no. 58 (2008).

Louÿs, Pierre, and Ōta Saburō and Araki Sueo, trans. *Aphrodite: mœurs antiques* [Aphrodite: ancient morals]. Tokyo: Kokusai Bunken Kankokai, 1928.
Lyang Hon Yeon. 'Kankoku Kaiga no Kindaika to Josei no Hyōgen' [Modernization of paintings in Korea and expression of female figures]. PhD diss., Kyoto Sangyō University, 2014.
Meguro Museum of Art, ed. *Sengo Bunka no Kiseki 1945–1995* [Japanese culture: the fifty postwar years]. Tokyo: Asahi Shinbun, 1995.
Motohashi Nobuhiro, and Tōra Miki. *Shin AV Jidai* [The new age of adult video]. Tokyo: Bungei Shunjū, 2010.
———. *Ero Hon Ōgon Jidai* [The golden age of pornographic books]. Tokyo: Kawade Shobō, 2015.
Naimushō Keihokyoku [Department of Security, The Home Ministry], ed. *Kinshi Tankōbon Mokuroku* [The catalogue of banned books]. 3 vols. Tokyo: Kōhokusha, 1976–1977.
Ogura Michiyo. 'Ogura Seizaburō to Sōtai-kai' [Ogura Seizaburō and the Sōtai-kai]. *Ningentankyū* 1, no. 5 (October 1950).
Onozawa Akane. *Kindai Nihon Shakai to Kōshō Seido: Minshū Shi to Kokusai Kankei Shi no Shiten Kara* [Modern Japanese society and the prostitution system: from the point of view of popular history and international relations]. Tokyo: Yoshikawa Kōbunkan, 2010.
Ōta Saburō. *Ratai no Shūzoku to Sono Geijutsu* [Customs and art of the nude]. Tokyo: Heibonsha, 1934.
Pan, Lynn. *Shanghai Style: Art and Design Between the Wars*. California: Long River Press, 2008.
Shimokawa Kōshi. *Nihon Ero Shashinshi* [The history of Japanese erotic photography]. Tokyo: Seikyūsha, 1995.
———, ed. *Seifūzokushi Nenpyō Taisho Shōwa Hen 1912–1945* [The chronological history of sex in the Taisho and Showa eras 1912–1945]. Tokyo: Kawade Shobō, 2009.
Sontag, Susan. *Regarding the Pain of Others*. New York: Picador, 2003.
Tagame Gengorō, ed. *Nihon no Gei Erothikku Āto* [Gay erotic art in Japan], vol. 1. Tokyo: Pot Publishing, 2003.
Takahashi Tetsu. *Kinsei Kindai 150 Nen Seifūzoku Zushi* [The illustrated history of sex: 150 years from the early modern to the modern period], vol. 2. Tokyo: Kuboshoten, 1968.
Tamura Taijirō. *Nikutai no Akuma* [The demon of the flesh]. Tokyo: Kodansha, 2006.
Tomita Akihiro (also known as Sasaoka Sakuji). *Heitai Gashū* [A picture book of soldiers]. Tokyo: Banchō Shobō, 1971.
Topiwala, Kirty, ed. *The Institute of Sexology*. London: Wellcome Collection, 2014.
Yamamoto Akira. *Kasutori Zasshi Kenkyū* [A study of Kasutori magazines]. Tokyo: Chūōkōronsha, 1998.
Zhang, Yingjin. 'Artwork, Commodity, Event: Representation of the Female Body in Modern Chinese Pictorials'. In *Visual Culture in Shanghai 1850s–1930s*, edited by C. Jason Kuo. Washington D.C.: New Academia Publishing, 2007.

Part III
Translation of Art within East Asia

9 Chinese Seal Carving in Modern Japan
Qian Shoutie's Relationship with Hashimoto Kansetsu

Aida Yuen Wong

Introduction

The 'Slender Iron' Qian Shoutie (1897–1967) (Figure 9.1), a seal carver based in Shanghai, was dubbed one of the 'Three Irons of Jiangnan' (*Jiangnan Santie*), along with Wu Changshuo (*Kutie*) (1844–1927) and Wang Daxin (*Bingtie*) (1869–1924).[1] A recent compilation of Qian's seals provides a glimpse into his stylistic range, while the predominance of signature seals enables a reconstruction of his patronage circle.[2] In addition to attracting noted Chinese artists and literati, he enjoyed wide renown in Japan, a fact corroborated by the numerous stamps he engraved for Japanese such as Tomioka Tessai (1837–1924), Nakamura Fusetsu (1866–1943), Nagao Uzan (1864–1942), and especially, Hashimoto Kansetsu (1883–1945). This essay delves into Qian Shoutie's career between the 1920s and the 1940s, partly to register the ambiguous position of artists involved in Sino-Japanese cultural exchange at the height of political enmity, and partly to shed light on seal carving, an often overlooked area in art historical scholarship.

Qian Shoutie's artistic maturation intersected with the rise of 'neo-literati painting' (*shin-nanga*) in Japan. One of the great exponents of this trend, Hashimoto Kansetsu, became Qian's patron, friend, advocate, and link to the Japanese art world. Historians of the older generation such as Miyazaki Ichisada remembered Kansetsu as a top-ranked artist, on a par with Yokoyama Taikan (1868–1958) and Takeuchi Seihō (1864–1942).[3] In 1919, Kansetsu was named a judge at the first Teiten (short for *Teikoku bijutsu-in tenrankai*, Imperial Academy of Fine Arts Exhibition), an honour reserved for the most respected members of the Japanese art world. Yet, virtually all pictorial series on Japanese modern masters published up to the 1980s omitted Kansetsu. The first monographic study of Kansetsu's life and art appeared in Japan only in 2007.[4] Kansetsu's posthumous reputation was probably marred by his imperialist service as a judge for the Sacred War Art Exhibitions of 1939 and 1944. Furthermore, his death, which coincided with the American bombings of Japan at war's end, might have 'precluded the usual memorial exhibition and related publications accorded artists of his stature'.[5] Kansetsu appears to have been an art historical conundrum, one made more complex by his taste for things Chinese.

Likewise, Qian has not yet been the object of extensive study. This may be due to the paucity of seal carving scholarship (relative to the scholarship on paintings and print media), especially in Western-language research, and for the further reason that Qian, like Kansetsu, fully belonged to neither Chinese nor Japanese art history. As an

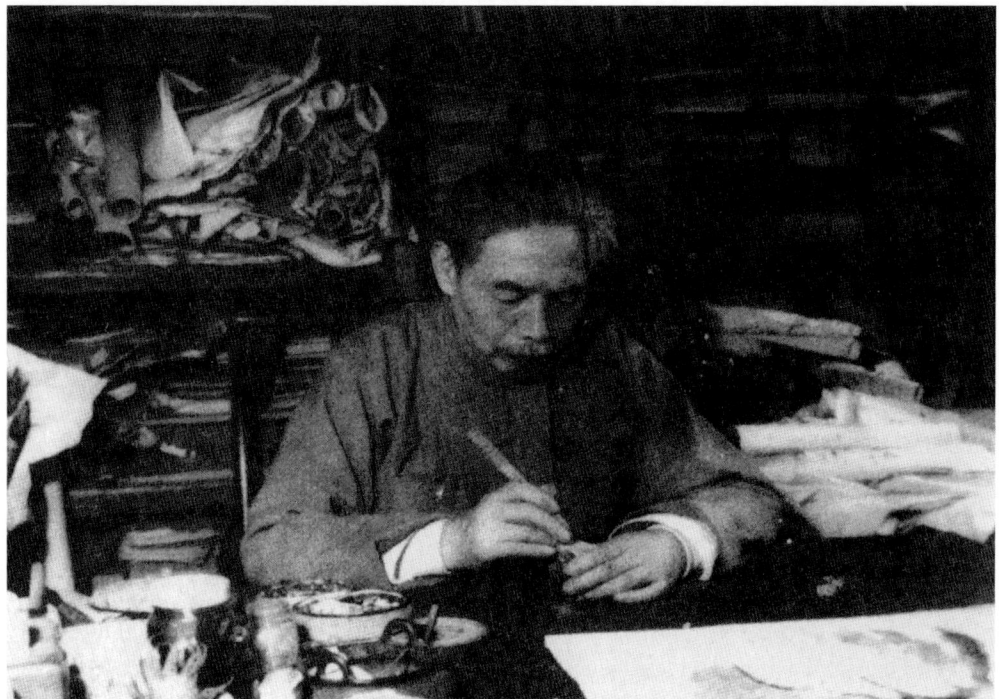

Figure 9.1 Photograph of Qian Shoutie
Published in *Qian Shoutie yincun* [Seals of Qian Shoutie], ed. Wu Yiren and Qian Dali, p. 1

alternative to the nation-centred historiography, this essay situates the relationship between Qian Shoutie and Hashimoto Kansetsu in the literati community, a community with a history that predates the modern nation and embodies social conducts distinct from nationalism.

Literati and the Social Dimension of Seals

The origins of seal carving in China go back at least 3,000 years. The first seals were made as emblems of authority and to authenticate official documents.[6] By the Eastern Jin dynasty (4th century), there were instances of collectors affixing seals on works of art to mark ownership.[7] In the Song and Yuan dynasties (10th–13th centuries), literati initiated the practice of stamping personal seals on paintings of their own creation. The partnering of seals with paintings in the construction of literati identity became prevalent from the Ming dynasty (1368–1644). Today, seal carving is admired, along with poetry, calligraphy, and painting, as *sijue* ('The Four Perfections'). Apart from revealing the artist's name, studio, or emotional–philosophical disposition, these vermilion stamps embody the Chinese love of antiquity. From the predominant use of archaic scripts to the delicate art of arranging characters on thumb-sized surfaces (*zhangfa*), seal carvers display their epigraphic sensibilities by drawing upon historical prototypes.

Seals are, in many ways, badges of refinement. For the connoisseur, the quality and colour of the stone can also bring great pleasure.

Not all painters make their own seals. Requesting seal-engravings from an expert calligrapher/carver has intrinsic value in the social life of the literati. The commissioning and gifting of seals signal mutual respect, and sometimes serve as repayments of 'elegant debts' that cement literati networks.[8] Before the fall of the Qing (1644–1911), the last imperial dynasty, the term 'literati' had referred to scholars who aspired to public office, passed the civil service examination, and practised poetry, calligraphy, painting, and music. This was the highest ideal that few fully attained. In the 20th century, after the abolition of the civil service examination, social interactions played an ever more critical role in perpetuating the literati arts. Professional artists, no longer disadvantaged as a social class, emulated the behaviour of the literati by forming coteries to promote kindred interests in poetry, calligraphy, and seal carving, and many of these professionals were instrumental in saving the literati arts from obsolescence.

For a long time, seals were regarded as a craft rather than an art that deserved high-minded consideration. Even during the Ming and Qing dynasties, when literati valued carving seals as a gentlemanly pursuit, it was always treated as auxiliary to painting and calligraphy. To elevate the status of seal carving, enthusiasts in the Late Qing and Early Republican periods, with the Xiling Seal Carving Society (*Xiling yinshe*, est. 1904) as the epicentre, held regular exhibitions and published seal albums, fostering pride in the medium.[9] Promoted as *zhuanke*, a name with a scholarly ring, seal engraving as an art form in modern China began to differentiate itself from the merely functional *yinzhang*. The enhanced status and institutional ferment attracted young artists to seal carving, including Qian Shoutie.

At age twelve, Qian Shoutie (formal name Ya; courtesy name Shuya) was apprenticed to the stele engraver Tang Boqian (dates unknown) of Suzhou. Tang ran a seal-carving and scroll-mounting business, and was widely respected as a connoisseur of old stelae and calligraphy books. Among those who frequented Tang's shop were Wu Changshuo and the poet-seal carver Zheng Wenzhuo (1856–1918). After Qian completed his apprenticeship, 'labouring like a slave' for six years,[10] he opened a small business carving stelae, but a higher ambition led him to the doorsteps of Wu and Zheng. He submitted himself to their tutelage, while at the same time honing his painting skills under the guidance of Yu Yuxiang (1874–1923). Building up momentum, Qian, now a budding, multitalented professional, moved to China's glittering cultural centre: Shanghai. In 1916, barely twenty years old, he joined the Haishang Tijin Guan Society of Seal Carving, Calligraphy, and Painting (*Haishang tijin guan jinshi shuhua hui*), and befriended Lu Qianfu (1851–1920), Wang Yiting (1867–1938), Huang Binhong (1865–1955), and other notables in the city.[11]

The 1920s was a time when popular diplomacy carried out by civilians, as an alternative to state diplomacy, had some success in easing political tension between China and Japan. Therefore, art professionals often took part in exchanges for more than just personal advancement. In the wake of the Great Kanto Earthquake of 1923, which decimated the Tokyo region and caused an estimated 90,000 casualties, artists from China stepped up to raise funds for disaster relief. Qian was among a group led by Wang Yiting who sold their paintings to benefit earthquake victims.[12]

In 1922, following a historic Sino-Japanese joint exhibition held in Tokyo, several Japanese artists including Kansetsu travelled together to Shanghai.[13] At a party thrown by the eminent doctor Xu Xiaopu, Kansetsu met Qian Shoutie for the first time. They became friendly and went sightseeing together. One of Kansetsu's goals on this trip was to find a good seal carver, and Qian was highly recommended by Pan Liangpu, a member of the Haishang Tijin Guan Society of Seal Carving, Calligraphy, and Painting.[14] The following year, Qian accepted an invitation to stay in Kansetsu's house in Kyoto, where he devoted much of his time carving seals for his host, but also consorting with local artists and literati. Kansetsu knew the general rules regarding the use of seals in paintings—their proper sizes and placements—but not the finer points of actually carving them, which required special techniques and aesthetic knowledge.[15] What could be better than to enlist the expertise of a Chinese seal carver, especially one who had a good grounding in painting and connections to Shanghai?

In 1924, Qian was back in China and assumed the Chairship of the National-style Painting Department at the Shanghai Academy of Fine Arts. The following year, Kansetsu sought Qian out again, and informed him that a special room had been set aside at the White Sand Village for him to carve seals.[16] According to Kansetsu's daughter, Takaori Taeko, Qian stayed for a whole year this time. His studio was complete with Chinese decor and an ample supply of precious *tianhuang* stones, chicken-blood stones, and other fine carving materials. Taeko recalled the sight of the Chinese house guest absorbed in his labour, sitting with a stone and knife in hand for hours on end. She also remembered his kindness, taking her fishing and giving her painting advice.[17]

Kansetsu's confidence in Qian Shoutie increased with each new contact, developing into a long-term patronage. Of the almost 400 surviving seals that Kansetsu used or collected, as many as 100 were Qian Shoutie's creations (Figure 9.2).[18] No single person, Chinese or Japanese, did more to shape Kansetsu's taste in seals. The number of seals by Kansetsu's next most patronized seal carver—the Japanese Sonoda Kōjō (1886–1968), a student and collector of antique Chinese seals who modelled himself on Wu Changshuo—was about twenty.[19] Kansetsu promoted Qian among the Japanese cultural community and helped launch exhibitions of his painting, calligraphy, and seal carving around Kyoto, Tokyo, and Osaka, at such venues as the Matsuzakaya Department Store and the Shiseidō Gallery.[20] Qian became known to Kosugi Misei (or Kosugi Hōan) (1881–1964), Nakamura Fusetsu, Nagao Kō (or Nagao Uzan), and Kawai Senrō, among other artists and seal lovers.[21] In those promising days, Qian's

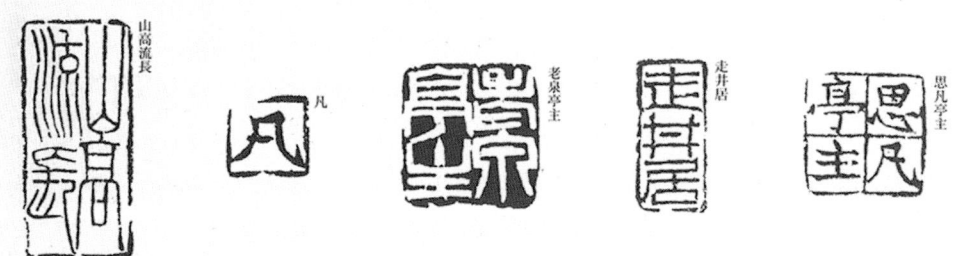

Figure 9.2 Select seals of Hashimoto Kansetsu by Qian Shoutie
Published in *Hashimoto Kansetsu* (Asahi Shinbunsha, 1994), p. 111

productivity surged as he began to attract a cohort of Japanese patrons. Qian's seal album published in the following year was inscribed by Nagao as well as Kansetsu, who wrote:

> In the fourth month of the *Guihai* year (1923), while taking my wife on a tour of Hangzhou and Suzhou, I urged Qian Shoutie to come back with me to my White Sand Village, where many of my former disciples would seek his [seal] carvings. They were all renowned and lofty figures in my country. Qian had recently published his seal album to record his accomplished hand and asked for my comments. Seal carving has never been my strong suit, so the task was difficult. Now that I have seen Qian's paintings, which are handsome and limpid, and profoundly capture the tune of the ancients, I know that his seal carving must be elegant. These are just a few words jotted down in leisure.[22]

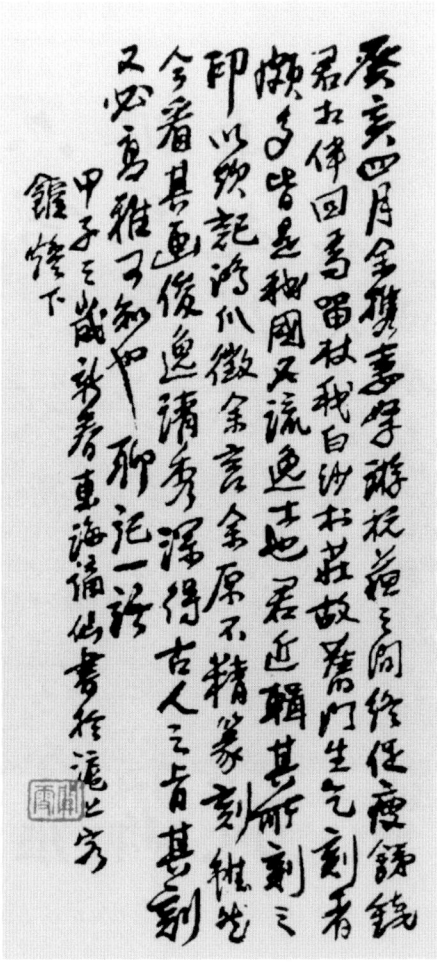

Figure 9.3 Hashimoto Kansetsu's poetic commentary on Qian Shoutie's seal album
Published in *Qian Shoutie yincun* [Seals of Qian Shoutie], ed. Wu Yiren and Qian Dali, p. 4

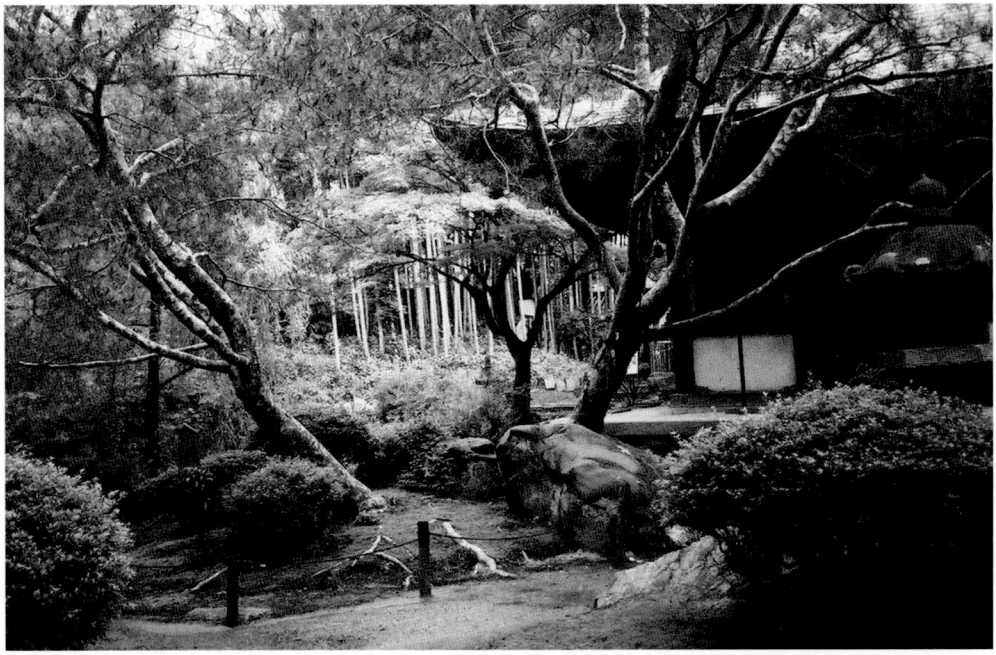

Figure 9.4 Hashimoto Kansetsu's residence in Kyoto, named Hakusasonsō (White Sand Village Residence), today's Hashimoto Kansetsu Memorial Museum

Kansetsu's residence was a garden estate at the foot of the historic Silver Pavilion. Called Hakusasonsō (White Sand Village Residence), today's Hashimoto Kansetsu Kinenkan (Hashimoto Kansetsu Memorial Museum), it was his private paradise (Figure 9.4). Every part of Hakusasonsō is lovingly designed and decorated with objects Kansetsu collected over the years—here a tearoom with a pond view, there a stone relief of the Buddha, and further on a small path, an antique lantern from the Heian period.[23] Like the consummate Edo-period literati Ishikawa Jōzan, creator of Shisendō (The Hall of the Poetry Immortals, Kyoto), Kansetsu intended his home to be an *inkyo* (hermitage) devoted to art and other private pursuits. A pair of calligraphic plaques *in situ* summarizes his sentiments: 'A House Built in the City/Stone Walls like Deep Mountains'.

Qian created several seals referring to the White Sand Village. One of them employs *kaishu* (Regular Script) on the *tian-zi* grid, a grid format derived from Qin-and-Han bronze seals (Figure 9.5). This seal appears in several of Kansetsu's paintings. Inspiration for the unusual combination of *kaishu* and a grid format (not necessarily a *tian-zi* grid) might have come from antique stelae (for example, the *Shipinggong zaoxiang ji* from the Longmen Grottoes). Qian's teacher, Wu Changshuo, also made use of this arrangement, but in Wu's case, it mostly occurred on the upright side of the stone (*biankuan*) rather than on the seal face.[24] Qian's *kaishu* on this 'White Sand Village' seal also contains traces of the Clerical Script, *lishu*.

Also notable is Qian's experimentation with distinctively Japanese-style compositions, as seen in a round seal featuring two characters squeezed into a small space in the

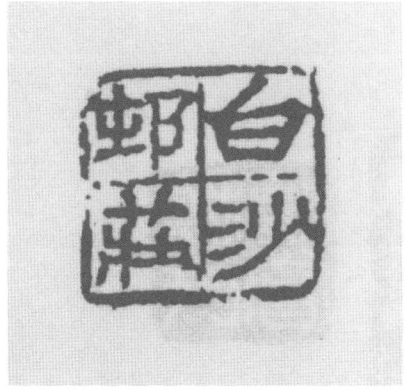

Figure 9.5   Qian Shoutie, 'White Sand Village Residence', ca. 1920s–1930s
Published in *Qian Shoutie yincun* [Seals of Qian Shoutie], ed. Wu Yiren and Qian Dali, p. 51

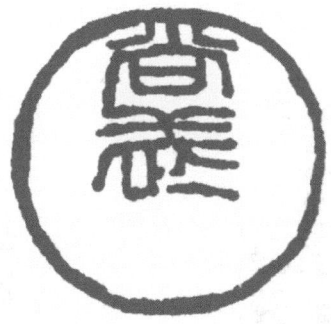

Figure 9.6   Qian Shoutie, 'Shangwu' seal in Japanese style, ca. 1920s–1930s
Published in *Qian Shoutie yincun* [Seals of Qian Shoutie], ed. Wu Yiren and Qian Dali, p. 44

upper centre, leaving three-quarters of the stamp face void (Figure 9.6). Such a work suggested Qian's willingness to please Japanese clients (or friends) on their native aesthetic terms. For the most part, however, his oeuvre retained a strong Chinese flavour that appealed to the *bunjin* set—Sinophiles and *nanga* painters.

Bridging Cultural Gaps

In Japan, where the literati or *bunjin* status was never strictly applied to scholars in administrative positions as it was in China, anyone with the means and cultural inclinations could freely and selectively acquire the trappings of a cultivated *bunjin*.[25] A number of painters in modern Japan partook of the *bunjin* culture by collecting seals. Takeuchi Seihō, a lover of haiku, possessed some 420 seals. Kansetsu, with about

400 seals, rivalled Seihō who also happened to be one of his early painting teachers. Aside from having been raised in a Confucian household, Kansetsu might have developed a similar passion under Seihō's influence despite their purportedly strained relationship. Other modern Japanese painters who owned large seal collections were Tomioka Tessai, Kōno Bairei (1844–95), and Imao Keinan (1845–1924). Engraving seals is a highly specialized skill that requires knowledge of classical scripts and a talent for micro-carving. All of the Japanese artists mentioned above made only a small number of their own seals, if any.[26] Aesthetic functions aside, painters used seals as part of their signatures and, often, as indexes of the circumstances or the states of mind under which their pictures were conceived, as seals routinely feature specially chosen poetic sayings and other private allusions. The collecting of seals grew to be a hobby among the literati circle in Japan, just as it had in China.

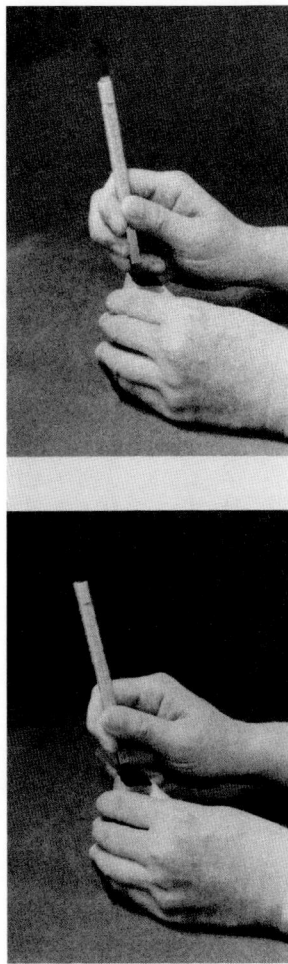

Figure 9.7 How to hold the knife for the double-hook (top) and single-hook (bottom) methods
Published in Ma Guoquan, 'Zhuanke jifa zhong de daofa wenti' [Issues concerning knife methods in seal carving techniques], p. 485

Although seal carving has a long and autonomous history in Japan, Japanese seal carvers of the late 19th and early 20th centuries respected their Chinese counterparts. Seals have varied sizes, in red or white legends; the engraved lines can be curved or straight, and the way of holding the knife and the cutting direction all affect the quality of the seal. The Japanese had traditionally carved seals on wood and followed a method the Chinese called 'single-hook' (*dangoushi*), which entails gripping the knife like a pen with the thumb and the index finger and driving the blade away from the carver's body. This method is best suited for making straight and neat lines. But the Chinese have also used the 'double-hook method' (*shuanggoushi*), where the thumb, index and the middle fingers are used to exert force on the top side of the knife while the fourth digit plays a supportive role behind. This way, the blade moves towards the body in slanting cuts. The result is a freer, less encumbered style that better approximates brush calligraphy (Figure 9.7).[27] Since the late 19th century, a number of Japanese had travelled to the continent to learn this and other sophisticated ways of seal carving. For example, Maruyama Tai'u visited Shanghai in 1878 to follow Xu Sangeng (1826–1890). Two decades later, Kawai Senrō sought Wu Changshuo's mentorship and became one of the earliest Japanese members of the Xiling Seal Carving Society, which had made Wu its first president.[28] Having also been Wu's follower, Qian Shoutie was assured a degree of respect in Japan.

Qian's artistry can be gleaned from seals he created with variations on the name 'Kansetsu'. In the centre of 'setsu' (snow) in one seal, a pair of three horizontal strokes pierced by a vertical line is sometimes added to encompass the motif of 'sweeping/cleaning' in the manner of *xiaozhuan* (small seal script) (Figure 9.8). In this archaic form, the augmented stroke count makes the character 'setsu' (pronounced *xue* in Chinese) visually analogous to 'kan' (pronounced *guan* in Chinese), as the two characters now exhibit the same tripartite composition with comparable inter-stroke density. Qian's seals, each thoughtfully designed, enhanced the scholarly aura that Kansetsu wished to create for his neo-literati paintings.

Figure 9.8 Qian Shoutie, 'Guanxue zijian' [Kansetsu's self-inspection], ca. 1920s–1930s
Published in *Qian Shoutie yincun* [Seals of Qian Shoutie], ed. Wu Yiren and Qian Dali, p. 51

Sinophilism as Form and Content

Kansetsu grew up in an environment steeped in *kangaku* (Chinese classical studies). Both his grandfather and father were Confucian scholars, adept in Chinese-style poetry, painting, and calligraphy. A deeply felt connection with China, both with its land and its classical writings, underlay his life's work. He made no fewer than twenty trips to China between the 1910s and the 1940s.[29] Although more Japanese artists and intellectuals visited China in the nineteenth and twentieth centuries than at any other period in history, twenty journeys was still remarkable. Kansetsu possessed first-hand experience and an empirical sense of what Chinese culture was like; this set him apart from most of the earlier Japanese Sinophiles, who based their fantasies of China on literary translations or on limited access to Chinese works transmitted by exceptional sojourners and travellers.[30] His jubilant portrait of Chinese river travellers in the pair of screens titled *Southern Country* (1914) in the Himeji City Museum[31] and his sketches of Chinese landscapes are evidence that he saw China as a living culture.[32] This is not to say that his paintings are devoid of fantasies, but in the end, the painter seems at least as interested in experiences from the Chinese perspective. This explains Kansetsu's commitment to exchanges with contemporary Chinese artists. He also amassed a large number of paintings from China and authored the first ever monograph on the Ming-Qing artist Shitao (1642–1707), an icon for both Chinese *guohuajia* (national-style painters) and Japanese *nangaka* (literati-style painters).[33]

For the frontispiece of his book, *Nanga e no dōtei* (The road to literati painting, 1925), Kansetsu chose an encomium by Wu Changshuo, who compared him with two canonical masters of the Five Dynasties (907–960), Jing Hao and Guan Tong:

> Jing and Guan awake the vanity of comparison.
> I have seen radiance emanating from mountains in ink.
> A deep anxiety grips me at the thought of wielding my brush again,
> As Mount Tai and Mount Hua could migrate to Fusang [Japan].[34]

Historians need not spend time assessing whether Kansetsu's works deserved such homage or speculating on Wu's sincerity. What the poem—written at a wine gathering—meant to record was an exchange of literati pleasantries. Kansetsu delighted in Wu Changshuo's praise, citing it as an affirmation of his own affinity with China's painting tradition.

In Japan, Kansetsu was better known for his figure paintings than for his landscapes, reflecting the continuous popularity of legends, folktales, and historical subjects in *nihonga* (Japanese-style painting) since the Meiji period (1868–1912). Kansetsu depicted many scenes from Chinese history and literature. Though hardly unprecedented, this thematic Sinophilism produced some memorable tableaux that underscored his literary background, one of his finest trademarks. In 1918, Kansetsu produced a pair of award-winning screens based on the ballad of the legendary female warrior Hua Mulan, who goes to battle in male disguise. By the time this painting was exhibited in 1918 at the twelfth Bunten (an abbreviation for *Monbushō bijutsu tenrankai*, the Ministry of Education Art Exhibition), he had already produced a body of ambitious and highly acclaimed pictures. Still in his thirties, he had built an unshakable reputation as one of the best talents of the age.

In many of his paintings, Kansetsu took a Chinese subject and interpreted it in a Japanese style.[35] This was a common enough strategy in Japanese painting, with ample examples from Edo-period Rimpa and the Kanō Schools, for instance. However, 'China as *content* and Japan as *style*' must not be taken as an axiom. In her book, literary historian Atsuko Sakaki perceives in Japan's Sinophilic tendencies a more organic relationship to China:

> I propose that Japan is like a sensitive subject wrapped in a blanket; it can and does change the shape of the blanket, its temperature, smell, and shade. It is hard to determine where the warmth and other sensual effects come from—whether from 'China', the blanket, or 'Japan', the body. Though it may feel as though the sensual effects are produced by the blanket and that these effects define the blanket, in fact they are coproduced by the blanket and the body—the object/subject. As the body tosses and turns, folds are made and unmade in the blanket. While the blanket might be feeling the warmth, sensing the smell, and seeing the color of the body (who knows?), its inanimate state is taken for granted and is not questioned.[36]

Sakaki views China and Japan as intimate entities that form a nexus of cross-cultural references. Indeed, some of Kansetsu's paintings are neither strictly Japanese nor Chinese. Certain Chinese themes were already so familiar in Japan that they could well be regarded as Japanese. For example, at the tenth Teiten in 1929, Kansetsu presented the tragic story of the Tang-dynasty imperial concubine Yang Guifei in a work entitled *Song of Everlasting Sorrow* (after the famous poem by Bai Juyi) using the *baimiao* or 'outline' method. Yang Guifei was no stranger to the local audience, as references to this plump beauty appeared in Japanese writings as early as Lady Murasaki Shikibu's *Genji Monogatari* (The tale of Genji, ca. 1000).[37] Taken together with the Chinese literary subject and the choice of *baimiao*, Kansetsu's style still demonstrates an aesthetic inclination grounded in Chinese conventions. Unlike the followers of Fukuzawa Yukichi (author of 'Datsu-A ron' or 'Dissociation from Asia', 1885), who saw sinicizing tendencies as detrimental to Japanese modernization, Kansetsu eagerly embraced and pursued them. The tenth Teiten in 1929, where the *Song of Everlasting Sorrow* was shown, marked a highpoint in Kansetsu's career. At age forty-six, he was selected to join the august panel of judges. In the same year his paintings were exhibited in Europe.[38] With their classical Chinese references, Kansetsu's paintings captivated both local and overseas audiences. The works of Kansetsu could be seen as having 'co-produced' literati aesthetics by occasionally partnering with Chinese-style carved seals—not to reference 'China' as a dichotomous Other that is purely 'content', but as a constitutive element of his literati style. Seals enhanced the scholarly resonance in Kansetsu's neo-literati paintings or *shin-nanga*.

Shin-nanga refers to an early 20th-century attempt to reform the devalued Chinese-inspired *nanga*, a Japanese literati painting tradition that had been in practice since the Edo period. Exemplified by such images as the ink bamboos of Gion Nankai (1677–1751) and the light-colour landscapes of Ike no Taiga (1723–1776), this tradition was carried forward in the Meiji period by Sinophiles such as Tanōmura Chokunyū (1816–1907) and Tomioka Tessai. In the judgment of some modernizers of late 19th-century Japan, these Edo-Meiji *nanga* (also called *bunjinga*) failed to depict external reality by ignoring naturalistic light and shadow and space-form relationships.[39] As the 20th century ushered in avant-garde streams from Europe (e.g. Post-impressionism and Cubism), this negative assessment was repudiated. Scopic regimes that departed from scientific perspectives gained a new legitimacy, providing the impetus for neo-literati painting during the interwar period. Its champions, including Hashimoto Kansetsu, further vitalized the *nanga* culture by forging alliances with China's contemporary art world.[40]

Kansetsu's co-founding in 1926 of the artists' group Society of Derobement (*Kaiisha*),[41] with the vision of advancing free artistic exchange, was a collaboration with Chinese artists, including Qian Shoutie, Liu Haisu (1896–1994), and Wang Yiting. Around the same time, Kansetsu joined the Sino-Japanese Association for Artistic Kinship (*Zhongri yishu tongzhi hui*) formed in Shanghai. Its Chinese members included Huang Binhong, Zhang Shanzi (1882–1940), and Zheng Wuchang (1894–1952), among other traditionalist brush painters.[42] While the proliferation of art societies is integral to modern culture, a common phenomenon in both East and West, the socialization of the art practice based on the pleasure of exchange is an old literati practice. Such Sino-Japanese societies as the Society of Derobement and the Sino-Japanese Association for Artistic Kinship represented updated forms of literati networking, institutional innovations adopted to facilitate modern practices such as group exhibitions and cross-cultural exchanges.

Persevering through Adversities

Qian Shoutie made at least four trips to Japan before the war. His first two sojourns (1923 and 1925) expanded his cultural horizons and strengthened his professional commitments. Back in Shanghai, he dedicated himself to the advancement of modern Chinese art. He co-founded the Chinese Painting Society (*Zhongguo huahui*) in 1931, an association of painters which grew to 300 members. That year, Qian joined a group of Chinese artists on an inspection tour to Japan, a trip highlighted by an audience with Emperor Hirohito.[43] That was also the year Qian had another exhibition in Japan, held in Tokyo's Shiseidō with the backing of Kansetsu, the writer Tanizaki Junichirō (1886–1965), and some sixteen other Japanese admirers.[44] Four years later, Qian decided to relocate his family to Japan, where he served as an editor-consultant for the calligraphy journal *Shoen*.[45] Little did he know how profoundly that decision would affect the rest of his life.

Chinese sojourners in Japan had a history of being politically active, and Qian's work at the calligraphy journal put him in contact with Guo Moruo (1892–1978), the Chinese antiquarian, patriot, and Communist-sympathizer then living under surveillance in Japan.[46] In 1937, with the escalation of war, Guo made a clandestine escape to China. It was a risky manoeuvre that succeeded with the help of Qian Shoutie, who put Guo in disguise and arranged for his transportation.[47] Lu Yan's recent study on Guo Moruo reveals the tantalizing detail that Qian 'was a covert Chinese intelligence agent . . . working for the semiofficial Japan Research Institute at Nanjing'.[48] Guo's departure prompted an investigation that led to Qian's arrest by Japanese police. According to one account, he refused to kneel in the courtroom and threw a metal inkpot at the judge. He was sentenced to four years in prison on charges of disturbance of order and attempted homicide.[49]

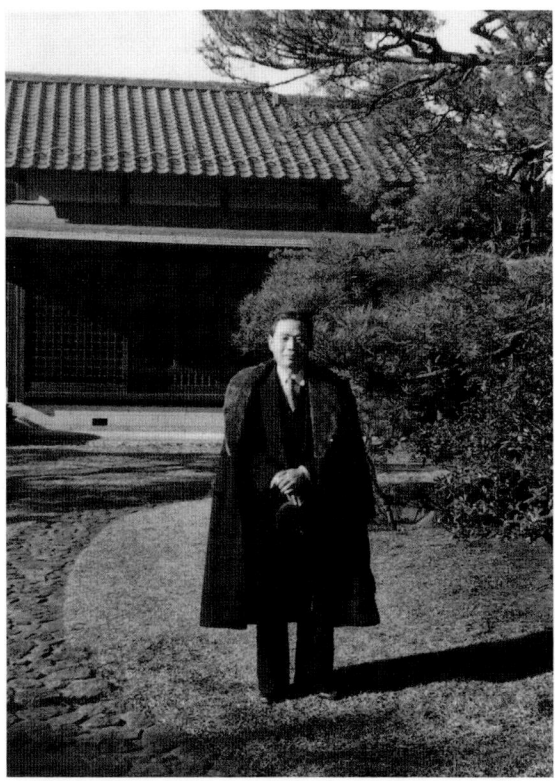

Figure 9.9 Qian Shoutie in Japan, 1947

Published in *Qian Shoutie nianpu* [Qian Shoutie's chronology], compiled by Liao Lu and Qian Mingzhi, p. 12

Qian's relationship with the Japanese literati community survived his imprisonment. His seditious acts only broadened his celebrity, it seemed. He continued to receive Japanese commissions while in prison, and his letters to family suggested a positive outlook and a vigorous existence.[50] In 1941, Qian was released before serving the full four-year term, in part thanks to the intercession of Kansetsu and other Japanese friends.[51] Qian was deported at once and ordered never to set foot in Japan again. But he did return, after the war in 1947, as the Cultural Secretary of the Chinese Diplomatic Delegation (Figure 9.9). By then, Kansetsu had passed away. Postwar vicissitudes closed the last chapter of Qian Shoutie's life. In the 1950s and 1960s, he devoted himself to producing, promoting, and teaching art, but was stigmatized by the Communist authorities as a 'Rightist'.[52] At the start of the Cultural Revolution, while old and sick, he was tormented for having been a 'spy', a *tewu* (special agent). Qian died of heart failure at age seventy in 1967.

The story of Hashimoto Kansetsu and Qian Shoutie illustrates the modus operandi of the literati arts. More than nationalism, mutual regard for traditionalist aesthetics reinforced by social fellowship was the foundation of their relationship. Politics influenced the tenor of Sino-Japanese cultural exchange, to be sure, but if privileged as the master narrative, politics could polarize historical experience along national lines, making it difficult to account for the nuances of interpersonal ties. As this study has shown, friendship and common cultural interests had the ability to transcend political differences. Kansetsu's infamous complicity in the imperialist cause did not lead him to abandon his captured friend who acted against the very same cause. Even in an age of hostility, the literati world endured as a stronghold of Sino-Japanese artistic interchange.

Notes

1 See Wu Yiren and Qian Dali, eds., *Qian Shoutie yincun* [Seals of Qian Shoutie], 2 vols. (Shanghai: Sanlian Shudian, 2000), vol. 1, p. 12.
2 Wu and Qian, *Qian Shoutie yincun*.
3 Miyazaki Ichisada, 'Hashimoto Kansetu to Kangaku' [Hashimoto Kansetsu and Sinology], *Miyazaki Ichisada zenshū* [The complete works of Miyazaki Ichisada], vol. 22 (Tokyo: Iwanami Shoten, 1992), p. 364.
4 Nishihara Daisuke, *Hashimoto Kansetsu: shi to suru mono wa Shina no shizen* [Hashimoto Kansetsu: taking the nature in China as my teacher] (Kyoto: Minerubua, 2007).
5 Paul Berry, 'Hashimoto Kansetsu 1883–1945', in *Modern Masters of Kyoto: The Transformation of Japanese Painting Traditions Nihonga from the Griffith and Patricia Way Collection*, ed. Michiyo Morioka and Paul Berry (Seattle: Seattle Art Museum distributed by the University of Washington Press, 2000), p. 225.
6 On the history and the aesthetics of seal carving see the introductory texts, Cui Zhi and Zheng Hong, *Zhuanke* [Seal carving] (Shanghai: Shanghai Wenyi Chubanshe, 2003); and Jason C. Kuo, *Word as Image: The Art of Chinese Seal Engraving* (Seattle: University of Washington Press, 1992). Legends also claim that, besides documentation and the assertion of authority, ancient seals were made to repel evil spirits. See Kuo, *Word as Image*, p. 18.
7 References to the early uses of seals in painting appear in Zhang Yanyuan, *Lidai minghua ji* [On famous paintings through the ages], *juan* 3, and in Lu Fusheng et al., eds., *Zhongguo shuhua quanshu* [Compendium of texts on Chinese calligraphy and painting] (Shanghai: Shanghai Shuhua Chubanshe, 1993), vol. 1, p. 130.
8 The function of art as payment of social obligations in literati culture is treated as the central subject in Craig Clunas, *Elegant Debts: The Social Art of Wen Zhengming, 1470–1559* (Honolulu: University of Hawai'i Press, 2004).
9 On the history of the Xiling Seal Carving Society, see Xiling Yinshe [Xiling Seal Carving Society], *Xiling Yinshe Bainian shiliao changbian* [Complete source materials on the one hundred years of the Xiling Seal Carving Society] (Hangzhou: Xiling Yinshe, 2003).
10 See Liao Lu and Qian Mingzhi, comps., *Qian Shoutie nianpu* [Qian Shoutie's chronology] (Shanghai: Shanghai Renmin Meishu Chubanshe, 2007), p. 2.
11 Ma Guoquan [Ma Kwok-kuen], *Jindai yinren zhuan* [Biographies of modern seal carvers] (Shanghai: Shanghai Shuhua Chubanshe, 1998), pp. 284–285.
12 See Liao and Qian, *Qian Shoutie nianpu*, p. 4.
13 This exhibition involved 400 paintings by some sixty artists (including the then little-known Qi Baishi) brought from the Beijing and Shanghai regions, and was held at the Tokyo Prefectural Institute of Awards for Commercial and Manufacturing Achievements. Contemporary Japanese artists also showed their works. See Aida Yuen Wong, *Parting the Mists: Discovering Japan and the Rise of National-Style Painting in Modern China* (Honolulu: University of Hawai'i Press, 2006), pp. 106–108.
14 Wu and Qian, *Qian Shoutie yincun*, p. 23; also Liao and Qian, *Qian Shoutie nianpu*, p. 3.
15 In his book, *The Road to Literati Painting*, Kansetsu devoted about a page to the art of seal carving. He emphasized the delight a seal could add to a painting, and how it could be used to balance a picture, depending on the size of the seal in relation to the line quality of the painted elements; if the picture is executed in bold strokes, for example, one could afford to use larger seals. See Hashimoto Kansetsu, *Nanga e no dōtei* [The road to literati painting], 5th ed. (Tokyo: Chūō Bijutsusha, 1925), pp. 72–73.

16 Liao and Qian, *Qian Shoutie nianpu*, p. 3.
17 See Takaori Taeko, 'Sen Sōtetsu san no koto' [About Mr Qian Shoutie] in Mizuno Kei, ed., *Hashimoto Kansetsu impu* [Album of Hashimoto Kansetsu's seals] (Tokyo: Tōkyōdō Chuppan, 1991), p. 208.
18 The figure 100 was based on a count by an expert of Sino-Japanese art exchange, Ajioka Yoshindo (formerly of the Shōtō Museum of Art in Tokyo). An earlier source cited sixty-seven. See Mizuno, *Hashimoto Kansetsu impu*, p. 3.
19 Mizuno, *Hashimoto Kansetsu impu*, p. 3; and also by Mizuno, 'Sonoda Kojō no ichimen' [One side of Sonoda Kojō], in Kyōto Kokuritsu Hakubutsukan [Kyoto National Museum], *Tenkokuka Sonoda Kojō: seitan 125 nen kinen: tokushu chinretsu* [Seal carver Sonoda Kojō: special exhibition in commemoration of the 125th anniversary of his birth] (Kyoto: Kyōto Kokuritsu Hakubutsukan), pp. 50–53.
20 Nishihara, *Hashimoto Kansetsu*, pp. 114–115.
21 Liao and Qian, *Qian Shoutie nianpu*, p. 3.
22 Hashimoto, *Nanga e no dōtei*, p. 5.
23 The history and components of this garden are described by an anonymous author in 'Hakusasonsō—Hashimoto Kansetsu Kinenkan' [The White Sand Village—Hashimoto Kansetsu Memorial Museum], *Nihon teien wo yuku* [Going to Japanese gardens] 4 (November, 2005): 26.
24 See Mao Ziliang, *Wu Changshuo liupai yinfeng* [Seal styles of the Wu Changshuo school] (Chongqing: Chongqing Chubanshe, 2011).
25 On the range of social roles played by Japanese literati see Yoko Woodson, 'Traveling Bunjin Painters and Their Patrons: Economic Life Style and Art of Rai Sanyo and Tanomura Chikuden (Patrons, Patronage, Literati Painters: Japan)' (PhD diss., University of California, Berkeley, 1983).
26 See Asahi Shinbunsha, *Hashimoto Kansetsu: Botsugo gojūnen kinen Hashimoto Kansetsuten* [Hashimoto Kansetsu: exhibition commemorating the fiftieth anniversary of his death] (Tokyo: Asahi Shinbunsha, 1994), pp. 110–111.
27 On the single-hook method, double-hook method, and other basic cutting techniques, see Ma Guoquan, 'Zhuanke jifa zhong de daofa wenti' [Issues concerning knife methods in seal carving techniques], in *Ma Guoquan yinxue lunji* [Collected writings on seal carving by Ma Guoquan] (Hong Kong: Sanyutang Ltd., 2011), pp. 483–493.
28 Uozumi Keizan of Kobe University discussed these Sino-Japanese connections in seal carving at the International Conference on East Asian Calligraphy Education (July 7–9, 2006). See www.unc.edu/~wli/CEG/Feature_Article.html (accessed March 31, 2007). For Wu Changshuo's relationship with the Japanese calligraphers/ seal carvers, see Matsumura Shigeki, 'Nihon ni okeru Go Shōseki no juyō—Meiji hen' [Reception of Wu Changshuo in Japan—Meiji chapter], *Chūgoku kingendai bunka kenkyū* [Studies of modern Chinese culture], no. 9 (March 2007): 39–84; see also Wong, *Parting the Mists*, ch. 4; early Japanese participation in the Xiling Seal Carving Society's activities is described in *Xiling Yinshe Bainian shiliao changbian*, pp. 33–36.
29 Kansetsu's frequent journeys to China put him in touch with local artists and satisfied a hunger for Chinese culture and customs that inspired his creativity. See Hashimoto Setsuya, *Shibontei zuisō* [Ruminations from the Shibon Pavilion] (Kyoto: Hakusasonsō, 1966), p. 50.
30 The nature of Japanese understanding of Chinese culture in pre-modern times has been discussed by a number of scholars, more recently, Thomas Lamarre, *Uncovering Heian Japan: An Archaeology of Sensation and Inscription* (Durham: Duke University Press, 2000); Atsuko Sakaki, *Obsessions with the Sino-Japanese Polarity in Japanese Literature* (Honolulu: University of Hawai'i Press, 2006), ch. 1; Josephine Baroni, *Obaku Zen: The Emergence of the Third Sect of Zen in Tokugawa Japan* (Honolulu: University of Hawai'i Press, 2000); Watanabe Akiyoshi, *Of Water and Ink: Muromachi-Period Paintings from Japan, 1392–1568* (Seattle: University of Washington Press, 1987).
31 'Southern Country' refers to Jiangnan, which the Chinese poet-emperor Li Yu used to describe the scenic Yangzi River region. Kansetsu's adoption of this title once again shows his command of Chinese literary classics.

32 Some of these sketches are collected in Hashimoto, *Nanga he no dōtei*.
33 Hashimoto Kansetsu, *Sekitō* [Shitao] (Tokyo: Godō, 1941) was first published in 1926. Incidentally, the cover of this book was inscribed and illustrated by Qian Shoutie (Qian Ya). For more on Shitao as an icon of modernity, see Wong, *Parting the Mists*, ch. 3.
34 Hashimoto, *Nanga he no dōtei*, frontispiece.
35 On Kansetsu's transculturalism, which incorporates Chinese, Japanese, and Western elements, see Inaga Shigemi, 'Hyōgen shugi to kiin seidō—hoku Shin jihen kara Taishō matsunen ni okeru Hashimoto Kansetsu no kiseki to Kyōto Shinagaku no shūhen' [Expressionism and spirit resonance—the trajectory of Hashimoto Kansetsu and the Sinology circle of Kyoto from the northern Qing incident to the end of Taisho], *Nippon kenkyū* 51 (2015): 97–125.
36 Sakaki, *Sino-Japanese Polarity in Japanese Literature*, pp. 12–13.
37 See Masako Nakagawa Graham, *The Yang Kuei-fei Legend in Japanese Literature* (Lewiston, NY: Edwin Mellen Press, 1998).
38 Asahi Shinbunsha, *Hashimoto Kansetsu*, p. 135.
39 Ernest Fenollosa, an American philosopher and art activist in Meiji Japan, launched a diatribe against literati painting in a lecture titled 'Bijutsu shinsetsu' (1882). His opinion directly or indirectly put champions of this centuries-long practice on the defensive. Fenollosa's essay is reproduced in Aoki Shigeru and Sakai Tadayasu, eds., *Nihon kindai shisō taikei: Bijutsu 17* [System of modern Japanese thoughts: fine arts 17] (Tokyo: Iwanami Shoten, 1989).
40 On the development of literati painting in the Edo and Meiji periods, see Yonezawa Yoshiho and Yoshizawa Chu, *Japanese Painting in the Literati Style*, trans. Betty Iverson Monroe (New York and Tokyo: Weatherhill/Heibonsha, 1974); Joan Stanley-Baker, 'The Transmission of Chinese Idealist Painting to Japan: Notes on the Early Phase (1661–1799)', *Michigan Papers in Japanese Studies*, no. 21 (Ann Arbor: University of Michigan, 1992); Maeda Tamaki, 'Tomioka Tessai's Narrative Landscape: Rethinking Sino-Japanese Traditions' (PhD diss., University of Washington, 2004; Kyōto Kokuritsu Kindai Bijutsukan, *Bunjinga no kindai: Tessai to sono shiyū tachi* [Destination of the literati school painting in modern ages: Tessai and his teachers and friends] (Kyoto/Tokyo: Kyōto Kokuritsu Kindai Bijutsukan, Tōkyō Kokuritsu Kindai Bijutsukan, 1998).
41 The name 'Kaiisha' denotes the spirit of naturalness, inspired by these words of Zhuangzi: *Jieyi panbo ying* 'undoing one's robe to realize the great infinite'.
42 Chen Zhenlian, *Jindai Zhongri huihua jiaoliu shi* [History of modern Sino-Japanese exchanges in painting] (Hefei: Anhui Meishu Chubanshe, 2000), pp. 390–391.
43 See Liao and Qian, *Qian Shoutie nianpu*, p. 4.
44 See Nishihara, *Hashimoto Kansetsu*, p. 113.
45 Liao and Qian, *Qian Shoutie nianpu*, p. 5.
46 Guo Moruo is best known in the antiquarian world as the author of, among other books, *Jiaguwen yanjiu* [Study of oracle bone script] and *Yin Zhou qingtongqi mingwen* [Inscriptions on Shang and Zhou bronzes]. In 1935, Guo also helped to introduce another Chinese artist-seal carver, Fu Baoshi, to the Japanese audience. Fu's solo exhibition at Tokyo's Matsuzakaya Department Store on May 10–14, 1935 drew the admiration of many of the same people who had attended Qian's shows. On Fu Baoshi's seal carving, including his experience in Japan, see Wang Benxing, *Fu Baoshi zhuanke yishu shijie* [The world of Fu Baoshi's seal carving art] (Beijing: Beijing Gongyi Meishu Chubanshe, 2004).
47 Guo Moruo's memoir contains the following passage that describes the day of his escape: 'At 5:30, I arrived in Tokyo and took a car to a friend's home in Yokohama. There I slipped into to an ill-fitting western suit and a pair of shoes for disguise. At 9:00, the friend accompanied me to the train station, where I hastened to Kobe on a speed train named Yan. This friend, whose name I shouldn't divulge here, bought my train ticket, ship ticket, and all. I don't know how to thank him'. The 'friend' was, of course, Qian Shoutie. The passage is cited in Liao and Qian, *Qian Shoutie nianpu*, p. 2.
48 Lu Yan, *Re-understanding Japan: Chinese Perspectives, 1895–1945* (Honolulu: University of Hawai'i Press, 2004), p. 184.
49 Yan, *Re-understanding Japan*, p. 11.

50 The letters to his (second) wife referred to the relatively good condition of the prison cell, his fine health, and a voracious appetite for reading. These letters are transcribed in Liao and Qian, *Qian Shoutie nianpu*, pp. 6–11.

51 See Ma Guoquan, *Jindai yinren zhuan*, p. 285.

52 In 1949 Qian stepped down from the position of Cultural Secretary and left for Hong Kong as the Communists took power. Wanting to play a role in rebuilding the motherland, he returned to Shanghai against the counsel of friends. For several years, Qian devoted himself to painting, seal carving, art education, and various cultural endeavours. He also taught at the Shanghai Painting Academy (*Shanghai Zhongguo huayuan*, est. 1956) and gained the respect of peers and students alike.

Bibliography

Anonymous. 'Hakusasonsō—Hashimoto Kansetsu Kinenkan' [The White Sand Village—Hashimoto Kansetsu Memorial Museum]. *Nihon teien wo yuku* [Going to Japanese gardens] 4 (November 2005).

Asahi Shinbunsha. *Hashimoto Kansetsu: Botsugo gojūnen kinen Hashimoto Kansetsuten* [Hashimoto Kansetsu: exhibition commemorating the fiftieth anniversary of his death]. Tokyo: Asahi Shinbunsha, 1994.

Baroni, Josephine. *Ōbaku Zen: The Emergence of the Third Sect of Zen in Tokugawa Japan*. Honolulu: University of Hawai'i Press, 2000.

Berry, Paul. 'Hashimoto Kansetsu 1883–1945'. In *Modern Masters of Kyoto: The Transformation of Japanese Painting Traditions Nihonga from the Griffith and Patricia Way Collection*, edited by Michiyo Morioka and Paul Berry. Seattle: Seattle Art Museum distributed by the University of Washington Press, 2000.

Chen Zhenlian. *Jindai Zhongri huihua jiaoliu shi* [History of modern Sino-Japanese exchanges in painting]. Hefei: Anhui Meishu Chubanshe, 2000.

Clunas, Craig. *Elegant Debts: The Social Art of Wen Zhengming, 1470–1559*. Honolulu: University of Hawai'i Press, 2004.

Cui Zhi and Zheng Hong. *Zhuanke* [Seal carving]. Shanghai: Shanghai Wenyi Chubanshe, 2003.

Fenollosa, Ernest. 'Bijutsu shinsetsu' (1882). Reproduced in *Nihon kindai shisō taikei: Bijutsu 17* [System of modern Japanese thoughts: fine arts 17], edited by Aoki Shigeru and Sakai Tadayasu. Tokyo: Iwanami Shoten, 1989.

Hashimoto Kansetsu. *Nanga he no dōtei* [The road to literati painting], 5th ed. Tokyo: Chūō Bijutsusha, 1925.

———. *Sekitō* [Shitao]. Tokyo: Godō, 1941.

Hashimoto Setsuya. *Shibontei zuisō* [Ruminations from the Shibun Pavilion]. Kyoto: Hakusasonsō, 1966.

Inaga Shigemi. 'Hyōgen shugi to kiin seidō—hoku Shin jihen kara Taishō matsunen ni okeru Hashimoto Kansetsu no kiseki to Kyōto Shinagaku no shūhen' [Expressionism and spirit resonance—the trajectory of Hashimoto Kansetsu and the Sinology circle of Kyoto from the northern Qing incident to the end of Taisho]. *Nippon kenkyū* 51 (2015): 97–125.

Kansetsu. See Hashimoto, Kansetsu.

Kuo, Jason C. *Word as Image: The Art of Chinese Seal Engraving*. Seattle: University of Washington Press, 1992.

Kyōto Kokuritsu Kindai Bijutsukan. *Bunjinga no kindai: Tessai to sono shiyū tachi* [Destination of the literati school painting in modern ages: Tessai and his teachers and friends]. Kyoto/Tokyo: Kyōto Kokuritsu Kindai Bijutsukan, Tōkyō Kokuritsu Kindai Bijutsukan, 1998.

Lamarre, Thomas. *Uncovering Heian Japan: An Archaeology of Sensation and Inscription*. Durham: Duke University Press, 2000.

Liao Lu and Qian Mingzhi, comps. *Qian Shoutie nianpu* [Qian Shoutie's chronology]. Shanghai: Shanghai Renmin Meishu Chubanshe, 2007.

Lu Fusheng et al., eds. *Zhonguo shuhua quanshu*. Shanghai: Shanghai Shuhua Chubanshe, 1993.

Lu Yan. *Re-understanding Japan: Chinese Perspectives, 1895–1945*. Honolulu: University of Hawai'i Press, 2004.

Ma Guoquan [Ma, Kwok-kuen]. *Jindai yinren zhuan* [Biographies of modern seal carvers]. Shanghai: Shanghai Shuhua Chubanshe, 1998.

———. 'Zhuanke jifa zhong de daofa wenti' [Issues concerning knife methods in seal carving techniques]. In *Ma Guoquan yinxue lunji* [Collected writings on seal carving by Ma Guoquan], edited by Huang Tian, 483–493. Hong Kong: Sanyutang Ltd., 2011.

Maeda Tamaki. 'Tomioka Tessai's Narrative Landscape: Rethinking Sino-Japanese Traditions'. PhD diss., University of Washington, 2004.

Mao Ziliang. *Wu Changshuo liupai yinfeng* [Seal styles of the Wu Changshuo school]. Chongqing: Chongqing Chubanshe, 2011.

Matsumura Shigeki. 'Nihon ni okeru Go Shōseki no juyō—Meiji hen' [Reception of Wu Changshuo in Japan—Meiji chapter]. *Chūgoku kingendai bunka kenkyū* [Studies of modern Chinese culture] no. 9 (March 2007): 39–84.

Miyazaki Ichisada. 'Hashimoto Kansetu to Kangaku' [Hashimoto Kansetsu and sinology], *Miyazaki Ichisada zenshū* [The complete works of Miyazaki Ichisada], edited by Miyazaki Ichisada, vol. 22. Tokyo: Iwanami Shoten, 1992.

Mizuno Kei, ed. *Hashimoto Kansetsu impu* [Album of Hashimoto Kansetsu's seals]. Tokyo: Tōkyōdō Chuppan, 1991.

Mizuno Kei. 'Sonoda Kojō no ichimen' [One side of Sonoda Kojō]. In *Tenkokuka Sonoda Kojō: seitan 125 nen kinen: tokushu chinretsu* [Seal carver Sonoda Kojō: special exhibition in commemoration of the 125th anniversary of his birth], edited by Kyōto Kokuritsu Hakubutsukan [Kyoto National Museum]. Kyoto: Kyōto Kokuritsu Hakubutsukan.

Nakagawa Graham, Masako. *The Yang Kuei-fei Legend in Japanese Literature*. Lewiston, NY: Edwin Mellen Press, 1998.

Nishihara Daisuke. *Hashimoto Kansetsu: shi to suru mono wa Shina no shizen* [Hashimoto Kansetsu: taking the nature in China as my teacher]. Kyoto: Minerubua, 2007.

Sakaki Atsuko. *Obsessions with the Sino-Japanese Polarity in Japanese Literature*. Honolulu: University of Hawai'i Press, 2006.

Stanley-Baker, Joan. *The Transmission of Chinese Idealist Painting to Japan: Notes on the Early Phase (1661–1799)*. *Michigan Papers in Japanese Studies*, no. 21. Ann Arbor: University of Michigan, 1992.

Takaori Taeko. 'Sen Sōtetsu san no koto' [About Mr. Qian Shoutie]. In *Hashimoto Kansetsu impu*, edited by Mizuno Kei. Tokyo: Tōkyōdō Chuppan, 1991.

Uozumi Keizan. Presented at the International Conference on East Asian Calligraphy Education, July 7–9, 2006. See www.unc.edu/~wli/CEG/Feature_Article.html. Accessed March 31, 2007.

Wang Benxing. *Fu Baoshi zhuanke yishu shijie* [The world of Fu Baoshi's seal carving art]. Beijing: Beijing Gongyi Meishu Chubanshe, 2004.

Watanabe, Akiyoshi. *Of Water and Ink: Muromachi-Period Paintings from Japan, 1392–1568*. Seattle: University of Washington Press, 1987.

Wong, Aida Yuen. *Parting the Mists: Discovering Japan and the Rise of National-Style Painting in Modern China*. Honolulu: University of Hawai'i Press, 2006.

Woodson, Yoko. 'Traveling Bunjin Painters and Their Patrons: Economic Life Style and Art of Rai Sanyō and Tanomura Chikuden (Patrons, Patronage, Literati Painters: Japan)'. PhD diss., University of California, Berkeley, 1983.

Wu Yiren and Qian Dali, eds. *Qian Shoutie yincun* [Seals of Qian Shoutie], 2 vols. Shanghai: Sanlian Shudian, 2000.

Xiling Yinshe [Xiling Seal Carving Society]. *Xiling Yinshe Bainian shiliao changbian* [Complete source materials on the one hundred years of the Xiling Seal Carving Society]. Hangzhou: Xiling Yinshe, 2003.

Yonezawa Yoshiho and Yoshizawa Chu. *Japanese Painting in the Literati Style*, translated by Betty Iverson Monroe. New York and Tokyo: Weatherhill/Heibonsha, 1974.

Zhang Yanyuan. *Lidai minghua ji* [On famous paintings through the ages], *juan* 3.

10 'National Painting' Unbound
Modernizing Ink Painting in the Sino-Japanese Art World

Tamaki Maeda

In the early 20th century, hundreds of Chinese students studied art in Japan.[1] Between 1905 and 1937, those who officially registered at major art schools alone numbered at least 129.[2] The number decreased dramatically after the outbreak of the Second Sino-Japanese War in 1937, but even during the war years, more than a dozen additional Chinese students attended those schools. A student of Zhejiang origin even registered at the Tokyo School of Fine Arts in April of 1945—just four months before Japan's defeat in the Asia-Pacific War (1937–1945).

The Chinese students in Japan were eager to learn 'foreign' ideas.[3] Li Shutong (1879–1940), who worked in Western-style oil painting, was a graduate of the Tokyo School of Fine Arts. Li taught at the Zhejiang First Normal College, implementing in his curriculum practices that were new to China, most conspicuously, in 1913, drawing from nude models. Artists of the so-called Lingnan School, notably Gao Jianfu (1879–1951) and his brother Gao Qifeng (1889–1933), learned from *nihonga*, painting in traditional media that often incorporated the optical realism found in European models.

Others who studied in Japan explored China's artistic past. Chen Hengque (Chen Shizeng, 1876–1923), Zhang Daqian (1899–1983), and Fu Baoshi (1904–1965) all spent their formative years in Japan. They are often categorized by scholars as *guohua* ('national painting') artists, who aimed to advance ink painting using techniques and styles found in works from China's imperial past. What did these traditionalists learn in Japan? How did their cross-national learning help advance their national art? More important, did their artistic vision and practice fit within the boundary of 'China', as the term 'national painting' implied? In keeping with these questions, this essay will explore works by Fu Baoshi.

Fu Baoshi's oeuvre exemplifies the development of semi-abstract painting by *guohua* artists. Compare two works: *Autumn Landscape with a Waterfall: In the Style of Wang Meng*, dated 1933, and *Landscape*, dated 1962 (Figure 10.1 and Plate 11). In the earlier painting, Fu painstakingly executes a rising rock formation on the right, contrasted with an equally careful depiction of a waterfall on the left. In the later work, however, meticulously rendered landscape elements are largely taken over by splashes, smudges, and sweeping strokes. We still register this work as a landscape because of the water running from upper right to lower left, and the three tiny figures looking at the waterfall. Otherwise, the painting could be abstract. The near formless forms, the traces of kinetic brush movement, and the materiality of ink remind us of works by 20th-century European and American painters such as Wassily Kandinsky (1866–1944) and Franz Kline (1910–1962). These two landscapes by Fu Baoshi point

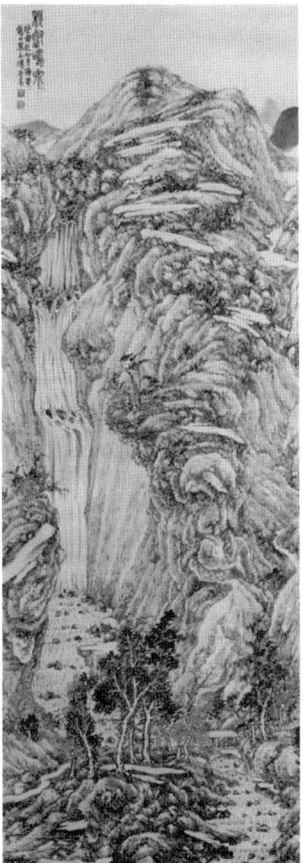

Figure 10.1 Fu Baoshi, *Autumn Landscape with a Waterfall: In the Style of Wang Meng* (Fang Huanghe Shanqiao: Qiuhuo mingquan tu), 1933. Hanging scroll, ink on paper, 135.5 × 54.0 cm

    Musashino Art University. In Musashino Bijutsu Daigaku and Chūgoku Bijutsu Gakuin Kōkanten Jikkō Iinkai, eds., *Fu Hōseki ten* [Fu Baoshi exhibition], p. 3

to a transformation of China's 'national painting' from literati painting to what we might call a 'modern' ink painting.

Using Fu Baoshi as an example, this essay investigates this evolution from literati to modern ink painting in light of Sino-Japanese artistic interchanges in the early 20th century. Fu looked back to the individualist painter Shitao (1642–1707), sharing visual interests with contemporary Japanese painters. Through his study with the art historian Kinbara Seigo (1888–1958), Fu familiarized himself with works by Chan (Zen) monk painters found in Japanese collections. Fu also explored a range of works by Japanese painters, including Sesshū Tōyō (1420–1506), Uragami Gyokudō (1745–1820), and Tomioka Tessai (1837–1924).

This essay first provides an overview of Fu Baoshi's stay in Japan, followed by an analysis of how Fu's theory and painting developed after his return to China. As I show,

Fu's production of modern ink painting transcended the national boundaries of China and Japan as well as the aesthetic categories of Chan (Zen) and literati art.

Fu Baoshi in Japan

Fu Baoshi first went to Japan in September 1932, at the age of twenty-nine.[4] Sino-Japanese cultural interchanges at this time were vital, even though Japanese military aggression in Manchuria had already caused tremendous strain. Fu's visit owed much to Xu Beihong (1895–1953), who himself had visited Tokyo, before studying at the École des Beaux-Arts in Paris. Xu wrote to the government official Xiong Shihui (1893–1974) to request funding for Fu's visit. Fu stayed in Japan for ten months, surveying art schools, museums, and libraries, and collecting books and exhibition catalogues. In June 1933 he returned to Nanchang to raise additional money.

Returning from Japan, Fu produced one of his earliest surviving works, the above-mentioned *Autumn Landscape with a Waterfall* (Figure 10.1). It is almost an exact copy of a work by the famous literati artist Wang Meng (1308–1385) reproduced in a high-quality collotype in *A Grand View of Famous Tang, Song, Yuan, and Ming Paintings* (*Tō Sō Gen Min meiga taikan*)—the catalogue of a 1928 exhibition held in the Tokyo Prefectural Museum and funded by the Japanese Ministry of Foreign Affairs.[5] This exhibition displayed more than 600 Chinese paintings, thanks to scholars, administrators, and collectors in China and Japan. Fu may have used the collotype reproduction as a model, given that he produced his painting immediately after his return from Japan. Also, in China, works by ancient masters such as Wang Meng were still often kept within the closed circle of connoisseurs. His choice of Wang Meng, coupled with the stylistic features discussed above, points to Fu's early career as an aesthetic descendant of the six Orthodox masters.[6]

Fu's second stay in Japan spanned from September 1933 to June 1935. This time he entered the Imperial Art School (present-day Musashino Art University) in Tokyo. Fu studied with Kinbara Seigo, an art historian and one of the founders of the school. Fu had probably encountered Kinbara's work in China, as his *Research on Early Chinese Painting Theory* (*Shina jōdai garon kenkyū*) had just been published there.[7] Aside from Kinbara, Fu worked in oil painting with Nakagawa Kigen (1892–1972), who had studied with Henri Matisse (1869–1954), and in sculpture with Shimizu Takashi (1987–1981), who had also studied in Paris.

During his second stay in Japan, Fu produced bird-and-flower paintings with bold brushstrokes (e.g. *Gourds*, ca. 1935). Perhaps responding to the needs of the art market in Japan, Fu's work became similar to that of the antiquarian artist Wu Changshi (1844–1927). Wu, though never travelling outside China, forged friendships with many Japanese notables, including the sculptor Asakura Fumio (1883–1964) and the scholar-artist Nagao Uzan (1864–1942), earning a considerable reputation.[8] In 1935, with Kinbara's assistance, Fu held a solo exhibition at Matsuzakaya Department Store in the upmarket Ginza District of Tokyo. It drew some leading figures in the art world, including the painters Yokoyama Taikan (1868–1958) and Nakamura Fusetsu (1866–1943) and the calligrapher-seal carver Kawai Senro (1871–1945) (who had studied with Wu Changshi in China). Masaki Naohiko (1862–1940), then the head of the Imperial Art Institute and a chief architect of the aforementioned 1928 exhibition, commented in his diary: 'Among [Fu's] paintings were excellent ones inspired by Wu Zhen (1280–1354) and Wang Meng [likely referring to Figure 10.1] but there were also roughly executed works recalling the Shanghai School.'⁹ Although the 'Shanghai School' is a vague term and no longer refers to any particular style, here Masaki probably had in mind works by Wu Changshi and his fellow artist from Shanghai Wang Yiting (1867–1938), who was also heavily involved in the Sino-Japanese artistic network.¹⁰

The shift in Fu's style, from orthodox landscape to the 'Shanghai School', was substantial, but neither went beyond existing norms of literati painting in China. Fu's choices of style were consistent with his perception of China's artistic past, as articulated in his *Developments in the History of Chinese Painting* (*Zhongguo huihua bianjian shigang*, 1929), published before his departure for Japan.¹¹ Starting with the beginning of painting in relation to ancient scripts, and continuing through the Qing dynasty, the book gives an overview of Chinese art, considering literati painting the most advanced genre of art. Of the one hundred painters of the Qing period listed in the book, Fu states that the six Orthodox masters were the most influential.¹² The last of the list is Wu Changshi, making the 'Shanghai School' the latest movement in Chinese painting.

Perhaps due to the success of his exhibition, Fu planned another show in Nagoya. His mother's sudden illness, however, drew him back to Nanchang. Fu seems to have planned to return to Japan, but instead, on the invitation of Xu Beihong, joined the National Central University in Nanjing.

In July 1937, Japan began a fully fledged assault on the northern coastal cities of China. This was followed by the Shanghai Incident of August 1937 and the Japanese military expansion to the south. Many citizens fled westward to the hinterland. Fu and his family went from Nanjing to Xuancheng, then to Nanchang, and eventually to his hometown Xinyu. In May 1938, Fu joined the anti-Japanese campaign led by the poet-activist Guo Moruo (1892–1978)—whom Fu had first met in Japan. Two years later he rejoined the National Central University, which had been relocated to Chongqing, the wartime capital. It was not until a year after Japan's surrender in 1945, that he (and his university) finally returned to Nanjing.

Fu Baoshi never again visited Japan.

Fu Baoshi's Theory of Painting

Political and military conflict altered Fu's life in unimaginable ways, but what he saw in Japan were important sources for his work afterwards, both in terms of writing and painting. Study in this foreign setting led him from an art built around literati painting to a broader focus on ink painting. Let us now consider Fu's theory of ink painting in relation to the development of art history in Japan.

The origin of art history in Japan can be traced back to ancient times.¹³ Its beginning as an academic discipline, however, has been credited to Okakura Kakuzō (1862–1913), who gave a lecture series on Japanese and Chinese art at the Tokyo School of Fine Arts in the 1890s.¹⁴ Following Okakura's lead, the Japanese government published the first periodized survey of Japanese art, *Histoire de l'Art du Japon*, for the Paris Exposition of 1900, and, in the following year, released its Japanese version, *A Manuscript of a Brief History of Japanese Art* (*Kōhon Nihon bijutsu ryakushi*). Once this basic narrative of national art was laid out, Japanese art historians expanded their research from Japanese to East Asian art—though it should be noted that this East Asian art focused primarily on Chinese and Japanese objects.[15]

Not surprisingly, Japanese historians first dealt with what was available in Japan. Okakura, who died in 1913, generally considered *kowatari*, or 'the old migration', as the canon of Chinese painting.[16] *Kowatari* refers to the objects imported to Japan before the 16th century, whose core was the Ashikaga shogunate collection. This collection, featuring works ascribed to members of the Song Academy and 12th- and 13th-century Chan (Zen) monks, was the most important basis for Japan's elevation of the so-called 'Song and Yuan painting' (known in Japan as *Sō-Genga*).[17] They were not only regarded, in Okakura's time, as the mainstream of Chinese painting, but were also important sources for the development of Japanese ink painting.

The strong emphasis on works by academy artists and Chan monk painters contrasts with art theories in China, notably that of Dong Qichang (1555–1636).[18] Dong famously proposed the concept that Chinese painting had been developed by artists of two opposing camps: literati (scholar-amateur) artists versus professional painters. Inspired by the two divisions in Chan Buddhism, Dong labelled the scholar-amateur line the Southern School, and the professional line, the Northern School. Himself a literati painter, Dong asserted the superiority of the Southern School over its Northern counterpart. It goes without saying that the history of Chinese painting is too complex to divide neatly into two camps, as Dong proposed, but his dichotomous idea was carried over by generations of scholar-connoisseurs and still affects our view of Chinese art. There were some ambiguities as to the historical reception of Chan artists, but, as we shall see, they were often lumped together with professional artists of the Northern School. Given this perception, Okakura's idea of Chinese art, elevating academy artists and Chan monk painters, appears diametrically opposed to Chinese scholars' view of Chinese art. Okakura's belief was consistent with the American art critic Ernest Fenollosa's (1853–1908) famous attack on literati painting in his 1882 lecture in Japan.[19]

Flourishing Sino-Japanese artistic exchanges in the early 20th century brought about shifting perceptions of Chinese painting in Japan. Following the demise of the Qing dynasty in 1911, a large number of paintings were imported to the archipelago.[20] Known as "the new migration" (*shinhakusai*), they included works kept among the closed circle of scholar-connoisseurs for centuries as well as those hidden in the Qing imperial collection. The new migration well represented the view of Chinese scholars—i.e., that literati painting was the canon of Chinese art. The most vital centre of this importation was Kyoto, where the Qing loyalist Luo Zhenyu (1866–1940), Sinologist Naitō Konan (1866–1934), and painter Tomioka Tessai were all active.[21] The wave of the new migration also reached Tokyo, generating a widespread art movement known as new literati painting or *shinnanga*.

Ōmura Seigai (1868–1927), a professor of art history at the Tokyo School of Fine Arts, reversed his teacher Okakura's view.[22] In 1914 the school held an exhibition of Ming and Qing literati painting from the collection of Lian Quan (1863–1932), a Qing scholar-official turned publisher-collector.[23] Ōmura, who edited its catalogue, must have been the chief architect of the exhibition. In 1921, Ōmura published *The Revival of Literati Painting* (*Bunjinga no fukkō*).[24] The next year, the artist-educator Chen Hengque, who had studied in Japan, translated Ōmura's work and included it in his *Research in Chinese Literati Painting* (*Zhongguo wenrenhua zhi yanjiu*), published in

Tianjin.²⁵ The rapidity of Chen's move demonstrates the simultaneity of art movements in China and Japan at this time.

Kinbara Seigo, Fu Baoshi's teacher at the Imperial Art School, belonged to the next generation of scholars engaged in East Asian art. While the mission of Naitō and Ōmura was ultimately to adopt Chinese scholars' views of Chinese painting, Kinbara, a formalist, tried to articulate an aesthetic of East Asian art based on the shared stylistic qualities of Japanese and Chinese painting. In the process, Kinbara took part in re-canonizing the old migration, in particular, the painting produced by Chan (Zen) monks of the 12th and 13th centuries.

Kinbara's study of Chinese art, especially his treatment of the period between the 10th and 13th centuries, must have been eye-opening for Fu Baoshi. He translated Kinbara's works, most notably his research on Tang and Song painting.²⁶ It was published in Shanghai in 1935, while Fu was still in Japan. Although the book includes reproductions of newly imported works—the works ascribed to the 'Southern School' artists Wang Wei (ca. 701–761), Dong Yuan (active in the 10th century), and Mi Fu (1051–1107), respectively—it places greater emphasis on the objects imported to Japan before the 16th century.

Perhaps still to incorporate an argument for the supremacy of literati painting, Kinbara discusses at length the broken-ink style of Wang Wei, whom Dong Qichang considered the origin of the scholar-artist lineage. But, when dealing with the subsequent eras, the book predominantly focuses on works by Chan painters. In his conclusion, Kinbara links Wang Wei and Muqi, a Chan painter active in the 13th century, under the umbrella of the Southern School.²⁷ His research thus portrays a lineage of Chinese literati painting that heavily emphasized ink as opposed to line. A few years later Kinbara refined his ideas in his book *Muqi*, arguing that because of his emphasis on ink, Muqi represents 'Southernization' of the Northern School of painting.²⁸

Kinbara's research may appear illogical for those accustomed to the idea of the supremacy of literati painting or Chan ink painting, but his argument has its basis in painstaking observation of visual elements.²⁹ Specifically, he links tight, precise outlines (*gongbi*), used for careful rendering of forms, with the Northern School, and looser, modulated lines, employed in a spirit of *xieyi* (expression of ideas), with the Southern School. For Kinbara, painting treatises were of less importance than the paintings themselves, though he was familiar with the literature in both Chinese and Japanese. The validity of his views versus that of the established categories is less important here than his attempt to equate the history of Chinese painting as a whole with the development of ink painting.

The significance of Kinbara's study for Fu was apparent in his shifting view of Chinese painting. In 1940, shortly after settling in Chongqing, Fu drafted an article: 'A Historical Analysis of "Landscapes", "*Xieyi*", and "Ink" in Chinese Painting' (published posthumously).³⁰ Here Fu reconsiders Chinese painting in light of the development of ink painting across the divide between the Southern and Northern Schools. Despite the title of the article, its scope extends beyond landscapes, and, most tellingly of his emerging view, Fu lists figurative works by Liang Kai (active 13th century) and Muqi, along with Wen Tong's (1018–1079) bamboo painting and Zheng Sixiao's (1241–1318) orchid painting, arguing that all four painters (two Chan painters and two scholar-amateurs) were crucial for the development of ink painting.³¹

In 1953, Fu published *Chinese Figurative and Landscape Painting*, his first historical survey of Chinese painting after his studies in Japan.[32] Written in the Maoist era, this time Fu denies the categorization of Chinese painting into the Southern and Northern Schools—asserting that the so-called 'literati' painters merely imitated the style of Chan painting, and therefore, that the notion of literati painting had no basis.[33] The statement was in tune with the Communist Party, denouncing the literati elite class in China's dynastic past, but it was also based on Fu's study that had begun almost two decades before in Japan.

In accordance with this statement, Fu's discussion of figurative painting concludes with the development from *baimiao* (plane-drawing) by Li Gonglin (1049?–1106) to the abbreviated style of Liang Kai and Shike (active 13th century)—pointing out that the subjectivism in later works was due to the Chan influence.[34] The chapter 'The Development of Ink Landscapes' groups together the scholar artists Mi Fu and Mi Youren (1074–1153), Chan painters Muqi and Yujian (active 13th century), and academy professionals Ma Yuan (active ca. 1190–1225) and Xia Gui (active ca. 1180–1230), arguing that all equally advanced ink landscapes.[35] Once again Fu presents Chan as the primary inspiration for this development.

The last painter that Fu discusses in his book is Shitao.[36] Although he does not specifically tie Shitao to Chan—which he could have done—Shitao was important for Fu's painting. Now let us turn to paintings by Fu Baoshi.

Fu Baoshi's Ink Painting

In 1942, while still in Chongqing, Fu produced *The Thatched Hut of Great Purity* (Figure 10.2). It is based on a quasi-historical legend that Shitao once wrote a letter to Bada Shanren (1826–1705) asking him to produce a painting of Shitao's cottage.[37] The letter is supposed to have said that 'the old hut stands on a gentle mound, and there are several ancient ailanthus trees. In the hut is a lone old man . . . not a monk, as I still have my hair and wear a cap'.

In *The Thatched Hut of Great Purity*, a gigantic ailanthus tree dominates the composition. Dwarfed by the tree is a humble hut; a scholar—presumably Shitao—looks up from a window. There is an abrupt change in the manner of execution between bold, wet brushstrokes delineating large trees and the fine strokes rendering the scholar and his surrounding objects. This painting recalls Shitao's signature style, in which the artist abbreviated natural elements into near-abstract patterns of brush and ink in order to express his untrammelled inner self.[38]

In Fu's time, Shitao as well as Bada Shanren represented the endurance of Han Chinese under foreign rule. Distant cousins, Shitao and Bada were descendants of the Ming imperial family who survived the Manchu conquest in the 17th century. The expression in the supposed letter '[I still] have my hair and wear a cap [*youfa youguan*]' is particularly poignant—suggesting that Shitao still kept a traditional hairstyle and headgear instead of wearing a queue in compliance with the norms of the Qing regime.[39] Fu's painting has thus been interpreted as an expression of nationalism, at the time when Republican China (1912–1949) was struggling to move forward from the fallen Qing rule (1644–1911) on the one hand, and facing a threat of Japanese invasion on the other.[40] Shitao's alleged independent attitude at such a time of political turmoil no doubt served as a source of strength for Fu and his contemporaries.

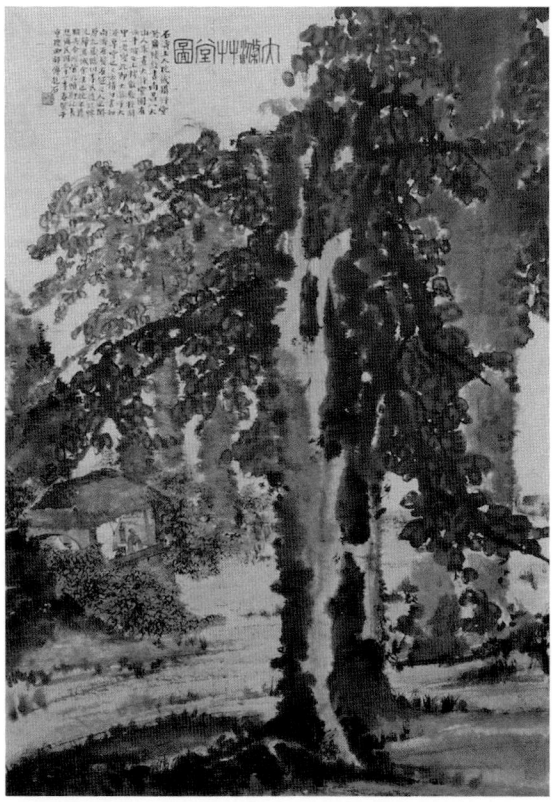

Figure 10.2 Fu Baoshi, *The Thatched Hut of Great Purity* (Dadi caotang tu), 1942. Hanging scroll, ink and colour on paper, 85.0 × 58.0 cm

Fu Family Collection. In Chen Lusheng, et al., *Fu Baoshi quanji* [Collected works of Fu Baoshi], vol. 1, p. 147

Inasmuch as *The Thatched Hut of Great Purity* appears to express Fu's patriotism, his works inspired by Shitao, including this painting, also demonstrate his close artistic ties with the Japanese art world.[41] Shitao attracted much attention there, starting in the early 20th century, when his works were introduced as part of the new migration of Chinese objects. As early as 1897, the seal carver Kuwana Tetsujō (1864–1937) purchased paintings in China, and his collection included the famous *A Waterfall on Mount Lu* by Shitao, now in the Sen'oku Hakkokan (Sumitomo Collection) in Kyoto.[42] Kuwana also owned a Shitao album *Returning Home*, now in the Metropolitan Museum of Art, New York, which bears a colophon brushed by Tomioka Tessai, quoting a passage by the 'Yangzhou Eccentric' artist Zheng Xie (1693–1765).[43] Luo Zhenyu, who sold hundreds of paintings in Japan for a living, had his *Landscape* by Shitao published in the art-journal *Kokka* in 1912 and 1916.[44] Painter Hashimoto Kansetsu (1883–1945), whose works Fu frequently referred to, released a book on Shitao in 1926.[45] It reproduces six works by Shitao—five owned by Japanese and another particularly famous piece, *Mount Huang Scroll* (1699), owned at that time by Kansetsu's friend Qian Shoutie

(1897–1967) (now in the Sen'oku Hakkokan).⁴⁶ The relationship between Kansetsu and Qian is expounded in Aida Yuen Wong's essay in the present volume.

Fu Baoshi carried his fascination with Shitao back to China. He compiled his first chronology of Shitao while in Japan in 1935, and published a series of writings on him in China in the following years.⁴⁷ In 1939 Fu released *Biographies of Chinese Artists in the late Ming* (*Mingmo minzu yiren zhuan*), a translation of a book by Yamamoto Teijirō (1870–1937).⁴⁸ President of the Taiwan Sugar Company and later a statesman, Yamamoto collected newly imported Chinese paintings in the early 20th century that became the basis for the Chōkaidō Art Museum in Japan. In 1939 Fu published poems and biographies of the four eccentric monks of the late Ming, including the sections on Shitao and Bada Shanren from Yamamoto's book.⁴⁹ Fu finished a new chronology of Shitao in 1941. In the following year, Fu produced *The Thatched Hut of Great Purity* and *Priest Shitao*. The aforementioned alleged letter by Shitao, which inspired Fu to paint *The Thatched Hut of Great Purity*, was apparently found in Kansetsu's book.⁵⁰

Another outcome of Fu's study in Japan was his exploration of the Chan ink painting from the Song and Yuan periods—which was in tune with his theory of ink painting discussed above. Fu's figurative paintings in the 1940s, for example, came close to the so-called apparitional painting (*wanglianghua*) produced by Chan monks.⁵¹ Art historian Shimada Shūjirō (1907–1994), in an article from the late 1930s, discusses that apparitional painting originally referred to works by the monk Zhirong (1114–1193). Although none of Zhirong's works has survived, his painting style can be found in works by Chan painters preserved in Japan, such as *Śākyamuni Descending from the Mountains* (1244).⁵² Apparitional painting is characterized by broad brushstrokes in extremely diluted ink delineating figures, coupled with fine lines in dark ink rendering details of the face (such as eyes and mouth). The robes of the figures are abbreviated, and done with free, casual strokes.

Aspects of apparitional painting can be found in Fu's *Beauty under Banana Leaves* (1945, Figure 10.3). Depicting an imaginary woman, this painting was based on a poem by Guo Moruo:

阮咸撥罷意低迷	Pausing her lute in a daze,
独坐瑶階有所思	She sits alone on a jade step, thinking—
一曲薰風無處寄	No one listens to her 'fragrant breeze'.
芭蕉葉綠上娥眉	Green banana leaves looming over, she raises her eyebrows.⁵³

In the painting, large banana leaves cast grey shadows on the ground. Executed with layers of dark ink in the boneless manner (*mogufa*), the leaves appear fresh like those of early summer. Seated beneath the plant is a young woman who, though absorbed in thought, turns her head as if noticing the gaze of the beholder. The loose, sparse lines of the woman's robe are almost obliterated, and the thinly applied dark ink forming her hair begins to dissipate. Rendered with these techniques, the figure appears to be materialized and dematerialized at the same time—echoing what the 4th-century Daoist Guoxiang called an apparition—a phenomenon that 'exists neither as a form nor as a shadow'.⁵⁴ Fu frequently depicted figures with an almost ghostlike appearance, as in his *Night Rain in Bashan* (1943), *Shi Le Seeking the Way* (ca. 1945), and *Amitabha* (1947). Although his techniques varied over time, half-emerging, half-dissolving forms preoccupied Fu from the 1940s onward.

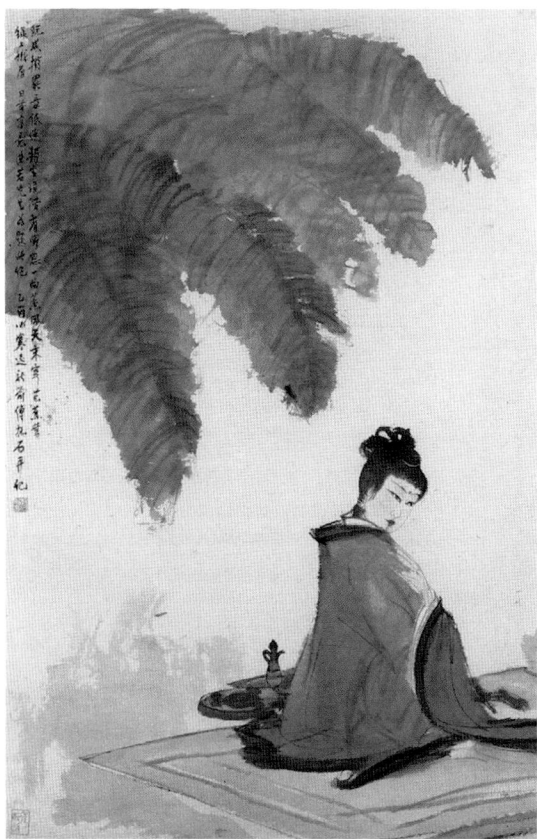

Figure 10.3 Fu Baoshi, *Beauty under Banana Leaves* (Yuan Xian bo ba yi dimi), 1945. Hanging scroll, ink and colour on paper, 85.2 × 54.5 cm

Nanjing Museum. In Xu Huping, et al., *Fu Baoshi Zhongguo hua: Fu Baoshi jiashu juanzeng, Nanjing Bowuyuan cang* [Chinese paintings by Fu Baoshi: donation of the Fu Baoshi family: collection of the Nanjing Museum], p. 30

Fu's experiment in the style of Chan painters is also apparent in his landscapes. *Evening Glow on a Fishing Village* (13th century) by Muqi is a well-known example of splashed-ink (*pomo*) painting by Chan monks.[55] Along with splashed-ink, Muqi extensively uses the boneless technique, avoiding outlines in rendering forms.[56] These techniques obscure the boundary between the solid and void in the pictorial realm. Also, Muqi's *Evening Glow* shows a fishing village at the front and distant mountains at the back, and between them is a band of water. Space recedes from the bottom to top as well as from right to left, as fishermen's boats gradually fade away to the left. A similar spatial treatment is present in *Returning Boats in Distant Shore*, attributed to Muqi. Here space recedes from bottom to top, and also from left to right, as mist obscures the scene on the right indicating an infinite expanse of water and sky. On the distant shore appear two boats, sailing back with the wind.

During the decade after his visits to Japan, Fu produced many landscapes with fishermen's boats. Although the subject alone is hardly unusual in East Asian painting, certain visual elements, coupled with the subject, recall Muqi. Fu's *Jutang Strait* (1944) is an imaginary landscape based on a poem by the Ming loyalist Lu Qian (Lu Banyin, 1621–1706).[57] Here Fu avoids precise outlines in rendering mountains and cliffs, and incorporates the splashed-ink technique to depict the mountains in front. The shape of the boats also recalls Muqi. Two more examples of Fu Baoshi's work from the 1940s, *Fisherman* and *Yangzi Gorge*, have splashy brushwork. These almost abstract traces of brush call the viewer's attention to the picture surface, against which space expands in an evocative manner. Rendered with the boneless technique, the rocks in both paintings appear weightless, as though they could dissolve into space.

Chan landscapes had a lingering effect in Fu's later works—as in his *After a Poem by Mao Zedong* (1961, Figure 10.4). Space here recedes from bottom to top, as well as from right to left. The coastline of the distant shore by Fu recalls the *Returning Boats* attributed to Muqi. At the lower left corner of the *Poem by Mao Zedong* is a remnant of the splashed-ink technique, appearing as small patches in dark ink, forming tree foliage. Behind the foliage lies a fishing village. This combination of splashed-ink and a fishing village also points to Muqi.

In addition to pictures by Shitao and Chan monks, Fu used a range of Japanese models for his new style of ink painting. His study of figurative works by contemporary artists like Hashimoto Kansetsu and Yokoyama Taikan is well known.[58] Here we shall take a fresh look at his Japanese models, in light of the abstraction in Fu's painting.

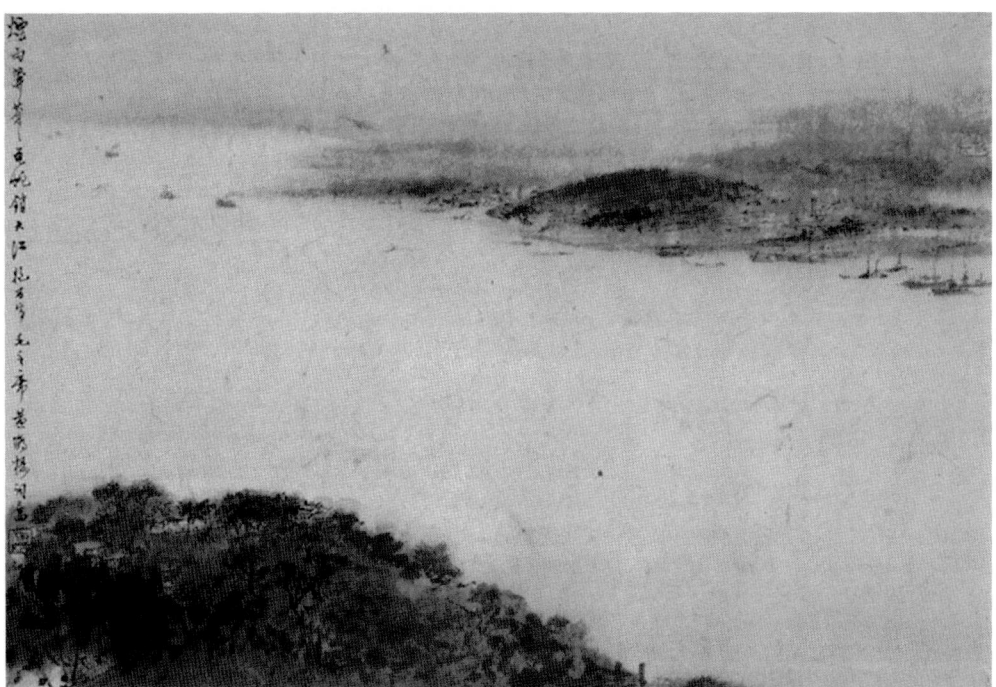

Figure 10.4 Fu Baoshi, *After a Poem by Mao Zedong* (Mao Zedong [Huanghelou] ciyi), 1961. Album leaf, ink on paper, 34.0 × 49.0 cm

Fu Family Collection. In Shibuya Kuritsu Shōtō Bijutsukan, ed., *Fu Hōseki: 20-seiki Chūgoku gadan no kyoshō: Nit-Chū bijutsu kōryū no kakehashi* [Fu Baoshi: a great master of 20th-century Chinese painting: a Sino-Japanese bridge in art exchanges], Figure 74

'National Painting' Unbound   199

Fu's *Washing Feet in a Stream* (1944) closely resembles *Serene Life by a Stream* (1921) by Tomioka Tessai. Both artists divide a long composition into the three-part structure of the fore-, middle-, and background, showing special recession from bottom to top. Tessai adopted the structure from the newly imported works in the 1910s and 1920s, but uses quicker and bolder strokes that only partially yield the shapes of rendered objects. Fu pushed the process of abstraction further by adding, quite literally, splashes of ink. They act to negate the spatial illusion in the painting and highlight the two-dimensionality of the pictorial surface.

Another subject that frequently appears in Fu's works in the 1940s is wet weather, as in *Evening Rain in Ba Mountains* (1944) and *Whispering Rain at Dusk* (1945, Figure 10.5).[59] Both depict rainy mountain vistas, whose foreground is done with dark ink that fades away as the scene shifts further into the distance. Fu covers the entire compositions with broad, diagonal strokes to depict the rainstorm and to charge the surface with a moist atmosphere. This technique was extensively used by Tomioka Tessai, as in his *Mountain Villa in a Rain Storm* (1920) and *Dongpo in a Straw Hat* (1912). In both Fu and Tessai's cases this brush method brings forth the materiality of ink itself.

In addition to rainscapes, Fu produced snowscapes, such as *Returning Home in Snowstorm* (1945) and *Landscape* (ca. 1944). In *Landscape*, Fu uses sparse lines for the contour and the texture of the soaring white mountains, and layers of dilute ink for the grey sky. Fu was probably familiar with works by the individualist literati painter

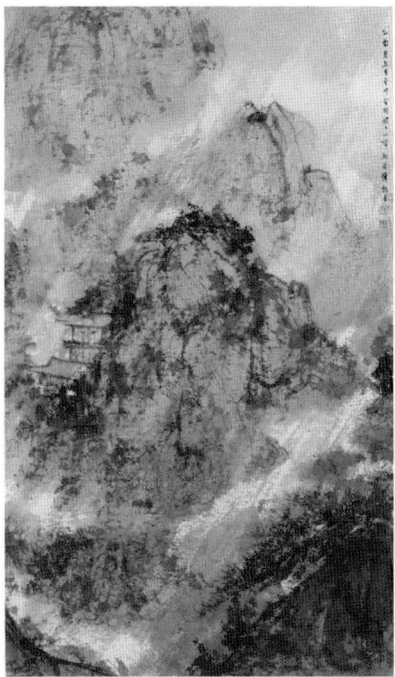

Figure 10.5 Fu Baoshi, *Whispering Rain at Dusk* (Xiaoxiao muyu), 1945. Hanging scroll, ink and colour on paper, 103.5 × 59.4 cm

Nanjing Museum. In Xu Huping, et al., *Fu Baoshi Zhongguo hua: Fu Baoshi jiashu juanzeng, Nanjing Bowuyuan cang* [Chinese paintings by Fu Baoshi: donation of the Fu Baoshi family: collection of the Nanjing Museum], p. 26

Uragami Gyokudō, who produced many mountainscapes of shifting weather, including *Mountains after Rain* (1810s) and *Eastern Clouds, Shifted Snow* (1811). Hashimoto Kansetsu, whose work Fu often consulted, was a pioneer in the research on Gyokudō. Paintings by Gyokudō often have a strong graphic quality, with emphasis on brushstrokes over rendering of forms, adding a sense of kinetic energy. A small lone figure in a landscape is a hallmark of Gyokudō's work—a motif that also appears frequently in Fu's work, including *Whispering Rain at Dusk*.

After the communist takeover in 1949, Fu produced paintings with subject matter that met the norms of the People's Republic of China. His *Crossing Dadu River* (1951) and *The Far Snows of Minshan Only Make Us Happy* (1953), both showing the heroism of the Red Army, were in tune with government-imposed 'thought remoulding'.[60] Fu, however, also continued his studies in traditional ink painting, including Japanese examples.

One of the most remarkable opportunities for Fu to explore Japanese painting was an exhibition of the monk painter Sesshū Tōyō held in Beijing in 1956—fifteen years before the normalization of diplomatic ties between the two nations. Fu was the sole editor of its well-researched, lavishly illustrated catalogue.[61] It bears a preface written by Guo Moruo. Comparing Sesshū, who studied in Ming China (1368–1644), and the writer Lu Xun (1881–1936), in Meiji Japan (1868–1912), Guo expresses his hope for further cultural exchanges between the two nations and closer friendships between their peoples.[62] More importantly, the catalogue offers Fu's *Portrait of Sesshū* (Figure 10.6)

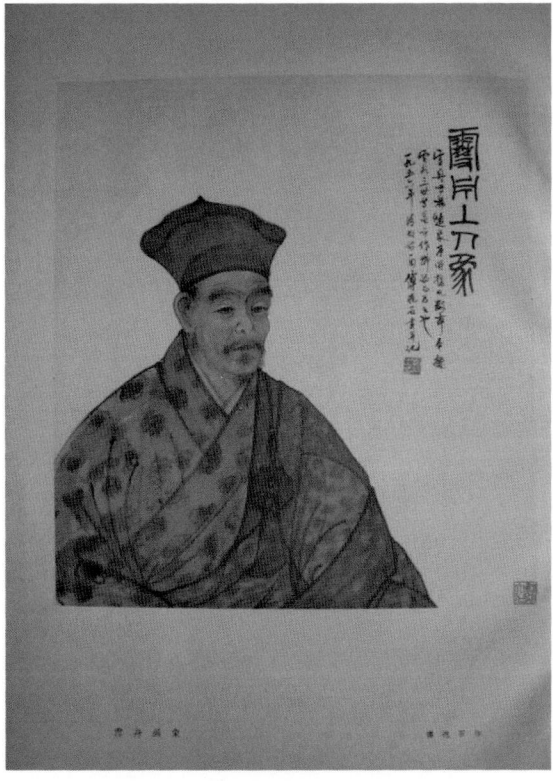

Figure 10.6 Fu Baoshi, *Portrait of Sesshū* (Xuezhou huaxiang), 1956
In Fu Baoshi, ed., *Xuezhou*, [Sesshū] n.p.

'National Painting' Unbound   201

as well as his essay 'Sesshū and his art' (*Xuezhou ji qi yishu*) and commentaries to forty-eight paintings by the Japanese artist. Fu conducted extensive research for the project, his up-to-date references even covering articles on Sesshū published in wartime Japan. The book includes several landscapes done with splashed-ink technique. Fu considers *Haboku Landscape* (1495, Figure 10.7) the most important in Sesshū's oeuvre, noting that he achieved his own style after studying in China.[63] The passage echoes Fu's experience of developing an ink painting of his own after studying in Japan.

Consider once again Fu Baoshi's 1962 *Landscape*, discussed at the beginning of this essay (Plate 11). The expressiveness of the brushstrokes, coupled with the scholars overlooking a waterfall, reminds us of Shitao. At the same time, the splashy manner points to a hallmark of Chan ink painting, exemplified by Sesshū's work. The age-old

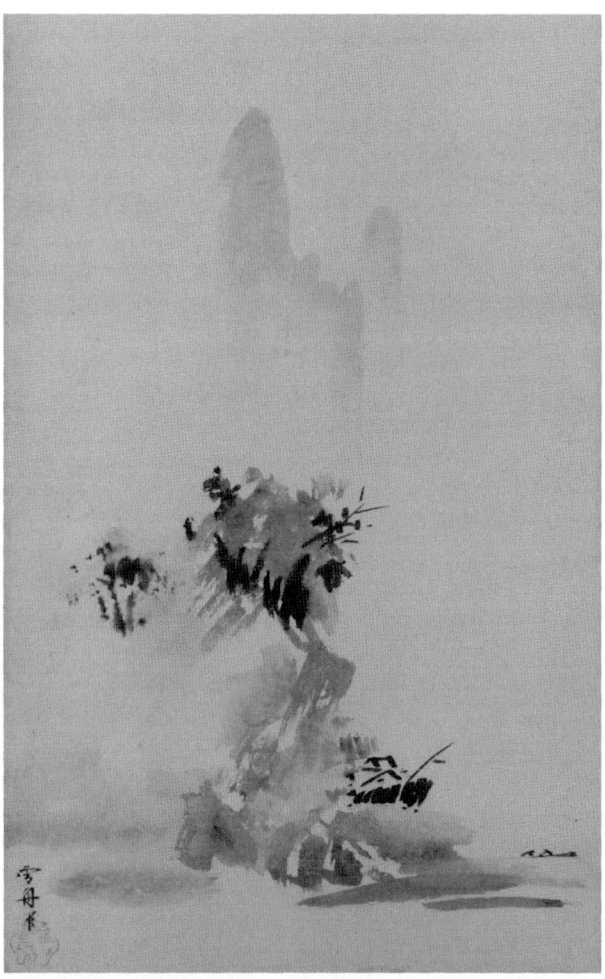

Figure 10.7 Sesshū Tōyō, *Haboku Landscape* (Haboku sansui zu) (detail), 1495. Ink on paper, 148.6 × 32.7 cm
Tokyo National Museum. Photograph provided by the Tokyo National Museum

literati ideal of expressing oneself through art and brush techniques typified by Chan art are combined to create a near-abstract, modern painting. Fu achieved this through his extensive studies of paintings by both Chinese and Japanese artists.

Conclusion

Is 'East Asian art history' possible? This question was central to the symposium leading up to the present publication. Underlying such a query is the tendency of scholars in the field to focus on artistic developments only within a national boundary—a tendency that was already present in the late 19th–early 20th centuries, at the outset of art history as an academic discipline in East Asia.[64] For many art historians of Japan and China of that generation, defining the history of art meant defining national identity. The pressing task was to unite the people under the emerging modern-state of Meiji Japan or Republican China, as well as to demonstrate their cultural advancement to foreign powers. This state-focused art history was important in laying the foundation for the discipline, but over decades it caused the essentialization of national aesthetics. Even today some still uncritically believe that 'literati art' is China's cultural essence and 'Zen art' is Japan's. Yet the histories of art in China and Japan are entangled, complex organisms, neither neatly dividable into artistic categories nor reducible to national aesthetics—as works by Fu Baoshi amply demonstrate.

For Fu Baoshi, Japan was a bountiful source of artistic inspiration, but it goes without saying that Fu, along with other people in China, suffered tremendously from Japanese imperialism. How did he then reconcile two seemingly contradictory impulses: a nationalist urge as a citizen of China versus a transnational artistic pursuit involving Japan? It is true that Fu joined an anti-Japanese campaign during the war. But shortly after the war, in 1947, Fu sent a letter to Kinbara—a fact that reveals Fu's generous broad-mindedness.[65] Living through an age of war and revolution, did he perhaps grow into an impartial thinker who considered a 'state' and its 'individuals' somewhat separately? Wasn't his new style of ink painting ultimately rooted in an art world that allowed interactions of diverse 'persons', regardless of their origins, but not so much in the political or military playing field centred on the collective 'nation'? Fu Baoshi and his art send us a clue to transnational art history: investigating art through 'individuals', as opposed to the 'nation', may yield a fuller understanding of the developments of art across East Asia, and even across the world.

Notes

1 This essay is in part based on: Tamaki Maeda, 'Rediscovering China in Japan: Fu Baoshi's Ink Painting', in *Writing Modern Chinese Art: Historiographic Explorations*, ed. Josh Yiu (Seattle: Seattle Art Museum, in association with University of Washington Press, 2009), pp. 70–81; and Tamaki Maeda and Aida Yuen Wong, 'Kindred Spirits: Fu Baoshi and the Japanese Art World', in *Chinese Art in an Age of Revolution: Fu Baoshi (1904–1965)*, ed. Anita Chung (New Haven: Yale University Press, 2011), pp. 35–41.
2 According to the list compiled in Tsuruta Takeyoshi, 'Ryūnichi bijutsu gakusei: kin hyakunen-rai Chūgoku kaigashi kenkyū 5' [Art students studied in Japan: research in the history of Chinese painting in the last hundred years 5], *Bijutsu kenkyū* [Art research] 367 (March 1997): 29–41. For Chinese art students in Japan, see also Yoshida Chizuko, *Kindai Higashi Ajia bijutsu ryūgakusei no kenkyū* [Research on East Asian international art students in modern times] (Tokyo: Yumani Shobō, 2009).
3 For China's learning from the Japanese art world, see Joshua A. Fogel, ed., *The Role of Japan in Modern Chinese Art* (Berkeley: University of California Press, 2012); Julia F. Andrews

and Kuiyi Shen, *The Art of Modern China* (Berkeley: University of California Press, 2012), pp. 26–113; and Aida Yuen Wong, *Parting the Mists: Discovering Japan and the Rise of National-Style Painting in Modern China* (Honolulu: University of Hawai'i Press, 2006).

4 For Fu's life and work in general, see Chung, ed., *Chinese Art*. For Fu's life in Japan in particular, see Ajioka Yoshindo, 'Kindai Nit-Chū bijutsu kōryū to Fu Hōseki' [Modern Sino-Japanese exchanges in art and Fu Baoshi], in *Fu Hōseki: 20-seiki Chūgoku gadan no kyoshō: Nit-Chū bijutsu kōryū no kakehashi* [Fu Baoshi: a great master of 20th-century Chinese painting: a Sino-Japanese bridge in art exchanges], ed. Shibuya Kuritsu Shōtō Bijutsukan (Tokyo: Yomiuri Shinbunsha, 1999), pp. 23–26. See also Musashino Bijutsu Daigaku and Chūgoku Bijutsu Gakuin Kōkanten Jikkō Iinkai, eds., *Fu Hōseki ten* [Fu Baoshi exhibition] (Kodaira: Musashino Bijutsu Daigaku Bijutsu Shiryō Toshokan, 1994).

5 Tōkyō Bijutsu Gakkō Bunkonai Tō Sō Gen Min Meiga Tenrankai, ed., *Tō Sō Gen Min meiga taikan* [A grand view of famous Tang, Song, Yuan, and Ming paintings], 4 vols. (Tokyo: Ōtsuka Kōgeisha, 1929). For the exhibition, see also Kuze Kanako, 'Gaimushō kiroku ni miru 'Tō Sō Gen Min meiga tenrankai' (1928-nen)' [An exhibition of famous Tang, Song, Yuan, Ming paintings (1928) seen through records of the Ministry of Foreign Affairs], *Nihon kenkyū* (2014) 50: 143–189.

6 The six Orthodox masters refer to: Wang Shimin (1592–1680), Wang Jian (1598–1677), Wang Hui (1632–1717), Wang Yuanqi (1642–1715), Wu Li (1632–1718), and Yun Shouping (1633–1690).

7 It was published in Yao Yuxiang ed., *Zhongguohua taolun ji* [Discussions on Chinese painting], (Beiping [Beijing]: Lida Shuju, 1932).

8 For the relationship between Wu Changshi and the Japanese art world, see Tōkyō Kokuritsu Hakubutsukan and Taitō Kuritsu Shodō Hakubutsukan, et al., eds., *Go Shōseki no sho, ga, in* [Wu Changshi's calligraphy, painting, and seal carving] (Tokyo: Taitōku Geijutsu Bunka Zaidan, 2011).

9 Masaki Naohiko, *Jūsan Shōdō nikki* [Jūsan Shōdō diary] (Tokyo: Tōkyō Chūōkōron Bijutsu Shuppan, 1966), 4: 1230.

10 For Wang Yiting and the Sino-Japanese artistic network in the early 20th century, see Walter B. Davis, 'Welcoming the Japanese Art World: Wang Yiting's Social and Artistic Exchanges with Japanese Sinophiles and Artists', in *The Role of Japan in Modern Chinese Art*, ed. Joshua A. Fogel (Berkeley: University of California Press, 2012), pp. 84–112, 321–328.

11 Fu Baoshi, *Zhongguo huihua bianjian shigang* (1929; reprint, Shanghai: Shanghai Guji Chubanshe, 1998).

12 Ibid., pp. 74–83. For the six Orthodox masters, see note 6 above.

13 For the development of art history in pre-modern Japan, see Sakazaki Shizuka, *Nihon ga no seishin* [The spirit of Japanese painting] (1942; reprint, Tokyo: Perikansha, 1995).

14 For the development of art history in Japan and China in the late 19th–early 20th century, including Okakura's lectures, see Tamaki Maeda, 'Inverting the Cultural Order: Naitō Konan and East Asian Art History', in *Japanese Art: Transcultural Perspectives*, ed. Christine Guth, Melanie Trede, and Mio Wakita (Leiden: Brill, forthcoming).

15 Ibid.; Dōshin Satō, *Modern Japanese Art and the Meiji State: The Politics of Beauty*, trans. Hiroshi Nara (Los Angeles: Getty Research Institute, 2011), pp. 153–182.

16 For the elevation of *kowatari* objects in modern Japan, see Christine Guth, *Art, Tea, Industry: Masuda Takashi and the Mitsui Circle* (Princeton: Princeton University Press, 1993).

17 Publications on *Sō-Genga* include: Tōkyō Kokuritsu Hakubutsukan, *Sō-Gen no kaiga* [Song and Yuan painting] (Kyoto: Benrido, 1962); and Ōsaka Shiritsu Bijutsukan [Osaka-City Museum], *Sō-Gen no bijutsu* [Art of the Song and Yuan] (Tokyo: Heibonsha, 1980).

18 For Dong Qichang's theory, see for example James Cahill, *The Distant Mountains: Chinese Painting of the Late Ming Dynasty, 1570–1644* (New York: Weatherhill, 1982); Susan Bush, *The Chinese Literati on Painting: Su Shih (1037–1101) to Tung Ch'i-Ch'ang (1555–1636)* (1971; reprint, Hong Kong: Hong Kong University Press, 2012).

19 Ernest F. Fenollosa, 'Bijustu shinsetsu' [A true theory of art], in *Bijutsu* [Fine arts], ed. Aoki Shigeru and Sakai Tadayasu, *Nihon kindai shisō taikei*, vol. 17 (Tokyo: Iwanami Shoten, 1989), pp. 35–65. For the reception of literati painting in Meiji Japan, see Christine Guth, 'Meiji Response to *Bunjinga*', in *Challenging Past and Present: The Metamorphosis of Japanese Art*, ed. Ellen P. Conant (Honolulu: University of Hawai'i Press, 2006), pp. 177–196.

20 For the importation to Japan of Chinese paintings in the 20th century, see Tamaki Maeda, '(Re-)Canonizing Literati Painting: The Kyoto Circle', in *The Role of Japan in Modern Chinese Art*, ed. Joshua A. Fogel (Berkeley: University of California Press, 2012), pp. 215–227, 353–358; Sobukawa Hiroshi, et al., *Chūgoku shoga tanbō: Kansai no shozō ka to sono meihin* [Exploring Chinese calligraphy and painting: collectors in Kansai and their famous works] (Tokyo: Nigensha, 2011).
21 For activities of this circle, see Maeda, '(Re-)Canonizing'; Tamaki Maeda, 'Luo Zhenyu and the "Legacy of the Southern School" in Japan and the West', in *Lost Generation: Luo Zhenyu, Qing Loyalists, and the Formation of Modern Chinese Culture*, ed. Chia-ling Yang and Roderick Whitfield (London: Saffron Books, in association with University of Edinburgh, 2012), pp. 123–141; and Tamaki Maeda, 'Tomioka Tessai's Narrative Landscape: Rethinking Sino-Japanese Traditions' (PhD diss., University of Washington, 2004).
22 For Ōmura Seigai, see Shioya Jun, Yoshida Chizuko, Ōnishi Junko, et al., *Ōmura Seigai no kenkyū* [Research on Ōmura Seigai] (Tokyo: Tōkyō Bunkazai Kenkyūjo, 2012).
23 Ōmura Seigai ed., *Shōbanryūdō gekiseki* [Dramatic ink traces in the Small Ten-Thousand Willows Studio] (Tokyo: Shinbi Shoin, 1914).
24 Ōmura Seigai, *Bunjinga no fukkō* [The revival of literati painting] (Tokyo: Kōgeisha, 1921).
25 Chen Hengque, comp., *Zhongguo wenrenhua zhi yanjiu* [Research in Chinese literati painting] (Tianjin: Tianjin Gui Shudian, 1922).
26 Kinbara Seigo, *Tang Song zhi huihua* [Paintings of the Tang and Song dynasties], trans. Fu Baoshi (Shanghai: Shangwu Yinshuguan, 1935).
27 Ibid., p. 55.
28 Kinbara Seigo, *Mokkei* [Muqi] (Tokyo: Atoriesha, 1939), p. 34.
29 Ibid. See also Kinbara Seigo, *Kaiga ni okeru sen no kenkyū* [Research on lines in painting] (Tokyo: Kokusho Kankōkai, 1976).
30 Fu Baoshi, 'Zhongguo huihua "shanshui" "xieyi" "shuimo" zhi shide kaocha' [A historical analysis of 'landscapes', 'xieyi', and 'ink' in Chinese painting], in *Fu Baoshi meishuwen ji* [Collection of writings on art by Fu Baoshi], comp. Ye Zonggao (Nanjing: Jiangsu Wenyi Chubanshe, 1986), pp. 239–253.
31 Ibid., p. 246.
32 Fu Baoshi, *Zhongguo de renwuhua he shanshuihua* [Chinese figurative and landscape painting, 1953], in *Fu Baoshi meishu wenji*, pp. 520–554.
33 Ibid., p. 541.
34 Ibid., p. 537.
35 Ibid., p. 545.
36 Ibid., pp. 552–553.
37 Chen Lusheng, et al., *Fu Baoshi quanji* [Collected works of Fu Baoshi] (Nanning Shi: Guangxi Meishu Chubanshe, 2008), 1: 146. For the authenticity of the letter, see Wen Fong, *Between Two Cultures* (New York: Metropolitan Museum of Art, 2001), pp. 106–111, 183–184.
38 For Shitao's painting style, see Jonathan Hay, *Shitao: Painting and Modernity in Early Qing China* (Cambridge: Cambridge University Press, 2001).
39 Chen, et al., *Fu Baoshi quanji*, 1: 146.
40 Ibid., and Chung, ed., *Chinese Art*, p. 72.
41 For the popularity of Shitao in the Sino-Japanese cultural sphere in the early 20th century, see Aida Yuen Wong, 'A New Life for Literati Painting in the Early Twentieth Century', *Artibus Asiae* 60, no. 2 (2000): 297–326.
42 For the Kuwana collection, see Kuwana Tetsujō, *Kyūka Inshitsu kanzō garoku* [A record of paintings authenticated and owned by Kyūka Seal Studio], 2 vols. (Kyoto: Bunseidō Shashin Seihansho, 1920).
43 Wen Fong, *Between Two Cultures*, p. 14.
44 *Kokka* 263 (1912); 313 (1916).
45 For Hashimoto Kansetsu and Shitao, see Shigemi Inaga, 'Western Modern Masters Measured on the East-Asian Literati Temple: Hashimoto Kansetsu and the Kyoto School of Sinology', in *Art/Histories in Transcultural Dynamics*, ed. Pauline Bachmann, et al. (Leiden: Wilhelm Fink, 2017), pp. 31–46.
46 Hashimoto Kansetsu, *Sekitō* [Shitao] (Tokyo: Chūō Bijutsusha, 1926).
47 For a list of Fu Baoshi's publications, see Chung, ed., *Chinese Art*, pp. 223–225.

48 Yamamoto Teijirō, *Mingmo minzu yiren zhuan* [Biographies of Chinese artists in the late Ming], trans. and ed. Fu Baoshi (Changsha: Shangwu Yinshuguan, 1939).
49 Fu Baoshi, 'Mingmo si jiseng' [Four eccentric monks of the late Ming] (1939), in *Fu Baoshi meishu wenji*, pp. 182–191.
50 Chung, ed., *Chinese Art*, p. 72; Hashimoto, *Sekitō*, pp. 23–24.
51 For apparitional painting, see Shimada Shūjirō, 'Mōryōga' [Apparitional painting], 2 parts, *Bijutsu kenkyū* 84 (1938): 4–13; 86 (1939): 8–16. For examples of apparitional painting, see Gregory Levine and Yukio Lippit, *Awakenings: Zen Figure Painting in Medieval Japan* (New York: Japan Society, 2007).
52 Yoshiaki Shimizu, 'Śākyamuni Descending the Mountain', in ibid., pp. 64–65; Shimada, 'Mōryōga', pt. 2: 8–16.
53 Translation mine.
54 Shimada, 'Mōryōga', pt. 1: 4.
55 For the splashed-ink technique, see Shimada Shūjirō, 'Concerning the I-p'in Style of Painting', trans. James Cahill, 3 parts, *Oriental Art*, n.s., 7, no. 2 (1961): 66–74; 8, no. 3 (1962): 130–137; 10, no. 1 (1964): 19–26.
56 For the boneless technique, see Yashiro Yukio, *Suibokuga* (Tokyo: Iwanami Shoten, 1969).
57 Shibuya Kuritsu Shōtō Bijutsukan, ed., *Fu Hōseki*, 139.
58 A number of publications deal with this issue, e.g. Chung, ed., *Chinese Art*.
59 For Fu's rainscapes, see also Aida Yuen Wong, 'Landscapes of National Empowerment: Fu Baoshi's Re-appreciation of the "Chinese" Rainscape Tradition from Japan', *Journal of History of Modern Art* 21 (December 2012): 175–197.
60 For the relationship between art and politics in post-1949 China, see, e.g. Julia F. Andrews, *Painters and Politics: In the People's Republic of China, 1949–1979* (Berkeley: University of California Press, 1994), and Jerome Silbergeld with Gong Jisui, *Contradictions: Artistic Life, the Social State, and the Chinese Painter Li Huasheng* (Seattle: University of Washington Press, 1993).
61 Fu Baoshi, ed. *Xuezhou* [Sesshū] (Beijing: Renmin Meishu Chubanshe, 1956).
62 Guo Moruo, 'Ti Xuezhou huace' [Title to Sesshū catalogue], in ibid., n.p. Guo also brushed the book title 'Xuezhou', which appears on the front cover page.
63 Ibid., pp. 14–15.
64 For a historiography of art history of this era, see Maeda, 'Inverting the Cultural Order', (forthcoming).
65 According to Kinbara's diary, the letter reached him on July 4, 1949. Kinbara Takurō, ed., 'Hongaku ryūgaku jidai no Fu Hōseki' [Fu Baoshi during his study in this school], in Musashino Bijutsu Daigaku and Chūgoku Bijutsu Gakuin Kōkanten Jikkō Iinkai, eds., *Fu Hōseki ten* [Fu Baoshi exhibition], p. 36.

Bibliography

Ajioka Yoshindo. 'Kindai Nit-Chū bijutsu kōryū to Fu Hōseki' [Modern Sino-Japanese exchanges in art and Fu Baoshi]. In *Fu Hōseki: 20-seiki Chūgoku gadan no kyoshō: Nit-Chū bijutsu kōryū no kakehashi* [Fu Baoshi: a great master of 20th-century Chinese painting: a Sino-Japanese bridge in art exchanges], edited by Shibuya Kuritsu Shōtō Bijutsukan. Tokyo: Yomiuri Shinbunsha, 1999.

Andrews, Julia F. *Painters and Politics: In the People's Republic of China, 1949–1979*. Berkeley: University of California Press, 1994.

Andrews, Julia F., and Kuiyi Shen, *The Art of Modern China*. Berkeley: University of California Press, 2012.

Bush, Susan. *The Chinese Literati on Painting: Su Shih (1037–1101) to Tung Ch'i-Ch'ang (1555–1636)*. Hong Kong: Hong Kong University Press, 2012.

Cahill, James. *The Distant Mountains: Chinese Painting of the Late Ming Dynasty, 1570–1644*. New York: Weatherhill, 1982.

Chen Hengque, comp. *Zhongguo wenrenhua zhi yanjiu* [Research in Chinese literati painting]. Tianjin: Tianjin Gui Shudian, 1922.

Chen Lusheng, et al. *Fu Baoshi quanji* [Collected works of Fu Baoshi]. Nanning Shi: Guangxi Meishu Chubanshe, 2008.

Davis, Walter B. 'Welcoming the Japanese Art World: Wang Yiting's Social and Artistic Exchanges with Japanese Sinophiles and Artists'. In *The Role of Japan in Modern Chinese Art*, edited by Joshua A. Fogel, 84–112, 321–328. Berkeley: University of California Press, 2012.

Fenollosa, Ernest F. 'Bijustu shinsetsu' [A true theory of art]. In *Bijustu* [Fine arts], edited by Aoki Shigeru and Sakai Tadayasu, 35–65. *Nihon kindai shisō taikei*, vol. 17. Tokyo: Iwanami Shoten, 1989.

Fogel, Joshua A., ed. *The Role of Japan in Modern Chinese Art*. Berkeley: University of California Press, 2012.

Fong, Wen. *Between Two Cultures*. New York: Metropolitan Museum of Art, 2001.

Fu Baoshi. 'Mingmo si jiseng' [Four eccentric monks of the late Ming] (1939). In *Fu Baoshi meishu wenji* [Collection of writings on art by Fu Baoshi], compiled by Ye Zonggao, pp. 182–191. Nanjing: Jiangsu Wenyi Chubanshe, 1986.

———. *Zhongguo de renwuhua he shanshuihua* [Chinese figurative and landscape painting, 1953]. In *Fu Baoshi meishu wenji* [Collection of writings on art by Fu Baoshi], compiled by Ye Zonggao, 520–554. Nanjing: Jiangsu Wenyi Chubanshe, 1986.

———. 'Zhongguo huihua "shanshui", "xieyi", "shuimo" zhi shide kaocha' [A historical analysis of 'landscapes', 'xieyi', and 'ink' in Chinese painting]. In *Fu Baoshi meishu wenji* [Collection of writings on art by Fu Baoshi], compiled by Ye Zonggao, pp. 239–253. Nanjing: Jiangsu Wenyi Chubanshe, 1986.

———. *Zhongguo huihua bianjian shigang*. Shanghai: Shanghai Guji Chubanshe, 1998.

Fu Baoshi, ed. *Xuezhou* [Sesshū]. Beijing: Renmin Meishu Chubanshe, 1956.

Guo Moruo. 'Ti Xuezhou huace' [Title to Sesshū catalogue]. In *Xuezhou* (Sesshū), edited by Fu Baoshi, n.p. Beijing: Renmin Meishu Chubanshe, 1956.

Guth, Christine M.E. *Art, Tea, Industry: Masuda Takashi and the Mitsui Circle*. Princeton: Princeton University Press, 1993.

———. 'Meiji Response to *Bunjinga*'. In *Challenging Past and Present: The Metamorphosis of Japanese Art*, edited by Ellen P. Conant, 177–196. Honolulu: University of Hawai'i Press, 2006.

Hashimoto Kansetsu. *Sekitō* [Shitao]. Tokyo: Chūō Bijutsusha, 1926.

Hay, Jonathan. *Shitao: Painting and Modernity in Early Qing China*. Cambridge: Cambridge University Press, 2001.

Inaga, Shigemi. 'Western Modern Masters Measured on the East-Asian Literati Temple: Hashimoto Kansetsu and the Kyoto School of Sinology'. In *Art/Histories in Transcultural Dynamics*, edited by Pauline Bachmann et al., 31–46. Leiden: Wilhelm Fink, 2017.

Kinbara Seigo. *Tang Song zhi huihua* [Paintings of the Tang and Song dynasties], translated by Fu Baoshi. Shanghai: Shangwu Yinshuguan, 1935.

———. *Mokkei* [Muqi]. Tokyo: Atoriesha, 1939.

———. *Kaiga ni okeru sen no kenkyū* [Research on lines in painting]. Tokyo: Kokusho Kankōkai, 1976.

Kinbara Takurō, ed. 'Hongaku ryūgaku jidai no Fu Hōseki' [Fu Baoshi during his study in this school]. In *Fu Hōseki ten* [Fu Baoshi exhibition], edited by Musashino Bijutsu Daigaku and Chūgoku Bijutsu Gakuin Kōkanten Jikkō Iinkai. Kodaira: Musashino Bijutsu Daigaku Bijutsu Shiryō Toshokan, 1994.

Kuwana Tetsujō. *Kyūka Inshitsu kanzō garoku* [A record of paintings authenticated and owned by Kyūka Seal Studio], 2 vols. Kyoto: Bunseidō Shashin Seihansho, 1920.

Kuze Kanako. 'Gaimushō kiroku ni miru Tō Sō Gen Min meiga tenrankai' (1928–nen)' [An exhibition of Famous Tang, Song, Yuan, Ming paintings (1928) seen through records of the Ministry of Foreign Affairs]. *Nihon kenkyū* 50 (2014): 143–189.

Levine, Gregory, and Yukio Lippit. *Awakenings: Zen Figure Painting in Medieval Japan*. New York: Japan Society, 2007.

Maeda, Tamaki. 'Tomioka Tessai's Narrative Landscape: Rethinking Sino-Japanese Traditions'. PhD diss. University of Washington, 2004.

———. 'Rediscovering China in Japan: Fu Baoshi's Ink Painting'. In *Writing Modern Chinese Art: Historiographic Explorations*, edited by Josh Yiu, 70–81. Seattle: Seattle Art Museum, in association with University of Washington Press, 2009.

———. '(Re-)Canonizing Literati Painting: The Kyoto Circle'. In *The Role of Japan in Modern Chinese Art*, edited by Joshua A. Fogel, 215–227, 353–358. Berkeley: University of California Press, 2012.

———. 'Luo Zhenyu and the "Legacy of the Southern School" in Japan and the West'. In *Lost Generation: Luo Zhenyu, Qing Loyalists, and the Formation of Modern Chinese Culture*, edited by Chia-ling Yang and Roderick Whitfield, 123–141. London: Saffron Books, in association with University of Edinburgh, 2012.

———. 'Inverting the Cultural Order: Naitō Konan and East Asian Art History'. In *Japanese Art: Transcultural Perspectives*, edited by Christine Guth, Melanie Trede, and Mio Wakita. Leiden: Brill, forthcoming.

Maeda, Tamaki, and Aida Yuen Wong, 'Kindred Spirits: Fu Baoshi and the Japanese Art World'. In *Chinese Art in an Age of Revolution: Fu Baoshi (1904–1965)*, edited by Anita Chung, pp. 35–41. New Haven: Yale University Press, 2011.

Masaki Naohiko. *Jūsan Shōdō nikki*. Tokyo: Tōkyō Chūōkōron Bijutsu Shuppan, 1966.

Musashino Bijutsu Daigaku and Chūgoku Bijutsu Gakuin Kōkanten Jikkō Iinkai, eds. *Fu Hōseki ten* [Fu Baoshi exhibition]. Kodaira: Musashino Bijutsu Daigaku Bijutsu Shiryō Toshokan, 1994.

Ōmura Seigai, ed. *Shōbanryūdō gekiseki* [Dramatic ink traces in the Small Ten-Thousand Willows Studio]. Tokyo: Shinbi Shoin, 1914.

———. *Bunjinga no fukkō* [The Revival of Literati Painting]. Tokyo: Kōgeisha, 1921.

Ōsaka Shiritsu Bijutsukan [Osaka-City Museum]. *Sō-Gen no bijutsu* [Art of the Song and Yuan]. Tokyo: Heibonsha, 1980.

Sakazaki Shizuka. *Nihon ga no seishin* [The spirit of Japanese painting]. Tokyo: Perikansha, 1995.

Satō, Dōshin. *Modern Japanese Art and the Meiji State: The Politics of Beauty*, translated by Hiroshi Nara. Los Angeles: Getty Research Institute, 2011.

Shimada Shūjirō. 'Mōryōga' [Apparitional painting], 2 parts. *Bijutsu kenkyū* 84 (1938): 4–13; 86 (1939): 8–16.

———. 'Concerning the I-p'in Style of Painting'. Translated by James Cahill. 3 parts. *Oriental Art*, n.s., 7, no. 2 (1961): 66–74; 8, no. 3 (1962): 130–137; 10, no. 1(1964): 19–26.

Shioya Jun, and Yoshida Chizuko, Ōnishi Junko, et al. *Ōmura Seigai no kenkyū* [Research on Ōmura Seigai]. Tokyo: Tōkyō Bunkazai Kenkyūjo, 2012.

Shibuya Kuritsu Shōtō Bijutsukan, ed. *Fu Hōseki: 20-seiki Chūgoku gadan no kyoshō: Nit-Chū bijutsu kōryū no kakehashi* [Fu Baoshi: a great master of 20th-century Chinese painting: a Sino-Japanese bridge in art exchanges]. Tokyo: Yomiuri Shinbunsha, 1999.

Silbergeld, Jerome, with Gong Jisui. *Contradictions: Artistic Life, the Social State, and the Chinese Painter Li Huasheng*. Seattle: University of Washington Press, 1993.

Sobukawa Hiroshi, et al. *Chūgoku shoga tanbō: Kansai no shozō ka to sono meihin* [Exploring Chinese calligraphy and painting: Collectors in Kansai and their famous works]. Tokyo: Nigensha, 2011.

Tōkyō Bijutsu Gakkō Bunkonai Tō Sō Gen Min Meiga Tenrankai, ed., *Tō Sō Gen Min meiga taikan* [A grand view of famous Tang, Song, Yuan, and Ming paintings], 4 vols. Tokyo: Ōtsuka Kōgeisha, 1929.

Tōkyo Kokuritsu Hakubutsukan and Taitō Kuritsu Shodō Hakubutsukan, et al., eds. *Go Shōseki no sho, ga, in* [Wu Changshi's calligraphy, painting, and seal carving]. Tokyo: Taitōku Geijutsu Bunka Zaidan, 2011.

Tōkyō Kokuritsu Hakubutsukan. *Sō-Gen no kaiga* [Song and Yuan painting]. Kyoto: Benridō, 1962.

Tsuruta Takeyoshi. 'Ryūnichi bijutsu gakusei: kin hyakunenrai Chūgoku kaigashi kenkyū 5' [Art students studied in Japan: research in the history of Chinese painting in the last hundred years 5], *Bijutsu kenkyū* [Art research] 367 (March 1997): 29–41.

Wong, Aida Yuen. 'A New Life for Literati Painting in the Early Twentieth Century'. *Artibus Asiae* 60, no. 2 (2000): 297–326.

———. *Parting the Mists: Discovering Japan and the Rise of National-Style Painting in Modern China*. Honolulu: University of Hawai'i Press, 2006.

———. 'Landscapes of National Empowerment: Fu Baoshi's Re-appreciation of the "Chinese" Rainscape Tradition from Japan'. *Journal of History of Modern Art* 21 (December 2012): 175–197.

Xu Huping, et al., *Fu Baoshi Zhongguo hua: Fu Baoshi jiashu juanzeng, Nanjing Bowuyuan cang* [Chinese paintings by Fu Baoshi: donation of the Fu Baoshi family: collection of the Nanjing Museum]. Beijing: Rongbaozhai, 2006.

Yamamoto Teijirō. *Mingmo minzu yiren zhuan* [Biographies of Chinese artists in the late Ming], translated and edited by Fu Baoshi. Changsha: Shangwu Yinshuguan, 1939.

Yao Yuxiang, ed. *Zhongguohua taolun ji* [Discussions on Chinese painting]. Beiping [Beijing]: Lida Shuju, 1932.

Yashiro Yukio. *Suibokuga*. Tokyo: Iwanami Shoten, 1969.

Yoshiaki Shimizu. 'Śākyamuni Descending the Mountain'. In *Awakenings: Zen Figure Painting in Medieval Japan*, edited by Gregory Levine and Yukio Lippit. New York: Japan Society, 2007.

Yoshida Chizuko. *Kindai Higashi Ajia bijutsu ryūgakusei no kenkyū* [Research on East Asian international art students in modern times]. Tokyo: Yumani Shobō, 2009.

11 Korean Lacquerwork Craftsmen Who Went to Japan

Change and Innovation in Korean Lacquerwork during the Colonial Period

Roh Junia

In the field of crafts, as in other art genres such as painting, Western terms and concepts were introduced to Korea via Japan.[1] Within the discourse on Korean modern craft in relation to Japan, however, it is generally said that production processes spread in the opposite direction. One often-cited example of Korean influence on the production of Japanese modern craft is how Yanagi Muneyoshi's (1889–1961) *mingei* (arts and crafts) movement was triggered by his enthusiasm for Korean ceramics. It is well known that famous Japanese ceramic artists such as Kitaoji Rosanjin (1883–1959) and Kawakita Handeishi (1878–1963) went to Korea to study and obtain clay for their work.

Examples such as these are intriguing in that the colony influenced the art of the metropole during the period of colonization and can be seen as a very significant point in describing the history of Korean art. However, it is important to note that these activities were motivated by the artists' personal interests in Korean ceramics of a former era rather than by interaction with Korean craftsmen. Such one-sided activities seldom brought significant changes to the production field in Korea.

In contrast, a number of Korean craftsmen who went to Japan were instrumental in changing the production of lacquerwork dramatically during the colonial period (1910–1945). In this essay, focusing on these previously neglected lacquerwork craftsmen, I examine how Korean lacquerwork production changed during the period by investigating two different cases of Korean craftsmen who spent time in Japan. First, I describe the case of several artisans who went to Takaoka, Toyama Prefecture, and evaluate how their exposure to new tools and techniques there influenced their work, especially regarding mother-of-pearl inlay, in Korea. Second, I discuss the spread of the Japanese dry-lacquer technique through Kang Chang-gyu (1906–1977), the only Korean student who attended the Tokyo School of Fine Arts (now Tokyo University of the Arts). Through these craftsmen who transcended geo-cultural boundaries, we can see various kinds of transfer in the field of lacquerwork that occurred within a relationship of mutual influence between Korea and Japan.

While lacquer craft developed in China, Japan, Vietnam, Thailand, and all across East Asian regions where lacquer trees naturally occur, the decorative techniques applied to lacquerware remained particular to their countries of origin. For example, the 'sprinkled-picture technique' is known to have developed mostly in Japan, and the mother-of-pearl inlay technique in Korea. The sprinkled-picture technique is called *maki-e* in Japanese and consists of lacquerware on which the design is made by sprinkling or spraying metallic powder, usually gold or silver, on wet lacquer with a dusting tube, sprinkler canister, or hair-tipped paint brush. The mother-of-pearl inlay technique in Korea is called *najeon*, which literally means nacre; the name indicates the material and technique at the same time. In this technique, linings of mother-of-pearl are cut into designs and either glued onto or inserted into the surface of the lacquer or wood.

In fact, mother-of-pearl inlay has been overwhelmingly the most popular decorative lacquerware technique in Korea, and for this reason, the term *najeon* is often used in Korea as a generic term for lacquerware. When Xu Jing (1091–1153), an envoy of the Song dynasty, went to Goryeo and saw the mother-of-pearl lacquerware produced there, his assessment was that: 'The lacquerware is extraordinarily sophisticated and could be regarded as highly valuable'. This demonstrates the long history that mother-of-pearl lacquerware has enjoyed in Korea.

During the Japanese colonial period, the General Government also actively encouraged the production of mother-of-pearl lacquerware. It was a typical Korean antique or souvenir that Japanese travellers visiting Joseon should buy. After the first Governor-General, Terauchi Masatake, went on an inspection of the southern region of Joseon—an area renowned for its sophisticated mother-of-pearl lacquerware, especially in the coastal city of Tongyeong—in 1913, he provided subsidies to encourage its production, fearing a decline in technology and output.

The Central Research Laboratory of Korea, which was established in 1912 directly under the General Government and which was the only engineering research institute operating during the entire Japanese colonial period, was also associated with mother-of-pearl lacquerware production. Lacquerware production was governed by the Department of Applied Chemistry. The Department's main roles were managing lacquer tree cultivation to secure the supply of lacquer liquid and promoting the export of Korean lacquerware to foreign countries. Imazu Akira, an engineer at the Central Research Laboratory, rated its mother-of-pearl lacquerware techniques highly: 'What is most distinctive among the Joseon lacquer crafts is the mother-of-pearl craftsmanship, which has a promising future'.[2]

Kimura Tenkō (1887–1950), another Central Research Laboratory engineer, was similarly fascinated by Joseon's mother-of-pearl lacquerware and valued mother-of-pearl lacquerware very highly:

> It is really solid in terms of quality. Its design is lavish and beautiful. It is strong and elegant at the same time. As the essence of Joseon art, lacquerware has earned praise, both in the past and at the present time, and at home and abroad. It constitutes one of the two pillars of Eastern Art, along with celadon of the Goryeo dynasty.[3]

Kimura was born in Takaoka and studied lacquerwork at a craft school there and in the Department of Applied Chemistry of a Tokyo craft high school. In 1915, he was appointed to work at the Central Research Laboratory of Korea, where he worked for the following five years. During that time, Kimura carried out a long-term project to discover differences in the quality of lacquerware based on the method of lacquer collection and the age of the lacquer tree. He enlisted the cooperation of craftsmen for the project, and it seems that he met Jeon Sung-gyu (1880–1940) in this way. Jeon was already a very famous mother-of-pearl-technique master and at that time ran a mother-of-pearl lacquerware factory in Joseon. We can surmise that he was more renowned than other Korean craftsmen because he was the only executive in the Joseon Lacquerware Association. The Association was founded in 1917 by forty-six Koreans and seventeen Japanese. The Chairman was Akira Imazu; both Kimura and Jeon were Secretary-Generals.[4]

When Kimura went back to Takaoka in October 1920, he decided to establish the Joseon Mother-of-Pearl Corporation to make and sell mother-of-pearl lacquerware in Japan. Kimura invited Jeon to move to Takaoka so he could pass on his mother-of-pearl inlay skills and work as chief engineer at the Joseon Mother-of-Pearl Corporation. Jeon accepted the offer and moved to Takaoka, bringing his pupils with him. After two and a half years, Jeon decided to return to Joseon with his best pupil, Kim Bong-ryong (1903–1994), to establish a private workshop in Samcheong-dong, Seoul, but he continued to provide products to the Joseon Mother-of-Pearl Corporation. Meanwhile, Jeon's other pupils stayed in Takaoka where they worked until the 1930s.

The Joseon Mother-of-Pearl Corporation manufactured household items characterized by 'an elegant Korean style and design'.[5] The products were usable in daily life, unlike elaborate artworks, and Kimura actually stated that his 'production motto is a popularisation of high art, directly from the manufacturer to the customer'.[6] They produced small pieces of furniture and articles such as tables, cupboards, mirrors, boxes for incense, braziers, boxes for ink stones, writing boxes, food trays, dishes, bowls, chopsticks, and vases as ready-made products, while at the same time offering customized designs as well. Their signature characteristic was that the articles were suitable for Japanese culture but were in a Korean style and used the Korean technique of mother-of-pearl inlay.

The Corporation developed products that were suited to the everyday lives of Japanese people, and targeted this market directly, supplying products to the Mitsukoshi Department Store in Tokyo and Shirokiya in Osaka. In addition, Kimura established a non-profit organization called the Joseon Art and Lacquerwork with Mother-of-Pearl Inlay Promotion Association, to which he appointed as advisers the mayor of Takaoka, the president of the Chamber of Commerce, and his lawyers, and to which he, alongside Jeon, served as Chairman.

Based on available maps, newspaper articles, magazines, and official reports, it appears that the Joseon Mother-of-Pearl Corporation operated from 1920 to about 1935, reaching its peak in the mid-1920s. The Corporation's works occasionally appear in auctions. They used Korean shell, which is much thicker than Japanese shell, and the design patterns and skills reflected the Korean style. This Korean style influenced the works of other lacquerware craftsmen in Takaoka. Most references on Takaoka lacquerware name Kimura Tenkō and a Korean craftsman. Unlike other craftsmen's lineages, which have been passed down to the present day, Kimura failed to cultivate future generations. Today, however, we see traces of Korean style in contemporary Takaoka lacquerwares. They seem to reflect the history of the Joseon Mother-of-Pearl Corporation in Takaoka, the city being the only location in Japan that makes lacquerware using only the mother-of-pearl inlay technique. The museums of Takaoka currently own and have on display the works of Kimura Tenkō as well as the Korean mother-of-pearl lacquerwares that Kimura had brought.

However, there can be no doubt that there was a much greater change among the Korean craftsmen who went beyond their national border than there was among the local craftsmen of Takaoka. At the time, there were more than 1,000 lacquerware craftsmen in Takaoka. Lacquerware was a major source of income for the city, so there was a good amount of infrastructure. Although Takaoka was a small provincial town, it also participated in an international exhibition because it happened to be the hometown of the famous Japanese art dealer Hayashi Tadamasa (1851–1906), who had been a general commissioner of the Japanese art section at the Universal Exposition in Paris in 1900. Furthermore, the craft school and research institute in Takaoka were established at a relatively early stage.

The Gallery for Merchandise of Takaoka was important because of its direct influence on Korean craftsmen. It was established as a showroom for consignment sales and samples—more than 100 from all around Japan and even from abroad—so craftsmen could study them. It supported craftsmen who participated in large and small exhibitions, managed a society of lacquerware craftsmen, and sometimes featured academic lectures by famous craftsmen from Tokyo. The Gallery was one channel through which Korean craftsmen learned many things during their time in Takaoka, even though they had not gone abroad with a view to study or train.

Most interestingly, it seems that it was in Takaoka that fretsaws were first used to cut mother-of-pearl. The metal fretsaw was first used in the United States and Germany in the 1890s.[7] It is unclear exactly when fretsaws were introduced to Japan and Korea, but it was certainly in Takaoka that Jeon discovered that a fretsaw could be used to cut mother-of-pearl; in most of his references to Korean lacquerwares with mother-of-pearl inlay, Jeon is recorded as saying that he got the idea of using a metal fretsaw to cut the mother-of-pearl while in Takaoka. Takaoka was famous for bronze works, and the fretsaw was already in use for metalwork as it is a very convenient tool for cutting delicate curves in hard materials. It is therefore slightly surprising that fretsaws had not previously been used in the mother-of-pearl works in Takaoka. As mentioned above, Korean shell is thicker than Japanese shell, so it is less flexible and more fragile. Previously, scissors had been employed to cut shell, but it was difficult to cut fragile material precisely. Needles or chisels could be used for more intricate designs, but because the shell surface is rough, using these tools allowed craftsmen to work only on a single layer at a time. In contrast, a fretsaw can cut several layers simultaneously. Craftsmen glued several layers of nacre together, usually from five to six up to a maximum of thirty. Then they sawed off thick combined layers from one side with a fretsaw, and lastly removed the glue with water to divide them again. Using this process, they could express delicate curves freely and could also reduce work hours. During the Joseon era, *kkeuneumjil* (a thin-slicing technique in which mother-of-pearl is cut in slender strips and then broken to the required length with a chisel), was chiefly used. Before use of the fretsaw, the decorations were geometric and slightly crude. Then with the fretsaw came *jureumjil* (filing technique), a technique of sawing out little pieces of mother-of-pearl. The tool enabled more natural-looking and sophisticated craftsmanship.

Regretfully, there are almost no modern pieces of mother-of-pearl lacquerware known to have been produced during the period of transition between the late Joseon dynasty (up to 1897) and the period of Japanese colonial rule. The current collection of Korean artefacts at the British Museum, which includes five pieces of mother-of-pearl lacquerware exhibited in the Japan-British Exhibition in 1910, provides some useful references, however. The mother-of-pearl lacquerware pieces are estimated to have been created before the exhibition, around 1908 or 1909. One of these pieces,

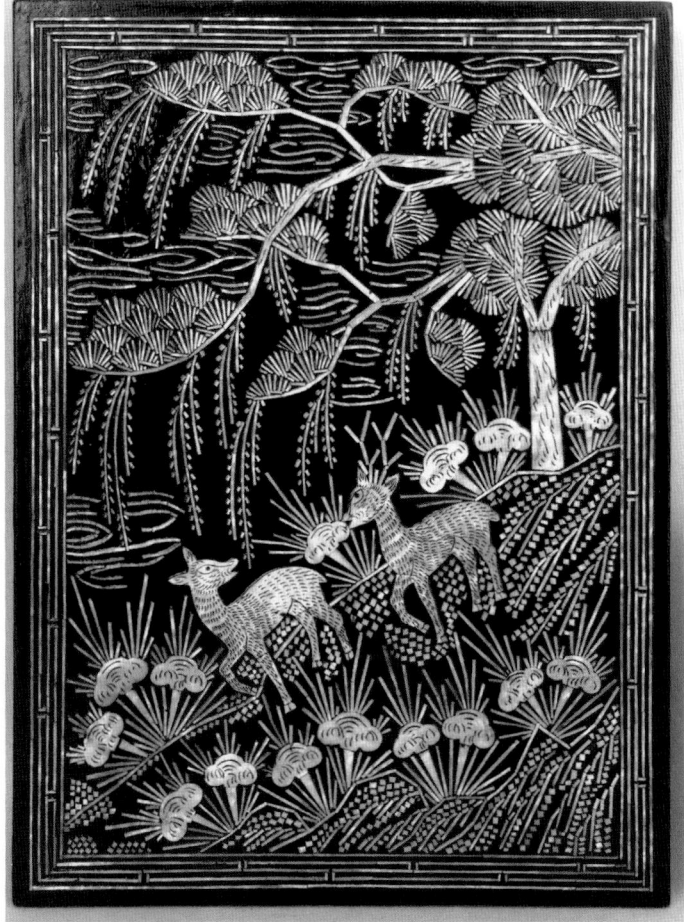

Figure 11.1 Plaque, early 20th century. Lacquered wood, inlaid with mother-of-pearl, 0.7 × 25.8 × 18.8 cm

British Museum

a plaque with a figure of a squirrel and a grape design on one side and a deer and fir on the reverse (Figure 11.1) mainly uses the thin-slicing technique and accordingly shows a strong sense of linear and geometric decoration. Where a wider piece of mother-of-pearl is attached, *mojobeop*, a technique of hair-line engraving on mother-of-pearl, is used to engrave many lines on the material. The gently curved bodies of a deer and a squirrel are represented impressively, but it is noticeable that the grapes are not perfectly round. Building on the late Joseon style used for production up until the 1910s, the introduction in the early 1920s of a filing technique using the fretsaw made it possible to overcome the limitations of earlier mother-of-pearl lacquerware in representing decorations and, in particular, in creating smooth curves—though of course, technical progress does not always mean aesthetic perfection.

Based on an examination of the products manufactured by the Joseon Mother-of-Pearl Corporation, it is possible to estimate more accurately when the filing technique using the fretsaw was first used. *Lidless Lacquered Box with Design Based on an Ancient Chinese Tale, in Mother-of-Pearl Inlay* (Figure 11.2), produced around 1923, is a thin rectangular box without a cover, which includes mother-of-pearl decorations on the edges and bottom. The filing technique is not used at all, and Korean thick nacre is used, rather than the thin nacre easily available in Japan, making the mother-of-pearl decorations more dimensional. Beginning with *Mountain Peony-Phoenix Lacquered Brazier with Mother-of-Pearl Inlay* (Figure 11.3), which was exhibited at the 11th *Nōten* (Crafts Exhibition of the Ministry of Agriculture and Commerce) in 1924, however, the filing technique using the fretsaw became quite visible. This octagonal brazier is finished in black lacquer in which thick nacre is used to display mountain peony and phoenix decorations on alternating sides. These decorations have apparently been cut out using a fretsaw, demonstrating that fretsaws were used for lacquerware before 1924.

After returning to Korea and establishing their private workshop in Seoul, Jeon and Kim became famous as recipients of bronze and silver medals at the Universal Exposition in Paris in 1925. It was very unusual for Koreans to receive awards at international exhibitions during the colonial period, so the recognition became big news. The official name of the exhibition was the *Exposition internationale des Arts décoratifs et industriels modernes*; it was also known as the 'Art Déco Expo', and it is generally considered as the first fully fledged design exposition. According to the purpose and rules of the exposition outlined in an official report, they strongly prohibited traditional art, requiring instead innovative design. The Governor-General displayed reproductions of Koryo celadons produced by Tomita Gisaku and lacquerwares made by Jeon and Kim as representatives of colonial Korea.[8] However, only lacquerwares won any awards. Because the exposition demanded innovative design, the celadon could not be considered for awards, even if they were of very high quality. In other words, the awards signal that Jeon's and Kim's lacquerwares were recognized as innovative designs. And that was possible because of the fretsaw they discovered in Takaoka. With delicate expressions and free curve cuttings, the Art Nouveau style could be applied to lacquerwares.

It should be noted that Tomita was not a craftsman but a businessman. He was the representative of a porcelain company and souvenir shop, whereas Kim and Jeon were artisans. They produced their works independently and participated in the exhibition under their own names. This suggests they were the earliest craftsmen in Korea who recognized modern crafts as art that correlated with one's identity as an artist. The Joseon Fine Art Exhibition was first held in 1922, but the craft section was added in 1932, through which it is said that the concept of 'craft as fine art' was introduced. In East Asia, especially in Korea, public exhibitions were very important for embedding the modern (i.e. usually Western) concept of art in the culture. Since Kim and Jeon had participated in a government exhibition in Takaoka in 1920, it can be said that their experience of public exhibitions began twelve years earlier than other Korean craftsmen's.

Jeon was accepted at the 13th and 16th Joseon Fine Art Exhibitions, and Kim was accepted every year between the 13th in 1934 and the 23rd in 1944. The accepted works featured complicated and delicate decorations with mother-of-pearl. There were

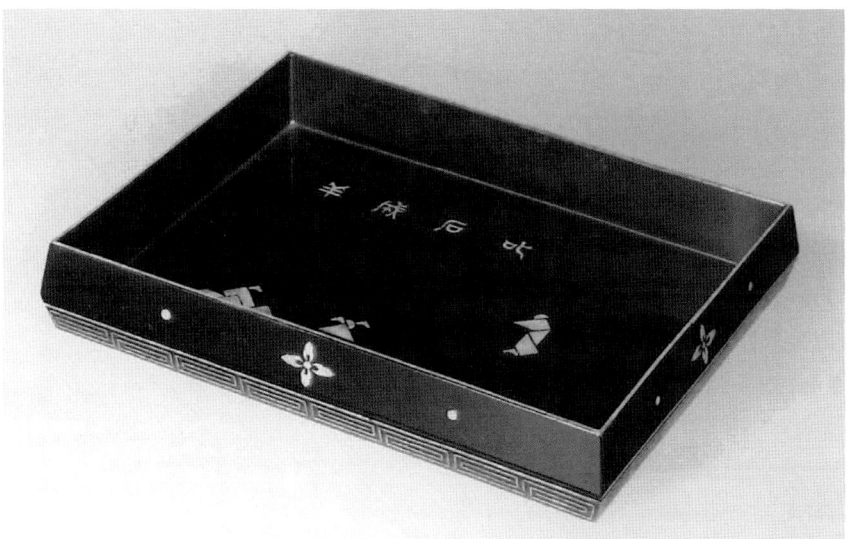

Figure 11.2 Jeon Sung-gyu (design by Kimura Tenkō), *Lidless Lacquered Box*, early 1920s. Lacquered wood, inlaid with mother-of-pearl, 5.1 × 23.0 × 30.3 cm

Gakushuin University Museum of History

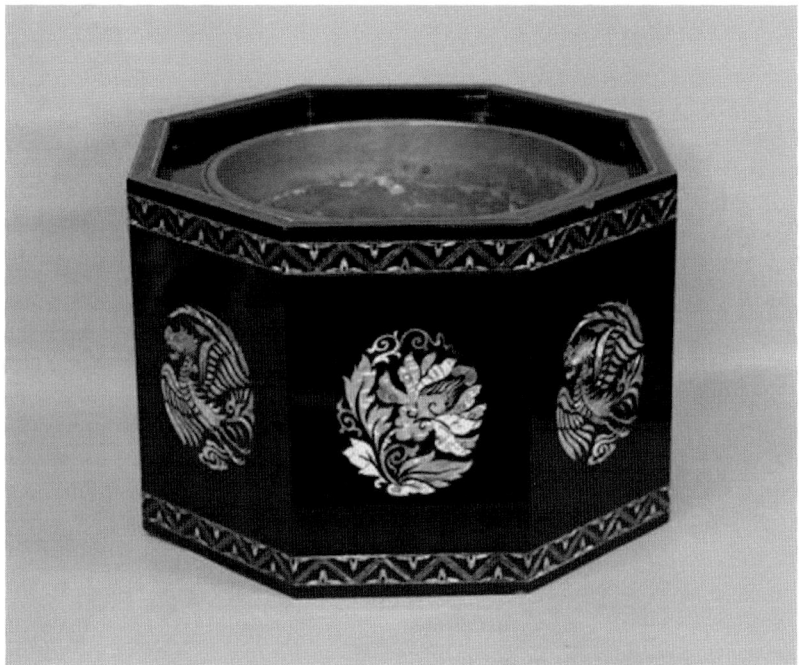

Figure 11.3 Jeon Sung-gyu, *Mountain Peony-Phoenix Lacquered Brazier with Mother-of-Pearl Inlay*. Lacquered wood, inlaid with mother-of-pearl

From the catalogue of the 11th Crafts Exhibition of the Ministry of Agriculture and Commerce (Nōten)

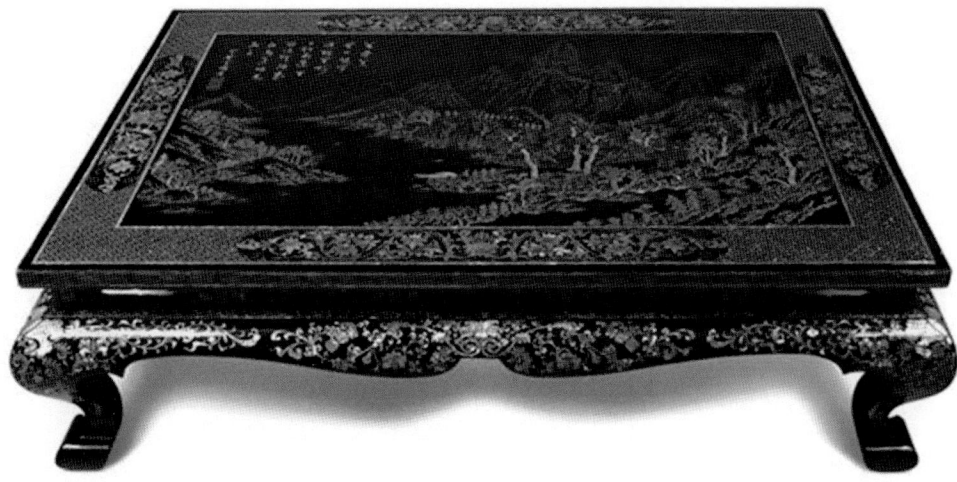

Figure 11.4 Jeon Sung-gyu, *Lacquered Dining Table*. Lacquered wood, inlaid with mother-of-pearl, ca. 1937, 35.3 × 121.1 × 85.3 cm

Korea Mother-of-Pearl Art Museum

no blank spaces, indicating superior skill. Compared with other craftsmen's works, they were much finer and more decorative.

Regretfully, their works from the Paris exhibition and the Joseon Fine Art Exhibitions have not survived, but similar ones remain. Jeon's *Lacquered Dining Table* with Landscape Design Inlaid with Mother-of-Pearl (Figure 11.4) is similar to the work accepted at the 16th Joseon Fine Art Exhibition. The table-top features a picturesque landscape bordered with ocean waves and a lotus scroll design following a tradition of Oriental landscape painting.[9] The skilful expression of Chinese characters and arabesque patterns on the top and side of the legs shows a superior grasp of the filing technique using the fretsaw.

As use of the fretsaw became widespread, the filing technique became the most used technique in modern Korean lacquerware. The decoration of mother-of-pearl became more and more skilful and splendid such that modern lacquerware sometimes looks quite extravagant. This style was completely opposite to the aesthetics of Yanagi Muneyoshi's *mingei* movement, which sought modern beauty that was artless and natural, distinct from Korean craft with its white porcelain, pottery, wooden furniture, and so on.

Kim Bong-ryong, who did not die until 1994, aged 92 (Jeon died in 1940), has been regarded as a master of the filing technique. Inspired by the glass vases of the Art Nouveau style, he skillfully adorned vases with plant patterns using mother-of-pearl. Usually, lacquerware is made of wood and hemp cloth, and objects produced are very light and unbreakable. However, Kim's vases are made of porcelain. This method was developed by Kimura when he worked at the Central Research Laboratory of Korea. The light and infrangible characteristics of lacquerware were lost, but instead, it enabled free moulding of lacquerware and made it strong in dry climates. Accordingly, it became suitable for exporting to Europe. After grating the surface of the celadon with emery cloth, he applied lacquer and then laid nacre on it. *Lacquered Ceramic Vase with Floral Scroll Design Inlaid with Mother-of-Pearl* (Plate 12) is a good example. The vase is marked by a long neck, and the beads and scrolls extending down the neck are very ornate and exquisite. The resplendent mother-of-pearl designs reflect light and glitter like jewels.[10]

Although the establishment of the Joseon Mother-of-Pearl Corporation and the later development of the filing technique in modern Korean mother-of-pearl lacquerware are not necessarily causally related, Jeon's visit to Takaoka certainly helped introduce the fretsaw to the mother-of-pearl lacquerware industry and made the filing technique a dominant process in modern mother-of-pearl lacquerware production.

After independence from Japan, when the Cultural Properties Protection Law was legislated in 1966, *najeonjang* (mother-of-pearl inlay) became eligible for 'intangible cultural property' status. Among the six pupils who had been to Takaoka with their master Jeon, three craftsmen—Kim Bong-ryong, Song Ju-an, and Sim Bugil—became Living National Treasures. Since lacquerwares with mother-of-pearl inlay constituted

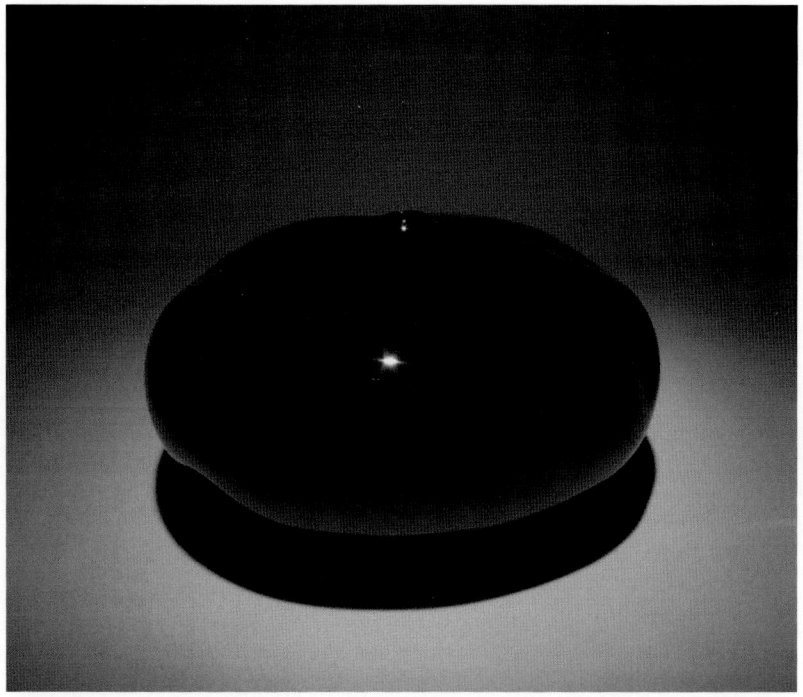

Figure 11.5 Chung Hae-cho, *Black Lustre 0819*. Lacquer, hemp cloth, 2008, 21.0 × 37.0 × 37.0 cm
British Museum

one-fifth of the entire selections of works in the Joseon Fine Art Exhibition, as I explain below in more detail, there must have been a number of craftsmen in Korea at that time. Among them, all those nominated as representatives of the nation had been to Takaoka. This suggests how influential the lacquerwork craftsmen who had spent time in Takaoka became.

The second case of Japanese influence on craft production processes that I will examine here is the development of the dry-lacquer technique in modern Korea. Since the British Museum reopened its Korean gallery in late 2014, it has displayed Chung Hae-cho's dry-lacquered work *Black Lustre 0819* (Figure 11.5), which the museum purchased in May 2013. The Victoria and Albert Museum (V&A) attracted a lot of attention around the same time when it acquired Chung's dry-lacquered work *Five Coloured Lustre 0831*. Considering that neither the British Museum nor the V&A had previously held a single piece of Korean lacquerware produced using the dry-lacquer technique, despite both having collected many pieces of mother-of-pearl lacquerware from the Goryeo (918–1392) and Joseon (1392–1897) dynasties in their Korean galleries, their choice to include dry-lacquer works rather than mother-of-pearl pieces when expanding their Korean collections came as something of a surprise. In fact, however, the proportion of modern Korean lacquerware made using the dry-lacquer technique is very high, to the extent that the dry-lacquer technique can be regarded as universal nowadays.

Dry lacquer (K: *geonchil*, J: *kanshitsu*) is a technique of East Asian sculpture and decorative arts in which a figure or vessel is fashioned with many layers of hemp cloth soaked with lacquer. The surface details are subsequently modelled using a mixture of lacquer, sawdust, powdered clay stone, and other materials. Dry lacquer has proved a very popular technique in Japan. In Korea, however, it was mostly used to make statues of Buddha. Analyses of Korea's state-designated cultural heritage show that dry-lacquer work was produced intensively from the late Goryeo dynasty to the early Joseon dynasty. What, then, re-established the dry-lacquer technique as a universal process in the modern period after so many years? To trace how the dry-lacquer technique re-emerged in the Korean peninsula, this paper examines works selected for the Craft Section of the Joseon Fine Art Exhibition during the Japanese colonial period.

Among the works accepted for the Joseon Fine Art Exhibition, the proportion of mother-of-pearl lacquerware was extremely high. Taking a look at the 527 pieces in the catalogues of the 11th to the 19th exhibitions, one finds that mother-of-pearl lacquerware accounted for the largest share, with 113 pieces.[11] This represents more than a fifth of all works accepted and is considerably greater than the number of ceramic pieces, which stood at about eighty. Non-mother-of-pearl lacquerware also accounted for a reasonably high share, with fifty works included.

What is particularly interesting is the differing percentages of Korean artists and Japanese artists for each category. Among the 113 pieces of mother-of-pearl lacquerware, seventy-five were produced by Koreans and thirty-eight by Japanese. Those produced by Koreans, in other words, were twice as numerous as those produced by Japanese. When it comes to non-mother-of-pearl lacquerware, however, we find a ratio that is almost exactly reversed: sixteen pieces were produced by Koreans and thirty-four by Japanese. It is also worth noting that nine out of the sixteen pieces produced by Koreans were created by a single maker, Kang Chang-gyu. More importantly still, Kang was the only Korean maker of dry-lacquered works to be accepted. It could be conjectured that, while studying in Japan, Kang acquired expertise in the dry-lacquer technique, which was no longer in common use across the Korean peninsula, and that he re-introduced the technique to Korea via the Joseon Fine Art Exhibition.

Kang is known to have gone to Japan at age sixteen. He studied lacquerwork at the Tokyo School of Fine Arts after attending Okayama Craft School. The Tokyo School of Fine Arts was the best school of its kind in Japan, intended for the most skilled to this day. Kang studied there for four years from 1929 to 1933. During the colonial period in Korea, there was no official art school or institute, so anyone who wanted to train as an artist, usually as a painter or sculptor, went to an art school in Japan, such as the Tokyo School of Fine Arts, Teikoku Art School, or Bunka Art School.

Consequently, they came back as the first generation of Korean modern artists. There were few students in the craft sector. At Tokyo School of Fine Arts, just two studied in the Department of Design, and only one studied in the Department of Lacquer Art. In the entire colonial period, Kang Chang-gyu was the only Korean craftsman who studied at an official university-level institute in Japan. He thus played a key role in spreading Japanese style to Korean lacquerware. Through his studies in Japan, he mastered techniques with Japanese lacquer—mainly dry lacquer and *maki-e*—that had not been popular in Korea before.

Kang studied in Japan at the time of an explosion of interest in Lelang lacquerware (known as *Nangnang* in Korean), examples of which had been discovered in good condition after more than 2,000 years of being buried underground.[12] Excavation and research projects on Lelang lacquerware were mainly led by professors at the Tokyo School of Fine Arts. Assistant Professor of the Department of Design (J: *zuan*) Oba Tsunekichi (1878–1958) went to Korea in 1916 at the request of Sekino Tadashi (1868–1935) in order to replicate Goguryeo and Lelang tomb murals discovered in Pyongyang for the Education and Management Bureau of the General Government. He noted the existence of extraordinary lacquerware items excavated in these tomb complexes and catalogued his findings in *Illustration of Lelang-Era Lacquerware Decorations*, which he subsequently donated to the Tokyo School of Fine Arts. After seeing Lelang lacquerware himself for the first time in Gyeongseong (now Seoul) in 1923, Rokkaku Shisui (1867–1950), a professor in the Department of Lacquer Art, was impressed by the technique and reportedly said: 'This is a technique that could not be imitated by current technology.'[13] He nonetheless began to explore how to replicate the technique, and in May 1928, after five years of research, he displayed a dozen replica Lelang lacquerware pieces that he had made himself, alongside the original models, in a presentation entitled *Exhibition of Lelang Lacquerware Restoration and Replication* held in a conference room of the Tokyo School of Fine Arts. Matsuda Gonroku (1896–1986), another professor in the Department of Lacquer at the Tokyo School of Fine Arts, is also known to have been involved in the repair and restoration of Lelang lacquerware between 1920 and 1925. The interest shown by professors such as these would naturally have been communicated to their students.

Thus, this 'neo-classicism' came into vogue in the realm of Japanese crafts, with many artworks influenced by Lelang lacquerware accepted to the Imperial Art Exhibition (*Teiten*). In 1927, craftsmen's longstanding desire for recognition was realized, in

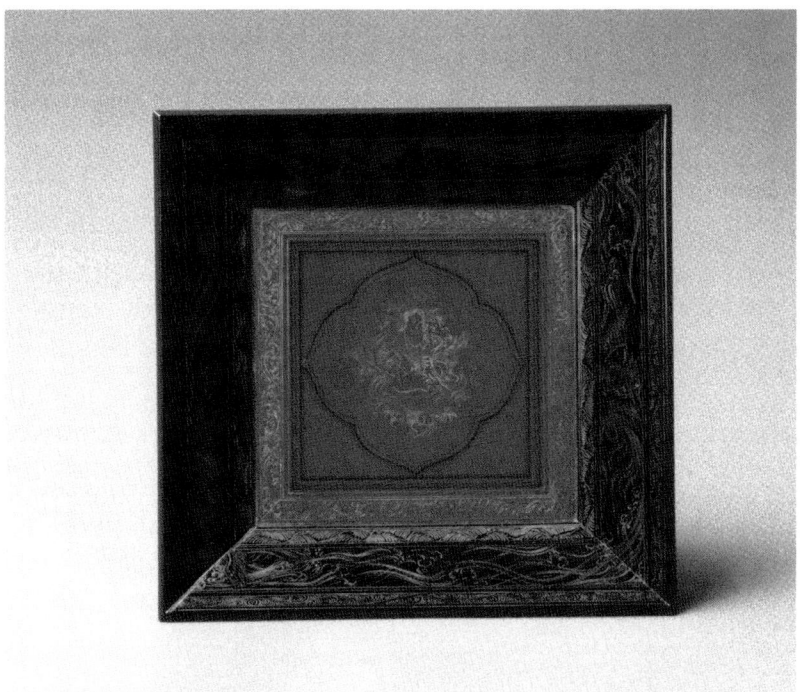

Figure 11.6 Rokkaku Shisui, *Square Tray with Design of Deva of Arts*. Lacquered wood, 1927, 2.2 × 19.6 × 19.6 cm

Hiroshima Prefectural Art Museum

the establishment of a craft division at the Exhibition of the Imperial Fine Arts Academy. At the first exhibition, craft artists who produced works with geometric forms, termed the Constructivists, attracted considerable attention. The central focus, however, was on the Neoclassical School, craft artists whose works were based on earlier examples or historical research.[14] Rokkaku Shisui, the leader of this trend, submitted works like *Square Tray with Design of Deva of Arts* (Figure 11.6) decorated with a fluid motif painted in the fine flowing lines of Lelang lacquerware. Such a trend could be explained as a cultural transfer reflecting an orientalist perspective in the period of imperialism. Naturally, the same trend was shown at the Joseon Fine Art Exhibition. Many Korean and Japanese artists and craftsmen who lived in Joseon produced works affected by relics from the Lelang and Goguryeo tombs.

Despite such explosive interest at the time, Kang was not interested in replicating Lelang lacquerware. He did not attempt to recreate the Joseon style, nor did he choose to pursue the traditional Japanese sprinkled-picture technique. Instead, he chose the dry-lacquer technique, directly confronting the challenges of the lacquer material itself. Kang's main fascination with Lelang lacquerware was the lacquer material. He also chose to make a dry-lacquer work as a graduation project. 'There was no rule or specific instruction for graduation work', wrote Kang's contemporary at the Tokyo School of Fine Arts, Terai Naoji, 'the students were able to get guidance whenever they wanted, but students had autonomy.'[15] It can thus be assumed that Kang's choice of dry-lacquer technique as a main method for his lacquerwork was an independent decision based on his own artistic interests.

Kang's praise of Lelang lacquerware reveals his thoughts about lacquer art. He noted with surprise that even though the wooden core had almost rotted, looking almost like a dried leaf, the lacquer-coated layer was separately preserved in its original form, with the colour just slightly dulled. He was excited by the thought that dry lacquer, using only lacquer without a core made of another material, could defy time; although organic material rots after a period of time, the lacquer material, itself derived from organic material, neither rots nor disappears. To Kang, the lacquer was a material that could 'dominate eternity'.[16]

Showing his talent in the world of plastic arts unrestrained by cliché or the need to replicate the local style, Kang overcame the stereotyped perception some had formed of this student from a colony. The dry-lacquer technique, with its focus on the shapes it created, was understood as more 'modern' than sprinkled-picture or mother-of-pearl inlay techniques, both of which focused on surface decorations.

The approach fitted well with the values of the Craft Section of the Imperial Art Exhibition, which, when adjudicating works, was influenced by Western movements such as Art Deco and Bauhaus. In Japan, at that time, the interest in nationalism within the field of craft, which had developed as part of a drive to increase productivity and as a result of policies promoting industry, had come to an end; the era of modernism was beginning. Kang's artistic choices were therefore favoured in Japan. He was accepted four times to the Imperial Art Exhibition, and from 1933 received six special acceptances at the Joseon Fine Art Exhibitions (at the 12th, 13th, 16th, 17th, 18th, and 19th). All of his exhibited works were dry-lacquered, and his Japanese style was quite distinctive. His pieces are characterized by their emphasis on surface smoothness and geometrical moulding. Surface decorations are excluded entirely, with just occasional *maki-e* or *urushi-e* (lacquer painting) techniques used in a discreet way.

Based on his impressive performance at the Imperial Art Exhibitions and the Joseon Fine Art Exhibitions, Kang established himself as the only craft artist to rival the Western artists of his day. Crowning his six special acceptances, in 1941 he was honoured with the Craft Section's Lifetime Achievement Award, a prize created to celebrate the 20th anniversary of the Joseon Fine Art Exhibition. He was appointed a 'Highly Commended Artist' at the 21st Exhibition and participated once again at the 23rd. He was the only Korean appointed to an honorary position in the Craft Section.

Kang was far more recognized than any of the craftsmen in mother-of-pearl lacquerware promoted for export by the General Government and commended by the Central Research Laboratory for their promising future. An interesting comparison can be made between Kang and Kim Bong-ryong, one of the most notable mother-of-pearl inlay craftsmen, who had been to Takaoka. Kim received awards at the Universal Exposition in Paris in 1925 before the Craft Section was created at the Joseon Fine Art Exhibition. He also received acceptances and special acceptances consecutively at the 13th to the 23rd Joseon Fine Art Exhibitions, but the additional honours that went to Kang were not granted to him.

There are two perspectives from which this can be understood. First, Kang was the only exhibitor in the Craft Section to come from the Tokyo School of Fine Arts.

He received his higher education in Japan, and his four acceptances at the Imperial Art Exhibition would likely have had a halo effect. The fact that he was associated with the Tokyo School of Fine Arts, an institution at the pinnacle of Japan's academic hierarchy, would also have been viewed positively at the colonial government's exhibitions, especially since the Craft Section judges were all faculty members at the Tokyo School of Fine Arts. Kang's professor Rokkaku judged at the 20th and the 23rd exhibitions, while Matsuda fulfilled this role at the 22nd.

Second, compared to mother-of-pearl lacquerware, which focuses on surface decorations, the dry-lacquer technique focuses on moulding. While design of the surface decoration is an important aspect of mother-of-pearl inlay, the dry-lacquer technique requires the design of three-dimensional figures. Might these characteristics have contributed to the dry-lacquer technique being understood as modern? It seems so. While mother-of-pearl inlay was traditional and considered to be the work of a 'craftsman', the dry-lacquer technique that Kang demonstrated was understood as modern and as the work of an 'artist'.

'What is craft, by the way? Craft is art. That is, an expression of beauty using the form and method of craft. In other words, it is a good production. An excellent example is Kang Chang-gyu's work selected for special acceptance',[17] commented Kang's contemporary, the painter Ra Hye-seok. The late art historian Lee Kyung-sung similarly noted:

> There were young craftsmen who stood firm against the mainstream of the exhibition-type craft movement on the stage of the Joseon Fine Art Exhibition, for example, Kang Chang-won [Kang Chang-gyu's other name] who studied at Tokyo School of Fine Arts, but most craftsmen and artisans adapted to the needs of the Japanese. To them, receiving the honour of being accepted to the art exhibition was equivalent to raising the value of their works. But they lacked a perception and understanding of modern craft; they just made better products with skills gained from practice and repetition. These products then got treated as art when they were accepted at the exhibition'.[18]

Even though there was no dry-lacquer production, other than Kang's, before Korea was liberated, the Ministry of Education Award, a top award in the Craft Section of the first National Art Exhibition of the Republic of Korea, went to Park Chul-joo, who exhibited *Dry-Lacquered Flower Vase*. The award, for which Kang was one of the judges, heralded a boom in dry-lacquer production after liberation. Since then, it has not been hard to find dry-lacquered works at National Art Exhibitions.

After liberation, craft degrees—mainly in ceramics and metal crafts—were created in colleges of arts and universities, although there were very few colleges that established degrees in lacquer craft. Most lacquer professors made their works using the dry-lacquer technique, and their students' dry-lacquered works have subsequently been awarded prizes at the National Art Exhibitions and various other significant exhibitions.

In traditional crafts, division of labour is taken for granted. It is extremely rare, for instance, for a mother-of-pearl lacquerware artist to work on his or her own

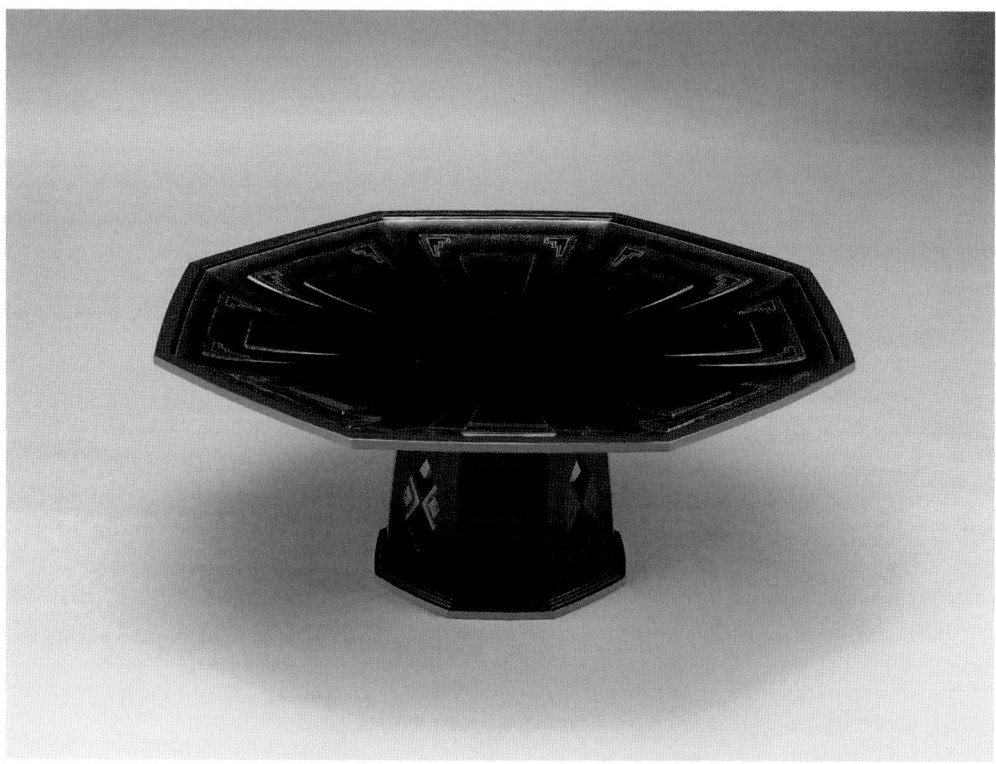

Figure 11.7 Kang Chang-gyu, *Dry-Lacquered Tray*. Lacquer, hemp cloth, 1933, 15.2 × 35.5 × 35.5 cm

National Museum of Korea

foundation (core), using wooden material. Where dry-lacquer technique is concerned, however, the moulding process, on which the designing of shapes in lacquer-coating is dependent, is viewed as crucial, and each work, therefore, is produced by a single individual working alone. The production method in which a single person takes charge from the design stage through to completion was understood as more 'modern' and closer to the ideal of the 'artist' or 'designer'. Furthermore, decorative mother-of-pearl is quite distant, in terms of its origin, from the modern minimalistic aesthetic, which avoids decorations.

Recently, one of Kang's works, *Dry-Lacquered Tray* (Figure 11.7), which reflects the dry-lacquer technique, was registered on the list of Cultural Properties. It was created for his graduation project at the Tokyo School of Fine Arts. His teacher recommended that he submit it to the 12th Joseon Fine Art Exhibition, and it earned an award for excellence. In September 2009 it was selected as one of the 20th-century craft works to be registered as a Cultural Property. In other words, like craftsmen who had been to Takaoka, the only Korean student of the Tokyo School of Fine Arts also became a national representative.

Kang's method and style were clearly influenced by Japanese style, as he studied and lived in Japan for almost twenty years beginning at the age of sixteen. The style of his work demonstrably changed through his experience in Japan and, as he gained influence, subsequently affected the craft of Korean lacquerwork. The Japanese influence on Kang attracted some negative reactions; seeing his works in the Joseon Fine Art Exhibition, one critic noted: 'Kang's work is creative and uses high-technique but it follows the tendency of the Japanese Imperial Art Exhibition's style. It is difficult to detect a Korean identity.'[19] Another critic commented that his work 'is not good because the harmony of gold powder, patterns, and colour makes it feel Edo'.[20]

This essay has considered the significant changes that several lacquer artists with connections to Japan made to modern lacquerware in Korea. These makers were positioned between two traditions: on the one hand, the mother-of-pearl lacquerware popular until the Joseon dynasty (that we see collected in the British Museum) and the works exhibited in the 1910 Japan-British Exhibition, and, on the other, examples such as the works of art most recently acquired by the British Museum and V&A.

The example of Chung Hae-cho's work purchased by the British Museum has no particular relationship with the Korean lacquerware made before the modern period and should instead be understood in the tradition of the dry-lacquer technique, which was initiated by Kang Chang-gyu. Chung was, in addition, an artist who studied in Japan, and it would be difficult to dispute that the technique and form of his art was strongly influenced by his stay in Japan. He created strange curvaceous shapes by applying lacquer to hemp cloth attached to polystyrene. A highly recognizable feature of his work, meanwhile, was his use of the five traditional Korean colours and his creation of colour rhythms characterized by beautiful lustre and distinctive contrast. What does it mean that this artwork has been recognized as a new tradition of Korea in the eyes of the outside world?

Understanding classicism through celadon of the Goryeo dynasty, and modernity through white porcelain of the Joseon dynasty, many Japanese artists studied Korean ceramics. As mentioned above, such study prompted a re-evaluation of Korean ceramics of former eras, but it had little influence on the manufacture of it. On the other hand, a few craftsmen's visits to Japan and the cultural exchanges that occurred there between Korean and Japanese craftsmen eventually caused revolutionary changes in the genre of Korean lacquerwork. The discovery of a new tool in Japan made the filing technique much easier, and it brought significant transformation in styles. The excessively decorative style was suitable for the Joseon Fine Art Exhibition and export to foreign countries. Meanwhile, an artist who studied in Japan broadened the appeal of *geonchil* and *maki-e* techniques that had not been popular in Korea. Perhaps even the origin of the concept of modern crafts or artistic consciousness in Korea can be found in lacquerware. While it is important to keep in mind the oppressive reality of colonization, the new tools and methods used by these craftsmen who had transcended geo-cultural boundaries certainly made a lasting impact. Lacquerware was negatively affected by rapid modernization during the second half of the 20th century, but it survived and even enjoyed a revival when Korea's economy was bolstered in the 1960s and 1970s. The transformation that occurred thanks to cultural exchanges among craftsmen during the period of colonization has made it a unique form of art that is both traditionally Korean and modern, encouraging the continued production of such lacquerware to this day.

Notes

1 Today, the English word 'craft' translates to *gong-ye* in Korean. The concepts of gong-ye that formed within the relationships between East and West, old and new, and empire and colony, were basically constructed under the influence of Japan, which dominated those relationships. Although its meaning was changed again and even self-imitated several times, the concept of *gong-ye* that was formed in the modern age became the fundamental base of *gong-ye* as we know it today. See Boyoon Her, The Formation of the Concept of *Gong-ye* in the Korean Modern Age, *Journal of Design History* 27, no. 4 (November 1, 2014): 335–350.
2 'Speech of chairman Imazu Akira on the meeting of Joseon Lacquerware Association', *Mae-il sin bo* [Korean daily news] (February 22, 1917).
3 Leaflet on the establishment of the Joseon Art and Lacquerwork with Mother-of-Pearl Inlay Promotion Association (attached to the *Lidless Lacquered Box with Design Based on an Ancient Chinese Tale, in Mother-of-Pearl Inlay*), January 1923 (Tokyo: Gakushuin University Museum of History Collection, no. 220).
4 'The meeting of Joseon Lacquerware Association', *Mae-il sin bo* (February 20, 1917).
5 Advertisement in the *Takaoka shōkō annai* [Takaoka commerce guide] (Takaoka: Takaoka Shōgyō Kaigisho, 1927).
6 Ibid.
7 Patrick Spielman, *The New Scroll Saw Handbook* (New York: Sterling Publishing, 2002), p. 37.
8 *Catalogue illustré de la Section Japonaise à l'Exposition internationale des Arts décoratifs et industriels modernes* (Paris: Commissariat général de la section japonaise, 1925).
9 Kim Bong-ryong, *Jungyo muhyung munwhajae No. 10: Najeonjang* [Important intangible cultural heritage no. 10: mother-of-pearl inlay master] (Seoul: Crosspoint Cultural Foundation, 2016), p. 159.
10 Ibid., p. 98.
11 My analysis was based on images and titles, and inevitably therefore includes a degree of error since some works were not identifiable.
12 Nangnang is the present-day name of the Han-dynasty Chinese colony of Lelang, situated in what is now North Korea.
13 Rokkaku Shisui, 'Lecture on excavated Lelang lacquerware', *Tokyo bijutsu gakkō kōyūkai geppō* 25 [Tokyo School of Fine Arts alumni monthly news 25], no. 3 (June 1926).
14 Ruth S. McCreery and Yamamoto Hitoshi, *Ekkyōsuru Nihonjin: kōgeika ga yume mita Ajia* [Japanese crossing borders: Asia as dreamed by craftspeople, 1910–1945] (Tokyo: Tokyo Kokuritsu Kindai Bijutsukan, 2012), p. 53.
15 Terai Naoji, 'Department of lacquer art of the early Showa era', in *Tokyo Geijutsu Daigaku hyakunenshi* [Centennial history of Tokyo National University of Fine Arts and Music], ed. Geijutsu Kenkyū Shinkō Zaidan and Tokyo Geijutsu Daigaku (Tokyo: Gyosei, 1987), p. 517.
16 Kim Sang-il, 'Chang-won Kang, the Dry-Lacquer Artist', *Shin yeo won* [New woman's garden] 29 (March 1974), p. 180.
17 Ra Hye-seok, 'The Impression on the Joseon Fine Art Exhibition', *Mae-il sin bo* (May 21, 1933).
18 Lee Kyung-sung, *Hankuk Geundae Misulsa (Gong-ye)* [Korean Modern Art History (Craft)] (Seoul: National Museum of Modern and Contemporary Art, Korea, 1975), p. 36.
19 Dam Seon-woo, 'Seeing the 12th Joseon Fine Art Exhibition: chaos and contradiction', *Choson il bo* [Choson daily news] (June 3, 1933).
20 Koo Bon-woong, 'Seeing the 13th Joseon Fine Art Exhibition', *Joseon Joong-ang il bo* [Choson central daily news] (June 6, 1934).

Bibliography

Advertisement in the *Takaoka shōkō annai* [Takaoka commerce guide]. Takaoka: Takaoka Shōgyō Kaigisho, 1927.
Anonymous. *Joseon chilgonghoe chonghoe* [The meeting of Joseon Lacquerware Association]. *Mae-il sin bo*, February 20, 1917.

———. *Chilgonghoe seoksangeseo heo-jang Imazu Akira sieui yon-seol* [Speech of chairman Imazu Akira on the meeting of Joseon Lacquerware Association]. *Mae-il sin bo* [Korean daily news], February 22, 1917.

———. Leaflet on the establishment of the Joseon Art and Lacquerwork with Mother-of-Pearl Inlay Promotion Association, attached to the *Lidless Lacquered Box with Design Based on an Ancient Chinese Tale, in Mother-of-Pearl Inlay*, January 1923. Tokyo: Gakushuin University Museum of History Collection, no. 220.

———. *Catalogue illustré de la Section Japonaise à l'Exposition internationale des Arts décoratifs et industriels modernes*. Paris: Commissariat général de la section japonaise, 1925.

Dam Seon-woo. *Je sibihoe Jomijeon ibu, samhureul bogo* [Seeing the 12th Joseon Fine Art Exhibition: chaos and contradiction]. *Choson il bo* [Choson daily news], June 3, 1933.

Her, Boyoon. 'The Formation of the Concept of *Gong-ye* in the Korean Modern Age'. *Journal of Design History* 27, no. 4 (November 1, 2014): 335–350.

Kim Bongryong. *Jungyo muhyung munwhajae No. 10: Najeonjang* [Important intangible cultural heritage no. 10: mother-of-pearl inlay master]. Seoul: Crosspoint Cultural Foundation, 2016.

Kim Sang-il. *Geonchil gong-ye, Kang Chang-won ong* [Chang-won Kang, the dry-lacquer artist]. *Shin yeo won* [New woman's garden] 29 (March 1974).

Koo Bon-woong. *Je sibsamhoe Joseon mijeoneul bom* [Seeing the 13th Joseon Fine Art Exhibition]. *Joseon Joong-ang il bo* [Choson central daily news], June 6, 1934.

Lee Kyung-sung. *Hanguk Geundae Misulsa (Gong-ye)* [Korean modern art history (craft)]. Seoul: National Museum of Modern and Contemporary Art, Korea, 1975.

McCreery, Ruth S. and Yamamoto Hitoshi. *Ekkyōsuru Nihonjin: kōgeika ga yume mita Ajia* [Japanese crossing borders: Asia as dreamed by craftspeople, 1910–1945]. Tokyo: Tokyo Kokuritsu Kindai Bijutsukan, 2012.

Ra Hye-seok. *Mijeoneui insang* [Impression of the Joseon Fine Art Exhibition]. *Mae-il sin bo*, May 21, 1933.

Rokkaku Shisui. *Rakurōhakkutsu shikki ni kansuru kōwa* [Lecture on excavated Lelang lacquerware]. *Tokyo bijutsu gakkō kōyūkai geppō 25* [Tokyo School of Fine Arts alumni monthly news 25] no. 3 (June 1926).

Spielman, Patrick. *The New Scroll Saw Handbook*. New York: Sterling Publishing, 2002.

Terai Naoji. *Shōwa shoki no shikkōka* [Department of lacquer art of the early Showa era]. In *Tokyo Geijutsu Daigaku hyakunenshi* [Centennial history of Tokyo National University of Fine Arts and Music], edited by Geijutsu Kenkyū Shinkō Zaidan and Tōkyō Geijutsu Daigaku. Tokyo: Gyosei, 1987.

12 The Concept of Art in the *Meishu Congshu*
From Foreign Loan to National Tradition

Liu Yu-jen

The *Meishu Congshu* (Book Collection on Art) was the first book collection in China dedicated to the subject of *meishu*, a neologism coined in Japanese as *bijutsu* and introduced into China as early as 1880, commonly thought of as a translation of the European concept of Art.[1] The first three series of the *Meishu Congshu* were published in installments from 1911 to 1918 by the Shanghai-based publisher Shenzhou Guoguangshe (Publishing house of the national glories of the divine land). The publisher took up the traditional practice of *congshu* (collections of writings by different authors), assembling existing Chinese texts considered relevant to the specified area of interest. A disparate array of writings about a variety of objects were thus collected and reorganized under the concept of *meishu*. The compilation of the *Meishu Congshu* exemplifies a moment in East Asian art history when local cultures encountered the European idea of Art and took it as the framing principle to look at similar discourses within their own traditions.

However, the transcultural trajectory by means of which the concept of *meishu* entered China lent the concept and its semantic connotations an unsettled character, in need of negotiating with local art-related knowledge and practices. The *Meishu Congshu* presupposes the relationship between the sorting concept and the selected texts as compatible and mutually defining. But how could existing Chinese texts be viewed as addressing the theme of *meishu*, an idea originating in Europe and with no equivalent in China? This demanded a process of adoption and domestication, contingent upon the editors' understanding and 'neologistic imagination' of the concept.[2]

The term *meishu* came to be widely acknowledged in China in the first decade of the 20th century, notably in the publications of the *Journal of National Essence* (*Guocui xuebao*, 1905–1912), which saw *meishu* as the essence of the Chinese nation, to be preserved and propagated. This nationalistic agenda prompted the same publisher to start an art periodical in 1908 called *Shenzhou guoguangji* (Collected national glories of the divine land, 1908–1912) to publicize visual reproductions of *meishu*, and in 1911 the book series under discussion, *Meishu Congshu*. The publisher's enterprises thus played an important role in spreading its nationalistic vision of *meishu*, thereby shaping the contemporary understanding of the term. To explore the process by which the (Euro-Japanese) concept of *meishu* was fitted into the existing knowledge system in China, this essay looks at the taxonomical construction of the *Meishu Congshu*, its modifications and rationales, throughout its publishing history. It sees the book series within the context of translingual practice, where the neologism *meishu* emerged as the Chinese counterpart for the European concept of

Art, and stresses *Meishu Congshu*'s agency in creating this new discursive field and articulating it with local traditions.

Although there exist today six series of the *Meishu Congshu*, this essay addresses only the first three—which were made before the Shenzhou Guoguangshe publishing house changed hands in 1928—since they differ significantly from the latter ones in publishing and editorial conditions and reflect the development of the concept of *meishu* from the time of the *Journal of National Essence*.³ By comparing the new classification system of *meishu* in the *Meishu Congshu* with that of *yishu* in the 18th-century imperial book collection *Complete Library of the Four Treasuries* (*Siku quanshu*, hereafter, the *Four Treasuries*), this essay demonstrates how this imported concept of *meishu* differed from the existing category of *yishu*, while at the same time was naturalized and endowed with an aura of tradition and authenticity in its new Chinese setting.

Meishu as the National Essence

Meishu Congshu was among the cultural endeavours initiated by the Society for Preserving National Learning (*Guoxue baocunhui*), a loosely organized group established in Shanghai in early 1905. Following the Boxer Rebellion (1900), which marked the culmination of China's successive defeats by Western powers and imperial Japan in the 19th century, the Society was formed in a mood of national crisis, emulating the National Essence Movement in Japan in the 1880s and 1890s. The Society sought to salvage the nation by preserving China's 'national learning' and hoped to inaugurate a Chinese Renaissance. To exert wider influence, the Society started the *Journal of National Essence* as its mouthpiece. Contributors included Chinese philologists and pro-revolution activists Zhang Binglin (1869–1935) and Liu Shipei (1884–1919), poet Huang Jie (1873–1935), and painter Huang Binhong (1865–1955).⁴ But the mastermind behind the Society was the editor Deng Shi (1877–1951), a cultural entrepreneur with a deep concern for China's fate. Deng was born in Shanghai and educated in keeping with traditional Confucian learning. Apart from running the day-to-day affairs of the Society and the *Journal*, he also established a library and reprinted rare texts by the ancients on behalf of the Society. Announcements requesting books for the library or for reprinting were frequently put out in the *Journal*, and the donations and letters from readers seen in the Society's reports, published every issue, testified to the positive reception of the Society's endeavours.⁵

The *Journal* equated 'national learning' with 'national essence', and from 1907 included a section entitled *Meishu* for relevant essays and images. *Meishu* was from then on promoted as an indispensable component of the 'national essence', possessing great capacity for motivating nationalistic sentiments in the Chinese people. The Society's enterprise in *meishu* publication thus received further development, with a separate publishing house, Shenzhou Guoguangshe, set up in 1908 to launch the art periodical *Shenzhou guoguangji*. Managed primarily by Deng Shi, the periodical employed the most up-to-date printing technologies for art reproduction, namely the halftone and collotype processes. Photographic images of works solicited from collectors in the southern Yangtze area, such as ancient rubbings, calligraphy, and paintings, were reproduced and distributed within China and beyond. It was through these publishing enterprises of the Society's that the nationalistic connotations of the term *meishu* were most powerfully manifested and consolidated.⁶ It was against this backdrop that the first three series of *Meishu Congshu* were compiled and released under Deng Shi's editorship.

The *Meishu Congshu* initially proposed five categories (*lei*) by which texts considered relevant to *meishu* were to be selected (or excluded) and grouped. Its publication stretched for a period of seven years, from 1911 to 1918.[7] Originally only one series was planned, to be released volume by volume on a monthly basis to make up a complete set of ten volumes.[8] But since this series was able to accommodate only a limited number of the texts available to the editor, a Continuing Series (*xuji*) was published in 1913 and 1914 to follow the first Primary Series (*zhengji*).[9] Due to the unexpectedly enthusiastic reception from within the country and abroad (Japan, Europe, and North America), a third Latter Series (*houji*) was released between 1915 and 1918.[10]

Paradoxically, the new field of *meishu* was substantiated by old texts written by authors of earlier generations.[11] This prompts the question of whether the *Meishu Conghsu* really aspired to introduce an authentic Western idea of Art, or was merely a rebranding of the old, existing concept of *yishu* (arts), a category codified in the imperially structured and widely accepted bibliographical classification system of the *Four Treasuries*.[12]

The *Meishu Congshu* in a Translingual Context

The tension between the old and the new framing concepts was complicated by the interpenetration of meanings of the two terms *meishu* and *yishu*. The latter (*geijutsu* in Japanese) was an established term existing in China since at least the 5th century, denoting 'skill';[13] in late 19th-century Japan it was also applied to translating the European concept of Art (like *bijutsu*) and subsequently travelled back to the modern Chinese language as a return loan from Japanese.[14] The editor's preference for *meishu* (a new semantic creation) over *yishu* (an existing semantic construction) for the title of the book collection could be regarded as an attempt to create a new discursive space equivalent to that of Art in European culture and sufficiently different from the existing idea of *yishu* in China. However, since the book collection gave no exposition of how *meishu* differed from the traditional *yishu*, the publishing endeavour of the *Meishu Congshu* could in reality have been little more than a new disguise for an old concept.

Scholars interested in the exact designation of the category *meishu* and its validity as a 'new' concept have paid particular attention to the degree to which the original idea (i.e. the Western concept of Art) was brought into China through translation as a package of ideas, for the term *meishu* is generally accepted as a translation of a foreign concept. However, by measuring the extent to which the European concept of Art was fully received in the Chinese context, one can hardly avoid imposing a modern conception of Art or 'fine arts' upon materials that were not necessarily produced out of the same concerns.

Such an approach is exemplified in articles by Chen Zhenlian and Ogawa Hiromitsu.[15] Both place the publication of *Meishu Congshu* in a linear development in which the European concept of 'fine arts' would eventually be received in its entirety in China. Chen thus highlights only the part that accords with what he regards as today's understanding of the term *meishu*, taking painting as the highest art form and embracing other categories of visual art, such as sculpture and seal carving. He is therefore amazed at the striking resemblance between the *meishu* seen in the *Meishu Congshu* and the definition of the term *meishu* today and concludes that the concept of *meishu* in the *Meishu Congshu* was 'ahead of its time', since, he argues, the meaning of the term had apparently been quite 'clear' (meaning it was very close to today's understanding) notwithstanding the fact that the neologism caused widespread conceptual confusion at the time.[16]

Although arriving at a different conclusion, the same approach is taken by Ogawa. Ogawa regards the European concept of Art as including painting, sculpture, crafts, and architecture. He examines these categories in relation to the texts selected and the categorizations proposed in the *Meishu Congshu*. He then concludes that the idea of *meishu* in this book collection is still based on the traditional notion of *yishu*, because texts on sculpture, or *diaoke*—a category he believes should have been included—are absent from the first three series. The lack of a category on architecture in this book collection was further attributed to the Japanese mediation, since architecture was not mentioned at all when the European concept of fine art was first introduced to Japan.[17]

This teleological approach fails to question whether the researcher's own conception of *meishu*, or the European concept of Art, is a valid measure at all. It is generally agreed that the European idea of Art with a capital A (and related terms 'Fine Arts' or 'Beaux Arts') assumed its modern shape in the 18th century, and is comprised of painting, sculpture, architecture, poetry, and music arts, which are often compared with each other and discussed on the basis of common principles. This particular grouping constitutes an area separated from, and even above, the crafts, the sciences, and other human activities.[18] Since the second half of the 19th century, however, the boundaries between Art and crafts have been constantly challenged, which affects each individual's conception of Art, too.[19] Perhaps this is why Chen and Ogawa have quite different understandings of 'the' European idea of Art. If in the present day the notion of Art is still far from fixed and unified, what can one rely upon in order to map out the situation more than a century ago? It is therefore not helpful to presuppose an idea of Art and check whether the *Meishu Congshu* fits these criteria or not.

The methodological peril one faces is even greater. In theory, the semantic meaning of *meishu* in the *Meishu Congshu* should have been contingent on the interaction between the three elements that may have been involved in the formulation, transmission, and reception of this translated term: the perceived original concept (say, 'the' European concept of 'fine arts'), the appropriated meaning in the mediated language (i.e. the Japanese *bijutsu*), and the 'neologistic imagination' in the host language (i.e. the Chinese *meishu*).[20] Yet not only had 'the' European concept of 'fine arts' itself been undergoing significant change since the second half of the 19th century, but the Japanese *bijutsu*, coined in 1872, was not originally devised to translate 'the' concept of 'fine arts' either: rather, it was seen in the same document as translating two German terms, *Kunstewerbe* (art and craft) and *bildende Kunst* (pictorial art), neither of which is the German equivalent of 'fine arts' (*schöne Kunst*).[21] It is therefore difficult to pin down what exactly the 'original' European concept was that the *Meishu Congshu* aimed to convey at the time of its publication, or to what extent the conception of *meishu* was mediated by the Japanese understanding of this European idea.

Given that we do not know exactly the targeted foreign concept the Chinese term *meishu* intended to address (if any), perhaps we should liberate the concept of *meishu* from the quest for its 'original' European and 'mediated' Japanese concepts. Instead, we should try to understand the concept as it was presented in the *Meishu Congshu*, and explore the 'neologistic imagination' enacted in the very act of text selection and grouping principles manifested in the book series. Furthermore, I propose that we place *meishu* in the cultural field where it appeared as a new mode of representation that rose, to borrow Bourdieu's idea, through 'position-taking' in a given cultural field, eventually challenging the position of an established concept.[22] In this particular case, the most likely candidate that *meishu* was to confront is the concept of *yishu* in China, for its position in the Chinese knowledge system would have been immediately seen as 'traditional' by the simple appropriation of the new framing and grouping concept of *meishu*. Only after this question is addressed can we properly assess how new and how foreign the concept of *meishu* seen in the *Meishu Congshu* was and how it differed from the past and present perceptions of Art.

Classification in the *Meishu Congshu*

According to the General Remarks (*lüeli*), the texts collected in the *Meishu Congshu* can be divided into five groups:[23]

- Calligraphy and Painting (*shuhua lei*)
- *Diaoke* [carving] and Seals, with Objects of the Studio Appended (*diaoke moyin lei, wenfang gepin fu*)
- Ceramic, Bronze, Jade, and Stone (*citong yushi lei*)
- Literary Arts: *Ci, Qu* Poems, and *Chuanqi* Drama (*wenyi lei, ciqu chuanqi*)
- Miscellaneous Notes (*zaji*)

It is also noted that specific attention would be paid to the category of 'Calligraphy and Painting', especially painting, for it was 'the finest among all forms of *meishu* of the Divine Land', a statement that echoes the publishing practices of the art periodical *Shenzhou guoguangji*.[24]

These categories served not only as principles for text selection but also for demarcating the scope and boundaries of this book collection. However, they also raise important questions ignored in former scholarly attempts but crucial to our understanding of this classifying scheme on its own terms. First, was this classification a stable one and consistent with that in the former publishing enterprises of the Society? Second, was the meaning of the category *diaoke* the same as its most common English rendition today, 'sculpture'? Third, how do we account for the presence of the texts that seem to be out of place in this classification system, such as the 'Manual on Growing Orchids'?[25] These questions can be probed by examining the advertising notices—retained in the initial edition but removed in reprints—of the book titles to be published or desired for contribution in the successive volumes.

These advertising announcements demonstrate the scope of the *Meishu Congshu* project and its subsequent revisions. The first of them was seen in the inaugural volume, with 133 titles, which, although unsorted, were arranged more or less in accordance

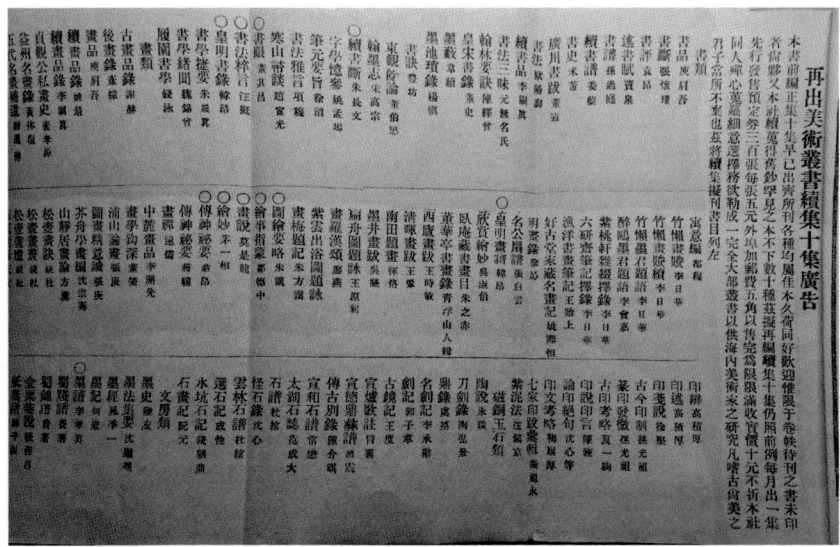

Figure 12.1 Advertisement for the ten-volume continuing series of the *Meishu Congshu*, *Meishu Congshu* 2, no. 10 (1914) SOAS Library
SOAS Library

with the order of the five categories proposed in the General Remarks.[26] In the First Series similar editorial notices are found in volumes 3 and 4.[27] All these lists constitute the original publishing plan for the *Meishu Congshu*, comprising 203 titles in total.[28] As this plan was too ambitious for a ten-volume series, the Second Series had to be launched. Another long list of the text titles intended for publication was likewise advertised in the first volume of the Second Series (1913). This is an important source for understanding the categorizing principles of the book collection (Figure 12.1). The list incorporates the titles listed in all previous notices with new ones added for a total of 224 titles, although only about 36 per cent of them were eventually printed in later volumes or series.[29] Significantly, all of the titles are categorized under the headings of Calligraphy (29 titles), Painting (109 titles), *Diaoke* and Seals (24 titles), Ceramic, Bronze, Jade, and Stone (17 titles), Objects of the Studio (30 titles), and Miscellaneous Notes (15 titles). This not only modifies the sorting principles proposed earlier, but also provides a general idea of which title goes into which category.[30]

One can hardly fail to notice the absence of the category of Literary Arts on the list. In fact, texts on *chuanqi* drama (considered to belong to the category of Literary Arts) were regarded in a later editorial notice of the first year (1911) as improper for the present project since they were by their nature not so much characteristic of *meishu* as of *wenxue* (literature).[31] Given that the Society had placed 'verse, prose, and *ci* and *qu* poems' (*shiwen ciqu*) in the domain of *meishu* in the *Journal of National Essence* (1906),[32] such abandonment, first of the texts on *chuanqi* drama and then of the whole category of Literary Arts, was a deliberate choice meant to differentiate *meishu* from the broader sense of Art that included forms of the visual, literary, and performing kind. The awareness of such a differentiation demarcated the domain of *meishu* in relation to other fields within the broader cultural field as being related to things visual, tangible, and non-textual, and narrowed it down as a subject parallel to, rather than inclusive of, Literature. Further, this awareness also implies that the discursive space of *wenxue* had been sufficiently established, to the extent that it seemed improper to discuss it indiscriminately as, or even alongside, *meishu*.³³

The compilation and publication of this book collection was an ongoing process. That the *Meishu Congshu* excludes from the outset the category of Metal and Stone [inscriptions] (*jinshi*) was in itself also a revision of the publisher's earlier classification of this category, which had originally been included as part of *meishu* in the *Journal of National Essence* and heavily reproduced in the art periodical *Shenzhou guoguangji*. Its absence was explained in the General Remarks as constituting a specialized area of study that deserved a separate book series and hence its exclusion from the present publication.³⁴

Furthermore, a close look at the text titles listed under the heading *Diaoke* and Seals also suggests a different perspective on the meaning of the term *diaoke* (琱刻 or 雕刻, both forms existing in the first edition of the *Meishu Conghsu*), which is now almost a standard translation for the Western notion of 'sculpture' and which may thus mislead us into thinking that the texts grouped under this category would have been about statues, statuettes, and high- or bas-reliefs. While *diaoke* literally means 'the skills of carving and chiselling', it became a categorical heading by the late 16th century in China. It refers primarily to small carved objects in precious stone, wood, bamboo, ivory, silver, and so on, or the carvings worked into daily objects and even on walnut shells. More importantly, grand statues or reliefs in architectural settings are hardly ever mentioned in the context of this category.³⁵ Therefore, when one translates the term *diaoke* in its traditional sense into English, it is more accurate to render it as 'carving' than 'sculpture'. This traditional understanding of *diaoke* still persisted in the *Meishu Congshu*, as evidenced by the inclusion of the title 'Records of Bamboo Carvers', originally prefaced in 1807, by Jin Yuanyu.³⁶

It is the listing of the text 'Manual for Formulating Movable Types', prefaced in 1774, that completes the picture of the range of things the term *diaoke* was able to signify, a meaning that has ceased to exist in modern vernacular Chinese; that is, to denote the act of book printing.³⁷ This signification is not at all absurd, given that the making of xylographic books entails the carving of wooden print blocks. One of the earliest examples of such usage is found in the title of a late 9th-century text, a work about raising funds for printing monastic codes, which uses the term *diaoke* to express the meaning, 'putting into print'.³⁸ Similar examples are frequent in later periods.³⁹ This neglected aspect of the term *diaoke* not only explains why a text on movable-type book printing could be grouped under the category of *Diaoke* and Seals, but also shows how inappropriate it is to assume that the term *diaoke* in the *Meishu Congshu* meant, in the early 20th century, exactly the same as its modern meaning, sculpture.

While placing a text about '*diaoke* as book printing' in the domain of *meishu* might seem bizarre to our modern eyes, it was perfectly consistent with the publisher's conception of *meishu*, a fact which can be easily seen in its rhetoric on publishing practices. The photolithographic reprint of the book *Complete Works of Xie Xifa* was advertised as preserving the 'essence of our nation's *meishu*' as it retained the appearance of each carefully printed page of the original book.[40] Articles on the history of book printing were also sorted in the *Meishu* section in the *Journal of National Essence*.[41] The appreciation of book printing should not, however, be hastily assumed to be a sign of the elevation of crafts into the realm of Arts, as one might expect in European art history of the same period, when the Arts and Crafts Movement called for overcoming the separation between arts and crafts.[42] Rather, it should be understood within the context of the traditional practice of book collecting in China, in which not only is the age and rarity of a book valued, but the style and quality of the block-carving also matters.[43] Hence 'Old-Carved Books of the Song and Yuan' was among the ten groups of 'Objects of *meishu*' advertised for contribution in the *Journal of National Essence*.[44] The culture of book collecting and connoisseurship in book printing in China still resonated in the 20th century, which saw printing and rare books placed in the field of *meishu* in the *Meishu Congshu*.

The list of 'to be published titles' in Series 2, volume 1 shows that the category 'Miscellaneous Notes' not only accommodated texts consisting of assorted notes on connoisseurship in general—on subjects such as antiques, books, and various 'superfluous things'—but also included treatises on subjects not covered in the other categories, such as the text entitled 'On Using Incense without Producing Smoke'.[45] The text 'Manual on Growing Orchids' must have been selected for this book collection out of the same concern and would have been grouped under the category of Miscellaneous Notes, since it could not be attached to any of the other categories but was still considered relevant to the knowledge of *meishu*. Similarly, texts on *qin* zithers were grouped under this category. In fact, even after the editors had been made aware of the inappropriateness of the presence of texts on Literary Arts in this book project, 'odd' texts whose subjects ranged from dresses to accessories for men,[46] from making tea to making sugar,[47] from flower arrangement to keeping pet fish,[48] were still published throughout the first three series of the *Meishu Congshu*. In other words, these titles never came to be considered irrelevant or inappropriate to this new field of *meishu*. While other more established categories such as Calligraphy and Painting, *Diaoke* and Seals, and so on, may have served as the core elements by which the concept of *meishu* was meant to be grasped by and registered in readers' minds, it is these 'odd' texts—in the sense that they are both unusual to today's conception of *meishu* and outside all the proposed categories except Miscellaneous Notes—that mark out the very boundaries of the idea of *meishu* as it was understood by the editors and embodied in the *Meishu Congshu*.

These 'odd texts' all concern the material enjoyments that a person of refined taste might indulge in, enjoyments which actually define the essence of *meishu* to the collection's editors and which, as we shall see below, give this concept of *meishu* a unique character that differentiates it from that of *yishu*. The subjects and objects addressed by these texts are not restricted to visual culture (using incense without causing smoke reduces the visual effect that the act of incense scenting can offer); rather they also bring pleasure through senses other than vision, such as smell, taste, and hearing. These pleasures exist in various aspects of material life and are only deemed worth pursuing when someone holds an appreciative attitude towards the world surrounding them. As shown in the selected text titles, such pleasures lie not only in the thing itself, but also in the relationship between the person and the thing (as in the case of keeping pets). This intimate relationship did not present any contradiction to the other groupings in this book collection, as the texts in these categories are all about the 'things' outside of the self to be enjoyed, and more or less correspond to the material culture created and indulged in by the cultivated literati. *Meishu*, in this book collection, can thus be understood as the incarnation of the literati's elegant, sensory leisure pursuits in the material world.

From the perspective that takes *meishu* as things to be enjoyed with an appreciative mind, the inclusion of the texts on *qin* zithers in this collection poses an intriguing question concerning how far the concept of *meishu* in the *Meishu Congshu* resembles the existing idea and grouping principle of *yishu*, particularly the one exemplified in the imperial book collection the *Four Treasuries*, which also accommodates texts on *qin* zithers. Do these texts on *qin* zithers appear in the *Meishu Congshu* for the same reason as they do in the *Four Treasuries*? Does the conception of *meishu* in the *Meishu Congshu* by and large reproduce the hierarchical structure of knowledge proposed in the *Four Treasuries*, where the category of *yishu* is situated? To probe these questions, it is necessary not only to trace the semantic development of both terms, but also to examine and compare the positions occupied by the categories of *yishu* and *meishu* within the knowledge system evident in these two book collections.

Positioning *Meishu* in the Chinese Knowledge System

The preference for the term *meishu* over *yishu* in the title of the *Meishu Congshu* was more likely a decision intended to differentiate the contents and concepts of *meishu* from those of *yishu* (particularly as seen in the *Four Treasuries*) than an attempt to rebrand the old concept of *yishu* with a fancy new name. Compiled in the 1770s and 1780s, the bibliographic classification of the *Four Treasuries* had enjoyed paradigmatic importance since the time of its release.[49] Its significance was so great that the editors of the *Journal of National Essence* felt the need to explain why the new journal's structure did not adhere to the model set forth by this imperial book collection, which treats *jinshi* as a category under the branch of History, not *meishu*.[50] The editors' awareness of this predominant bibliographic classification thus implies that the use of the term *meishu* in the *Meishu Congshu* was a deliberate departure from the *Four Treasuries* tradition: an attempt to open up a new discursive space no longer subject to this tradition.

Differentiation implies a certain degree of resemblance between the things to be differentiated. *Meishu* and *yishu* bear similarities to one another in more than just their similar semantic construction of 'x + *shu*' (skills, or methods). Like *meishu*, the category *yishu* in the *Four Treasuries* is broken down into several subcategories, such as 'Calligraphy and Painting', '*Qin* Zither Music Scores', 'Seal Carving', and 'Miscellaneous Skills' (including *jie* drum beating, *jiegu*, and *go* game playing, *qi*).[51] Two of these same subcategories in *yishu* also appear as grouping categories in the classification of the *Meishu Congshu* (i.e. 'Calligraphy and Painting' and 'Seal Carving'); and texts on *Qin* Zithers are incorporated into this early 20th-century book collection as well, although not as an independent category of its own. In addition, *yishu* in the *Four Treasuries* also significantly distinguished itself from not only the field of Divination (*shushu*) but also from practical skills and abilities such as Gardening and Medicine, which might otherwise have been accommodated within the category of *yishu* if one considers the comprehensive meaning of the term, which embraces all kinds of skills and abilities (like 'arts' in English in the sense of 'skills'). The fact that the *yishu* in the *Four Treasuries* centres on the accomplishments pursued by a man of leisure enhances the impression that the two terms in both contexts seem to address the same thing.

However, *yishu* and *meishu* are in fact different in meaning as well as in their positions within the knowledge system. First, all the subcategories in *yishu* are grouped on the grounds of their being the many 'accomplishments' pursued by the literati, skills to be mastered and abilities to be possessed, whereas the texts that appeared in the *Meishu Congshu* are more on the topic of 'things' outside the self, things intended to be enjoyed by an appreciative mind. Such a distinction explains the fact that no texts on *go* games or drum beating were published in the *Meishu Congshu*. The skill-orientated meaning of the term *yishu* can also be observed in its subcategory, 'Miscellaneous *Skills*': this accommodates 'odd' texts relevant to *yishu* but unable to form a distinct group of their own. A look at the historic usage of the character *yi* shows its association with the acquired abilities related to leisure pursuits of intellectuals, as in the phrase extracted from Confucius's *Analects*, 'to ramble among *yi*' (*youyuyi*). The *yi* here refers to the 'six arts' (*liuyi*) supposed to be mastered by a cultivated person, including rituals, music, archery, charioteering, language, and arithmetic.[52] However, these are skills to be acquired by an individual through constant and persistent practice, rather than 'things' situated in the outside world that are meant for us to appreciate, to form a relationship with, as are the subjects included in the *Meishu Congshu*.[53]

Second, the classification in the *Four Treasuries* also demonstrates a highly hierarchical structure in which *yishu* occupies a rather low position, best demonstrated in the 'Complete Annotated Catalogue of the *Four Treasuries*'. This document, compiled by the editors of this imperial book collection, gives a lengthy exposition of the hierarchical order of the classification and the principles for grouping individual texts.[54] Classics (*jing*), the first branch in the '*Jingshi ziji*' (Classics, History, Philosophers, and Belles-letters) classification system codified in the *Four Treasuries*, was the highest and most revered, whereas the category of *yishu*, placed in the third branch, *zi*, is defined in a negative tone as being for texts on insignificant but pursuable subjects. For instance, *qin* music is included in this category because it was considered inappropriate for inclusion in the higher category of Music under the branch of Classics: according to the editors of the imperial book collection, *qin* music had by that time been abused by the free creation of the commoners and therefore no longer qualified as 'elegant music' suitable for State rituals or grouped under the 'Music' category. It was also argued that the various kinds of game playing—in spite of their having been mentioned in *Book of Rites*—were not really about rituals and should be 'downgraded' (from Classics) to *yishu* (*tuilie yishu*). As for gambling, dancing, and so on, the editors of the *Four Treasuries* regarded these as trivial skills and maintained that simply grouping them together under 'Miscellaneous Skills' would save a great deal of trouble with sorting. Even the presence of 'Calligraphy and Seal Carving' in *yishu* was justified by stressing how improper it would have been to have put them in the category of *xiaoxue*, the study of the origin and development of words, under the branch of Classics.[55] In other words, from the point of view of the editors, *yishu* consisted merely of minor skills—those less significant than those that constituted real learning, such as Classics—which nonetheless were considered to be acceptable as a kind of knowledge.

This attitude towards *yishu* did not cast a shadow over *meishu* seen in the *Meishu Congshu*, largely because the term *yishu* was not appropriated in this early 20th-century book collection. Perhaps the use of *meishu* was a deliberate challenge to the hierarchical structure of knowledge in the *Four Treasuries*—in which *meishu* had no place (and would not have been regarded as serious learning even if it had)—given both the high position Classics enjoyed and the slighting references *yishu* received in this imperial book collection. Employing the neologism *meishu* was probably a better way to introduce a new concept, one that would not be subject to the previously superior position of Classics and that would more easily have addressed the needs of the time as representing the essence of the nation. In fact, in the *Meishu Congshu*, *meishu* was praised even more highly than Classics and was regarded as the only subject of learning that could win the competition for survival in the world. As Deng Shi stated in the Preface to the *Meishu Congshu*:

> Since European learning began to have an effect on China, the traditional learning of our nation has suffered from decline. The times have changed, and so has the trend. Six *Classics* have now become no more than unwanted dregs, and Confucius's thinking seems like empty promises. Only [our] learning of *meishu* has been universally hailed as unique and peerless. One has to turn to the Orient when it comes to *meishu* . . . This is what we yellow race specialises in and which makes us proudly distinguished from other nations. [自歐學東漸，吾國舊有之學遂以不振。蓋時會既變，趨向遂殊，六經成糟粕，義理屬空言，而惟美術之學則環球所推為獨絕。言美術者，必曰東方。... 此則吾黃民之特長而可巍然示異於他國者也]⁵⁶

This is not to say that *meishu* had truly risen above the Classics to the top of the Chinese knowledge system. Nevertheless, this extract reveals the freedom granted by the neologism *meishu* to the reasoning by which *meishu*, as a new subject of learning, was able to emerge, while at the same time the traditional knowledge system and its hierarchical structure seem to have remained intact.

It should be borne in mind that the specific newness of *meishu*—such as how it differed from *yishu*, as discussed above—was never clearly spelled out in *Meishu Congshu*, while the actual *meishu* texts all seem to be old. Consequently, although the employment of the neologism *meishu* liberated this new concept from being subject to the inherent hierarchy of the tradition, the presence of these old texts enabled *meishu* to be incorporated into a project aimed at preserving the national essence, even though the grouping concept was actually new and fundamentally different from the traditional *yishu*.

Moreover, the discursive power of *meishu* was acquired largely through its alliance with the predominant nationalist discourse, which rendered it of indispensable importance to the nation. Hence Deng argued that *meishu* was the only comfort one could still turn to in this time of great turmoil, and such comfort was the key to keeping one's love for the nation alive:

> Were there none of *meishu*'s comforting, the hearts of the nation's people would surely die. While a perishing nation may still be restored, a dead heart can never be brought back to life. These books of dozens of *juan*s, which make worries forgotten and anger appeased, are merely hoping to rescue the dying hearts of the people

of such a nation. [使無美術以解釋而慰藉之，則一國之人心死矣。國死可復興，心死無復活，然則此十數卷忘憂捐忿之書，聊拯一國方死未死之人心]⁵⁷

In other words, the significance of *meishu* lay also in the fact that it was believed to be able to help China out of her predicament in relation to the imperial powers, for it kept hope alive. As 'things' to console one's mind, and with the strong support of nationalist discourse, *meishu* was no longer a deprecated, insignificant subject like *yishu*, but was elevated to the point of being not only one of the most important subjects of national learning, but also one of the most attractive tropes in the discourse on national essence.

Conclusion

The introduction of the European concept of Art into East Asia in the second half of the 19th century brought in a new mode of representation that had never previously been imagined. It inspired different ways in which the locals strove to create an equivalent in their own cultures. The book series *Meishu Congshu* was one such endeavour. It was produced under the nationalistic rhetoric in early 20th-century China, associated in particular with the preservation of the national essence. It employed the neologism *meishu*, distinct in semantic construction from the existing term *yishu*, to mark out a space occupying a higher position in the value system of culture, just like Art in European culture. However, *Meishu Congshu* came up with a grouping that did not so much follow the European model as integrated the existing collecting and appreciation culture in China. During this process, objects of scholars' enjoyments and leisure pursuits were transformed into *meishu*, which differentiated *meishu* from the traditional sense of *yishu*, a term denoting skills or personal accomplishments, rather than external things. The concept of *meishu* in early 20th-century China should thus be understood as an appropriation rather than a translation of the European concept of Art. By substantiating this new mode of representation with existing writings, the *Meishu Congshu* makes this new concept seem traditional and native to China. *Meishu* as an imported concept was in this way naturalized as a national tradition.

Notes

1 Frederico Masini, *The Formation of Modern Chinese Lexicon and Its Evolution toward a National Language: The Period from 1840 to 1898* (Berkeley: University of California, 1993), pp. 188–189.
2 Lydia Liu, *Translingual Practice: Literature, National Culture, and Translated Modernity—China, 1900–1937* (Stanford: Stanford University Press, 1995), pp. 26–27; 39–41. This approach sees 'translation' as premised on hypothetical 'tropes of equivalence', and examines the ways meaning is negotiated and invented by local and subjective imaginations of the neologism in question.
3 The fourth series was compiled by Huang Binhong and Sun Tagong from 1928 to 1936 after the publisher was taken over by Chen Mingshu in 1928, and the fifth and sixth series were published in Taiwan in 1964 and 1975 by Yiwen Yinshuguan [Yee Wen publishing company].
4 For research on the journal, see essays in *The Limits of Change: Essays on Conservative Alternatives in Republican China* (Cambridge, Mass.: Harvard University Press, 1976), ed. Charlotte Furth, pp. 57–89, 90–112; Tze-ki Hon, *Revolution as Restoration: Guocui*

xuebao and China's Path to Modernity, 1905–1911 (Leiden: Brill, 2013); Fa-ti Fan, 'Nature and Nation in Chinese Political Thought: The National Essence Circle in Early Twentieth-Century China', in *The Moral Authority of Nature* (Chicago: University of Chicago Press, 2004), ed. Lorraine Daston and Fernando Vidal, pp. 409–437.

5 For Deng's role, see Liu Yuzhen, 'Zhaoxiang fuzhi niandai lide Zhongguo meishu: Shenzhou guoguangji de fuzhi taidu yu wenhua biaoshu' [Chinese art in the age of photographic reproduction: the art periodical *Shenzhou guoguangji*], *Guoli Taiwan daxue meishushi yanjiu jikan* 35 (2013): 202–206; Hong Zaixin, 'Cong Minzu zhuyi dao xiandai zhuyi: Deng Shi, Huang Binhong xueshu sixiang guanxi kaolüe' [From nationalism to modernism: a brief examination of the thought of and relationship between Deng Shi and Huang Binhong], *Meishu xuebao* 2013, no. 3: 29–40; 2013, no. 4: 26–31.

6 Yu-jen Liu, 'Second Only to the Original: Rhetoric and Practice in the Photographic Reproduction of Art in Early Twentieth-Century China', *Art History* 37, no. 1 (2014): 68–95. Liu Yuzhen, 'Zhaoxiang fuzhi', pp. 185–244.

7 Publishing dates: Ogawa Hiromitsu, 'Bijutsu sōsho no kankō ni tsuite: Yōroppa no gainen "Fine Arts" to nihon no yakugo "bijutsu" no dōnyū' [Regarding the publication of *Meishu Congshu*: introduction of the European concept of 'Fine Arts' and the Japanese translated term '*Bijustu*'], *Bijutsushi ronsō* 20 (2004): 49.

8 'Xinhainian xinchu jingkan Meishu congshu guanggao' [Advertisement for the new production in *Xinhai* year of exquisitely edited *Meishu Congshu*], *Goucui xuebao* 6, no. 11 (1910). The *Guocui xuebao* I consulted is the edition in the SOAS Library, London, which still retains its original binding.

9 'Zaichu Meishu Congshu xuji shiji guanggao' [Advertisement for the ten-volume continuing series of *Meishu Congshu*], *Meishu Congshu* 1, no. 10 (1911). Initial editions of the *Meishu Congshu*, which retain the original advertisements, can be found at SOAS Library (c.FF.99/73350) and Hong Kong University Library (特山908.80). The observations below are based on these two sets.

10 'Zaichu Meishu Congshu houji shiji guanggao' [Advertisement for the ten volumes of the latter series of the *Meishu Congshu*], *Meishu Congshu* 2, no. 10 (1914). This advertisement, torn out of the SOAS copy, can be found in the Hong Kong University Library edition.

11 Most of the texts in the first three series of the *Meishu Congshu* were writings of the Ming and Qing periods. The most recently composed texts are Xu Zhiheng (1877–1935), *Yinliuzhai shuoci* [Studio of Drinking Stream on the subject of porcelain]; and Deng Shi, *Tanyilu* [Notes on art], *Meishu Congshu* 3, no. 6 (1916); 3, no. 10 (1918).

12 Ji Yun et al. (eds.), *Yingyin Wenyuange Siku quanshu* [Complete library of the *Four Treasuries* in the Wenyuan Hall], photographic reprint of the 18th-century edition (Taipei: Commercial Press, 1986). Compiling history of the *Four Treasuries*: Kent Guy, *The Emperor's Four Treasuries: Scholars and the State in the Late Ch'ien-lung Era* (Cambridge, Mass.: Harvard University Press, 1987).

13 One of the earliest usages of the term *yishu* is found in Fan Yie (398–445), *Hou Han Shu* [History of the Later Han], *Siku* edition, vol. 252, *juan* 5, 10.

14 Masini, *Formation of Modern Chinese Lexicon*, p. 213.

15 Chen Zhenlian, 'Meishu yuyuan kao: Meishu yiyu yinjin shi yanjiu' [The etymology of '*meishu*': a study on the introduction of '*meishu*' as a translated term]', *Meishu yanjiu* (2004), no. 1: 14–23; and Ogawa, 'Bijutsu sōsho', pp. 33–54.

16 Chen Zhenlian, 'Meishu yuyuan kao', pp. 18–19.

17 Ogawa, 'Bijutsu sōsho', pp. 33, 40–41.

18 Paul Kristeller, 'The Modern System of the Arts: A Study in the History of Aesthetics, Part I', *Journal of the History of Ideas* 12, no. 4 (1951): 497–498.

19 Larry Shiner, *The Invention of Art: A Cultural History* (Chicago: University of Chicago Press, 2001), pp. 225–301.

20 Lydia Liu, *Translingual Practice*, pp. 26–27.

21 Kitazawa Noriaki, *Me no shinden: 'bijutsu' juyōshi nōto* [Temple of the eye: on the reception of *bijutsu*] (Tokyo: Bijutsu shuppansha, 1989), pp. 139–145.

22 Pierre Bourdieu, *The Field of Cultural Production: Essays on Art and Literature* (New York: Columbia University Press, 1993), pp. 131–141.

23 'Lüeli', *Meishu Congshu* 1, no. 1 (1911), 1b.

24 Yu-jen Liu, 'Second Only to the Original', p. 89.
25 Liu Wenqi, *Yilanji*, *Meishu Congshu* 1, no. 1 (1911).
26 'Meishu congshu daikan shumu' [List of book titles to be published in the *Meishu Congshu*], *Meishu Congshu* 1, no. 1 (1911).
27 'Meishu congshu xu daikan shumu' [Continuing list of book titles to be published in the *Meishu congshu*], and 'Meishu congshu zhengkan shumu' [List of book titles desired for publishing in the *Meishu congshu*], *Meishu Congshu* 1, no. 3 (1911), 1–2. *Meishu Congshu* 1, no. 3 (1911); 'Meishu congshu sanxu daikan shumu' [Second continuing list of book titles to be published in the *Meishu congshu*], *Meishu Congshu* 1, no. 4 (1911).
28 Apart from the 133 titles in *Meishu Congshu* 1, no. 1, there are twenty-eight intended titles and thirty desired titles in *Meishu Congshu* 1, no. 3; and sixteen titles in *Meishu Congshu* 1, no. 4. However, four titles in *Meishu Congshu* 1, no. 4 overlapped with those already appearing in *Meishu Congshu* 1, no. 3.
29 On this list there are only eighty titles that were eventually released in the Second and Third Series.
30 'Zaichu Meishu congshu xuji shiji guanggao' [Advertisement for the ten-volume continuing series of the *Meishu congshu*], *Meishu Congshu* 2, no. 1 (1913).
31 'Fugao' [Appended notice (to *Meishu congshu sanxu daikan shumu*)], *Meishu Congshu* 1, no. 4 (1911), 1b. This notice is not seen in the reprints.
32 'Zheng meishupin zhonglei' [Types of art objects requested], *Goucui xuebao* 2, no. 8 (1906).
33 The modern meaning of *wenxue* as 'literature' was not widely accepted until the first decade of the 20th century: Theodore Huters, *Bringing the World Home: Appropriating the West in Late Qing and Early Republican China* (Honolulu: University of Hawai'i Press, 2005), pp. 76–80.
34 'Lüeli', 1b, 2a.
35 Examples: Zhang Yingwen, 'Lun diaoke' [On carvings], in *Qingmizang* [Pure and arcane collecting], *Siku* edition, vol. 872, *juan* 1, 26b–27a; Gao Lian, 'Lun tihong woqi diaoke xiangqian qimin' [On carved red lacquer, Japanese lacquer, carvings, and inlayed objects and vessels], in *Zunsheng bajian* [Eight discourses on the art of living], *Siku* edition, vol. 874, *juan* 14, 73–78; and Wen Zhenheng, 'Hailun tongyu diaoke yaoqi' [General views on bronzes, jades, carvings and kilned objects], in *Zhangwuzhi* [Superfluous things], *Siku* edition, vol. 872, *juan* 7, 23–25.
36 Jin Yuanyu, *Zhurenlu*, *Meishu Congshu* 2, no. 5 (1913).
37 Jin Jian, *Juzhenban chengshi*, *Meishu Congshu* 3, no. 8 (1917).
38 Sikong Tu (837–908), 'Wei dongdu Jing'aisi jianglüseng Huique huamu diaoke lüshu' [Statements written for Monk Huique who preaches Vinaya at the Jing'ai Temple in eastern capital on raising contributions for carving monastic codes], *Sikong Biaosheng wenji* [Collected works by Sikong Biaosheng], *Siku* edition, vol. 1083, *juan* 9, 4.
39 For example, see *Siku quanshu zongmu tiyao* [Annotated catalogue of the *Complete Collection of Four Treasuries*], ed. Yongrong et al. (Shanghai: Commercial Press, 1933), ii, *juan* 86, 1793, where the author uses the expression '*weiji diaoke*' [has yet to be carved] to indicate that a certain text had never been published in print form by a certain time.
40 'Xie Gaoyu xifa quanji' [Complete works of Xie Gaoyu], in 'Guocui congshu disanci chuban guanggao' [Advertisement for the third release of the book series *Guocui congshu*], *Guocui xuebao* 2, no. 8 (1906), inside back cover.
41 Such as Huang Jie, 'Banjikao' [On printed books], *Guocui xuebao* 4, no. 10; 4, no. 12 (1908).
42 Shiner, *Invention of Art*, 227; Elizabeth Cumming and Wendy Kaplan, *The Arts and Crafts Movement* (London: Thames and Hudson, 1991).
43 Concerns about the style of carved characters, layout, and paper used involving connoisseurship in rare books are exemplified in Ye Dehui, *Shulin qinghua* [Elegant talks on books] (Taipei: Shijie shuju, 1961), esp. *juan* 6.
44 'Zheng meishupin zhonglei'.
45 Dong Yue (1620–1686), *Feiyan xiangfa*, *Meishu Congshu* 2, no. 4 (1913).
46 Zhang Chou, *Yiefukao* [Studies in the garments for the wild], *Meishu Congshu*, 2, no. 10 (1914), on the sartorial styles and accessories for recluses; and Wang Tingding, *Zhangshan xinlu* [New notes on canes and fans], *Meishu Congshu* 2, no. 8 (1914), documenting various styles of canes and fans.

47 Zhang Qiande, *Chajing* [Book of tea], *Meishu Congshu* 2, no. 10 (1914), on the production and the making of tea; and Wang Zhuo, *Tangshuangpu* [Treatise on frost-like sugar], *Meishu Congshu* 3, no. 5 (1916), on making sugar.
48 Yuan Hongdao, *Pingshi* [History of vase flowers], *Meishu Congshu* 1, no. 6 (1911), on flower arrangement; and Zhang Qiande, *Zhusha yupu* [Treatise on vermilion fish], *Meishu Congshu* 2, no. 10 (1914), on how to keep small red fish with a hint of yellow colour as pets.
49 Chang Bide and Pan Meiyue, *Zhongguo muluxue* [Chinese bibliology] (Taipei: Wenshizhe, 1986), p. 216.
50 'Diliunian Guocui xuebao gengding limu' [Change in classification from the 6th year of the *Guocui xuebao*], *Guocui xuebao* 6, no. 1, 1b.
51 *Siku quanshu zongmu tiyao*, iii, *juan* 113, 2370.
52 Chichung Huang, *The Analects of Confucius* (Lun Yu): *A Literal Translation with an Introduction and Notes* (New York: Oxford University Press, 1997), p. 87.
53 For example, although 'Manual on Growing Orchids' appears at first glance to be a text on gardening, in the text the orchid is treated as if it were a human being to be taken care of and loved.
54 'Siku quanshu fanli' [General remarks on the *Four Treasuries*], in *Siku quanshu zongmu tiyao*, i, 1–7.
55 *Siku quanshu zongmu tiyao*, iii, *juan* 112, 2321.
56 Deng Shi, 'Xulüe' [Preface], *Meishu Congshu* 1, no. 1 (1911), 1b.
57 Ibid., 2b.

Bibliography

Anonymous. 'Diliunian Guocui xuebao gengding limu' [Change in classification from the 6th year of the *Guocui xuebao*]. *Guocui xuebao* 6, no. 1 (1910).
———. 'Zheng meishupin zhonglei' [Types of art objects requested]. *Goucui xuebao* 2, no. 8 (1906).
———. 'Xie Gaoyu xifa quanji' [Complete works of Xie Gaoyu]. In 'Guocui congshu disanci chuban guanggao' [Advertisement for the third release of the book series *Guocui congshu*]. *Guocui xuebao* 2, no. 8 (1906).
———. 'Xinhainian xinchu jingkan Meishu Congshu guanggao' [Advertisement for the new production in *Xinhai* year of exquisitely edited *Meishu Congshu*]. *Goucui xuebao* 6, no. 11 (1910).
Bourdieu, Pierre. *The Field of Cultural Production: Essays on Art and Literature*. New York: Columbia University Press, 1993.
Chang Bide, and Pan Meiyue. *Zhongguo muluxue* [Chinese bibliology]. Taipei: Wenshizhe, 1986.
Chen Zhenlian. 'Meishu yuyuan kao: Meishu yiyu yinjin shi yanjiu' [The etymology of '*meishu*': a study on the introduction of '*meishu*' as a translated term]. *Meishu yanjiu* 2003, no. 4: 60–71; 2004, no. 1: 14–23.
Cumming, Elizabeth, and Wendy Kaplan. *The Arts and Crafts Movement*. London: Thames and Hudson, 1991.
Deng Shi. 'Xulüe' [Preface]. *Meishu Congshu* 1, no. 1 (1911).
———. *Tanyilu* [Notes on art]. *Meishu Congshu* 3, no. 10 (1918).
Deng Shi, general ed. 'Fugao' [Appended notice (to *Meishu Congshu sanxu daikan shumu*)]. *Meishu Congshu* 1, no. 4 (1911), 1b.
———. 'Meishu Congshu daikan shumu' [List of book titles to be published in the *Meishu Congshu*]. *Meishu Congshu* 1, no. 1 (1911).
———. 'Meishu Congshu sanxu daikan shumu' [Second continuing list of book titles to be published in the *Meishu Congshu*]. *Meishu Congshu* 1, no. 4 (1911).
———. 'Meishu Congshu xu daikan shumu' [Continuing list of book titles to be published in the *Meishu Congshu*]. *Meishu Congshu* 1, no. 3 (1911).

———. 'Meishu Congshu zhengkan shumu' [List of book titles desired for publishing in the *Meishu Congshu*]. *Meishu Congshu* 1, no. 3 (1911).

———. 'Zaichu Meishu Congshu xuji shiji guanggao' [Advertisement for the ten-volume continuing series of *Meishu Congshu*]. *Meishu Congshu* 1, no. 10 (1911).

———. 'Lüeli' [General remarks]. *Meishu Congshu* 1, no. 1 (1911).

———. 'Zaichu Meishu Congshu xuji shiji guanggao' [Advertisement for the ten-volume continuing series of the *Meishu Congshu*]. *Meishu Congshu* 2, no. 1 (1913).

———. 'Zaichu Meishu Congshu houji shiji guanggao' [Advertisement for the ten volumes of the latter series of the *Meishu Congshu*]. *Meishu Congshu* 2, no. 10 (1914).

Dong Yue. *Feiyan xiangfa* [On using incense without producing smoke]. *Meishu Congshu* 2, no. 4 (1913).

Fan Fa-ti. 'Nature and Nation in Chinese Political Thought: The National Essence Circle in Early Twentieth-Century China'. In *The Moral Authority of Nature*, edited by Lorraine Daston and Fernando Vidal, 409–437. Chicago: University of Chicago Press, 2004.

Fan Yie. *Hou Han Shu* [History of the Later Han], *Siku* edition, vol. 252.

Furth, Charlotte, ed. *The Limits of Change: Essays on Conservative Alternatives in Republican China*. Cambridge, Mass.: Harvard University Press, 1976.

Gao Lian. 'Lun tihong woqi diaoke xiangqian qimin' [On carved red lacquer, Japanese lacquer, carvings, and inlayed objects and vessels]. In *Zunsheng bajian* [Eight discourses on the art of living], *Siku* edition, vol. 874, *juan* 14.

Guy, Kent. *The Emperor's Four Treasuries: Scholars and the State in the Late Ch'ien-lung Era*. Cambridge, Mass.: Harvard University Press, 1987.

Hon, Tze-ki. *Revolution as Restoration: Guocui xuebao and China's Path to Modernity, 1905–1911*. Leiden: Brill, 2013.

Hong Zaixin. 'Cong Minzu zhuyi dao xiandai zhuyi: Deng Shi, Huang Binhong xueshu sixiang guanxi kaolüe' [From nationalism to modernism: a brief examination of the thought of and relationship between Deng Shi and Huang Binhong]. *Meishu xuebao* 2013, no. 3: 29–40; 2013, no. 4: 26–31.

Huang, Chichung. *The Analects of Confucius* (Lun Yu): *A Literal Translation with an Introduction and Notes*. New York: Oxford University Press, 1997.

Huang Jie. 'Banjikao' [On printed books]. *Guocui xuebao* 4, no. 10; 4, no. 12 (1908).

Huters, Theodore. *Bringing the World Home: Appropriating the West in Late Qing and Early Republican China*. Honolulu: University of Hawai'i Press, 2005.

Ji Yun et al., eds. *Yingyin Wenyuange Siku quanshu* [Complete library of the four treasuries in the Wenyuan Hall], photographic reprint of the 18th-century edition. Taipei: Commercial Press, 1986.

Jin Jian. *Juzhenban chengshi* [Manual for formulating movable type]. *Meishu Congshu* 3, no. 8 (1917).

Jin Yuanyu. *Zhurenlu* [Records of bamboo carvers]. *Meishu Congshu* 2, no. 5 (1913).

Kitazawa Noriaki. *Me no shinden: 'Bijutsu' juyōshi nōto* [Temple of the eye: on the reception of *bijutsu*]. Tokyo: Bijutsu shuppansha, 1989.

Kristeller, Paul Oskar. 'The Modern System of the Arts: A Study in the History of Aesthetics, Part I'. *Journal of the History of Ideas* 12, no. 4 (1951): 496–527.

Liu, Lydia. *Translingual Practice: Literature, National Culture, and Translated Modernity—China, 1900–1937*. Stanford: Stanford University Press, 1995.

Liu Wenqi. *Yilanji* [Manual on growing orchids]. *Meishu Congshu* 1, no. 1 (1911).

Liu, Yu-jen. 'Second Only to the Original: Rhetoric and Practice in the Photographic Reproduction of Art in Early Twentieth-Century China'. *Art History* 37, no. 1 (2014): 68–95.

Liu Yuzhen. 'Zhaoxiang fuzhi niandai lide Zhongguo meishu: Shenzhou guoguangji de fuzhi taidu yu wenhua biaoshu' [Chinese art in the age of photographic reproduction: the art periodical *Shenzhou guoguangji*]. *Guoli Taiwan daxue meishushi yanjiu jikan* 35 (2013): 185–244, 258.

Masini, Frederico. *The Formation of Modern Chinese Lexicon and Its Evolution toward a National Language: The Period from 1840 to 1898*. Berkeley: University of California, 1993.

Ogawa Hiromitsu. 'Bijutsu sōsho no kankō ni tsuite: Yōroppa no gainen "Fine Arts" to nihon no yakugo "bijutsu" no dōnyū' [Regarding the publication of *Meishu Congshu*: introduction of the European concept of 'Fine Arts' and the Japanese translated term '*Bijutsu*']. *Bijutsushi ronsō* 20 (2004).

Shiner, Larry. *The Invention of Art: A Cultural History*. Chicago: University of Chicago Press, 2001.

Sikong Tu. 'Wei dongdu Jing'aisi jianglüseng Huique huamu diaoke lüshu' [Statements written for Monk Huique who preaches Vinaya at the Jing'ai Temple in eastern capital on raising contributions for carving monastic codes]. *Sikong Biaosheng wenji* [Collected works by Sikong Biaosheng], *Siku* edition, vol. 1083, *juan* 9.

Wang Zhuo. *Tangshuangpu* [Treatise on frost-like sugar]. *Meishu Congshu* 3, no. 5 (1916).

Wang Tingding. *Zhangshan xinlu* [New notes on canes and fans]. *Meishu Congshu* 2, no. 8 (1914).

Wen Zhenheng. 'Hailun tongyu diaoke yaoqi' [General views on bronzes, jades, carvings and kilned objects]. In *Zhangwuzhi* [Superfluous things], *Siku* edition, vol. 872, *juan* 7.

Xu Zhiheng. *Yinliuzhai shuoci* [Studio of Drinking Stream on the subject of porcelain]. *Meishu Congshu* 3, no. 6 (1916).

Ye Dehui. *Shulin qinghua* [Elegant talks on books]. Taipei: Shijie shuju, 1961.

Yongrong et al., eds. *Siku quanshu zongmu tiyao* [Annotated catalogue of the *Complete Collection of Four Treasuries*]. Shanghai: Commercial Press, 1933.

Yuan Hongdao. *Pingshi* [History of vase flowers]. *Meishu Congshu* 1, no. 6 (1911).

Zhang Chou. *Yiefukao* [Studies in the garments for the wild]. *Meishu Congshu* 2, no. 10 (1914).

Zhang Qiande. *Chajing* [Book of tea]. *Meishu Congshu* 2, no. 10 (1914).

———. *Zhusha yupu* [Treatise on vermilion fish]. *Meishu Congshu* 2, no. 10 (1914).

Zhang Yingwen. 'Lun diaoke' [On carvings]. In *Qingmizang* [Pure and arcane collecting], *Siku* edition, vol. 872, *juan* 1.

Glossary

Notes: (C) Chinese, (K) Korean, (J) Japanese
Names are given as 'Surname First name' and listed alphabetically. Emperors' formal names are listed under 'Emperor'.

People

Adaniya Masayoshi (J) 安谷屋正義
Amida (J) 阿弥陀
Annami (J) 安阿弥
Asakura Fumio (J) 朝倉文夫
Ashikaga Yoshimasa (J) 足利義政
Ashikaga Yoshimitsu (J) 足利義満
Ashikaga Yoshinori (J) 足利義教
Ashimine Kanemasa (J) 安次嶺金正
Ashitomi Chōshō (J) 安次富長昭
Bada Shanren (C) 八大山人
Cao Fuxing (C) 曹弗興
Chen Hengke, Chen Hengque (C) 陳衡恪 (Chen Shizeng 陳師曾)
Chen Zhenlian (C) 陳振濂
Cheong Hae-cho (K) 鄭解朝
Cho Taek-won (K) 趙澤元
Chu Suiliang (C); Cho Suiryō (J) 褚遂良
Dai Jin (C) 戴進
Deng Shi (C) 鄧實
Dōkyō (J) 道鏡
Dong Qichang (C) 董其昌
Dong Yuan (C) 董源
Emperor Go-Shirakawa (J) 後白河天皇
Emperor Huizong of Song (Song Huizong) (C) 宋徽宗
Emperor Kanmu (J) 桓武天皇
Emperor Renzong (C) 仁宗
Emperor Saga (J) 嵯峨天皇
Emperor Shōmu (J) 聖武天皇
Emperor Taizong of Tang (Tang Taizong) (C) 唐太宗
Emperor Tenji (J) 天智天皇

Emperor Tenmu (J) 天武天皇
Emperor Toba (J) 鳥羽天皇
Emperor Uda (J) 宇多天皇
Emperor Wu of Liang (Liang Wudi) (C) 梁武帝
Emperor Xianzong (C) 憲宗
Emperor Xuanzong of Tang (Tang Xuanzong) (C) 唐玄宗
Emperor Yongle (C) 永樂帝
Empress Genmei (J) 元明天皇
Empress Kōmyō (J) 光明皇后
Fu Baoshi (C) 傅抱石
Fujita Bunzō (J) 藤田文蔵
Fujishima Takeji (J) 藤島武二
Fujita Tsuguharu (J) 藤田嗣治
Fujiwara Fuhito (J) 藤原不比等
Fujiwara no Michinaga (J) 藤原道長
Fujiwara no Yorimichi (J) 藤原頼通
Fujiwara no Yukinari (J) 藤原行成
Fukuzawa Yukichi (J) 福沢諭吉
Furusawa Iwami (J) 古沢岩見
Gao Jianfu (C) 高劍父
Gao Qifeng (C) 高奇峰
Geiami (J) 芸阿弥
Gion Nankai (J) 祇園南海
Guan Tong (C) 關仝
Guo Moruo (C) 郭沫若
Guo Xi (C) 郭熙
Guo Xiang (C) 郭象
Gushiken Itoku (J) 具志堅以徳
Gushiken Seiji (J) 具志堅聖児
Guze Kannon (J) 救世観音
Haebaru Chōkō (J) 南風原朝光
Hamada Chimei (J) 浜田知明
Han Xiu (C) 韓休
Hang Zhiying (C) 杭穉英
Hasegawa Kiyoshi (J) 長谷川潔
Hashimoto Kansetsu (J) 橋本関雪
Hayashi Tadamasa (J) 林忠正
Higa Keijō (J) 比嘉景常
Hirafuku Hyakusui (J) 平福百穂
Hirafuku Suian (J) 平福穂庵
Hu Weiyong (C) 胡惟庸
Hua Mulan (C) 花木蘭
Huang Binhong (C) 黃賓虹
Huang Jie (C) 黃節
Huang Tu-Shui (C) 黃土水
Ike no Taiga (J) 池大雅
Imao Keinen (J) 今尾景年

Imazu Akira (J) 今津明
Inokuma Gen'ichirō (J) 猪熊弦一郎
Ishii Hakutei (J) 石井柏亭
Ishikawa Jōzan (J) 石川丈山
Isshi Kii (J) 一枝希維
Itaya Hazan (J) 板谷波山
Itō Hirobumi (J) 伊藤博文
Itō Seiu (J) 伊藤晴雨
Itō Shinsui (J) 伊藤深水
Iwakura Tomomi (J) 岩倉具視
Jeon Sung-gyu (K) 全成圭
Jianzhen (C); Ganjin (J) 鑑真
Jin Shan (C) 金善
Jin Shi (C) 金湜
Jin Xuecheng (C) 金学成
Jin Yuanyu (C) 金元鈺
Jing Hao (C) 荊浩
Jōchō (J) 定朝
Jōun (J) 如雲
Kang Chang-gyu (K) 姜昌奎
Kannon (J) 観音
Kanokogi Takeshirō (J) 鹿子木孟郎
Kawai Senrō (J) 河井仙朗 (Kawai Senro (J) 河井荃廬)
Kawakita Handeishi (J) 川喜田半泥子
Kim Bong-ryong (K) 金奉龍
Kim Bong-su (K) 金鳳洙
Kim Gwanho (K) 金觀鎬
Kim Jun-geun (K) 金俊根
Kimura Shōhachi (J) 木村荘八
Kimura Tenkō (J) 木村天紅
Kinbara Seigo (J) 金原省吾
Kinjō Yasutarō (J) 金城安太郎
Kitamura Shikai (J) 北村四海
Kitaōji Rosanjin (J) 北大路魯山人
Kobori Tomoto (J) 小堀鞆音
Koiso Ryōhei (J) 小磯良平
Kojima Torajirō (J) 児島虎次郎
Kōno Bairei (J) 幸野楳嶺
Kosugi Misei (J) 小杉未醒 (Kosugi Hōan 小杉放庵)
Kuroda Seiki (J) 黒田清輝
Kusunoki Masashige (J) 楠木正成
Kuwana Tetsujō (J) 桑名鉄城
Lee Qoede (K) 李快大
Li Cheng (C) 李成
Li Gonglin (Li Longmian) (C) 李公麟 (李龍眠)
Li Shutong (C) 李叔同
Lian Quan (C) 廉泉

Liang Kai (C) 梁楷
Liu Haisu (C) 劉海粟
Liu Shipei (C) 劉師培
Lü Qian (C) 呂潛 (Lü Banyin (C) 呂半隠)
Lu Lianfu (C) 陸廉夫
Lu Xun (C) 魯迅
Luo Zhenyu (C) 羅振玉
Ma Yuan (C) 馬遠
Maruyama Tai'u (J) 円山大迂
Masaki Naohiko (J) 正木直彦
Matsuda Gonroku (J) 松田権六
Men Wuguan (C) 門無関
Mi Fu (C) 米芾
Mi Youren (C) 米友仁
Mitsui Takaharu (J) 三井高陽
Mitsutani Kunishirō (J) 満谷国四郎
Miyamoto Saburō (J) 宮本三郎
Morikawa Kyoriku (J) 森川許六
Motoori Norinaga (J) 本居宣長
Muqi, Muxi (C) 牧谿
Nadoyama Aijun (J) 名渡山愛順
Nagai Kafū (J) 永井荷風
Nagamine Sōkyo (J) 長嶺宗恭
Naganuma Moriyoshi (J) 長沼守敬
Nagao Uzan 長尾雨山 (J) (Nagao Kō 長尾甲)
Naitō Konan (J) 内藤湖南
Nakagawa Kigen (J) 中川紀元
Nakamura Fusetsu (J) 中村不折
Oba Tsunekichi (J) 小場恒吉
Oda Nobunaga (J) 織田信長
Ogiwara Morie (J) 荻原守衛 (Rokuzan 碌山)
Ogura Seizaburō (J) 小倉清三郎
Oguri Sōtan (J) 小栗宗湛
Okada Saburōsuke (J) 岡田三郎助
Okakura Kakuzō (J) 岡倉覚三 (Okakura Tenshin 岡倉天心)
Okamoato Tarō (J) 岡本太郎
Ōkawa Tatsuji (J) 大川辰次
Ōmi no Mifune (J) 淡海三船
Ōmine Seikan (J) 大嶺政寛
Ōmine Shinichi (J) 大嶺信一
Ōmura Seigai (J) 大村西崖
Ōnaga Hiroyoshi (J) 大長広義
Ono Saseo (J) 小野佐世男
Ōshima Katsujirō (J) 大島勝次郎
Ōshima Takajirō (J) 大島高次郎
Ōshiro Kōya (J) 大城皓也
Ōta Saburō (J) 太田三郎

Ōuchi Masahiro (J) 大内政弘
Ouyang Xun (C); Ōyō Jun (J) 歐陽詢
Pai Un-soung (K) 裵雲成
Pan Liangpu (C) 潘良圃
Park Chul-joo (K) 朴鐵柱
Qian Shoutie (C) 錢瘦鐵 (Qian Ya (C) 錢厓 or Qian Shuya (C) 錢叔厓)
Ra Hye-seok (K) 羅蕙錫
Rokkaku Shisui (J) 六角紫水
Saigō Takamori (J) 西郷隆盛
Sekino Tadashi (J) 関野貞
Sesshū Tōyō (J) 雪舟等楊 (Sesshū 雪舟)
Shike (C) 石恪
Shimada Shūjirō (J) 島田修二郎
Shimizu Takashi (J) 清水多嘉志
Shitao (C) 石濤
Sim Bugil (K) 沈富吉
Song Ju-an (K) 宋周安
Sonoda Kojō (J) 園田湖城
Sun Yi (C) 孫億
Takahashi Tetsu (J) 高橋鐵
Takamura Kōtarō (J) 高村光太郎
Takamura Kōun (J) 高村光雲
Takata Rikizō (J) 高田力蔵
Takeuchi Seihō (J) 竹内栖鳳
Tamanaha Seikichi (J) 玉那覇正吉
Tamura Taijirō (J) 田村泰次郎
Tang Boqian (C) 唐伯謙
Tanizaki Junichirō (J) 谷崎潤一郎
Tanomura Chokunyū (J) 田能村直入
Terai Naoji (J) 寺井直治
Terauchi Masatake (J) 寺内正毅
Tomioka Tessai (J) 富岡鉄斎
Tomita Akihiro (J) 富田晃弘 (Sasaoka Sakuji 笹岡作治)
Tomita Gisaku (J) 富田儀作
Tsukioka Yoshitoshi (J) 月岡芳年
Tsurumi Mitsuzō (J) 鶴見三三
Umehara Ryūzaburō (J) 梅原龍三郎
Uragami Gyokudō (J) 浦上玉堂
Wada Eisaku (J) 和田英作
Wada Sanzō (J) 和田三造
Wang Hui (C) 王翬
Wang Jian (C) 王鑑
Wang Meng (C) 王蒙
Wang Shimin (C) 王時敏
Wang Wei (C) 王维
Wang Xianzhi (C); Ō Kenshi (J) 王獻之
Wang Xizhi (C); Ō Gishi (J) 王羲之

Wang Yiting (C) 王一亭
Wang Yuanqi (C) 王原祁
Wen Tong (C) 文同
Wu Changshi, Wu Changshuo (C) 吳昌碩
Wu Li (C) 吳歷
Wu Zhen (C) 吳鎮
Wuzhun Shifan (C) 無準師範
Xia Gui (C) 夏珪
Xiang yi tian (C) 香一天
Xiao Yan (C) 蕭衍 (personal name of Emperor Wu of Liang)
Xiong Shihui (C) 熊式輝
Xu Beihong (C) 徐悲鴻
Xu Jing (C) 徐兢
Xu Sangeng (C) 徐三庚
Xu Xiaopu (C) 徐小圃
Yabu Ken (J) 屋部憲
Yamada Shinzan (J) 山田真山
Yamagata Aritomo (J) 山縣有朋
Yamaguchi Zuiu (J) 山口瑞雨
Yamamoto Azumi (J) 山本安曇
Yamamoto Hōsui (J) 山本芳翠
Yamamoto Keiichi (J) 山元恵一
Yamamoto Morinosuke (J) 山本森之助
Yamamoto Teijirō (J) 山本悌二郎
Yamanoguchi Baku (J) 山之口獏
Yan Hui (C) 顏輝
Yanagi Muneyoshi (J) 柳宗悦
Yanagita Kunio (J) 柳田国男
Yang Guifei (C) 楊貴妃
Yasui Sōtarō (J) 安井曾太郎
Yokoyama Taikan (J) 横山大観
Yonehara Unkai (J) 米原雲海
Youn Eul-sou 尹乙洙 (K)
Yu Shinan (C); Gu Seinan (J) 虞世南
Yu Yushuang (C) 俞語霜
Yuasa Ichirō (J) 湯浅一郎
Yuehu (C) 月湖
Yujian (C) 玉澗
Yun Shouping (C) 惲壽平
Zhang Binglin (C) 章炳麟
Zhang Daqian (C) 張大千
Zhang Shanzi (C) 張善孖
Zhang Sigong (C) 張思恭
Zhang Yanyuan (C) 張彥遠
Zheng Sixiao (C) 鄭思肖
Zheng Wenzhuo (C) 鄭文焯
Zheng Wuchang (C) 鄭午昌

Zheng Xie (C) 鄭燮
Zhirong (C) 智融
Zhiyong (C) 智永

Institutions

Chōkaidō (J) 澄懐堂
Chōsen bijutsu raden fukyūkai (J) 朝鮮美術螺鈿普及会
Chōsen bijutsu tenrankai (also known as Senten) (J) 朝鮮美術展覧会、鮮展
Chōsen no raden sha (J) 朝鮮之螺鈿社
Gonin ten (J) 五人展
Guoxue baocunhui (C) 國學保存會
Haishang Tijin guan jinshi shuhua hui (C) 海上題襟館金石書畫會
Hakuba-kai (J) 白馬会
Imperial Wenyuan Library (Wenyuan ge) (C) 文淵閣
Joseon chilgolhoe 朝鮮漆工会 (K)
Jung-ang siheomso 中央試験所 (K)
Kaiisha (J) 解衣社
Kanten (J) 官展
Kōbu bijutsu gakkō (J) 工部美術学校
Manshūkoku bijutsu tenrankai (also known as Manten) (J) 満州国美術展覧会、満展
Monbushō bijutsu tenrankai (also known as Bunten) (J) 文部省美術展覧会、文展
Naikoku kangyō hakurankai (J) 内国勧業博覧会
Naimushō Keihokyoku (J) 内務省警保局
Nika-kai (J) 二科会
Nishimui (J) ニシムイ(北森)
Nitten (J) 日展
Okinawawa Taimusu-sha shusai sōgō bijutsuten (also known as Okiten) (J) 沖縄タイムス社主催総合美術展、沖展
Pari Nihon Bijutsuka Tenrankai (J) 巴里日本美術家展覧会
Seinen chōsokai (J) 青年彫塑会
Sen'oku Hakkokan (J) 泉屋博古館
Shenzhou guoguangshe (C) 神州國光社
Shinbunten (J) 新聞展
Shirakaba (J) 白樺
Shōsōin (J) 正倉院
Sōto-kai (J) 創斗会
Shunyō-kai (J) 春陽会
Taiwan bijutsu tenrankai (also known as Taiten) (J) 台湾美術展覧会、台展
Taiwan sōtokufu tenrankai (also known as Futen) (J) 台湾総督府美術展覧会、府展
Tansei-kai (J) 丹青会
Teikoku bijutsu-in tenrankai (also known as Teiten) (J) 帝国美術院展覧会、帝展
Tokyo bijutsu gakkō (J) 東京美術学校

Tokyo kangyō hakurankai (J) 東京勧業博覧会
Yi tu xue tang (C) 藝徒學堂
Zhe School (Zhepai) (C) 浙派
Zhongguo huahui (C) 中國畫會
Zhongri yishu tongzhi hui (C) 中日藝術同志會

Other

baimiao (C) 白描
Bijutsu (J) 美術 (see meishu) (C)
Bingata (J) 紅型
Bunjinga no fukkō (J) 文人画の復興
Byōbu kasen tō chō (J) 屏風花氈等帳
Chan (C); Zen (J) 禅
Chōkoku (J) 彫刻
Chuanqi (C) 傳奇
Ciqu chuanqi (C) 詞曲傳奇
Citong yushi lei (C) 磁銅玉石類
Congshu (C) 叢書
Dabao tie (C); Daihō jō (J) 大報帖
Dai Ō sho (J) 大王書
Daishō Ō shinseki sho (J) 大小王真跡帳
Daitō kinseirō mae kanraku zu byōbu (J) 大唐勤政楼前歓楽図屏風
Daitō koyō kyūden ga byōbu (J) 大唐古様宮殿画屏風
Datsu-A ron (J) 脱亜論
Diaoke moyin lei (C) 琱刻摹印類
Diaoke (C) 琱刻; (C) 雕刻
Fujiwara-kō shinseki byōbu chō (J) 藤原公真跡屏風帳
Fusō ryakki (J) 扶桑略記
Geijutsu 藝術 (J) (see yishu) (C)
Gomotsu on'e mokuroku (J) 御物御画目録
gongbi (C) 工筆
Gonki (J) 権記
Guocui xuebao (C) 國粹學報
Guohua (C) 國畫
Gyo byōbu ichihyaku jō (J) 御屏風壹佰疊
Hetu (C); Kato (J) 河図
Higashiyama Gomotsu (J) 東山御物
Houji (C) 後集
Huang ting jing (C); Kōtei gyō (J) 黄庭経
Jiegu (C) 羯鼓
Jing (C) 經
Jingshi ziji (C) 經史子集
Jinshi (C) 金石
Juka kōshi zu byōbu (J) 樹下高士図屏風
Kaiga (J) 絵画
Kaisho (J) 会所

Kara-e (J) 唐絵
Karamono kazari (J) 唐物飾り
Kegon-kyō (J) 華厳経
Kisaeng, Gisaeng (K) 妓生
Kizō sōgaku zu (J) 騎象奏楽図
Kōgei (J) 工芸
Kōhon Nihon bijutsu ryakushi (J) 稿本日本美術略史
Kojin ga byōbu (J) 古人画屏風
Kojin kyūden byōbu (J) 古人宮殿屏風
Kokka chinpō chō (J) 国家珍宝帳
Kokka (J) 国華
Kong shizhong tie (C); Kō jichū jō (J) 孔侍中帖
Kowatari (J) 古渡り
Koyō honzō ga byōbu (J) 古様本草画屏風
Koyō kyūden ga byōbu (J) 古様宮殿画屏風
Koyō sansui ga byōbu (J) 古様山水画屏風
Kudara ga byōbu (J) 百済画屏風
Kundaikan sōchō ki (J) 君台観左右帳記
Kuni zu byōbu (J) 国図屏風
Lanting xu (C); Rantei jō (J) 蘭亭序
Lei (C) 類
Lidai minghuaji (C) 歷代名畫記
Lingnan (C) 嶺南
Liuyi (C) 六藝
Lüeli (C) 畧例
Maiba byōbu (J) 舞馬屏風
Manyōshū (J) 万葉集
Matsuzakaya (J) 松坂屋
Meishu Congshu (C) 美術叢書
Meishu 美術 (C) (see bijutsu) (J)
Meizhi tie (C); Maishi jō (J) 妹至帖
Mingei (J) 民芸
Mingmo minzu yiren zhuan (C) 明末民族藝人傳
Mogufa (C) 沒骨法
Nanga e no dōtei (J) 南画への道程
Nihonga (J) 日本画
Ō Gishi rinsho byōbu (J) 王羲之臨書屏風
Ogoe (J) 御後絵
Ōyō Jun shinseki byōbu (J) 欧陽詢真跡屏風
Pomo (C) 潑墨
Qi (C) 棋
Qianziwen (C); Senjimon (J) 千字文
Qin (C) 琴
Sang luan tie (C); Sō ran jō (J) 喪乱帖
Sansui ga byōbu (J) 山水画屏風
Sansui zu tsuitate (J) 山水図衝立
Shangshu (C); Shōsho 尚書

Shenzhou guoguangji (C) 神州國光集
Shijo ga byōbu (J) 子女画屏風
Shina jōdai garon kenkyū (J) 支那上代画論研究
Shinhakusai (J) 新舶載
Shiwen ciqu (C) 詩文詞曲
Shō Ō sho (J) 小王書
Shuju yaku chō (J) 種々薬帳
Siku quanshu (C) 四庫全書
Soga yoasobi byōbu (J) 素画夜遊屏風
Sō-Genga (J) 宋元画
Tō daiwajō tōseiden (J) 唐大和上東征伝
Tō Sō Gen Min meiga taikan (J) 唐宋元明名画大觀
Torige ryūjo zu byōbu (J) 鳥毛立女図屏風
Tō-Shin u shōgun ō Gishi no shohō (J) 搨晋右将軍王羲之書法
Tōyō shumi (J) 東洋趣味
Tuhui baojian (J) 図絵宝鑑
Wanglianghua (C) 魍魎画
Xieyi (C) 写意
Xuezhou ji qi yishu (C) 雪舟及其藝術
Yamato-e (J) 大和絵
Yōga (J) 洋画
Youfa youguan (C) 有髮有冠
Zenna-zō (J) 善那像
Zhencao qianziwen (C); Shinsō senjimon (J) 真草千字文
Zhongguo huihua bianqian shigang (C) 中國繪畫變遷史網
Zhongguo wenrenhua zhi yanjiu (C) 中國文人画之研究

Index

References to illustrations are in **bold**.

Adaniya Masayoshi 110, 112–13; *Child Eating* 116; *Nostalgia* 116–17, **117**; *Tower* 116, **Pl.7**
apparitional painting 196, **197**
art history: frameworks 53–4, **55**; Japan 191–2; national 56; *see also* East Asian art history; European Art History; Japanese Art History
Ashikaga shoguns 16
Ashikaga Yoshimasa 25
Ashikaga Yoshimitsu 19
Ashikaga Yoshimori 18
Ashimine Kanemasa: *Crowd* 115, **116**; *I am tired* 115
authenticity 22, 106; definition 6

Beijing, Palace Museum 54
Belting, Hans 5
bijutsu (fine art): modernization 135; origins of term 128–9, 131, 132; *see also* plastic arts
Boxer Rebellion (1900) 228
Bruegel, Pieter, *The Sermon of St. John the Baptist* 88
Buddhism, dedication of Shōsōin collection 35–6
Buddhist statues: cult/exhibition value 129–30; *kaichō* project 130; museum exhibits 130
Bunten art exhibitions 141–3, 144

calligraphy, Shōsōin collection 34, **35**, 36–8
censorship: of geisha images 154–5; Japan 153
China, national essence 228
Chinese Painting Society (1931) 180
chōkoku 132; definition 141; modernization 135
Christianity, and European art history 52, 57
clay modelling 137

Complete Library of the Four Treasuries 228, 235
cultural nationalism 136
culture *see* high culture

Dai Jin, *High Mountains and Flowing Rivers* **22**, **27**
Deng Shi 228, 237
Dong Qichang, art theory 192
Dower, John, *War without Mercy* 160
dry-lacquer technique 221, 222; lacquer hemp cloth **217**, 218; statues 218; tray **223**; vase 222

East Asia, scope of term 6–7
East Asian art, transnationality of 1
East Asian art history: arrangement by nation states 52; and *Meishu Congshu* (Book Collection on Art) 227; possibility of 8–9, 202; as regional art history 56, 57, 58, **59**; as single organic system 8
Eckardt, Andre 85; *A History of Korean Art* 86
Edo period (1603–1868) 126; pornography 152
eroticism: homoerotic 160–1, **160**; Korea 155; as wartime propaganda 158, **159**, 160, **Pl.10**; *see also* pornography
ethnocentrism 55
European art history: and Christianity 52, 57; chronological displays 52, 54
exhibitions: *Aesthetic Perfection* (2014) 16; *Southern Song Paintings* 1616

Fenollosa, Ernest 137
Five People Exhibition Group, Okinawan art 112–13
folding screen paintings: 39–40, 42–3, **Pl.3**; *Nobleman under the trees* **41**
folk crafts, Okinawa 108, 118

France-Japon magazine 91, 95; article on Pai Un-soung **92**
Fu Baoshi: *After a Poem by Mao Zedong* 198, **198**; *Amitabha* 196; *Autumn Landscape with a Waterfall* 188, **189**, 190, 201, Pl.11; *Beauty under Banana Leaves* 196, **197**; *Biographies of Chinese Artists in the late Ming* 196; *Chinese Figurative and Landscape Painting* 194; *Crossing Dadu River* 200; *Evening Glow on a Fishing Village* 197; *Evening Rain in Ba Mountains* 199; *Fisherman* 198; influences on 189, 190; ink painting 10, 188, **189**, 190, 191–4, **195**, 196, **197**, 198, **198**, 199, **199**, Pl.11; *Jutang Strait* 198; *Night Rain in Bashan* 196; *Portrait of Sesshū* 200; *Priest Shitao* 196; *Returning Home in Snowstorm* 199; Shanghai School style 191; *Shi Le Seeking the Way* 196; solo exhibition 190–1; *The Far Snows of Minshan Only Make Us Happy* 200; *The Thatched Hut of Great Purity* 194–5, **195**, 196; *Washing Feet in a Stream* 199; *Whispering Rain at Dusk* 199, **199**, 200; *Yangzi Gorge* 198
Fujishima Takeji 105; and Orientalism 68–9; *Orientalism* 69–70, **69**; *Rear Wooden Gate . . . Mausoleum of Confucius* 75, **76**; *Sunrise in Inner Mongolia* 70, **71**; *The Rising Sun Shines in the Six Directions* 70
Fujita Tsuguharu 105–6, 117; *Grandchildren* 106, **107**
Fukuoka Asian Art Museum 65, 83

Geiai, *Landscape* 25, **26**, 27
Geiami, *Viewing Waterfall* 25, **26**
geisha images, censorship of 154–5
global: definition 5–6; local framework **23**, 24
global art 5
global history 15
glossary of names: institutions 250–1; other 251–3; people 244–50
Gomotsu on'e mokuroku catalogue 17–18; artists 18; triptychs 19
Guangzhou Museum of Art 21
Guo Bochuan, *The Forbidden Palace of Peking* 77
Guo Xi 17

Haebaru Chōkō 108
Hamada Chimei 153
Hamburg Museum of Ethnology 90
Hanson, Dian, *My Buddy: World War II Laid Bare* 160–1

Hashimoto Kansetsu 169; friendship with Qian Shoutie 172, 181, 196; Kyoto residence 174, **174**; *nihonga* style paintings 178–9; praise by Wu Changshuo 178; Sinophilism 178, 179; *Song of Everlasting Sorrow* 179; *Southern Country* (screens) 178
Heian period, Treasure House 44–5
Higashiyama Gomotsu 16
high culture, and sub-culture 60
Hirafuku Hyakusui 103
Huizong: *Four Seasons Landscapes* 18, 24; *Peach Blossom and Dove* 18
Huizong, Emperor 18
hybridity 3

identity: definition 6; Okinawa 117
Ishii Hakutei 154
Ishikawa Kinichirō 77
Isshi Kii, *Landscape* 25, **27**

Japan: art history 191–2; austerity 152; censorship 153; Chinese seal carving 169; Chinese students in 188; Domestic Industrial Expositions (1877–90) 133, **134**, **135**, **136**; Fifteen Years' War (1931–45) 153; Korea-boom 60; Korean lacquerwork craftsmen 209; literati 175–6; neo-literati painting 169; sculpture genre 127, 132–3; wartime art 152; *see also* Tokyo
Japanese art history 53; ideology 56
Japanese Artist Exhibitions (Paris), exhibition hall **93**
Japanese-British Exhibition (1910) 212
Jeon Sung-gyu 210–11
Jin Shan 22
Jin Shi 16
Joseon Lacquerware Association 211
Joseon Mother-of-Pearl Corporation 211, 217; products 214
Journal of National Essence, contributors 228

Kang Chang-gyu 218–19, 220–1, 221–2; *Dry-Lacquered Tray* 223, **223**
kara-e (Chinese-style paintings) 8, 16, **17**, 20; definition 17; generative power of 25–8, 29; made in China/Japan continuum 28
karamono display 19–20
karamono-kazari main room, image 18, **19**
Kim Bok-jin 141
Kim Gwanho, *Sunset* 155
Kimura Tenkō 210
Kinbara Seigo, *Research on Early Chinese Painting Theory* 190
Kinjō Yasutarō 104

kisaeng (Korean dancer) motif 156
Kitamura Shikai 142–3
Kobori Tomoto 103
Kojima Kaoru 68
Kojima Torajirō: *Autumn* 71–2, **72**; *Belle de Matin* 71, 72
Kokka chimpō chō catalogue 33–4, 35
Korea: censorship 155; erotica 155; Guimet Museum in 19th century 87; mother-of-pearl lacquerware 210; *see also* Korean lacquerwork craftsmen
Korea National Museum 54
Korean art 83–4; in Germany 85–6
Korean lacquerwork craftsmen, Japan 209
Korean War 84
Koreans, in Paris 93
Kuroda Seiki 67, 105; *Maïko (Dancing Girl)* 72, **Pl.4**; *Morning Toilette* 154

lacquerware *see* mother-of-pearl lacquerware
landscape scrolls 20–2, 25
Lee Mi-na 83
Lee Qoede, *Dancer Taking a Rest* 156–7
Li Cheng 17
Li Gonglin 18
Liang Kai 18
Liaoning Provincial Museum 21
literati: Japan 175–6; meaning 171
literati art movement 192–3

Ma Yuan 18; *Grand Views of Rivers and Mountains* (attrib) **21**; *guanyin* 20; *Patriarchs of the Zen Sect* 20; *Superior Views of One Thousand Cliffs* 22
Manchurian Incident (1931) 92
Matsuzaki Shinji, *Exterior View of the Fine Art Gallery* **134**
Meiji period 128; constitution 135
meishu: and European Art concept 227–8, 238; as National Essence 228–9
Meishu Congshu (Book Collection on Art): advertisement for 232, **232**; book printing 233–4; carved objects 233; in Chinese Knowledge System 235–8; classification of texts 231–5, 236; and East Asian art history 227; Literary Arts, absence 232–3; organization 229; publication 227; *qin* zithers 235; scope 231–2; in translingual context 229–31
Michelangelo, *The Last Judgment* 88
Ming dynasty (1368–1644) 170
Mitsui Takaharu 90
mother-of-pearl lacquerware: box 214, **215**; brazier 214, **215**; ceramic vase 217, **Pl.12**; dining table 216, **216**; exhibitions 214, 218–19; filing technique 216, 217; Korea 210; plaque 212–13, **213**; *see also* dry-lacquer technique
Muqi 18, 20; *Evening Glow* 197; *Returning Boats in Distant Shore* 197
Muromachi period (1336–1573) 2, 8, 15–16, 16, 25

Nadoyama Aijun 105, 110; *Hot-blooded man in a Southern Country* 107; *In the Ryūkyū Classical Idiom* 107; *Nostalgia* 110–11, **110**
Naganuma Moriyoshi 143
nanga painting tradition, reform 179–80
nation: and border disputes 4; concept of 3–4
national: definitions 2, 3; *see also* transnational
nationalism 3; *see also* cultural nationalism
networks, external connections 24
New Boundaries in Modern Japanese Art History conference (2013) 1
nihonga (Japanese-style painting) 103, 188; in colonial ideologies 104, 117; Hashimoto Kansetsu paintings 178–9; Okinawa 103–4
nudes (female): as art 154; banned in Japan 154; and social morals 154

Ogiwara Morie (Rokuzan), *Woman* 144, 145, **Pl.9**
Oguri Sōtan, *Eight Views of Landscape* (attrib) 27
Okada Saburōsuke 67–8
Okakura Tenshin 130–1, 137
okimono (decorative object), sculpture as 131–2
Okinawa 7; art education 103–5; Battle of (1945) 108–9, 115; Beggars' March (1955) 115; folk crafts 108, 118; gaze from mainland 108; history 102; identity 117; Japanization of 104; *nihonga* paintings 103–4; US Occupation 102, 109–10; *yōga* paintings 104–5, 117
Okinawan art 102–3, 109; abstraction 114–17; artists 110; Five People Exhibition Group 112, 112–13; local colour 107–8; modernism 112–14
Ōmine Seikan 105; *Landscape of Nishihara Village* 111, **111**
Ōmura Seigai 140
Onchi Kōshirō, *White walls [Impressions of Suzhou]* 7
Ono Saseo: *A Market on the Island of Bali* 158; *Big Waves and the Beauty of Health* 158
Orientalism, and Fujishima Takeji 68–9
Ōta Saburō, *Customs and Art of the Nude* 154

Pai Un-soung 83; biography 84; connections 90–1; criticism of 95; and *France-Japon* magazine 91, **92**, 93; hybrid art 89; at Japanese Artist Exhibitions (Paris) 93–4; painting in Chinese ink in atelier **89**; reputation 96; solo exhibition, invitation letter 91, **91**; works: *Baron Mitsui and His Works* 90, 91, **Pl.6**; *Family Portrait* 87–8, **88**; *Self-Portrait* 85, **86**; *Self-Portrait with Hat* 86, **86**, 87
painters, in their paintings 88
paintings *see* folding screen paintings; screen paintings; *yōga* paintings
pantograph method 137
Park Chul-joo, *Dry-Lacquered Flower Vase* 222
plastic arts 126, 127, 132, 141; decorative 135; definition 145n.1; domain of craftsmen 133; premodern 129; reproducible 140
pornography: definition 152; Edo period (1603–1868) 152; magazines 157; posters 157; underground 155; *see also* eroticism

Qian Shoutie: album, Hashimoto's commentary on **173**; apprenticeship 171; artistic names 172; artistry, example 177, **177**; death (1967) 181; friendship with Hashimoto Kansetsu 172, 181, 196; imprisonment 180–1; photographs 169, **170**, **181**; political activities 180; seals of Hashimoto Kansetsu 172, **177**; 'Shangwu' seal, Japanese style **175**; 'White Sand Village Residence' seal **175**
Qing dynasty (1644–1911) 171

Ragusa, Vincenzo 132
Raphael, *The School of Athens* 88
regions, boundary problems 57
Renan, Ernest 3–4
Rodin, Auguste, *The Words of Rodin* 144
Rodinism 144
Rokkaku Shisui, *Square Tray with Design of Deva of Arts* 220
Rokuzan *see* Ogiwara Morie
Runge, Kurt 90
Russo-Japanese War (1904–5) 65, 144

screen paintings 41; *Landscape* **42**; *Musicians Riding Elephants* **42**; *see also* folding screen paintings
sculpture: in bronze **138**, **140**; clay models 137; as craftwork 133; non-sculpture items 141; as *okimono* (decorative object) 131–2; in wood **139**

sculpture genre (Japan) 127, 132–3; Buddhist influence 144; criticism of 143; modernization 136–43
sculpture programme, Tokyo School of Fine Arts 140
seal carvings (Chinese): artists 171; collectors 175–6; Japan 169, 177; origins 170; techniques **176**, **177**; use 176
Sesshū: *Haboku Landscape* 201; *Long Landscape Scroll*: 25, 27, **Pl.1**; multilayering 28–9; 'Xia Gui' style 28; Yamaguchi regional context 28, **29**
Small Landscape Scroll 25, **26**
Shanghai 157
Shanghai Academy of Fine Arts 172
Shanghai Incident (1937) 191
Shitao 189, 194; *A Returning Home* (album) 195; *A Waterfall on Mount Lu* 195; *Landscape* 195; *Mount Huang Scroll* 195–6
Shōmu, Emperor 32
Shōsōin collection (treasure): additions 34, 35; calligraphy 34, **35**, 36–8; catalogue 33, **Pl.2**; contents 33–4; dedication to Buddhism 35–6; formation 32; medicines 36; paintings, folding screens 39–40, 43, **Pl.3**; removals from 8, 36, 43; weapons 34, **36**
Sino-Japanese Association for Artistic Kinship 180
Sino-Japanese War (1894–5) 65
Smith, Anthony 4
Society of Derobement 180
Society for Preserving National Learning 228
Sontag, Susan, *Regarding the Pain of Others* 153
Southern Song dynasty 20
Southern Song paintings 16
Sugimura Yōtarō 94–5

Taishō era (1912–26) 143
Taiwan, *yōga* paintings 77–8
Taiwan Art Exhibition 142
Takahashi Tetsu, *The Graphical History of Sex*, images 155, **156**
Takamura Kōtarō: criticism of sculpture genre 143; *Hand*, bronze 139, **140**
Takamura Kōun 136–7; *Portrait of Saigō Takamori* **138**
Tamanaha Seikichi: on art 115; *Portrait of an Elderly Mother* 113–14, **113**; *Shipwrecks* 114–15, **114**
Tamura Taijirō, *Nikutai no Mon* (*Gate of the Flesh*) 154
Tang dynasty 40
Teiten exhibitions 65, 70, 77, 169, 179, 219

Tenpyō era 32
Tokyo, Great Kantō Earthquake (1923) 157, 171
Tokyo Industrial Exposition 142
Tokyo National Museum 54
Tokyo School of Fine Arts 67, 103, 105, 136, 219; foundation 136; graduates 77, 110, 141; sculpture programme 140; wood carving 136, 137; *see also* Tokyo University of the Arts
Tokyo University of the Arts 209
Tomioka Tessai: *Dongpo in a Straw Hat* 199; *Mountain Villa in a Rain Storm* 199; *Serene Life by a Stream* 199
Tomita Akihiro, 'Bathing of Soldiers' **160**
tōyō, definitions 57
TrAIN (Transnational Art, Identity and Nation) Research Centre 2, 3
transcultural 5
transnational: and cultural borders 4–5; definitions 2–3; *see also* hybridity; transcultural
triptych format display 19–20
Tsurumi Mitsuzō 92

ukiyo-e art 10, 53
Umehara Ryūzaburō 74–5; Beijing Period works 76, 77; *Chang-an Streets* 76; *Diary of Peking* 76, 77; *Forbidden City* 76, Pl.5; *Scenery of Taiwan* 75
Uragami Gyokudō: *Eastern Clouds, Shifted Snow* 200; *Mountains after Rain* 200

value system circles 6
Vasari, Giorgio 133, 135
Vienna World's Fair (1873), classifications and divisions **128**

Wang Meng 190
Wang Xizhi, *Letter on the Disturbances* 37, 38
women, violence against 153

world art 5
Wu Changshuo, praise of Hashimoto Kansetsu 178
Wuzhun Shifan 18

Xia Gui 18, 25; painted scrolls 30n.8; *Pure and Remote Views of Mountains and Streams* **21**, 22, 27; *Rivers and Mountains for Ten Thousand Miles* 22; *Twelve View of Landscape* 21, 27; and 'Xia Gui' style 28
Xiling Seal Carving Society (1904) 171

Yamada Shinzan 103–4, 105; *Establishment of the Ryūkyū Domain* 104, 117
Yamaguchi region 28, 29
Yamaguchi Zuiu 103
Yamamoto Azumi 144
Yamamoto Hōsui, *Watch under the Moon at Chinese Station* 67
Yamamoto Keiichi 110
Yamamoto Morinosuke 105
Yamato Takeru statue 134, **Pl.8**
yamato-e (Japanese-style paintings) 16, **17**
Yan Hui 20
Yasui Sōtarō, *A Portrait of Chin-Jung* 73–4, **73**
yōga (Japanese Western-style paintings): exhibitions 65, 78; Okinawa 104–5, 117; painters 66 (table), 67–9; research 78; scope 66; Taiwan 77–8
Yonehara Unkai: *Portrait of Edward Jenner*, in bronze 137, **138**; *Portrait of Edward Jenner in Wood* **139**
Yongle, Emperor 22–3
Yuehu 18, 20

Zen Buddhism 18
Zhang Sigong 18
Zhe School 21, 22
zō wo tsukuru jutsu: meaning 131, 132; *see also chōkoku*